EDENS ZERO

12

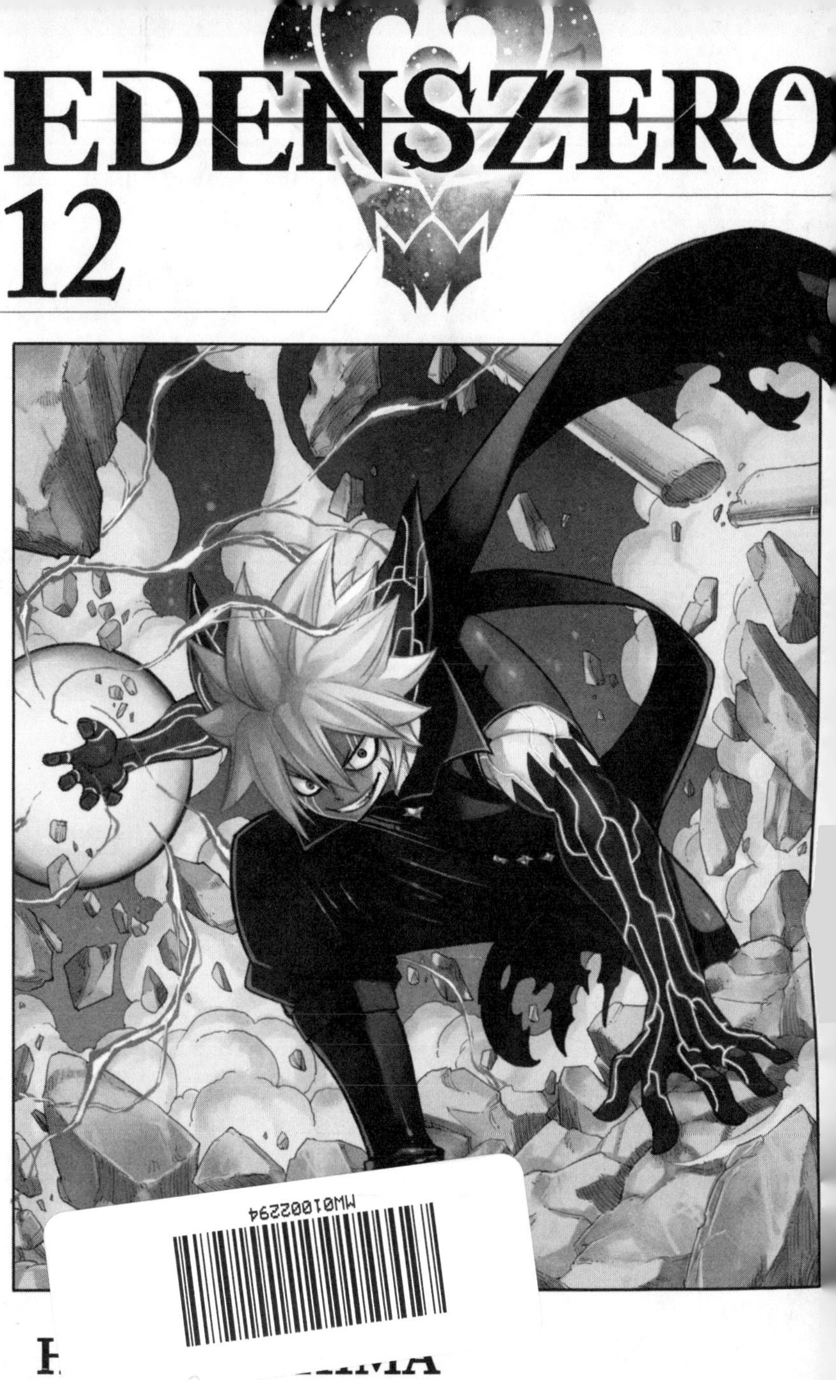

H IMA

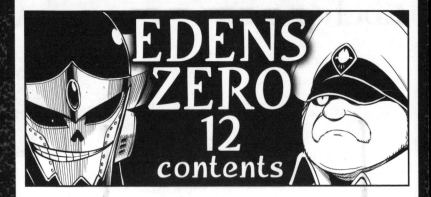

EDENS ZERO 12 contents

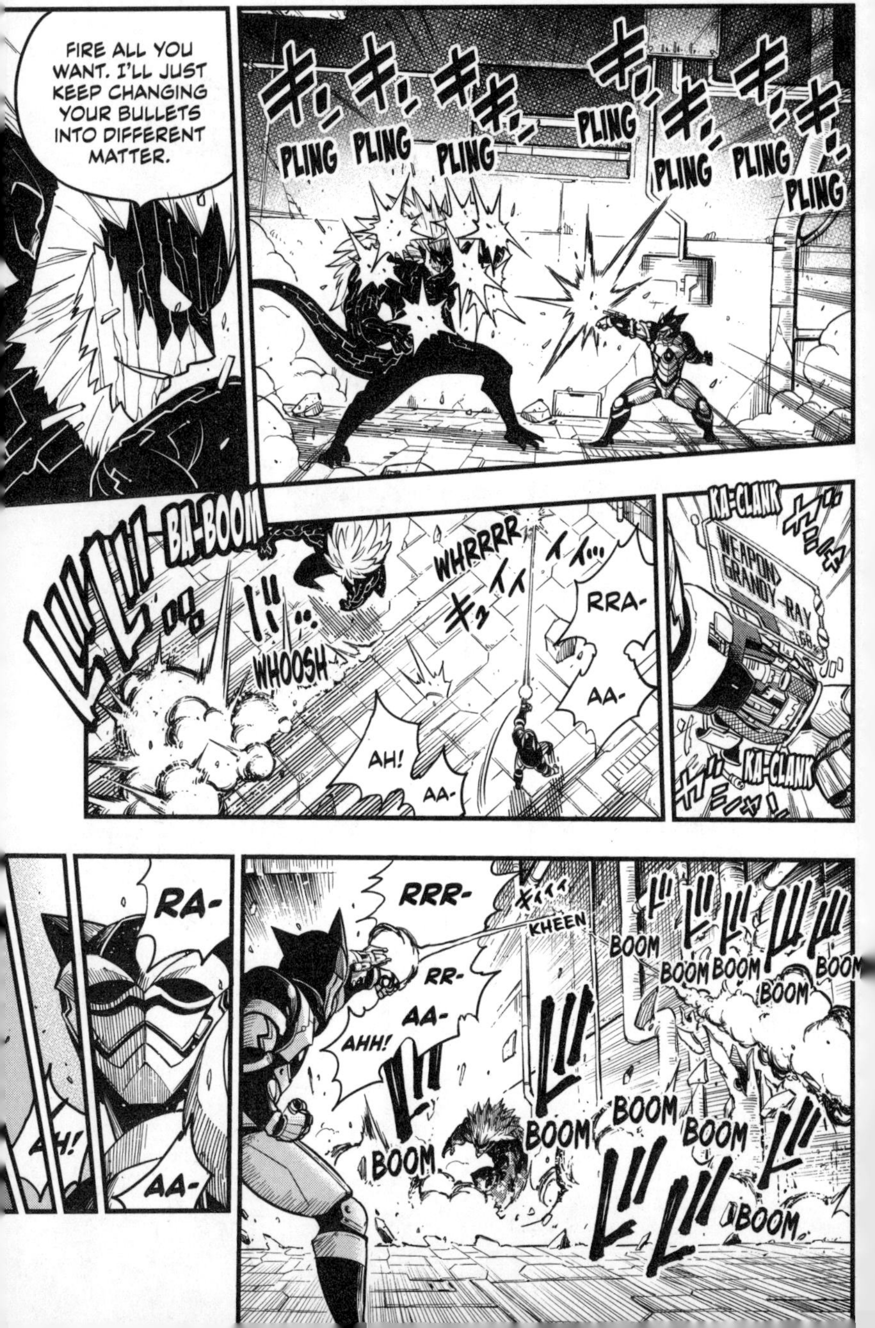
PLING PLING PLING PLING PLING PLING PLING
FIRE ALL YOU WANT. I'LL JUST KEEP CHANGING YOUR BULLETS INTO DIFFERENT MATTER.
KA-CLANK
WEAPON: GRANDY-RAY
GR
KA-CLANK
WHRRRR
RRA-
AA-
BA-BOOM
WHOOSH
AH!
AA-
RRR-
KHEEN
BOOM BOOM BOOM BOOM BOOM
RR-
AA-
AHH!
BOOM BOOM BOOM BOOM BOOM
RA-
AH!
AA-

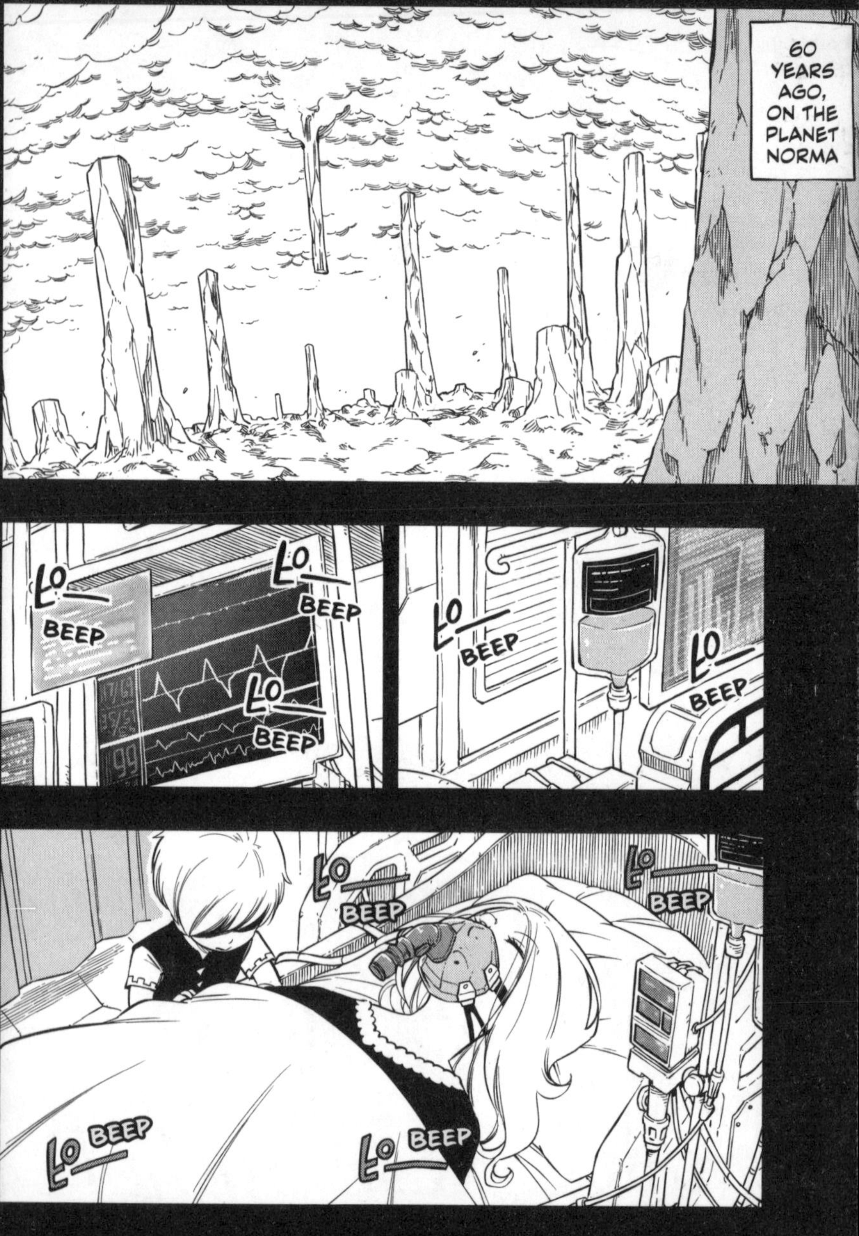
60 YEARS AGO, ON THE PLANET NORMA
BEEP
BEEP
BEEP
BEEP
BEEP
BEEP
BEEP
BEEP
BEEP

EDENSZERO

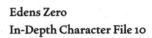

Edens Zero
In-Depth Character File 10

PINO'S ANALYSIS

'T PUSH

Name: Mosco Versa-0

Powers: Harite (Sumo Slap)

Likes: Sister, little animals

Dislikes: Ghosts

Attack: ☆

Defense: ☆

Marksmanship: ☆

Ether Power: ☆

Intelligence: ☆

Mystery Button: ☆☆☆☆☆

Memo

Moscoy! I can't help wanting to imitate Mr. Mosco's catchphrase. He appears to be Miss Sister's minion, as he is always by her side. He was once brainwashed and controlled by the fake Sister, but now he is back to normal. I'm beside myself with curiosity about that button on his tummy.

CHAPTER 96: A YOUNG MAN'S MEMORIES

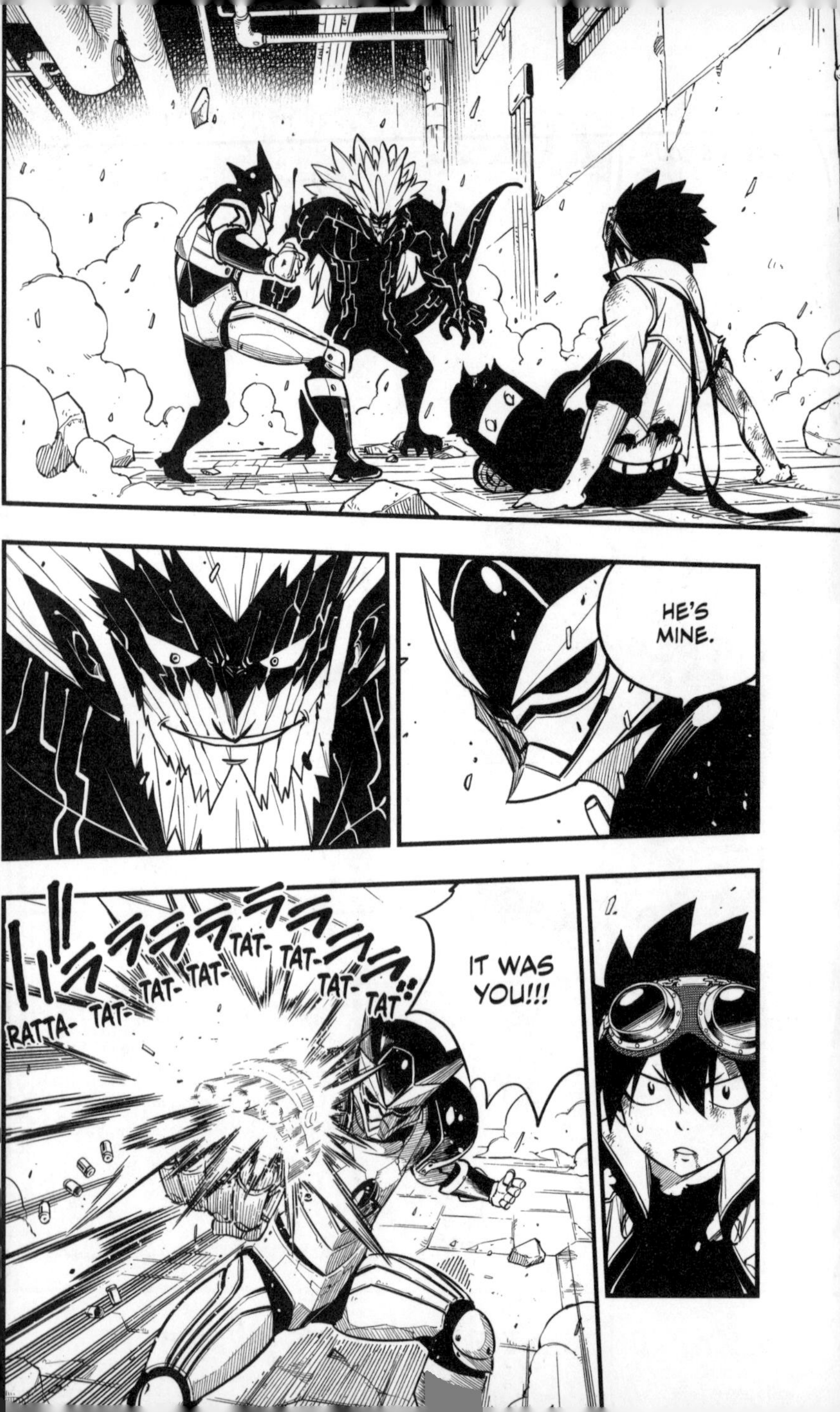
HE'S MINE.
IT WAS YOU!!!
RATTA-TAT-TAT-TAT-TAT-TAT-TAT-TAT

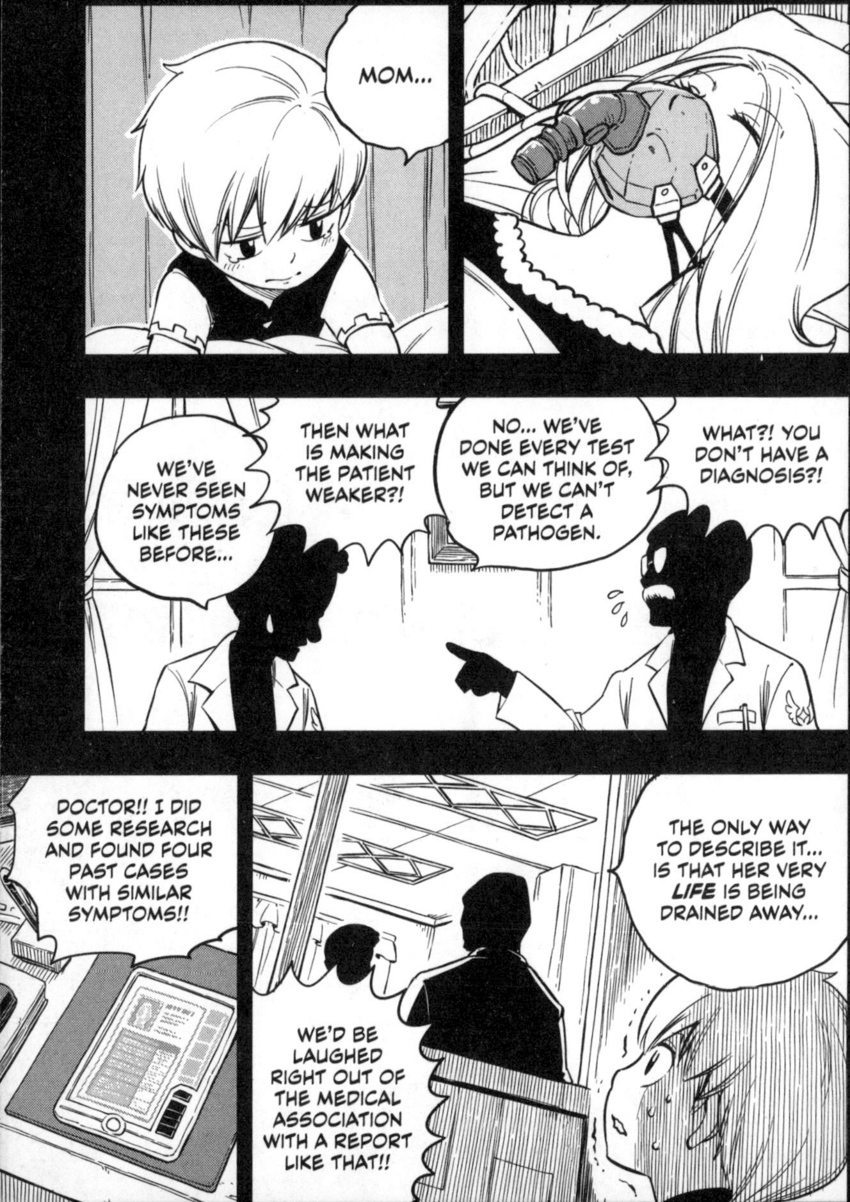
MOM...
WHAT?! YOU DON'T HAVE A DIAGNOSIS?!
NO... WE'VE DONE EVERY TEST WE CAN THINK OF, BUT WE CAN'T DETECT A PATHOGEN.
THEN WHAT IS MAKING THE PATIENT WEAKER?!
WE'VE NEVER SEEN SYMPTOMS LIKE THESE BEFORE...
THE ONLY WAY TO DESCRIBE IT... IS THAT HER VERY *LIFE* IS BEING DRAINED AWAY...
WE'D BE LAUGHED RIGHT OUT OF THE MEDICAL ASSOCIATION WITH A REPORT LIKE THAT!!
DOCTOR!! I DID SOME RESEARCH AND FOUND FOUR PAST CASES WITH SIMILAR SYMPTOMS!!

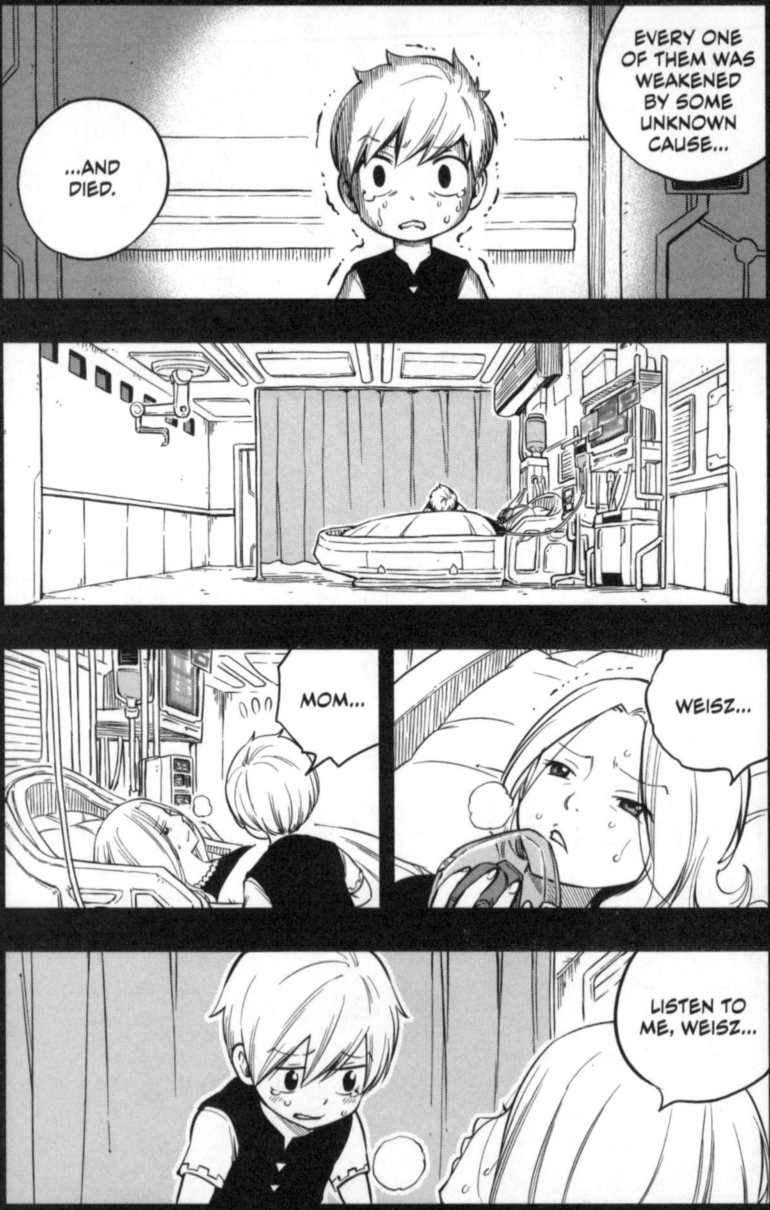
EVERY ONE OF THEM WAS WEAKENED BY SOME UNKNOWN CAUSE...
...AND DIED.
WEISZ...
MOM...
LISTEN TO ME, WEISZ...

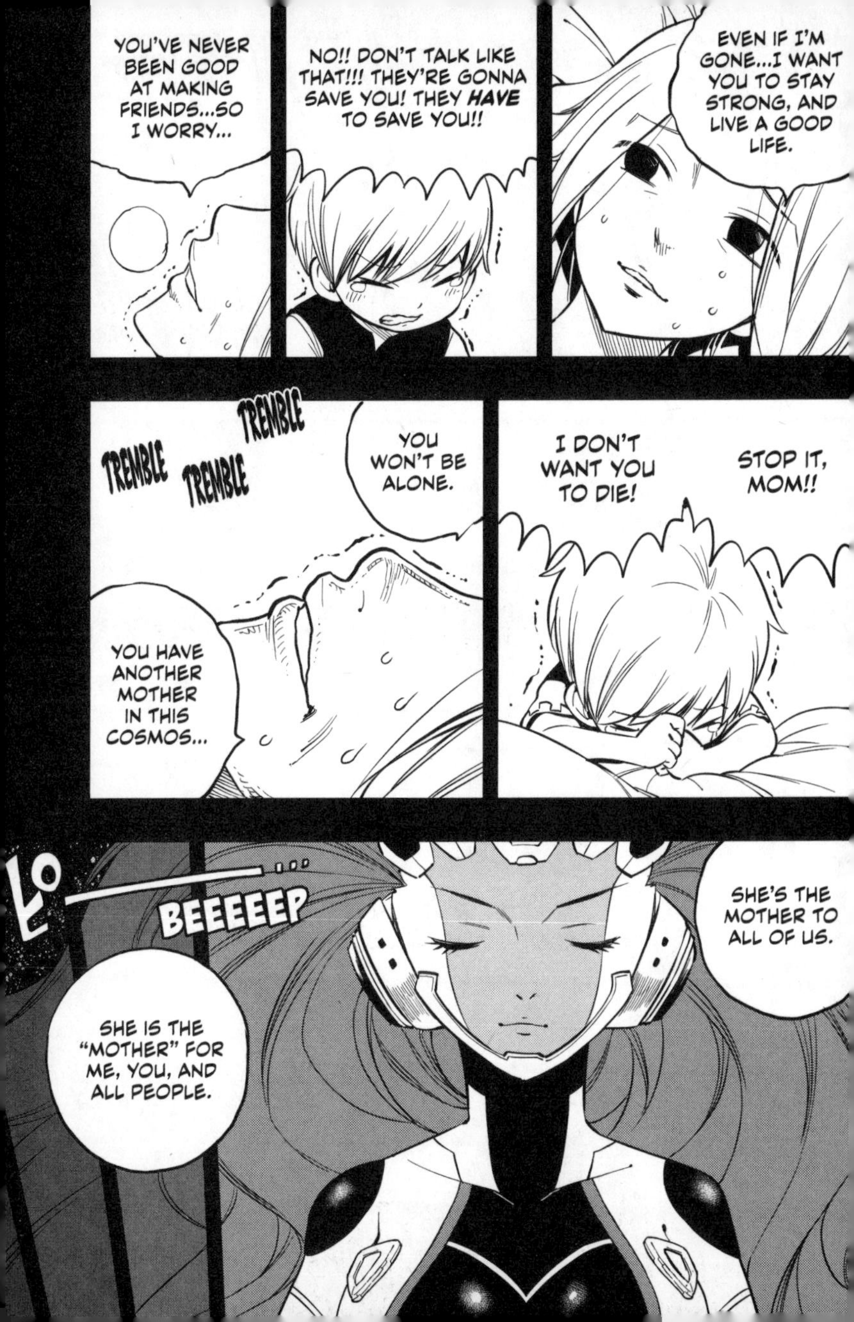
EVEN IF I'M GONE...I WANT YOU TO STAY STRONG, AND LIVE A GOOD LIFE.
NO!! DON'T TALK LIKE THAT!!! THEY'RE GONNA SAVE YOU! THEY *HAVE* TO SAVE YOU!!
YOU'VE NEVER BEEN GOOD AT MAKING FRIENDS...SO I WORRY...
STOP IT, MOM!!
I DON'T WANT YOU TO DIE!
YOU WON'T BE ALONE.
TREMBLE
TREMBLE
TREMBLE
YOU HAVE ANOTHER MOTHER IN THIS COSMOS...
SHE'S THE MOTHER TO ALL OF US.
BEEEEEP
SHE IS THE "MOTHER" FOR ME, YOU, AND ALL PEOPLE.

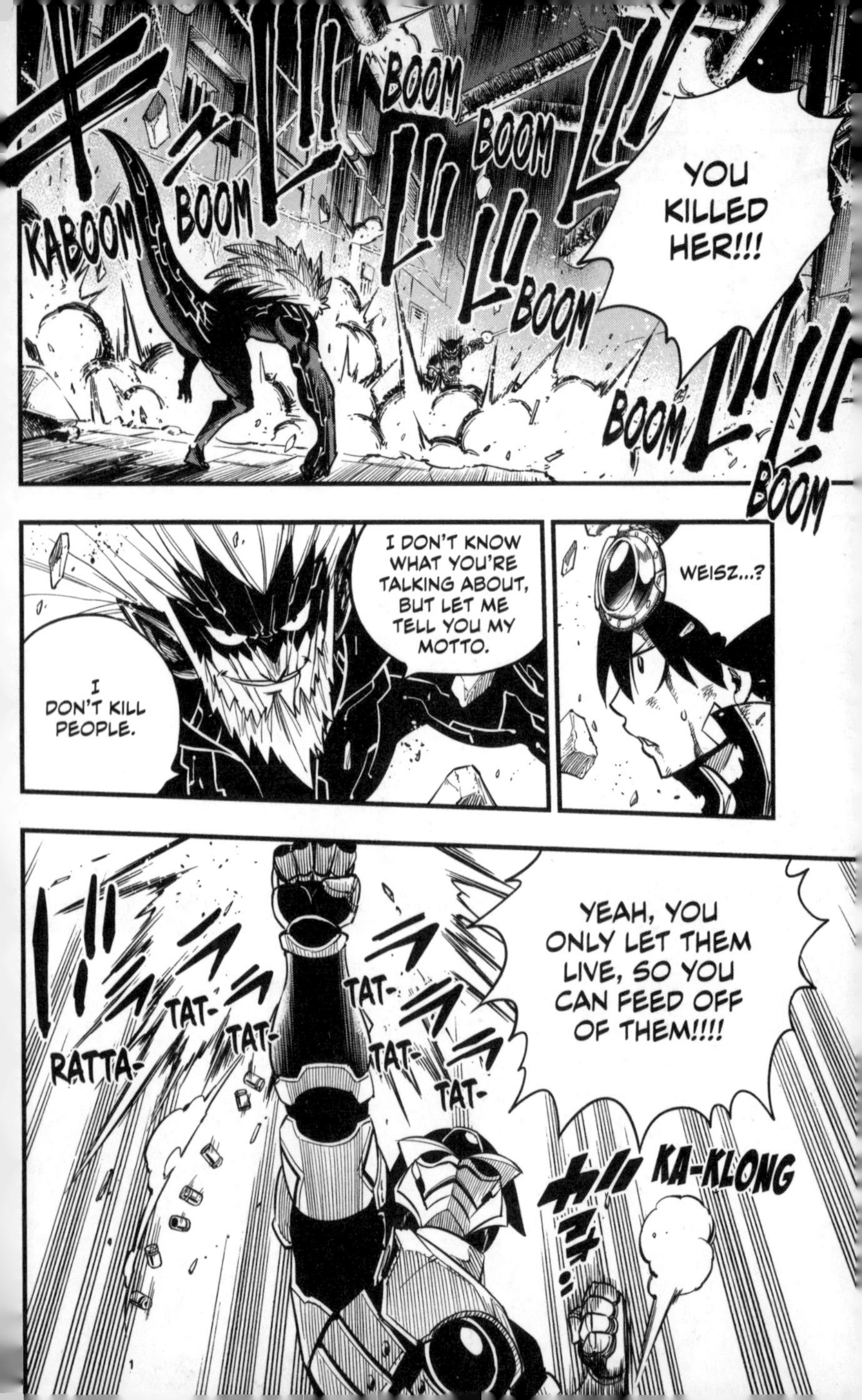
YOU KILLED HER!!!
BOOM
BOOM
BOOM
BOOM
BOOM
KABOOM
BOOM
WEISZ...?
I DON'T KNOW WHAT YOU'RE TALKING ABOUT, BUT LET ME TELL YOU MY MOTTO.
I DON'T KILL PEOPLE.
YEAH, YOU ONLY LET THEM LIVE, SO YOU CAN FEED OFF OF THEM!!!!
KA-KLONG
TAT-TAT-TAT-
RATTA-TAT-TAT-

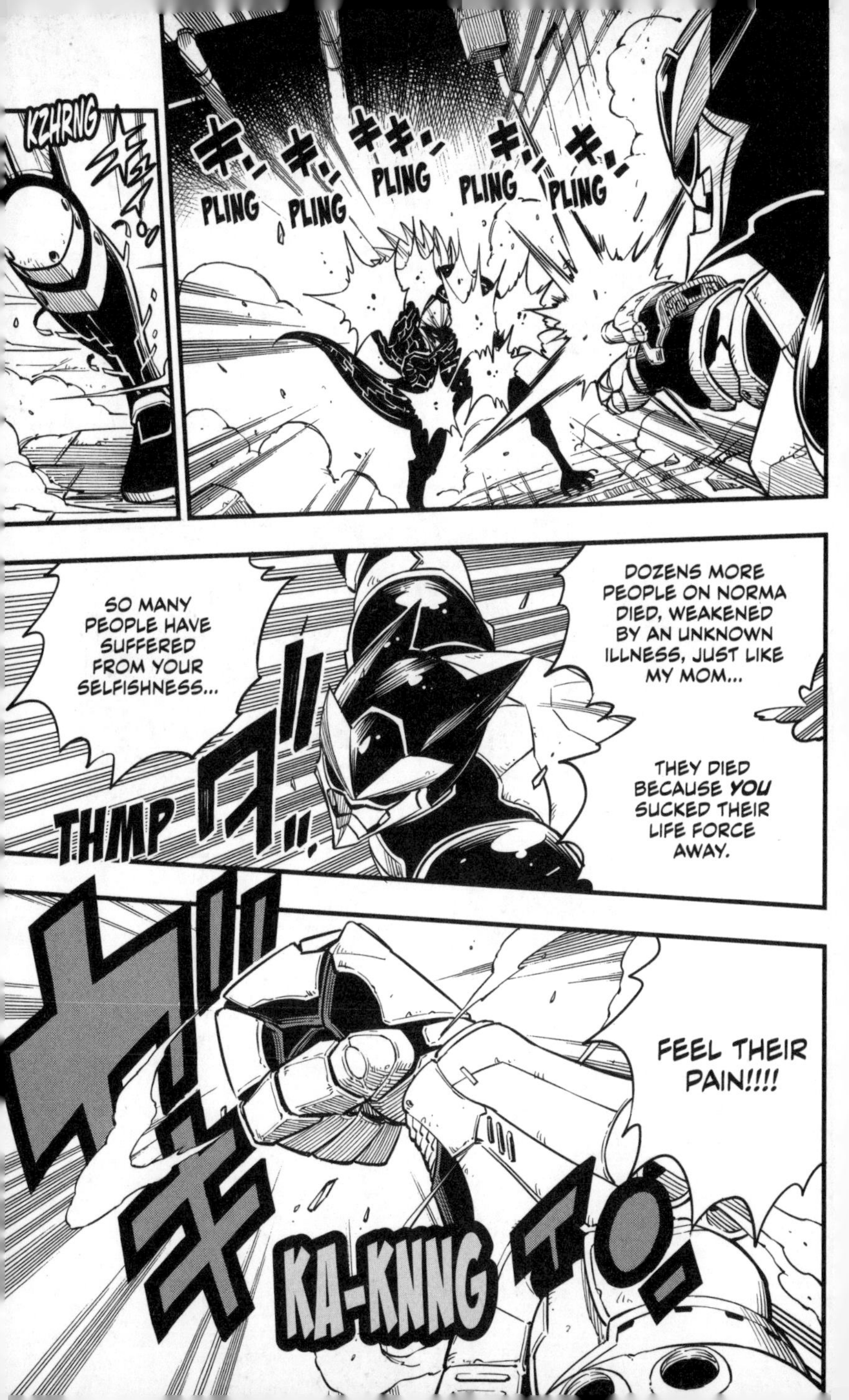
PLING
PLING
PLING
PLING
PLING
KZHRNG
DOZENS MORE PEOPLE ON NORMA DIED, WEAKENED BY AN UNKNOWN ILLNESS, JUST LIKE MY MOM...
THEY DIED BECAUSE *YOU* SUCKED THEIR LIFE FORCE AWAY.
SO MANY PEOPLE HAVE SUFFERED FROM YOUR SELFISHNESS...
THMP
FEEL THEIR PAIN!!!!
KA-KNNG

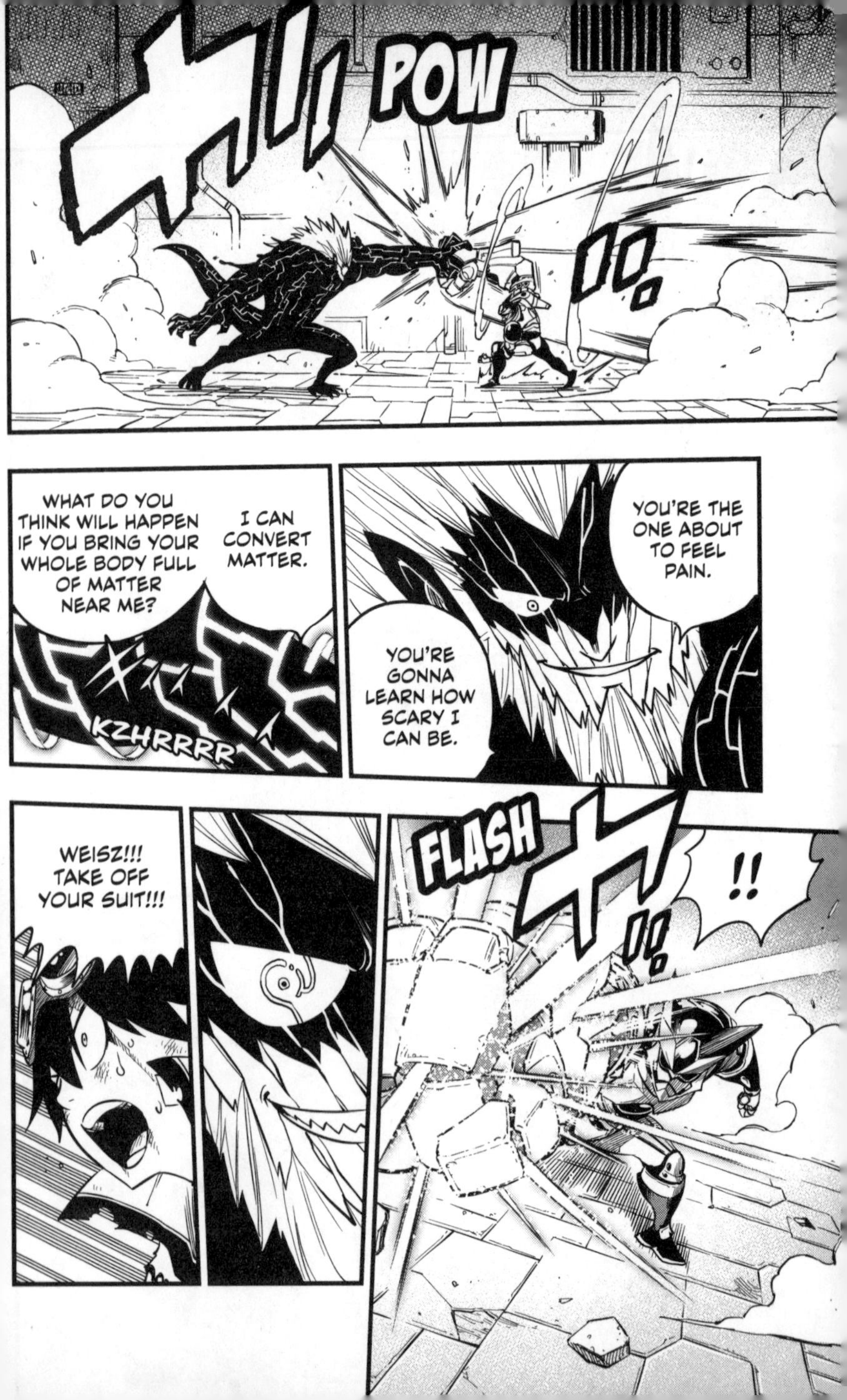
POW
YOU'RE THE ONE ABOUT TO FEEL PAIN.
YOU'RE GONNA LEARN HOW SCARY I CAN BE.
I CAN CONVERT MATTER.
WHAT DO YOU THINK WILL HAPPEN IF YOU BRING YOUR WHOLE BODY FULL OF MATTER NEAR ME?
KZHRRRR
FLASH
!!
WEISZ!!! TAKE OFF YOUR SUIT!!!

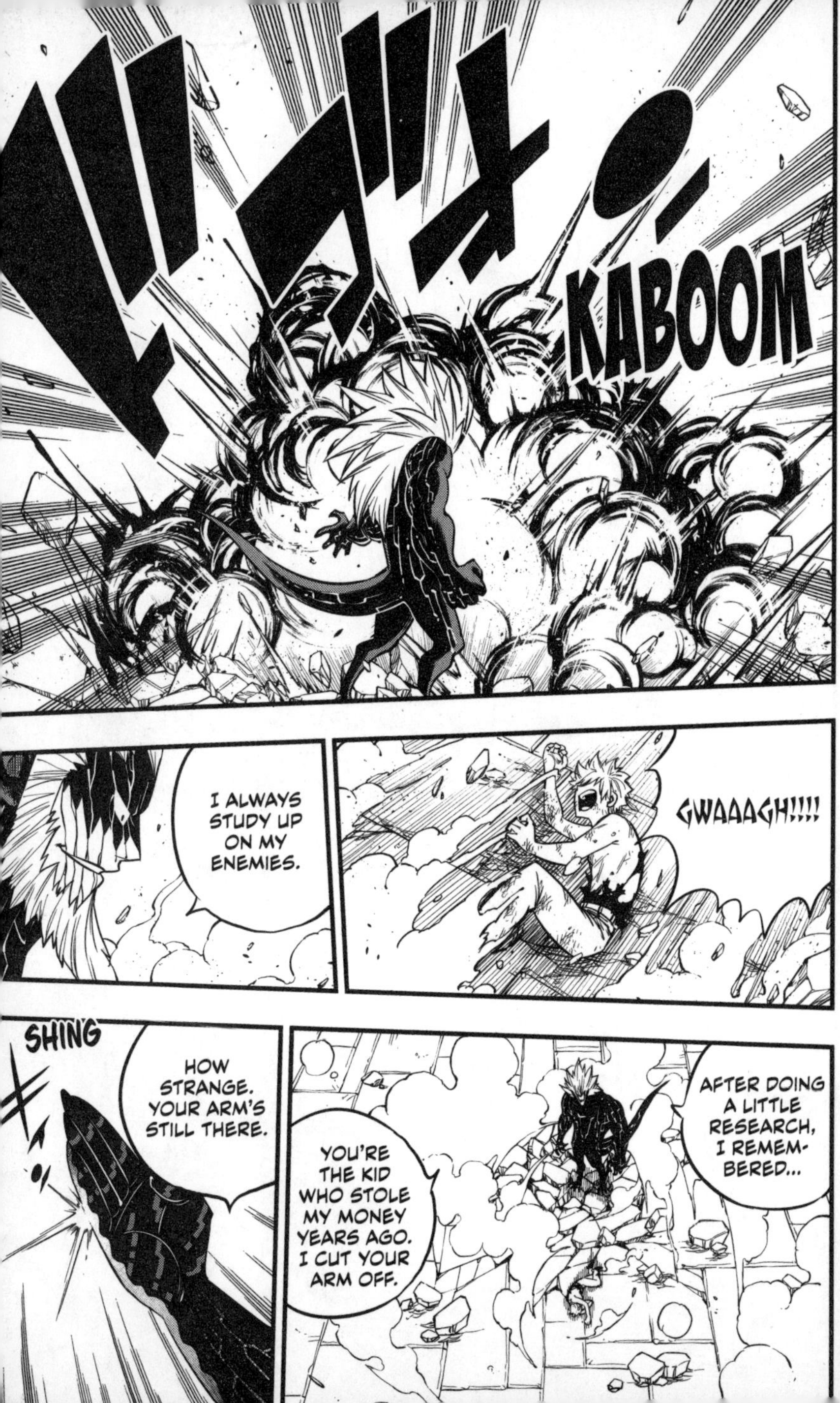
KABOOM
GWAAAGH!!!!
I ALWAYS STUDY UP ON MY ENEMIES.
AFTER DOING A LITTLE RESEARCH, I REMEM-BERED...
YOU'RE THE KID WHO STOLE MY MONEY YEARS AGO. I CUT YOUR ARM OFF.
SHING
HOW STRANGE. YOUR ARM'S STILL THERE.

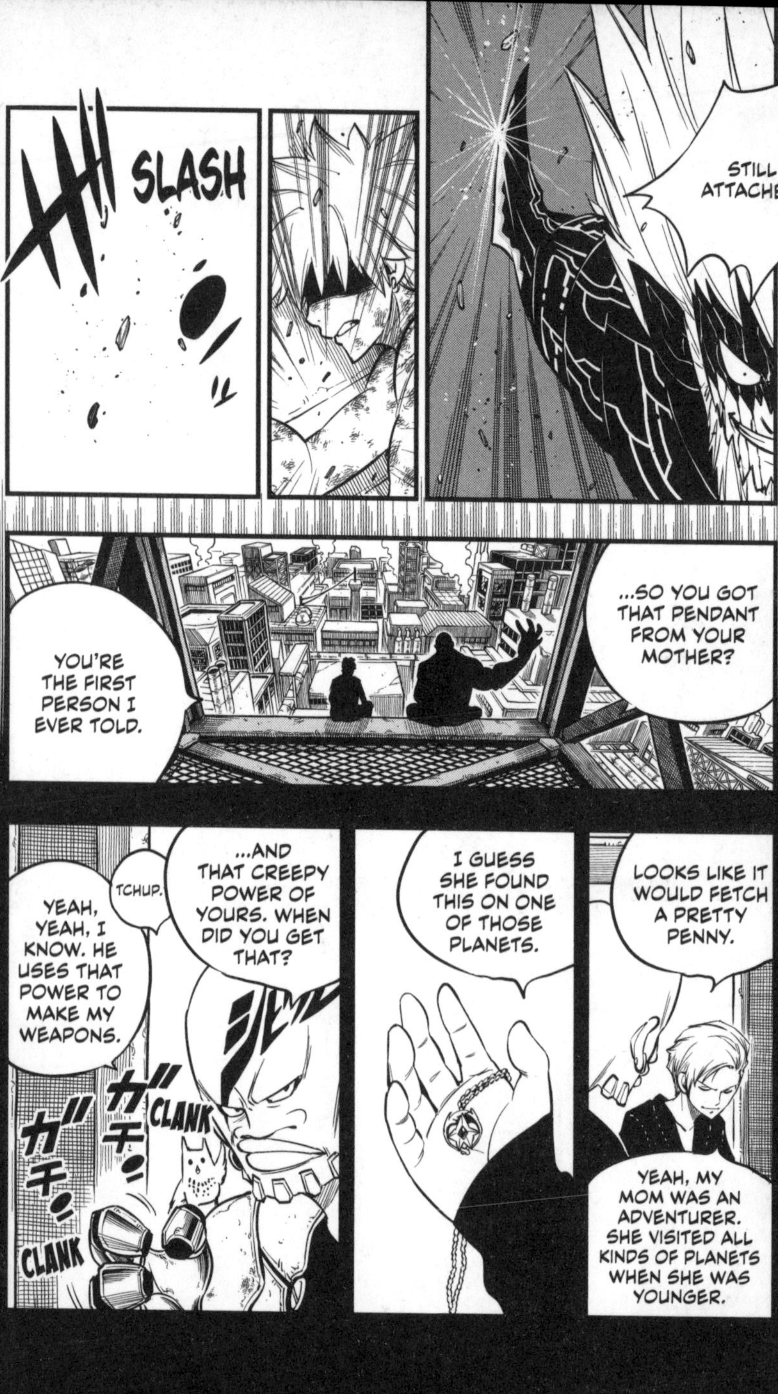
STILL ATTACHED.
SLASH
...SO YOU GOT THAT PENDANT FROM YOUR MOTHER?
YOU'RE THE FIRST PERSON I EVER TOLD.
LOOKS LIKE IT WOULD FETCH A PRETTY PENNY.
YEAH, MY MOM WAS AN ADVENTURER. SHE VISITED ALL KINDS OF PLANETS WHEN SHE WAS YOUNGER.
I GUESS SHE FOUND THIS ON ONE OF THOSE PLANETS.
...AND THAT CREEPY POWER OF YOURS. WHEN DID YOU GET THAT?
TCHUP.
YEAH, YEAH, I KNOW. HE USES THAT POWER TO MAKE MY WEAPONS.
CLANK
CLANK

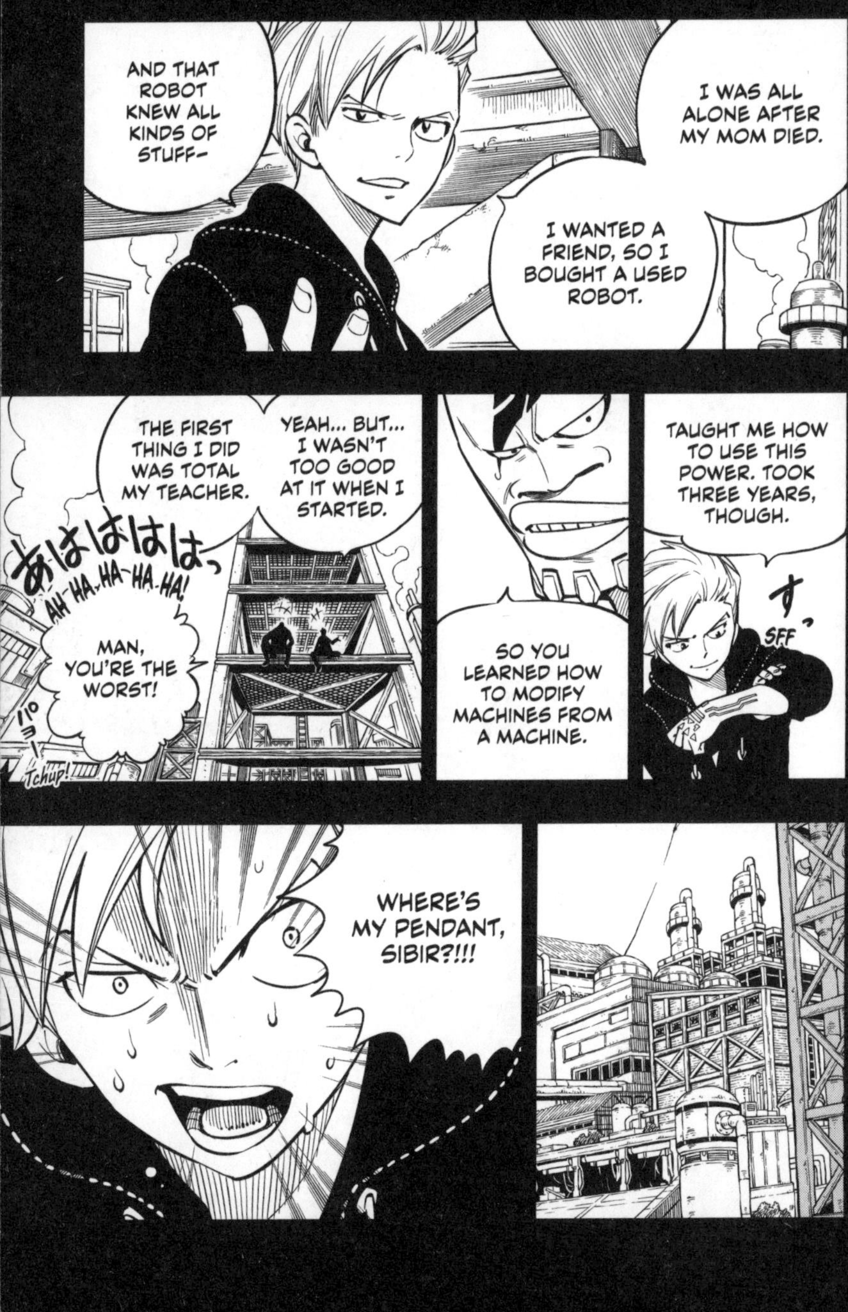
I WAS ALL ALONE AFTER MY MOM DIED.
I WANTED A FRIEND, SO I BOUGHT A USED ROBOT.
AND THAT ROBOT KNEW ALL KINDS OF STUFF–
TAUGHT ME HOW TO USE THIS POWER. TOOK THREE YEARS, THOUGH.
す
SFF
SO YOU LEARNED HOW TO MODIFY MACHINES FROM A MACHINE.
YEAH... BUT... I WASN'T TOO GOOD AT IT WHEN I STARTED.
THE FIRST THING I DID WAS TOTAL MY TEACHER.
あははははっ
AH-HA-HA-HA-HA!
MAN, YOU'RE THE WORST!
Tchup!
WHERE'S MY PENDANT, SIBIR?!!!

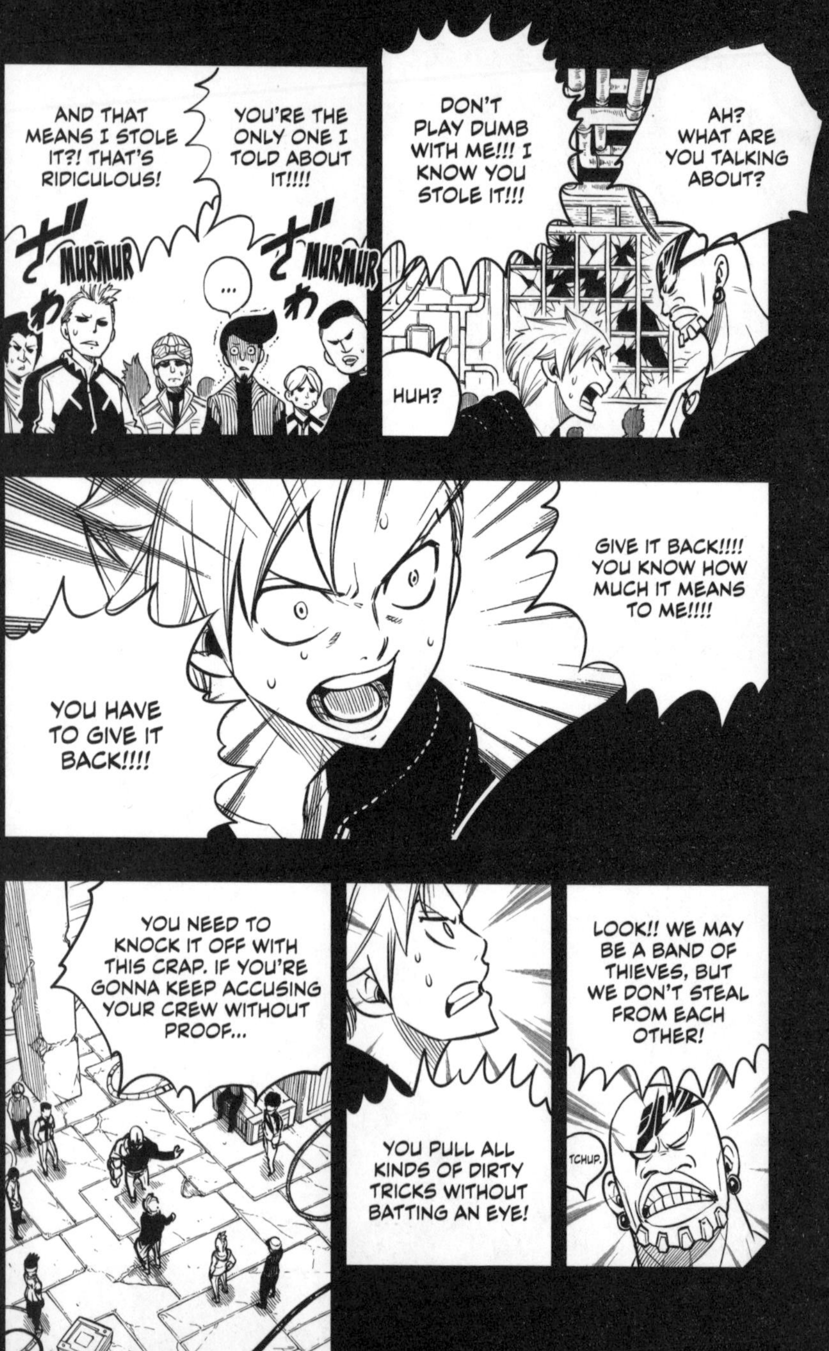
AH? WHAT ARE YOU TALKING ABOUT?
DON'T PLAY DUMB WITH ME!!! I KNOW YOU STOLE IT!!!
HUH?
YOU'RE THE ONLY ONE I TOLD ABOUT IT!!!!
AND THAT MEANS I STOLE IT?! THAT'S RIDICULOUS!
ざわ MURMUR
...
ざわ MURMUR
GIVE IT BACK!!!! YOU KNOW HOW MUCH IT MEANS TO ME!!!!
YOU HAVE TO GIVE IT BACK!!!!
LOOK!! WE MAY BE A BAND OF THIEVES, BUT WE DON'T STEAL FROM EACH OTHER!
TCHUP.
YOU PULL ALL KINDS OF DIRTY TRICKS WITHOUT BATTING AN EYE!
YOU NEED TO KNOCK IT OFF WITH THIS CRAP. IF YOU'RE GONNA KEEP ACCUSING YOUR CREW WITHOUT PROOF...

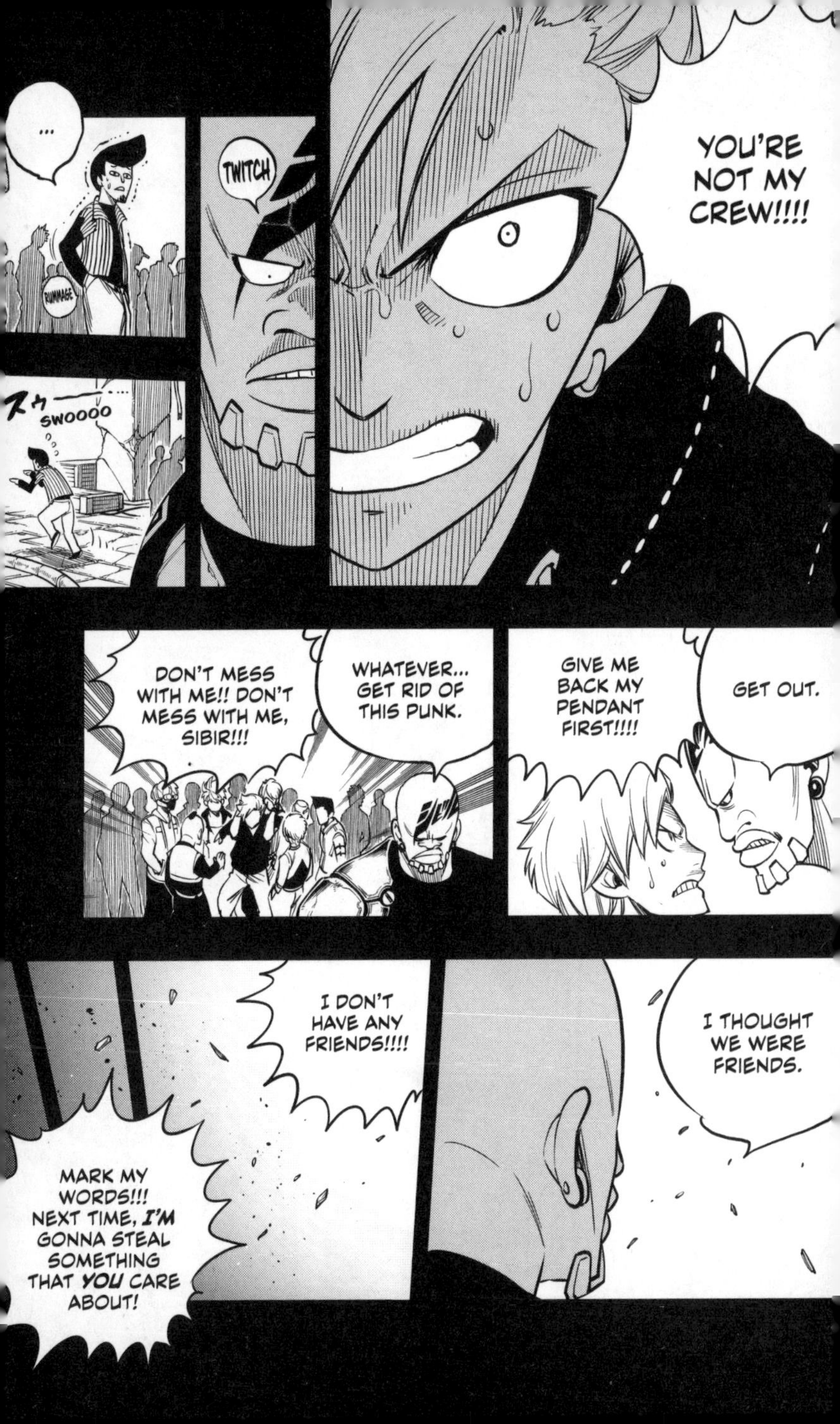

YOU'RE NOT MY CREW!!!!
TWITCH
...
RUMMAGE
SWOOOO
GET OUT.
GIVE ME BACK MY PENDANT FIRST!!!!
WHATEVER... GET RID OF THIS PUNK.
DON'T MESS WITH ME!! DON'T MESS WITH ME, SIBIR!!!
I THOUGHT WE WERE FRIENDS.
I DON'T HAVE ANY FRIENDS!!!!
MARK MY WORDS!!! NEXT TIME, *I'M* GONNA STEAL SOMETHING THAT *YOU* CARE ABOUT!

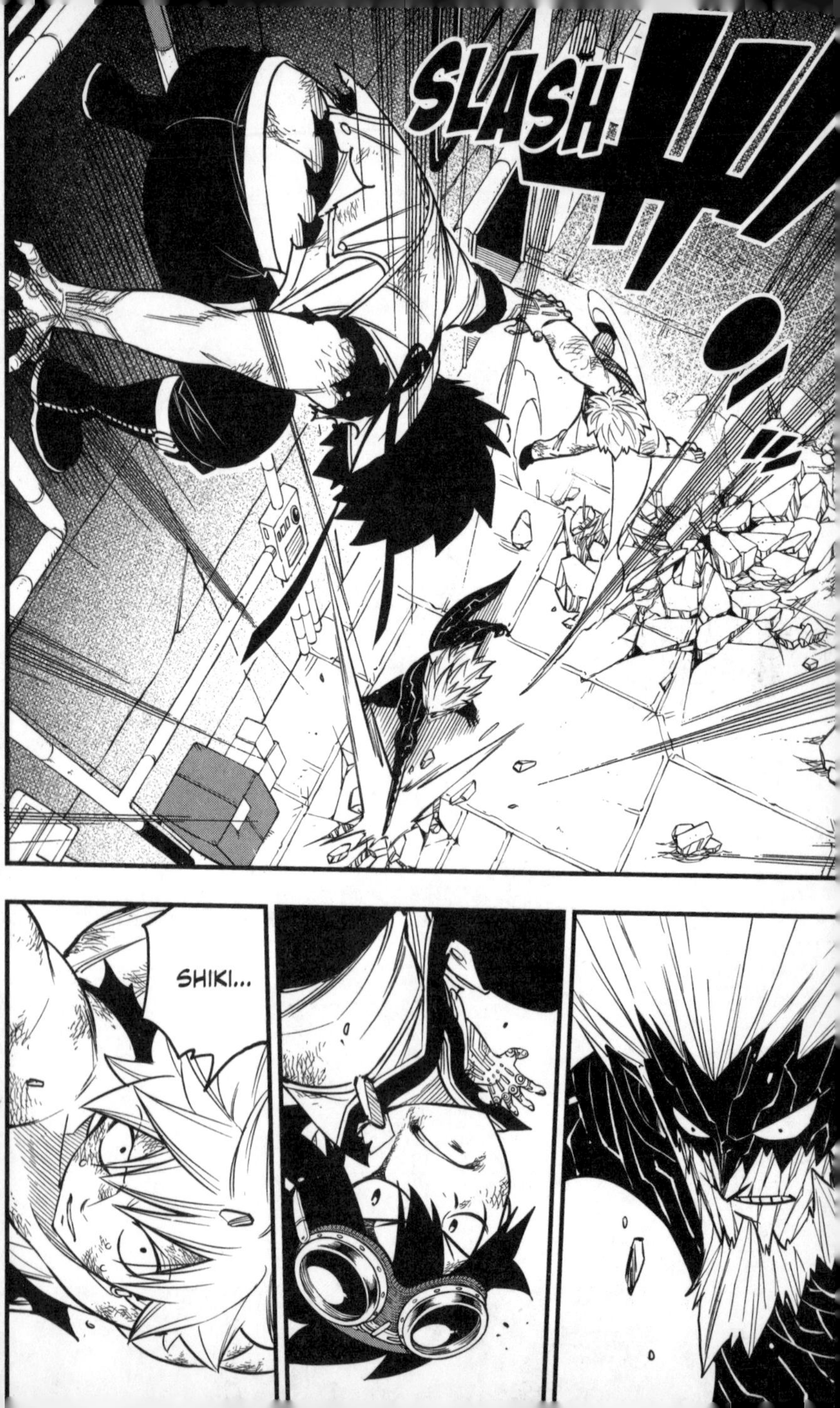
SLASH
SHIKI...

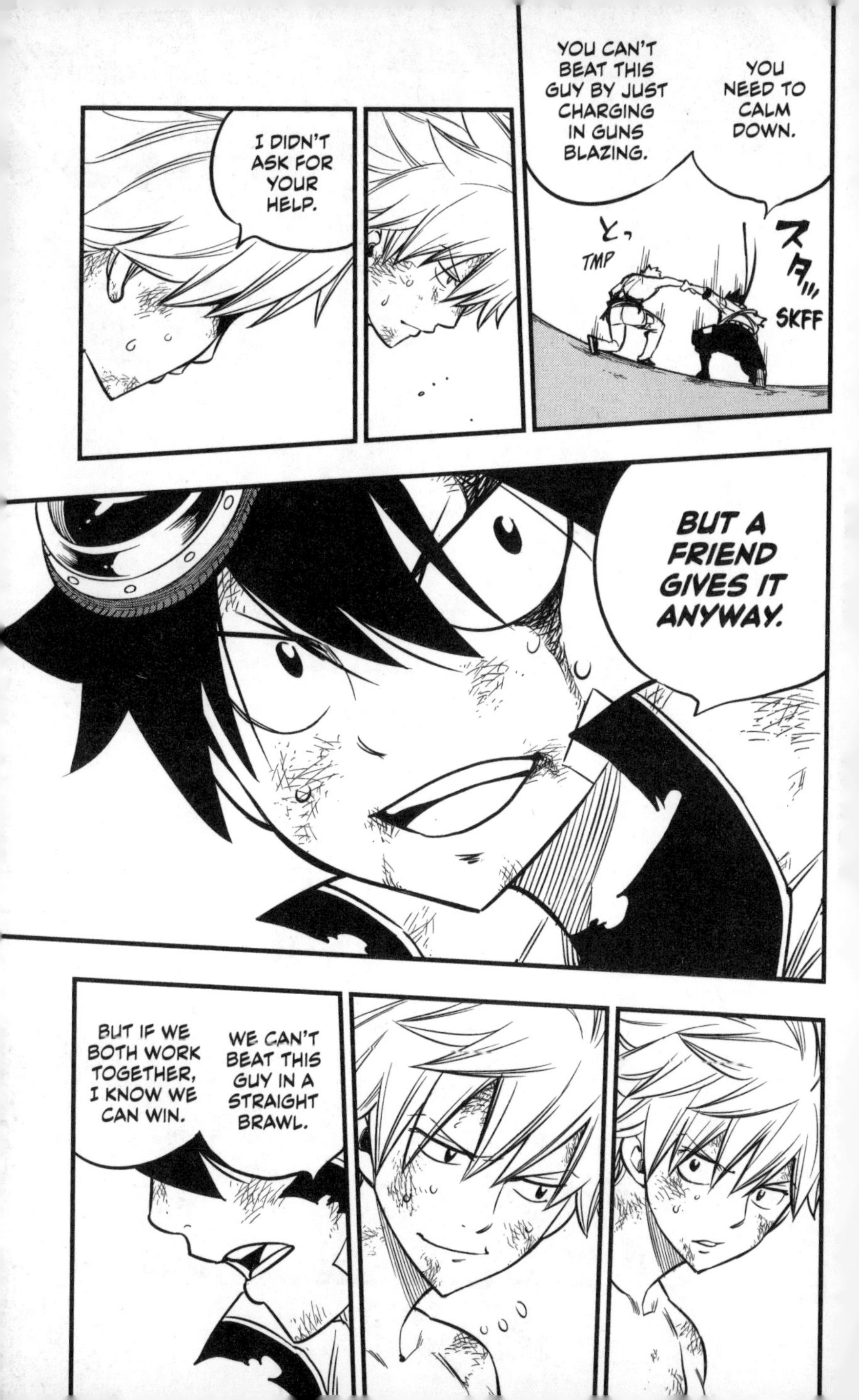
YOU NEED TO CALM DOWN.
YOU CAN'T BEAT THIS GUY BY JUST CHARGING IN GUNS BLAZING.
スタ
SKFF
と
TMP
...
I DIDN'T ASK FOR YOUR HELP.
BUT A FRIEND GIVES IT ANYWAY.
WE CAN'T BEAT THIS GUY IN A STRAIGHT BRAWL.
BUT IF WE BOTH WORK TOGETHER, I KNOW WE CAN WIN.

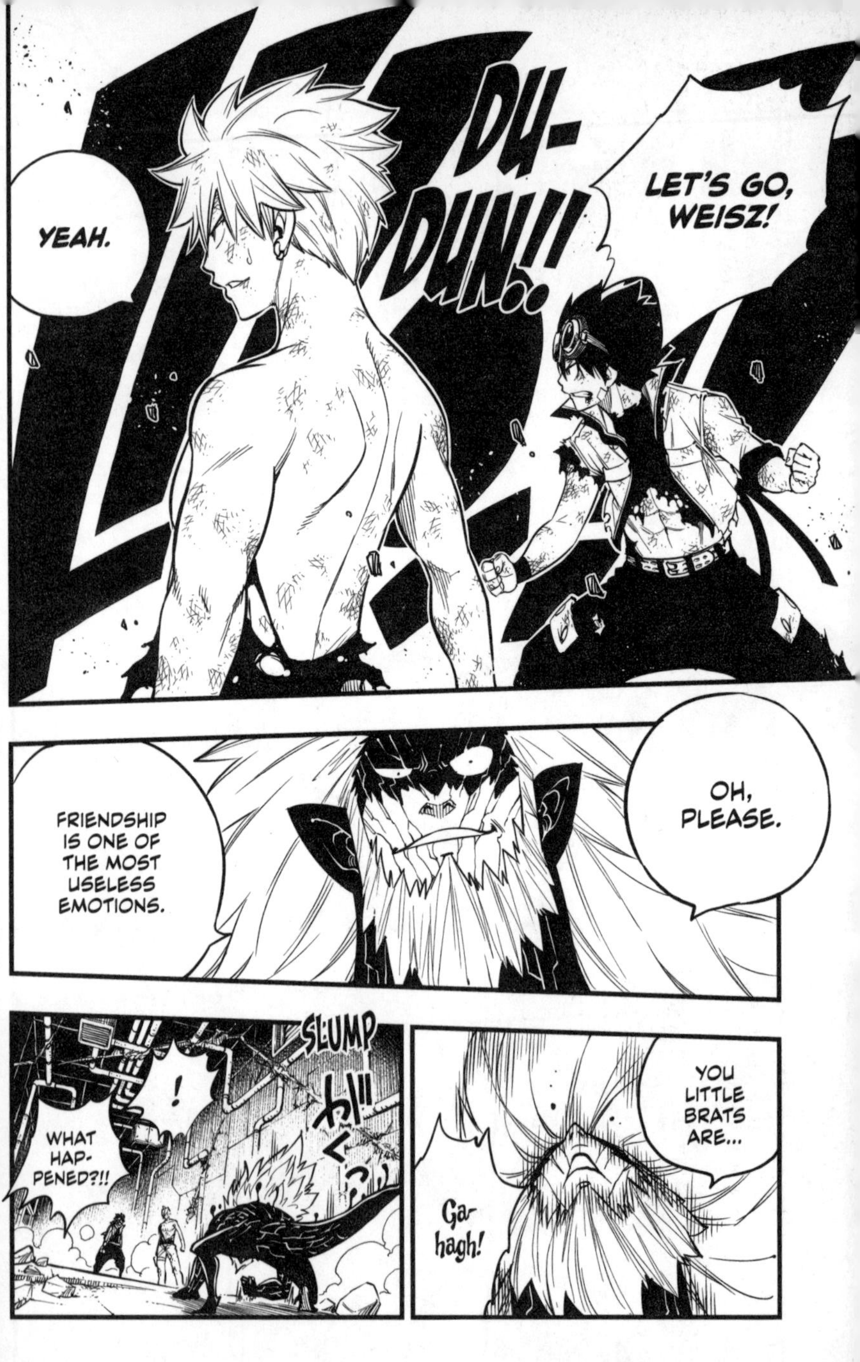
LET'S GO, WEISZ!
DU-DUN!!
YEAH.
OH, PLEASE.
FRIENDSHIP IS ONE OF THE MOST USELESS EMOTIONS.
YOU LITTLE BRATS ARE...
Ga-hagh!
SLUMP
!
WHAT HAP-PENED?!!

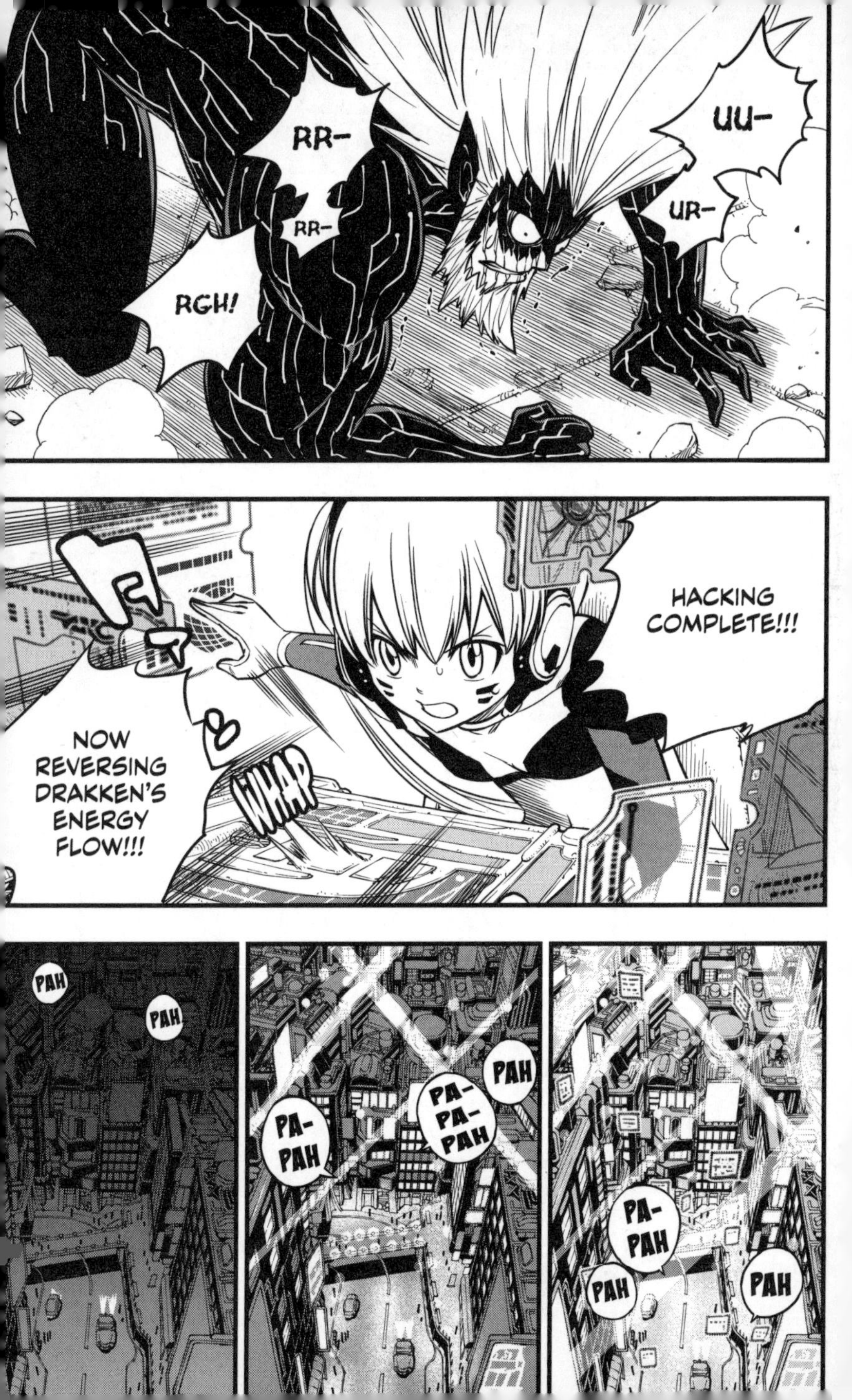
UU-
UR-
RR-
RR-
RGH!
HACKING COMPLETE!!!
WHAP
NOW REVERSING DRAKKEN'S ENERGY FLOW!!!
PA-PAH
PAH
PAH
PAH
PA-PA-PAH
PA-PAH
PAH
PAH

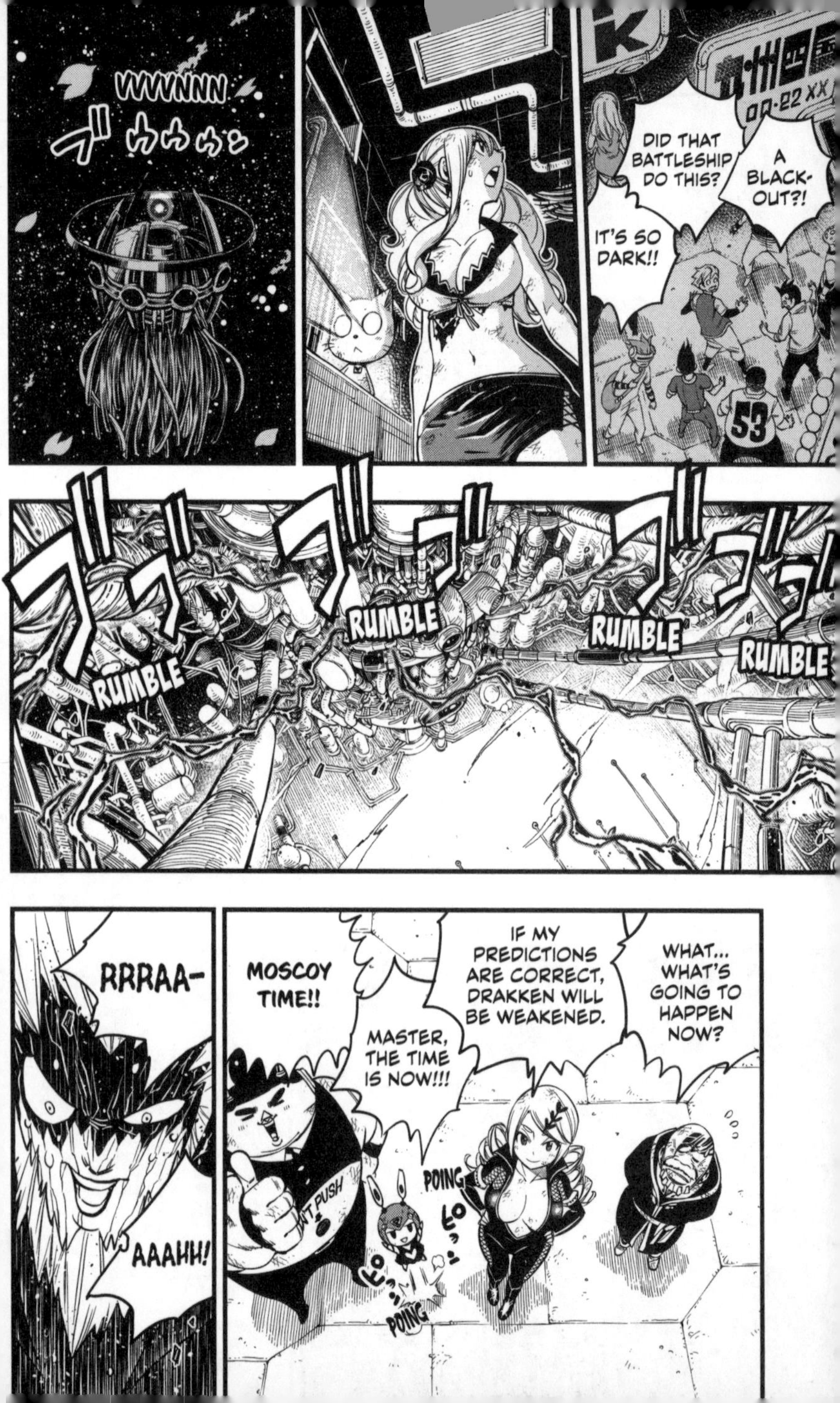
A BLACK-OUT?!
DID THAT BATTLESHIP DO THIS?
IT'S SO DARK!!
VVVVNNN
RUMBLE
RUMBLE
RUMBLE
RUMBLE
WHAT... WHAT'S GOING TO HAPPEN NOW?
IF MY PREDICTIONS ARE CORRECT, DRAKKEN WILL BE WEAKENED.
MOSCOY TIME!!
MASTER, THE TIME IS NOW!!!
POING
PUSH
POING
RRRAA-
AAAHH!

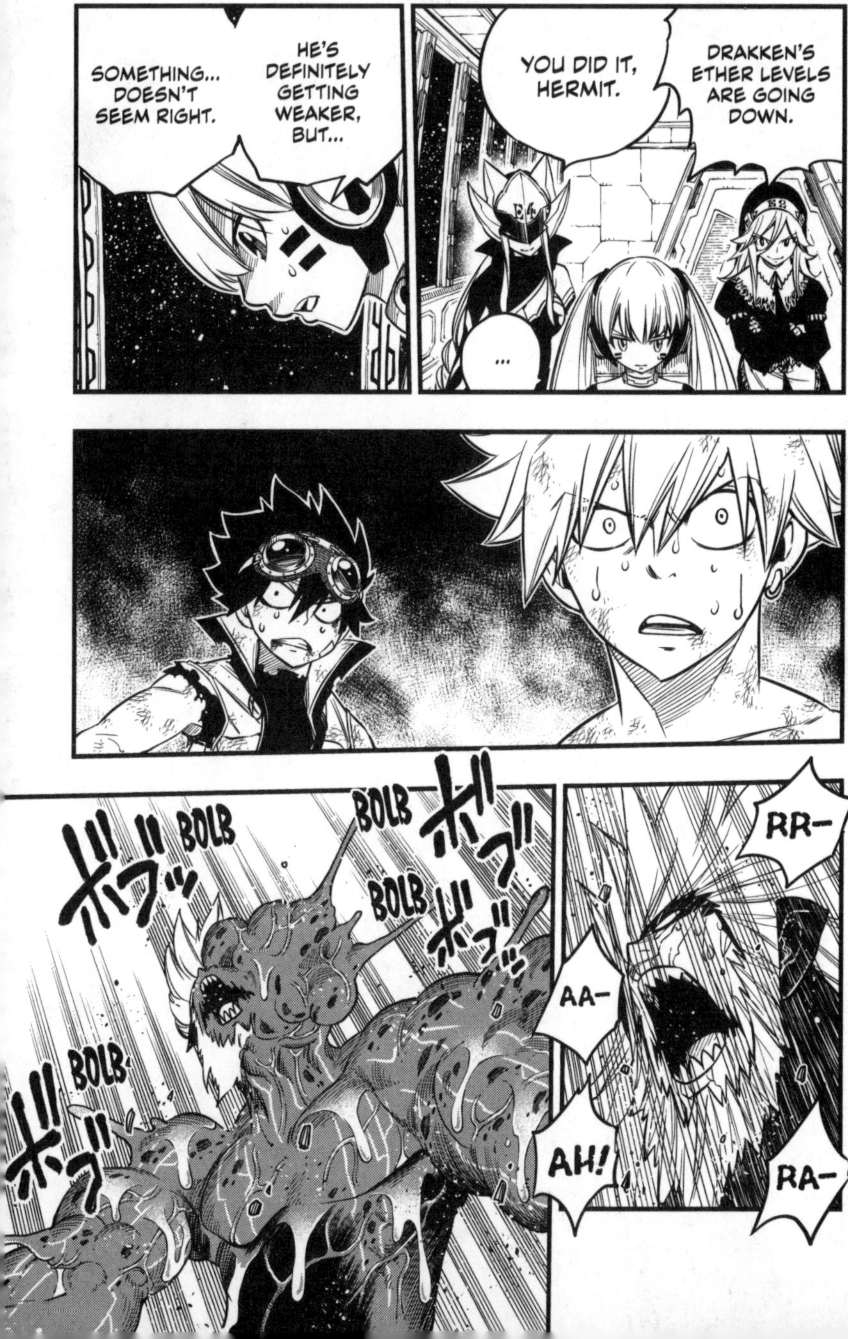
DRAKKEN'S ETHER LEVELS ARE GOING DOWN.
YOU DID IT, HERMIT.
...
HE'S DEFINITELY GETTING WEAKER, BUT...
SOMETHING... DOESN'T SEEM RIGHT.
RR-
AA-
RA-
AH!
BOLB
BOLB
BOLB
BOLB

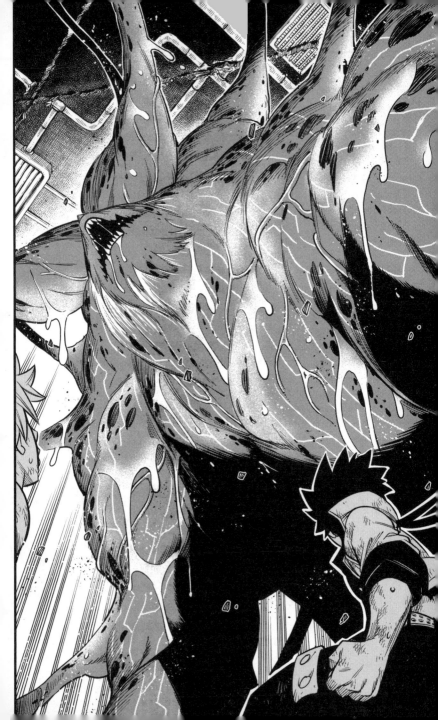

EDENS ZERO

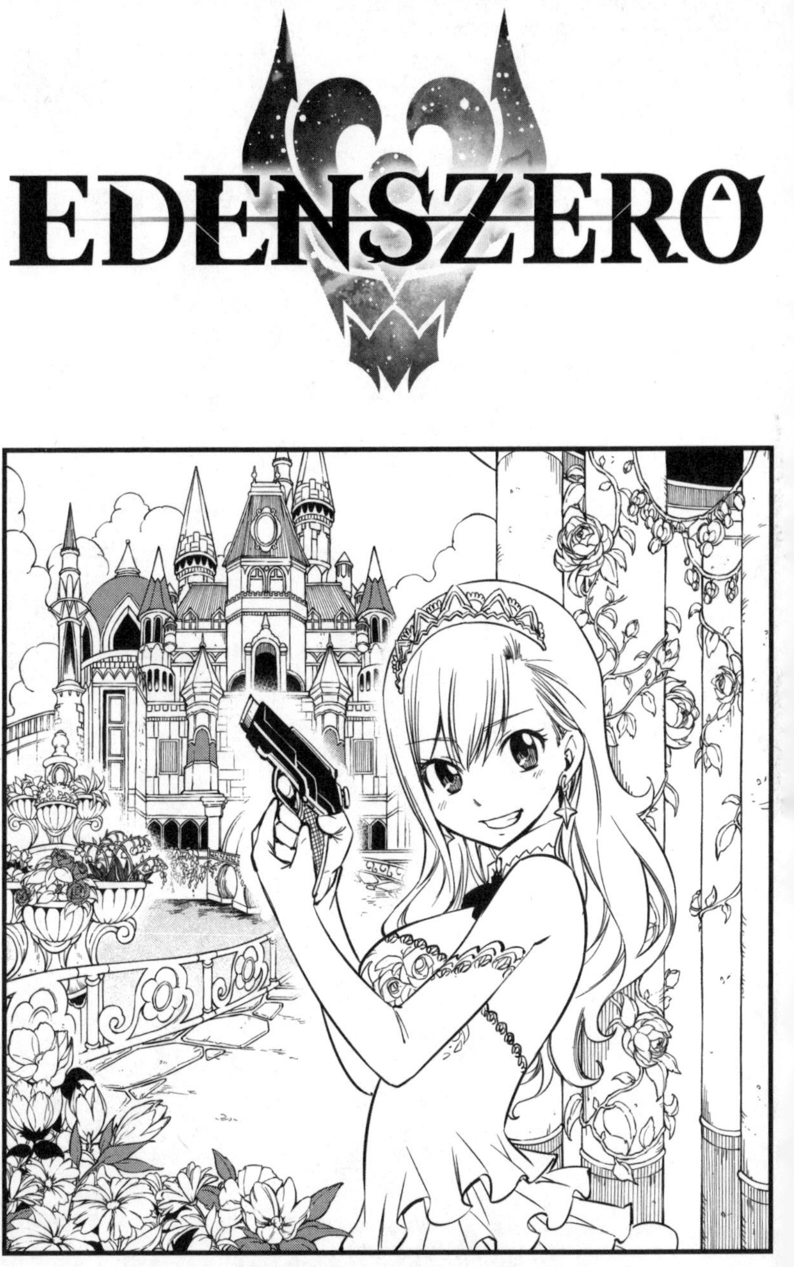

CHAPTER 97: THE TIME IS NOW

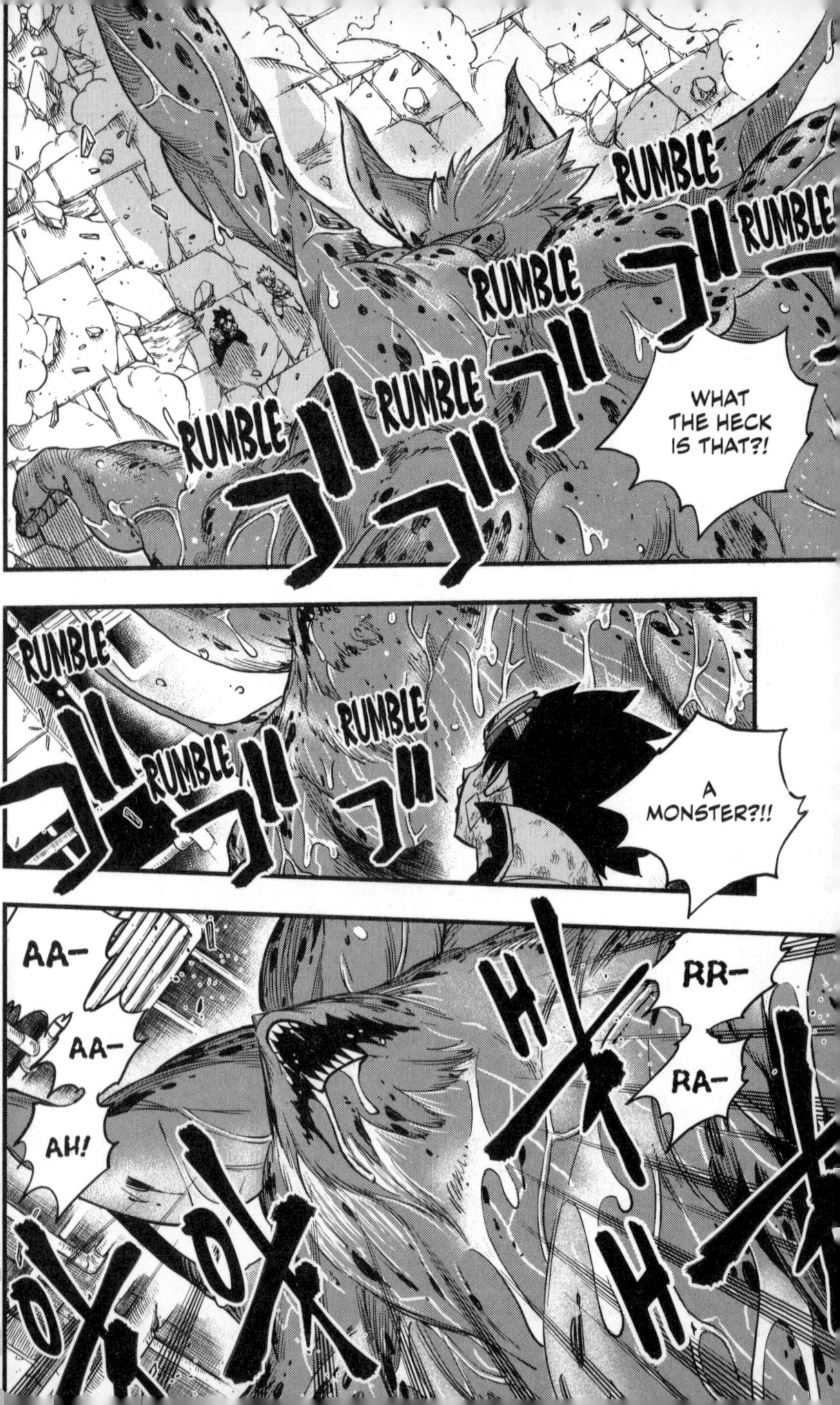
RUMBLE
RUMBLE
WHAT THE HECK IS THAT?!
RUMBLE
RUMBLE
RUMBLE
A MONSTER?!!
RUMBLE
RUMBLE
RUMBLE
RR-
RA-
AA-
AA-
AH!

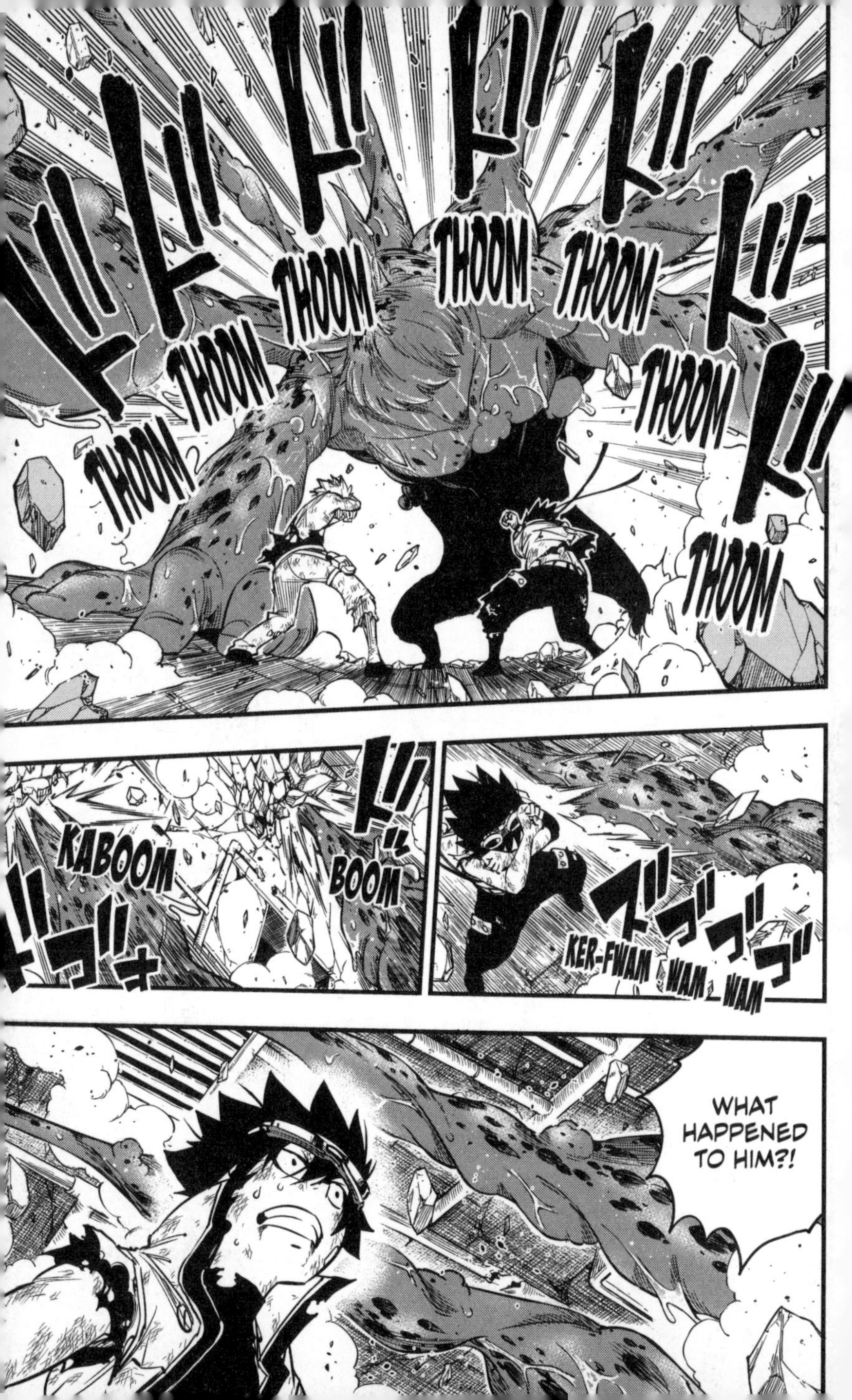
THOOM
THOOM
THOOM
THOOM
THOOM
THOOM
THOOM
KER-FWAM
WAM
WAM
KABOOM
BOOM
WHAT HAPPENED TO HIM?!

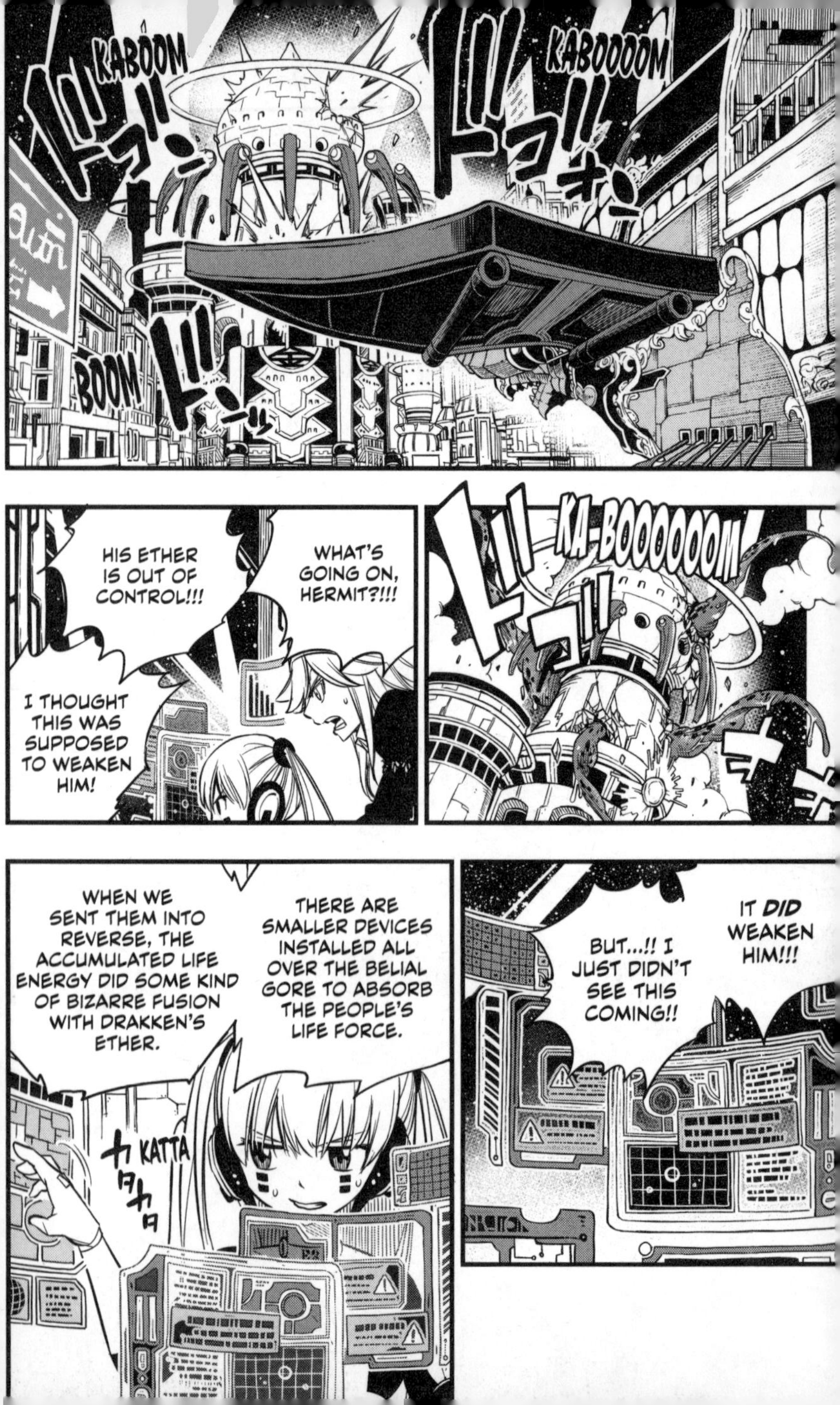
KABOOOOM
KABOOM
BOOM
KA-BOOOOOOM!
WHAT'S GOING ON, HERMIT?!!!
HIS ETHER IS OUT OF CONTROL!!!
I THOUGHT THIS WAS SUPPOSED TO WEAKEN HIM!
IT *DID* WEAKEN HIM!!!
BUT...!! I JUST DIDN'T SEE THIS COMING!!
THERE ARE SMALLER DEVICES INSTALLED ALL OVER THE BELIAL GORE TO ABSORB THE PEOPLE'S LIFE FORCE.
WHEN WE SENT THEM INTO REVERSE, THE ACCUMULATED LIFE ENERGY DID SOME KIND OF BIZARRE FUSION WITH DRAKKEN'S ETHER.
KATTA

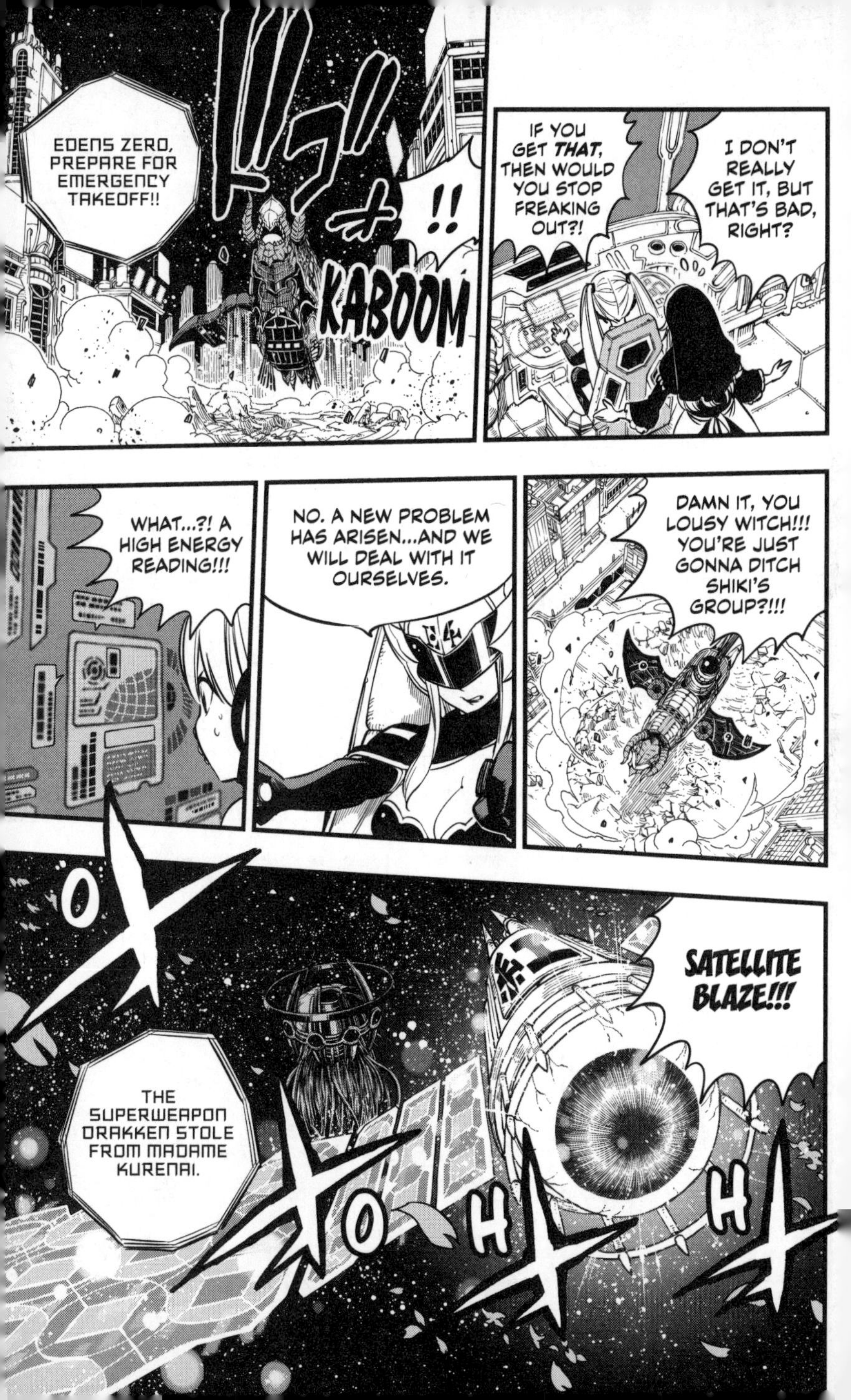
I DON'T REALLY GET IT, BUT THAT'S BAD, RIGHT?
IF YOU GET *THAT*, THEN WOULD YOU STOP FREAKING OUT?!
!!
KABOOM
EDENS ZERO, PREPARE FOR EMERGENCY TAKEOFF!!
DAMN IT, YOU LOUSY WITCH!!! YOU'RE JUST GONNA DITCH SHIKI'S GROUP?!!!
NO. A NEW PROBLEM HAS ARISEN...AND WE WILL DEAL WITH IT OURSELVES.
WHAT...?! A HIGH ENERGY READING!!!
SATELLITE BLAZE!!!
THE SUPERWEAPON DRAKKEN STOLE FROM MADAME KURENAI.
O
O H H

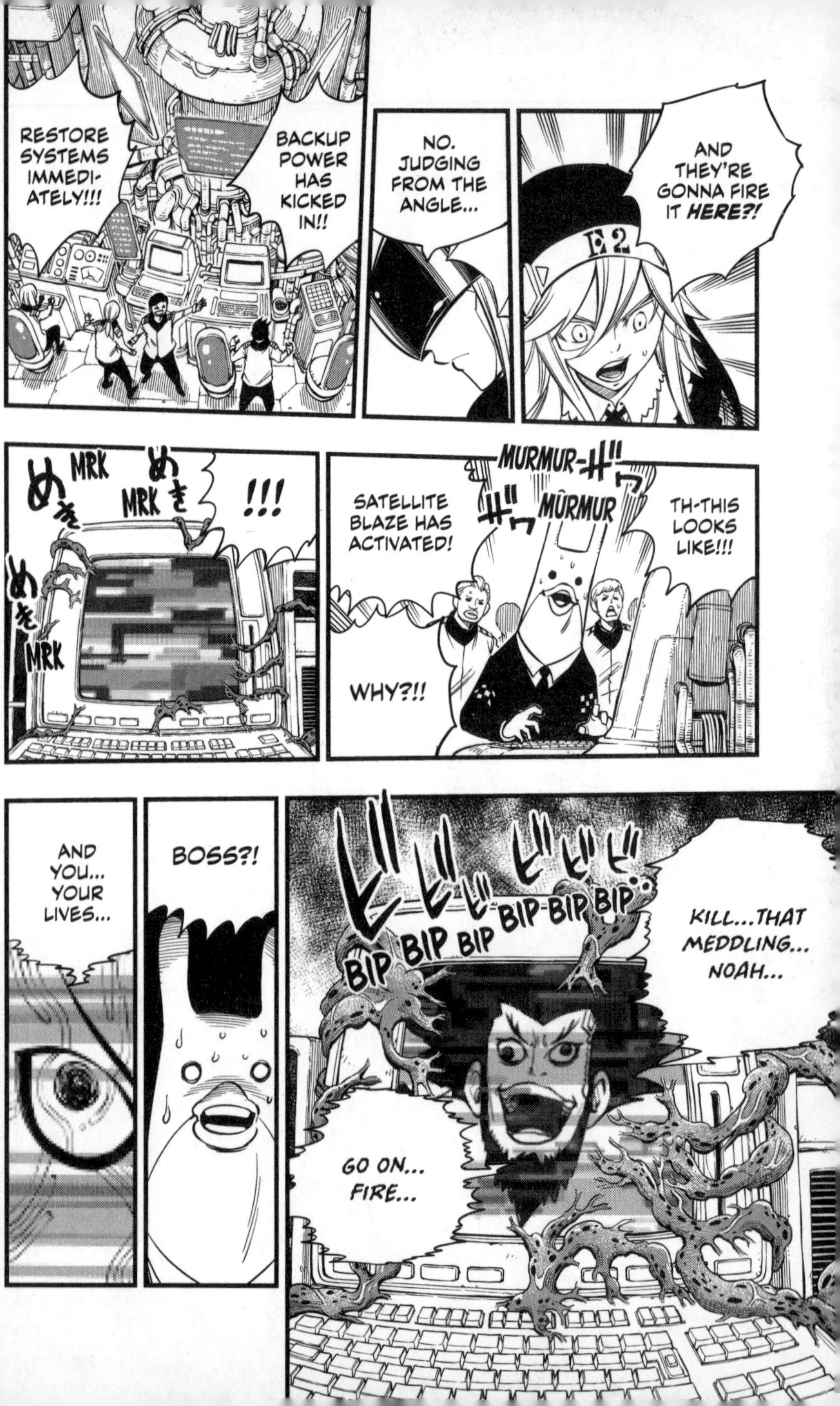
AND THEY'RE GONNA FIRE IT *HERE?!*
NO. JUDGING FROM THE ANGLE...
BACKUP POWER HAS KICKED IN!!
RESTORE SYSTEMS IMMEDI-ATELY!!!
TH-THIS LOOKS LIKE!!!
MURMUR-ザワ
ザワ MURMUR
SATELLITE BLAZE HAS ACTIVATED!
WHY?!!
!!!
めき MRK
めき MRK
めき MRK
KILL...THAT MEDDLING... NOAH...
ビビビ BIP-BIP BIP
ビビ BIP BIP BIP
GO ON... FIRE...
BOSS?!
AND YOU... YOUR LIVES...

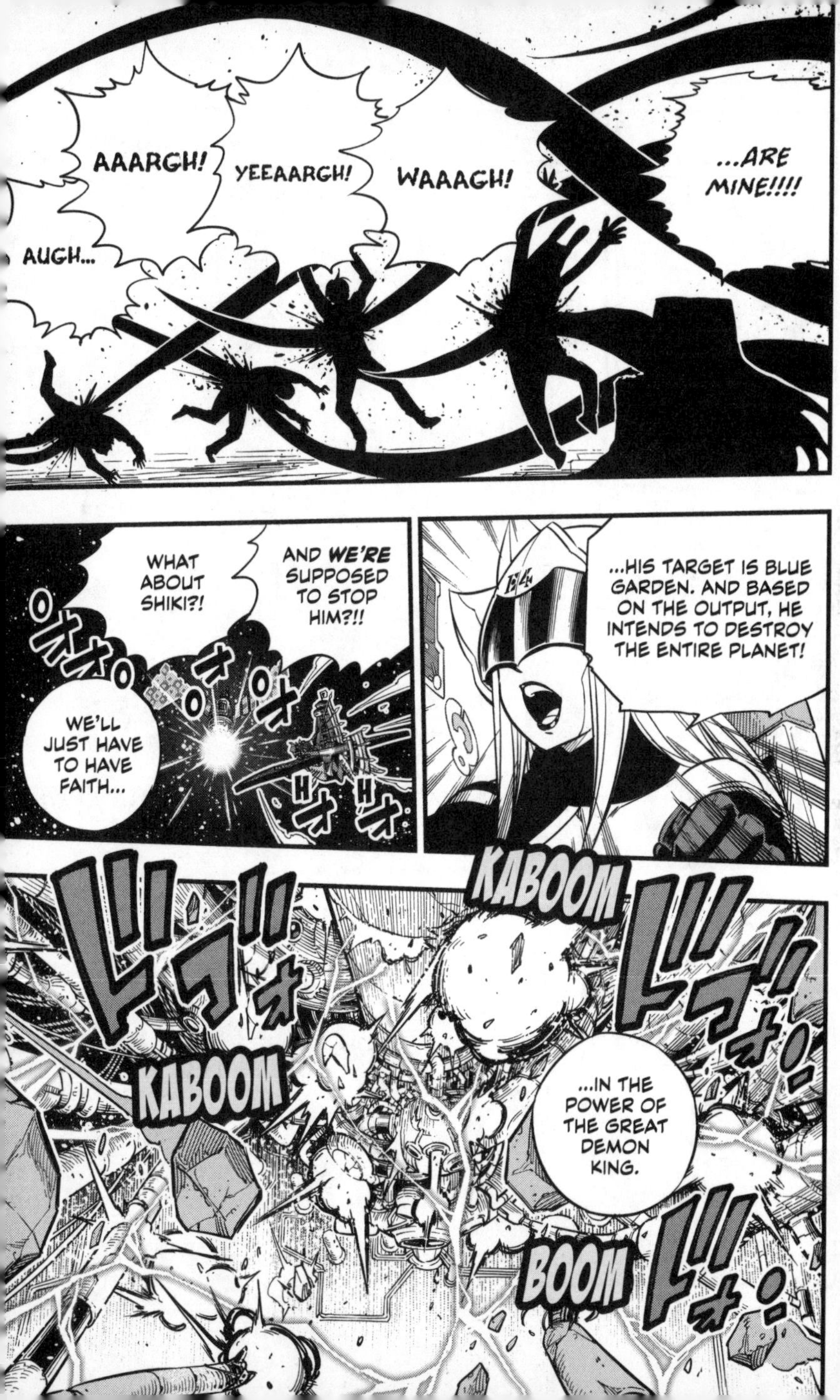
...ARE MINE!!!!
WAAAGH!
YEEAARGH!
AAARGH!
AUGH...
...HIS TARGET IS BLUE GARDEN. AND BASED ON THE OUTPUT, HE INTENDS TO DESTROY THE ENTIRE PLANET!
AND WE'RE SUPPOSED TO STOP HIM?!!
WHAT ABOUT SHIKI?!
WE'LL JUST HAVE TO HAVE FAITH...
KABOOM
...IN THE POWER OF THE GREAT DEMON KING.
KABOOM
BOOM

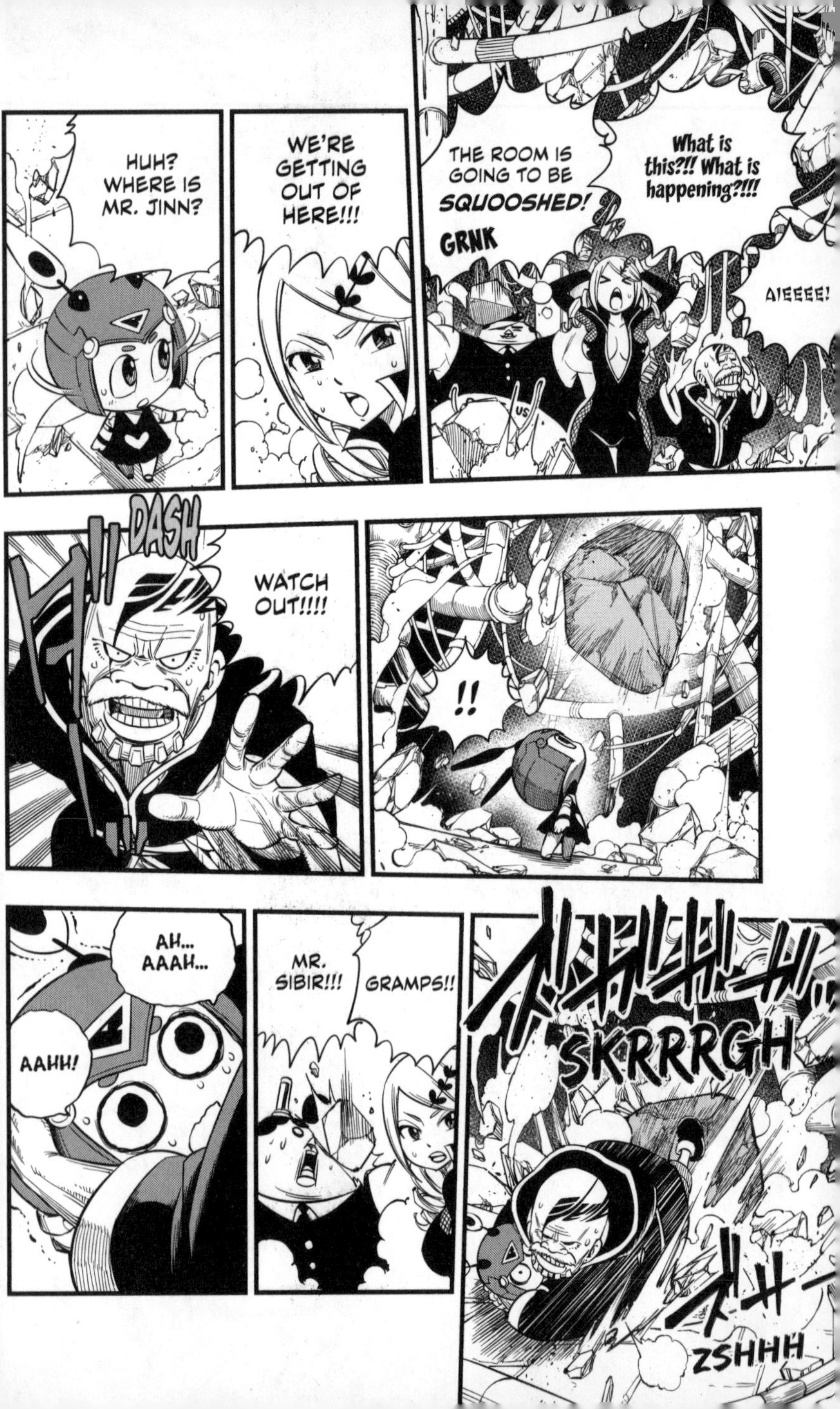
What is this?!! What is happening?!!!
THE ROOM IS GOING TO BE SQUOOSHED!
GRNK
AIEEEE!
WE'RE GETTING OUT OF HERE!!!
HUH? WHERE IS MR. JINN?
!!
DASH
WATCH OUT!!!!
SKRRRGH
ZSHHH
MR. SIBIR!!!
GRAMPS!!
AH... AAAH...
AAHH!

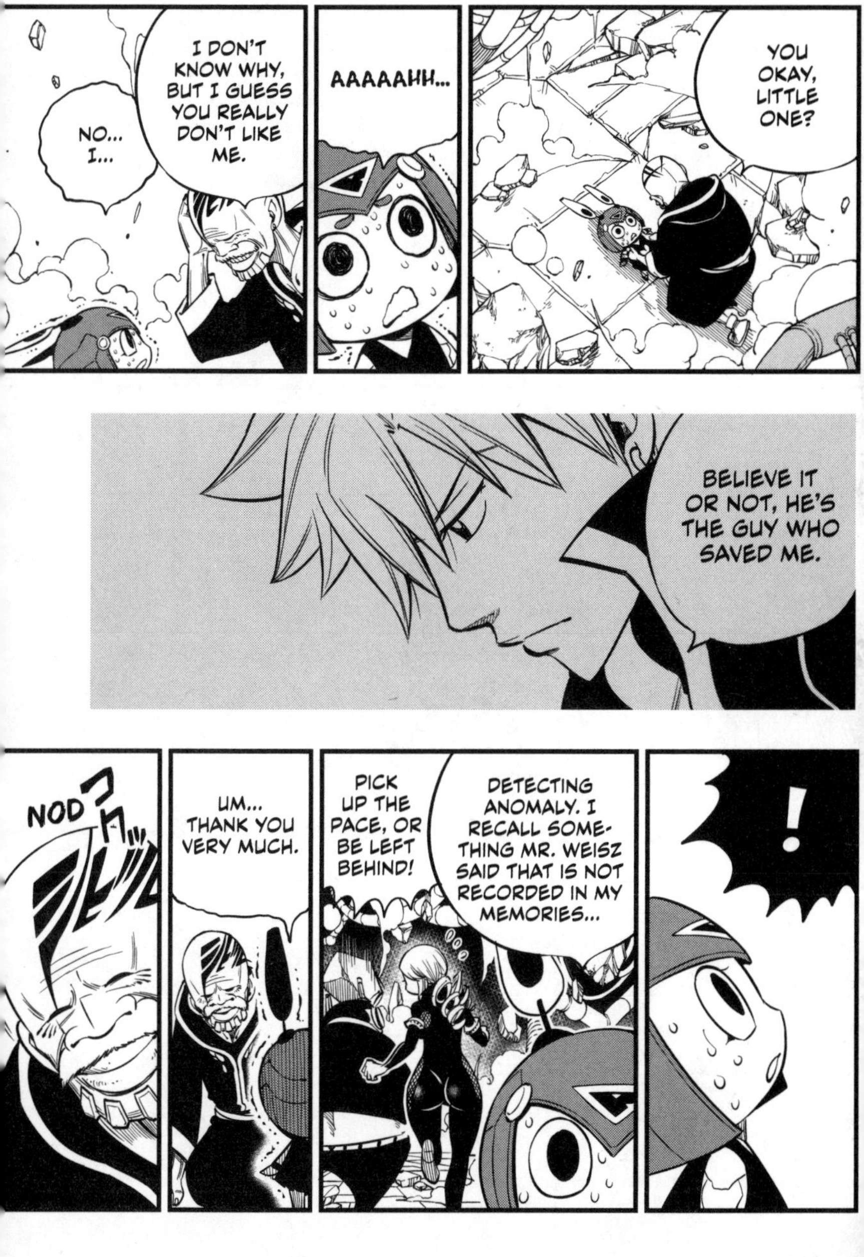
YOU OKAY, LITTLE ONE?
AAAAAHH...
I DON'T KNOW WHY, BUT I GUESS YOU REALLY DON'T LIKE ME.
NO... I...
BELIEVE IT OR NOT, HE'S THE GUY WHO SAVED ME.
!
DETECTING ANOMALY. I RECALL SOMETHING MR. WEISZ SAID THAT IS NOT RECORDED IN MY MEMORIES...
PICK UP THE PACE, OR BE LEFT BEHIND!
UM... THANK YOU VERY MUCH.
NOD

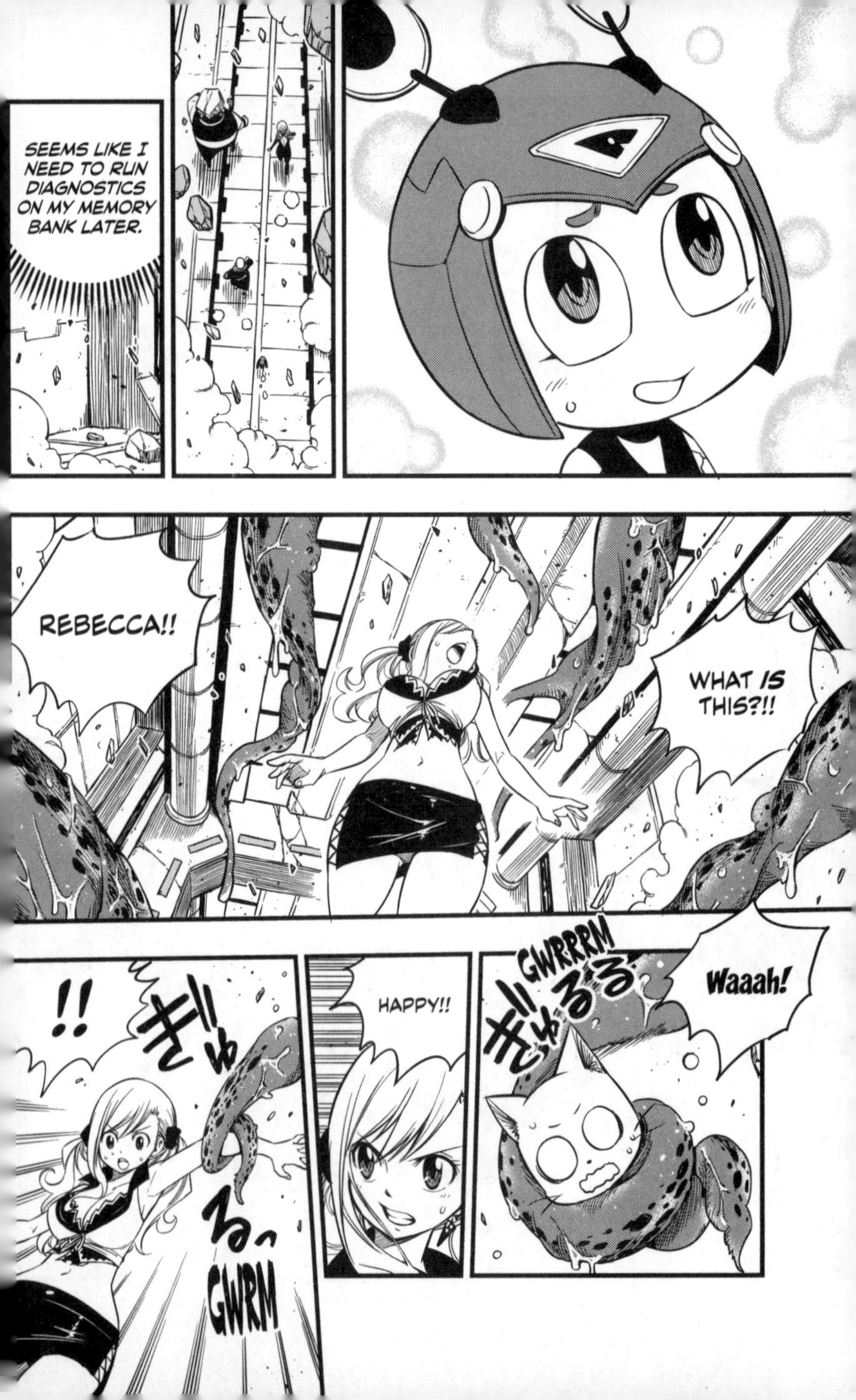
SEEMS LIKE I NEED TO RUN DIAGNOSTICS ON MY MEMORY BANK LATER.
WHAT IS THIS?!!
REBECCA!!
Waaah!
GWRRRM
ぎゅるる
HAPPY!!
!!
ぎゅ
る
GWRM

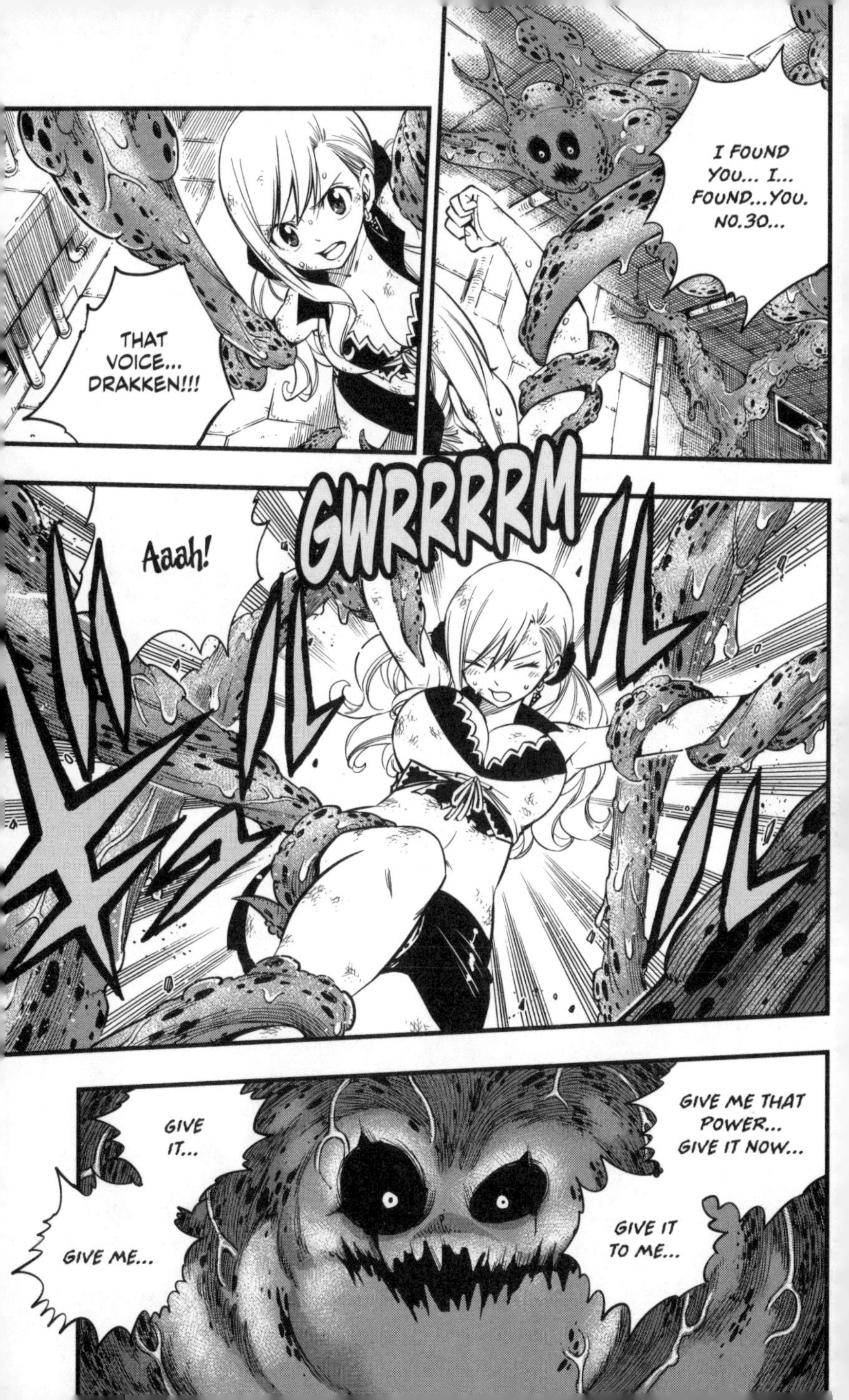
I FOUND YOU... I... FOUND...YOU. NO.30...
THAT VOICE... DRAKKEN!!!
GWRRRRM
Aaah!
GIVE ME THAT POWER... GIVE IT NOW...
GIVE IT...
GIVE IT TO ME...
GIVE ME...

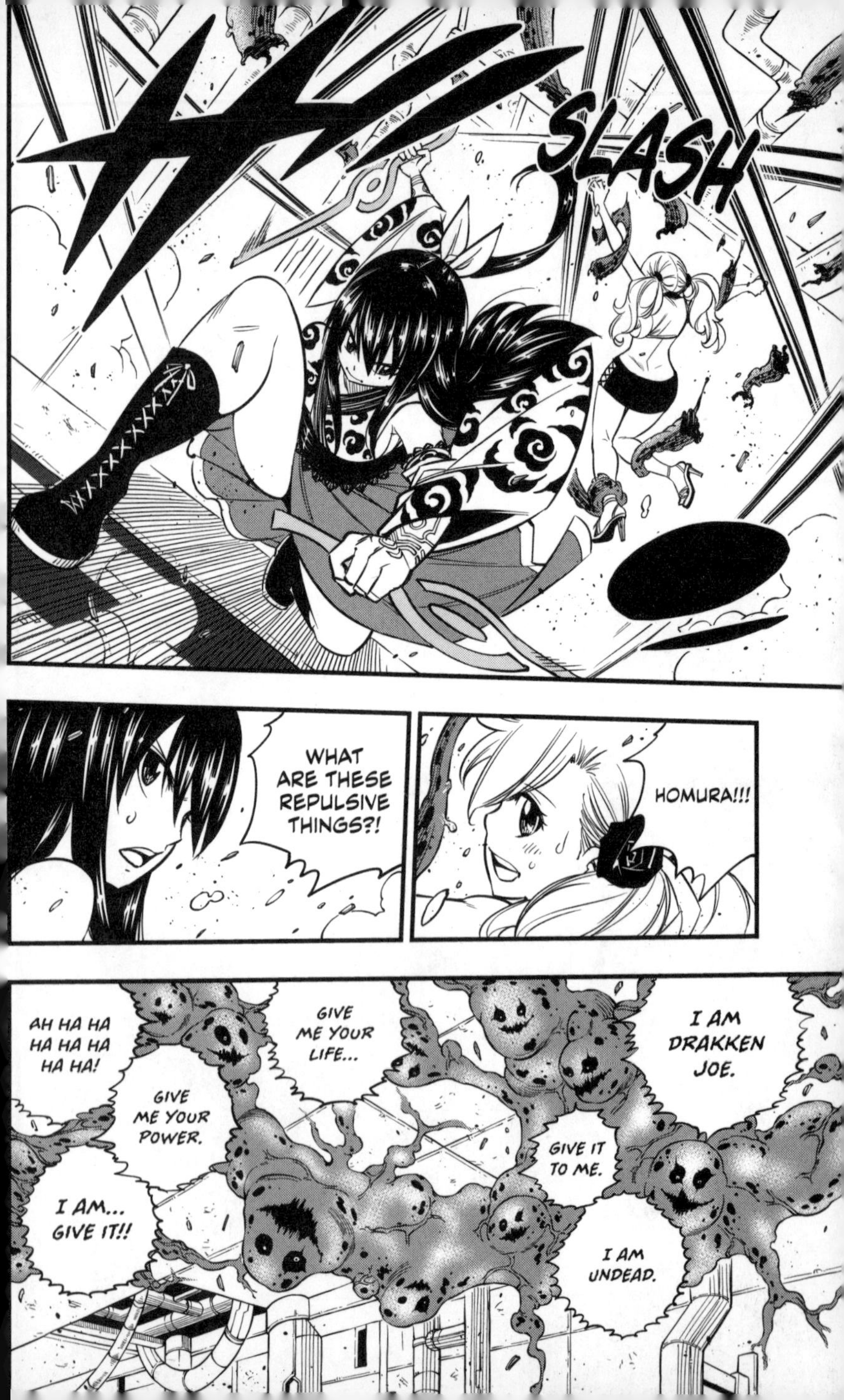
SLASH
HOMURA!!!
WHAT ARE THESE REPULSIVE THINGS?!
I AM DRAKKEN JOE.
GIVE ME YOUR LIFE...
AH HA HA HA HA HA HA HA!
GIVE IT TO ME.
GIVE ME YOUR POWER.
I AM UNDEAD.
I AM... GIVE IT!!

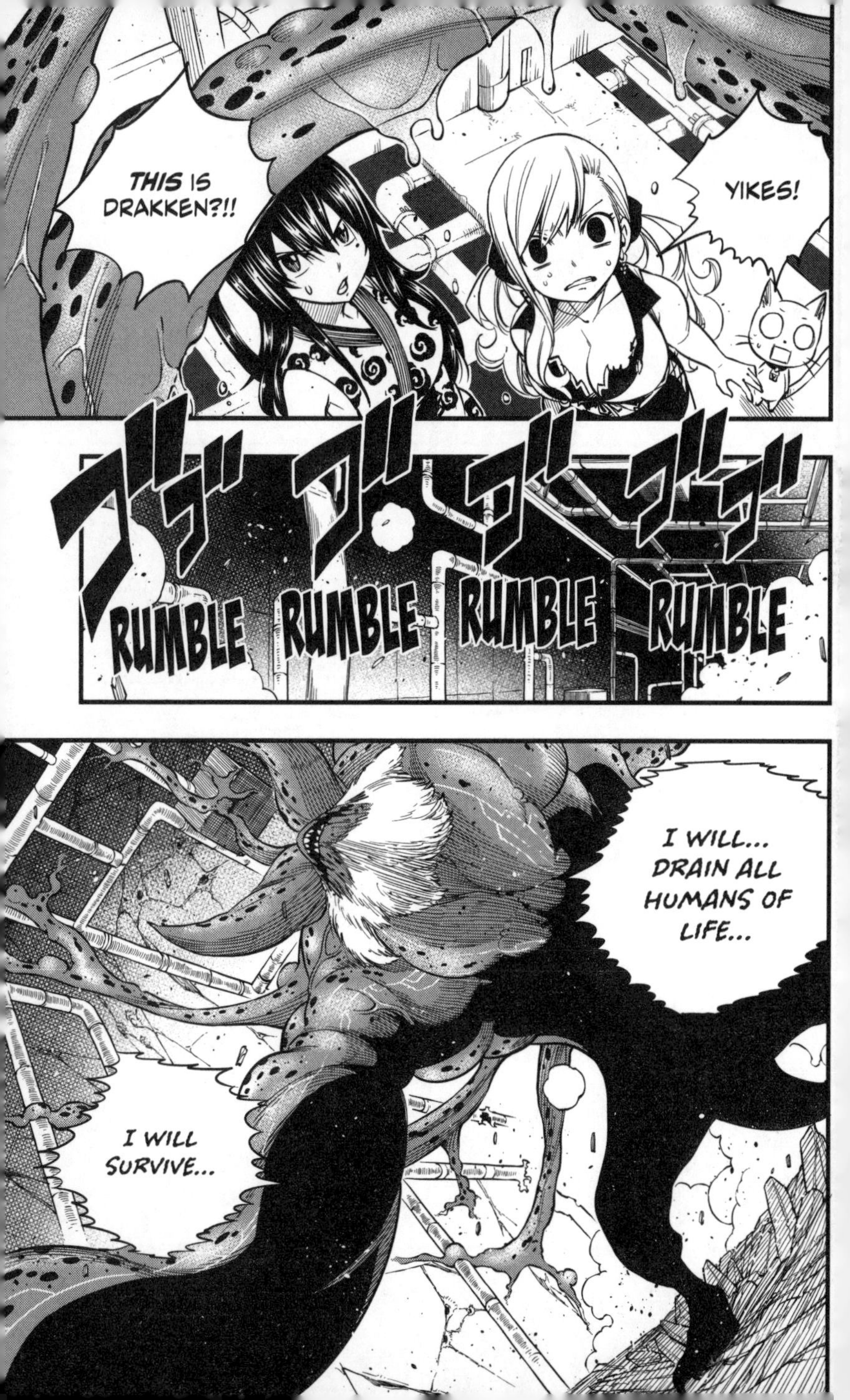
YIKES!
THIS IS DRAKKEN?!!
RUMBLE RUMBLE RUMBLE RUMBLE
I WILL... DRAIN ALL HUMANS OF LIFE...
I WILL SURVIVE...

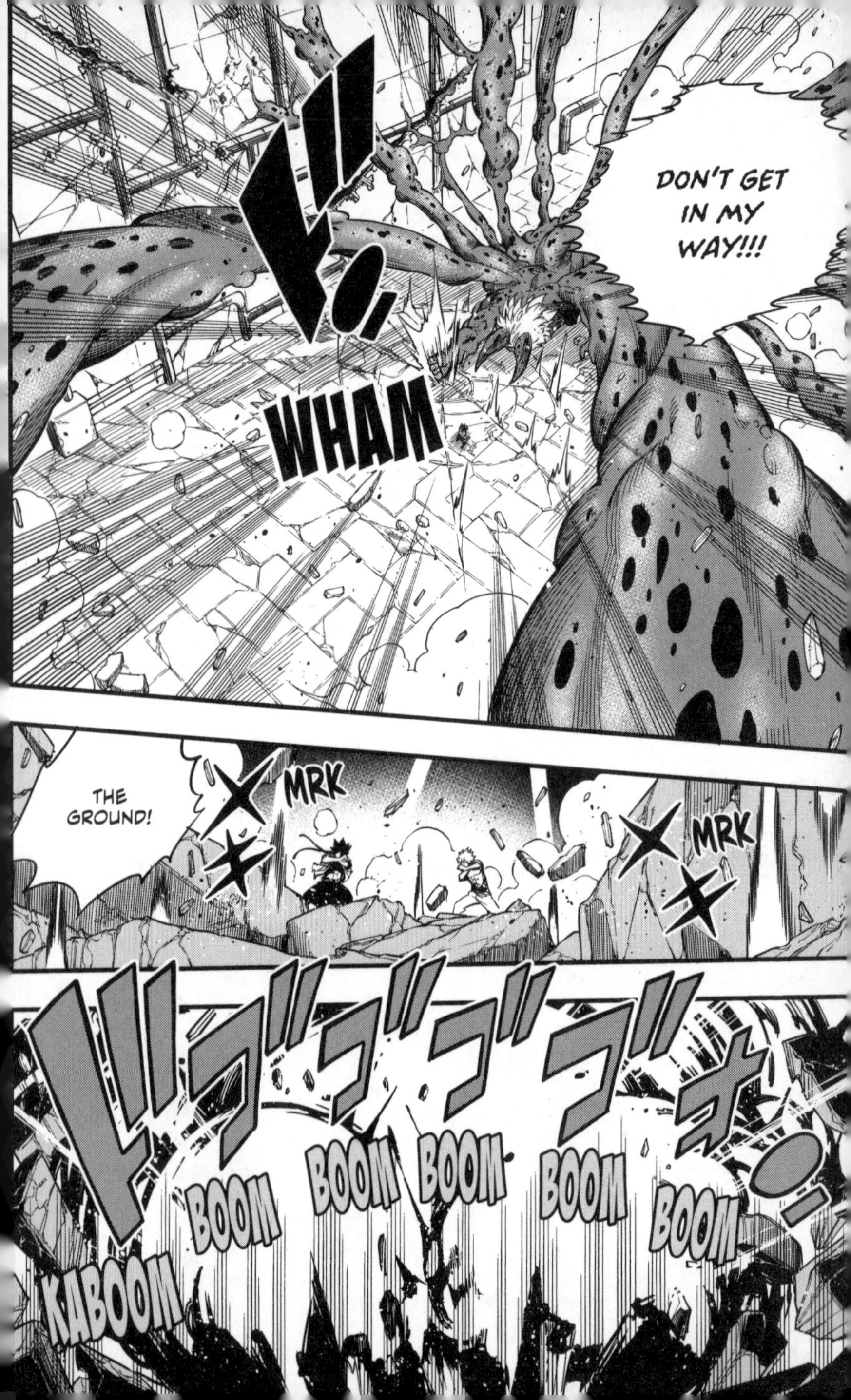
DON'T GET IN MY WAY!!!
WHAM
MRK
THE GROUND!
MRK
KABOOM BOOM BOOM BOOM BOOM BOOM

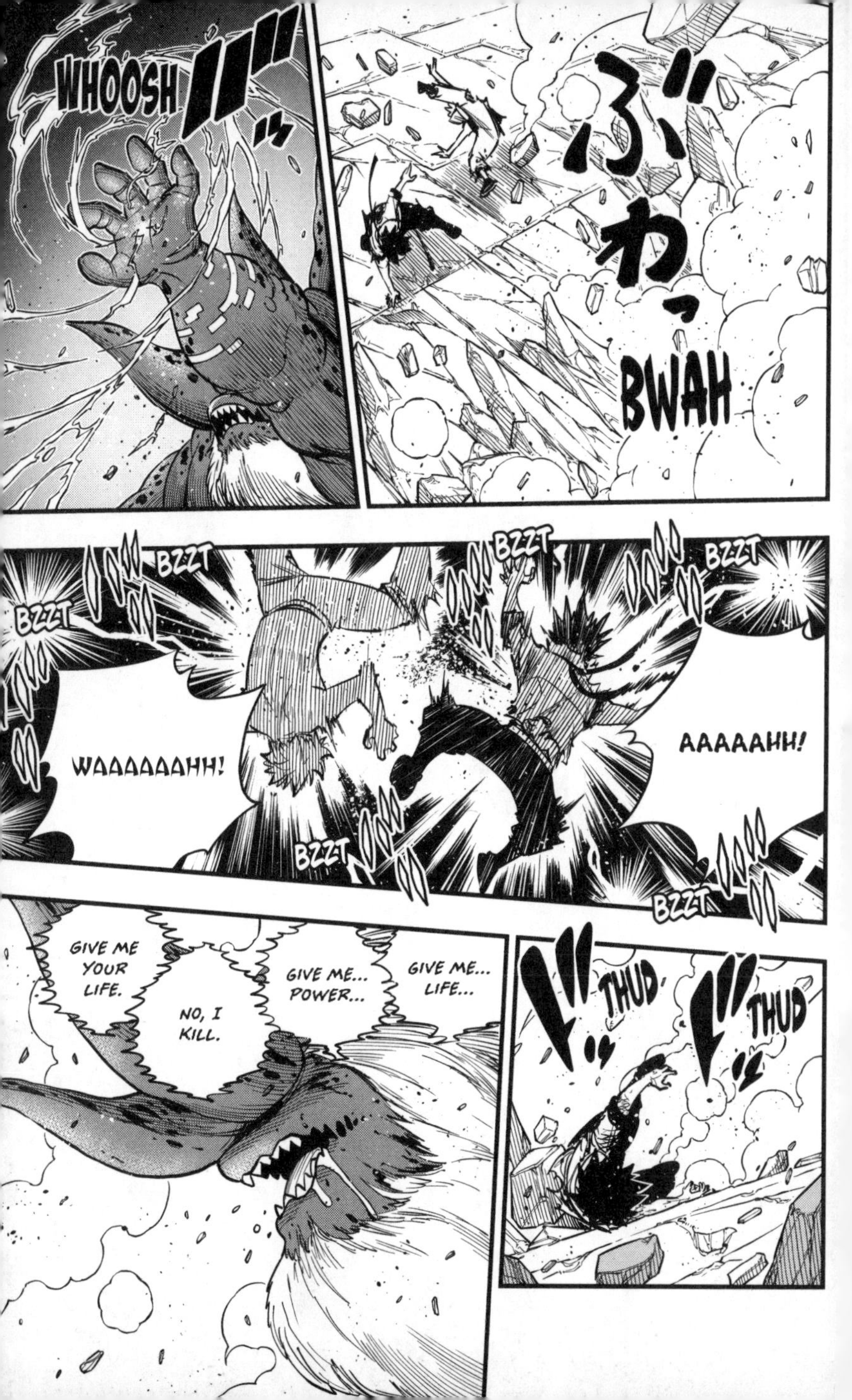
ぶわっ
BWAH
WHOOSH
BZZT
BZZT
AAAAAHH!
BZZT
BZZT
WAAAAAAHH!
BZZT
BZZT
THUD
THUD
GIVE ME... LIFE...
GIVE ME... POWER...
NO, I KILL.
GIVE ME YOUR LIFE.

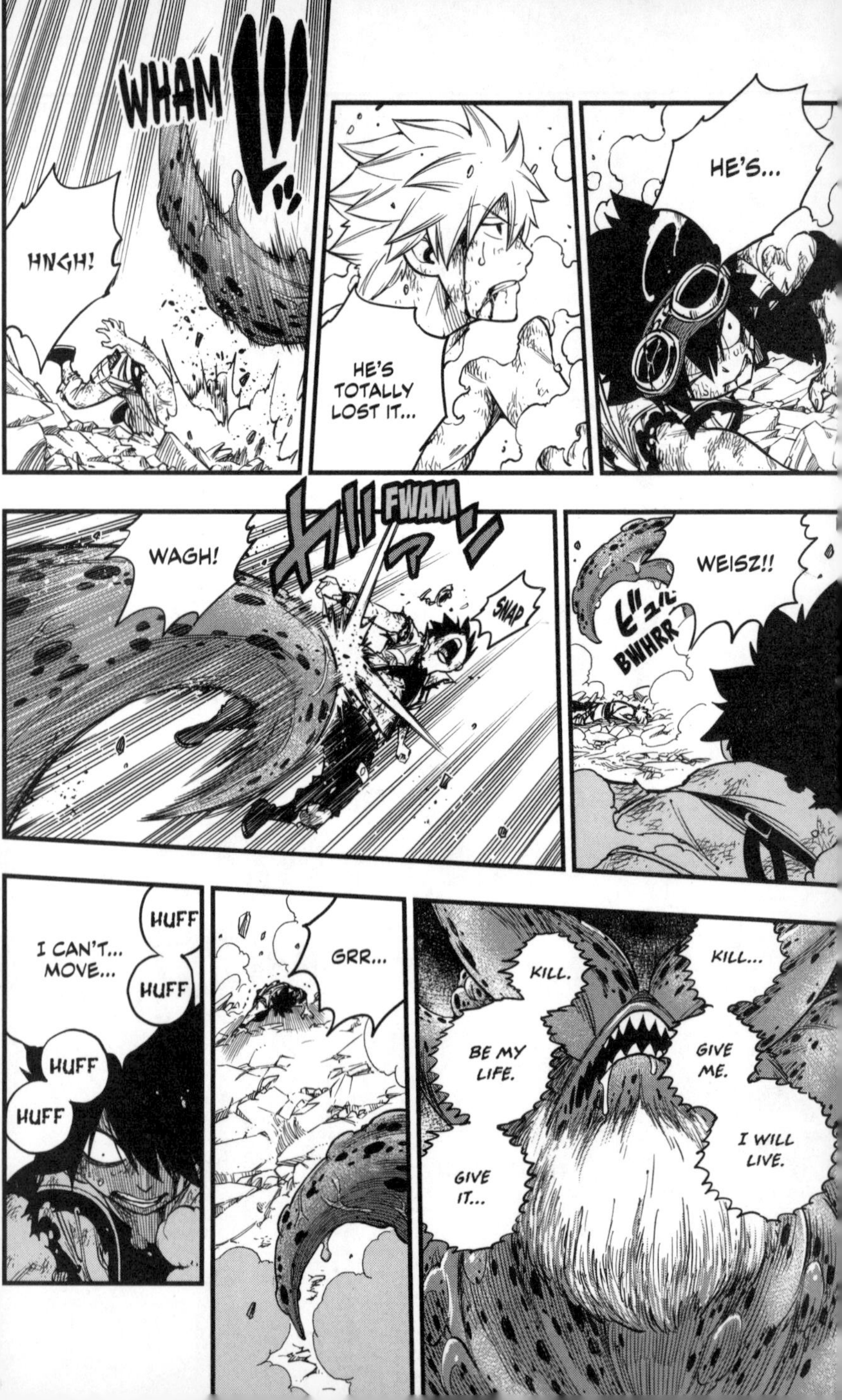
HE'S...
HE'S TOTALLY LOST IT...
WHAM!!!
HNGH!
WEISZ!!
BWHRR
FWAM
WAGH!
SNAP
KILL...
GIVE ME.
I WILL LIVE.
KILL.
BE MY LIFE.
GIVE IT...
GRR...
HUFF
HUFF
I CAN'T... MOVE...
HUFF
HUFF

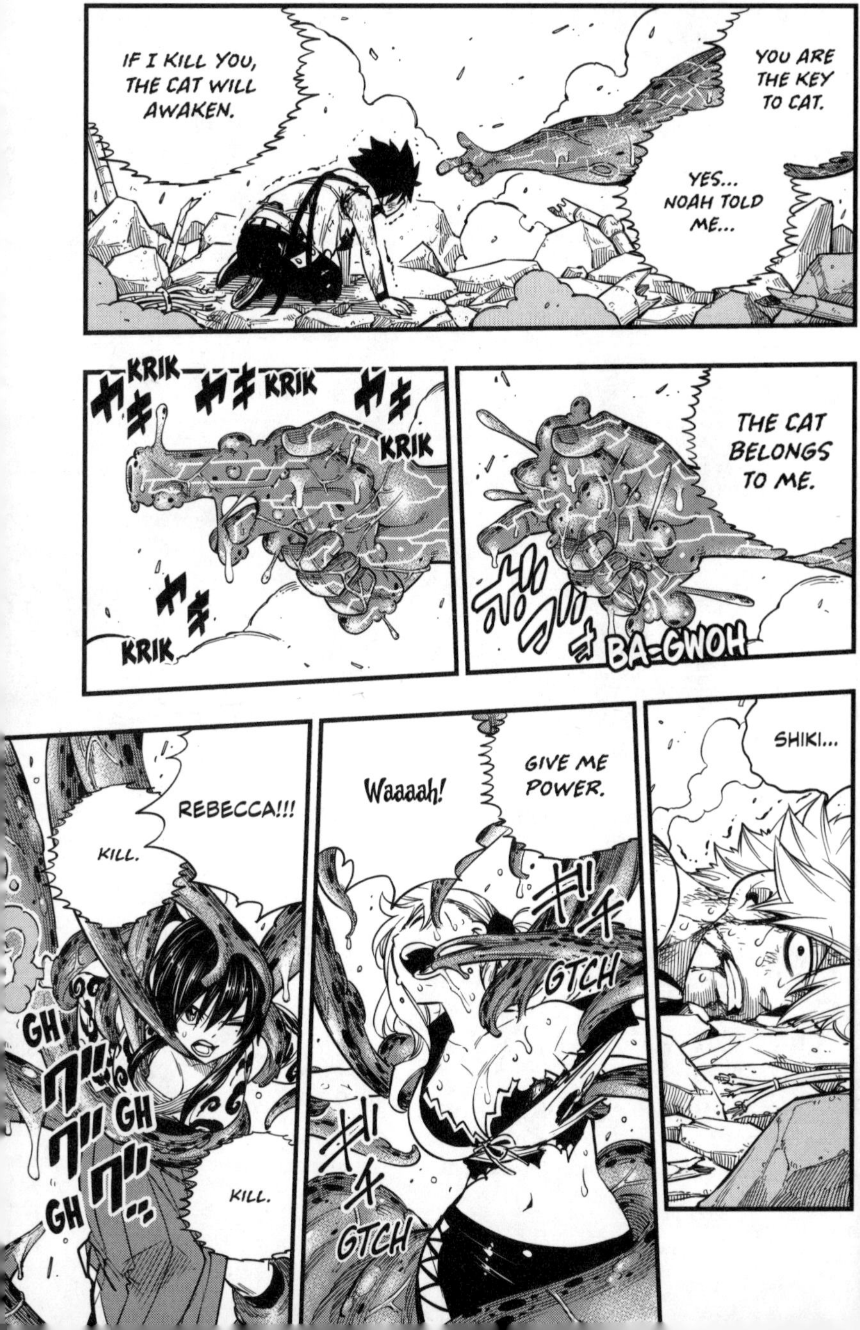
YOU ARE THE KEY TO CAT.
YES... NOAH TOLD ME...
IF I KILL YOU, THE CAT WILL AWAKEN.
THE CAT BELONGS TO ME.
BA-GWOH
KRIK
KRIK
KRIK
KRIK
SHIKI...
GIVE ME POWER.
Waaaah!
GTCH
GTCH
REBECCA!!!
KILL.
KILL.
GH
GH
GH

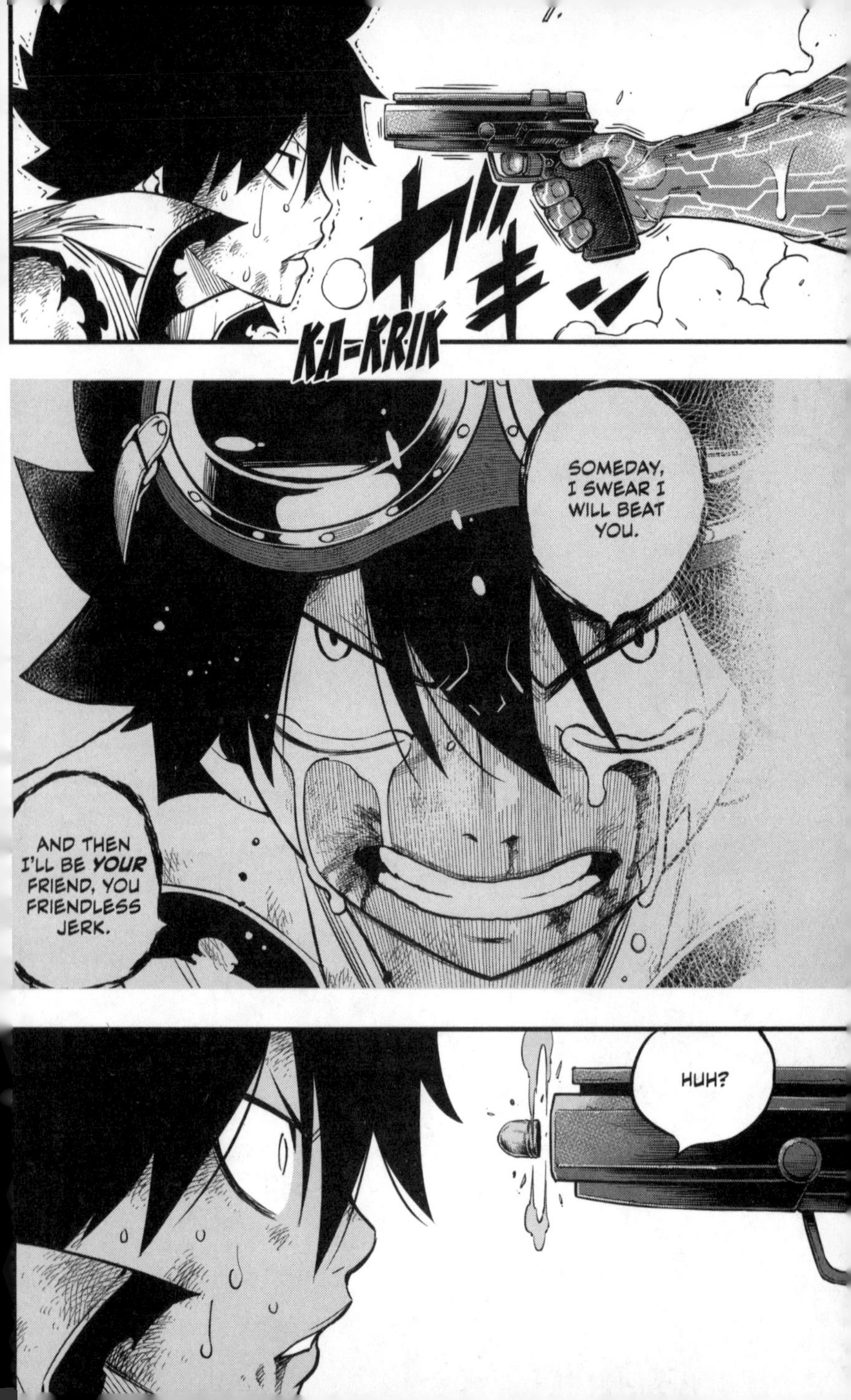
KA-KRIK
SOMEDAY, I SWEAR I WILL BEAT YOU.
AND THEN I'LL BE YOUR FRIEND, YOU FRIENDLESS JERK.
HUH?

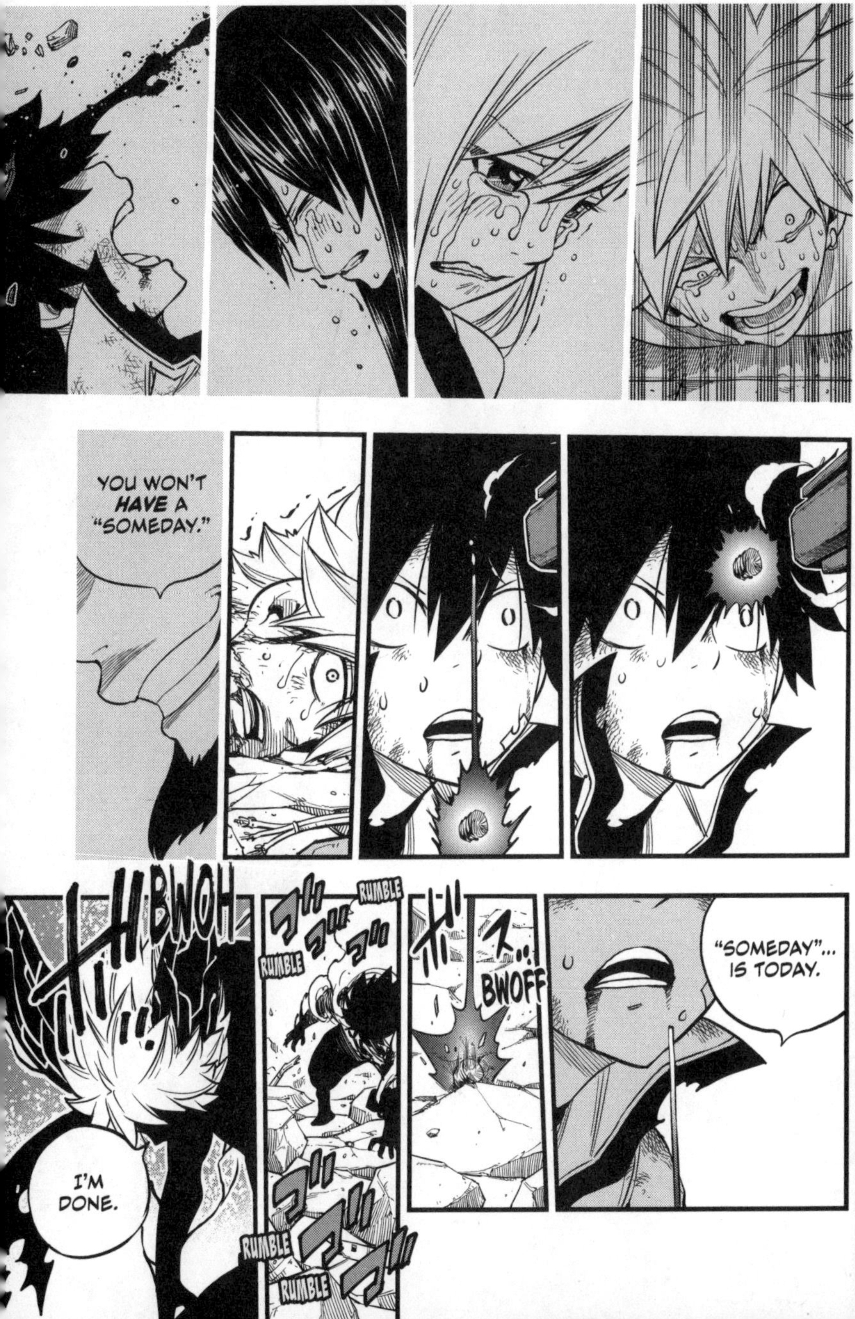
YOU WON'T *HAVE* A "SOMEDAY."
"SOMEDAY"... IS TODAY.
BWOFF
RUMBLE
RUMBLE
RUMBLE
RUMBLE
BWOH
I'M DONE.

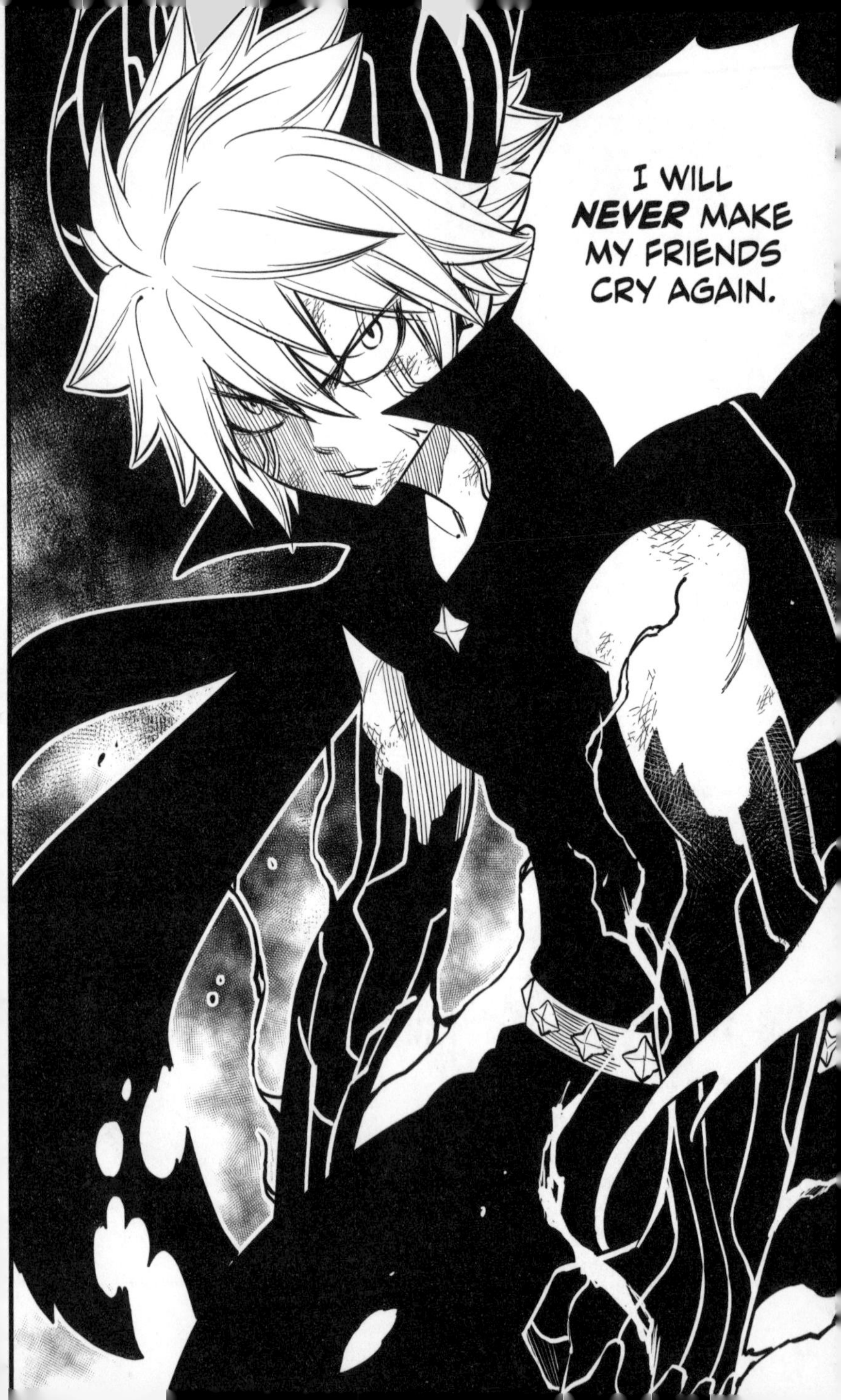
I WILL NEVER MAKE MY FRIENDS CRY AGAIN.

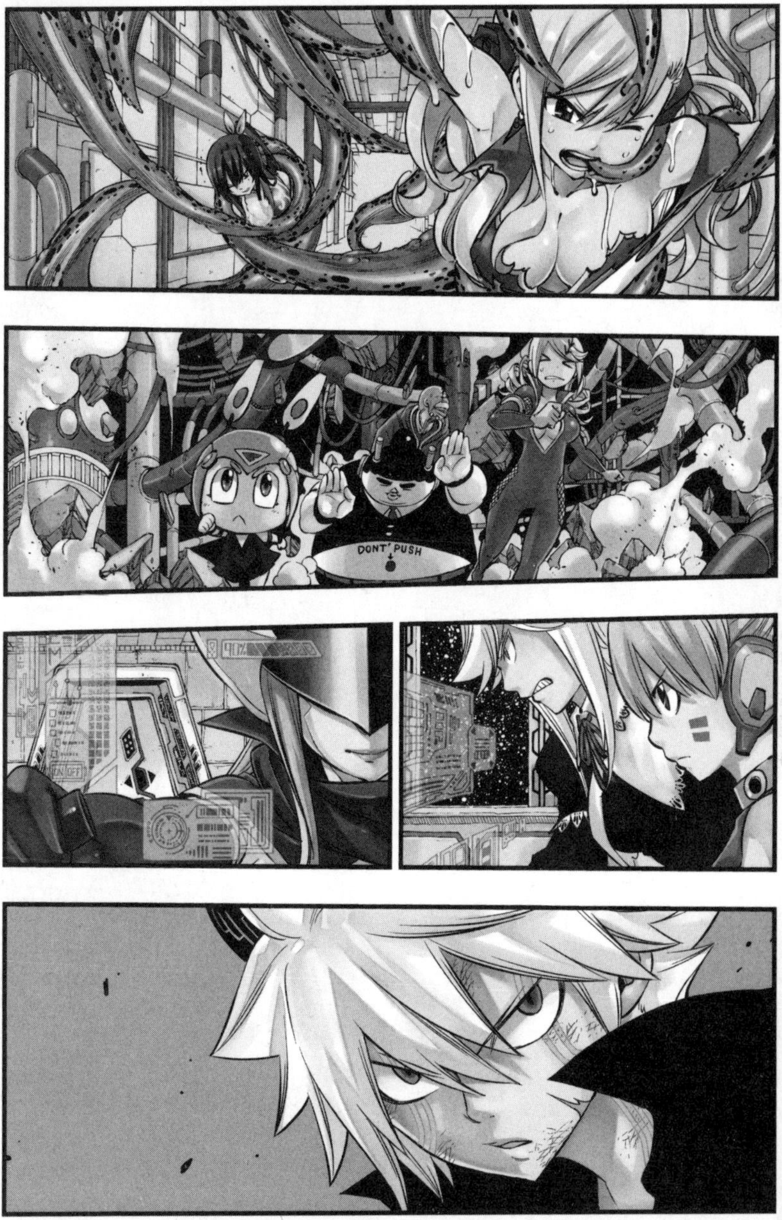
DONT' PUSH
ON OFF

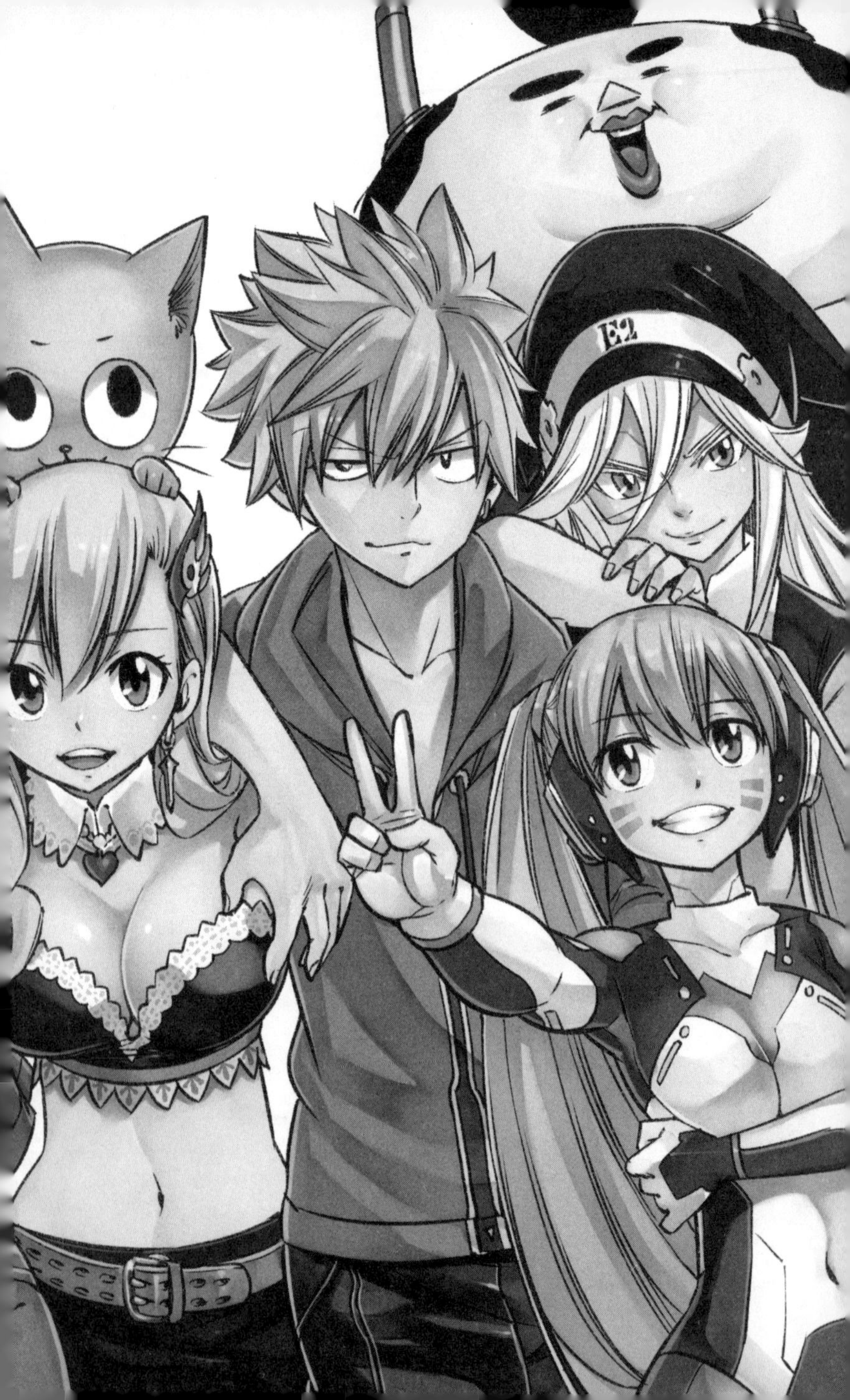
E2

CHAPTER 98: ADVENT OF THE DEMON KING

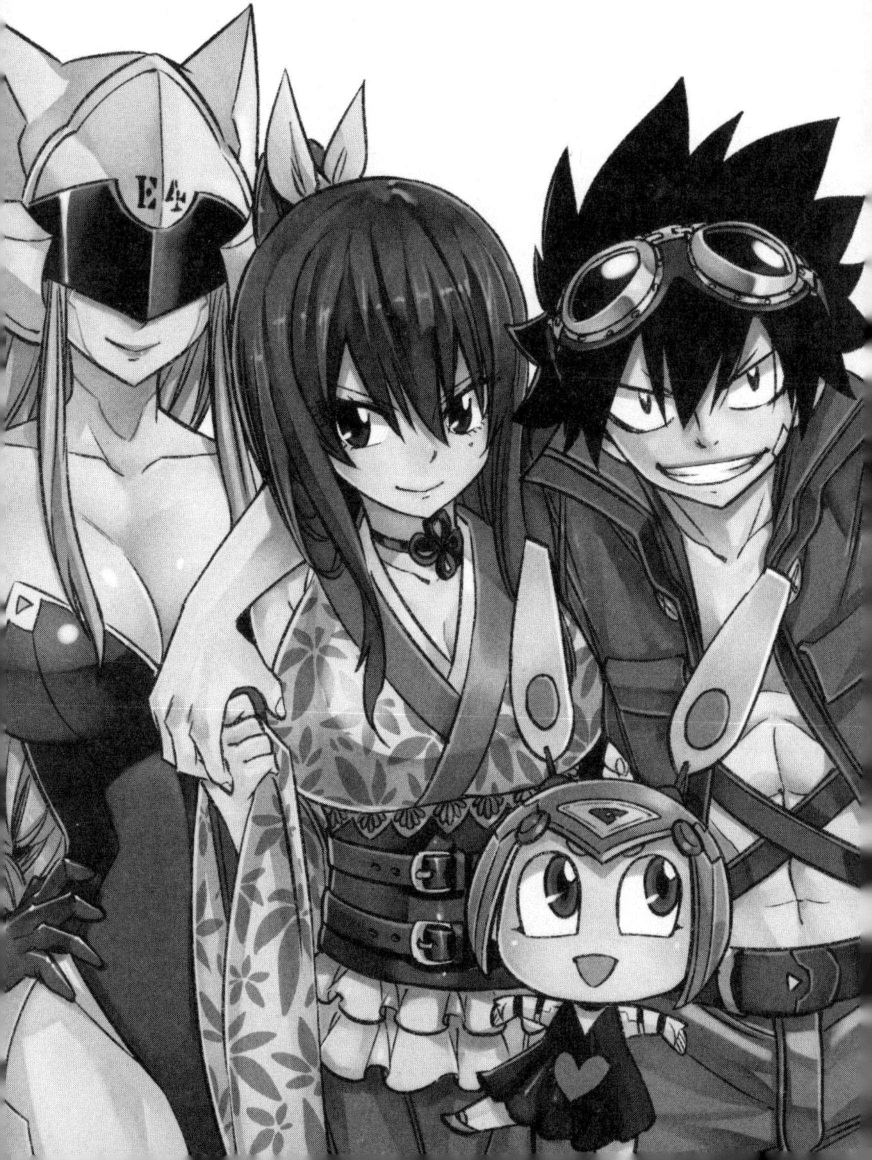

EDENSZERO

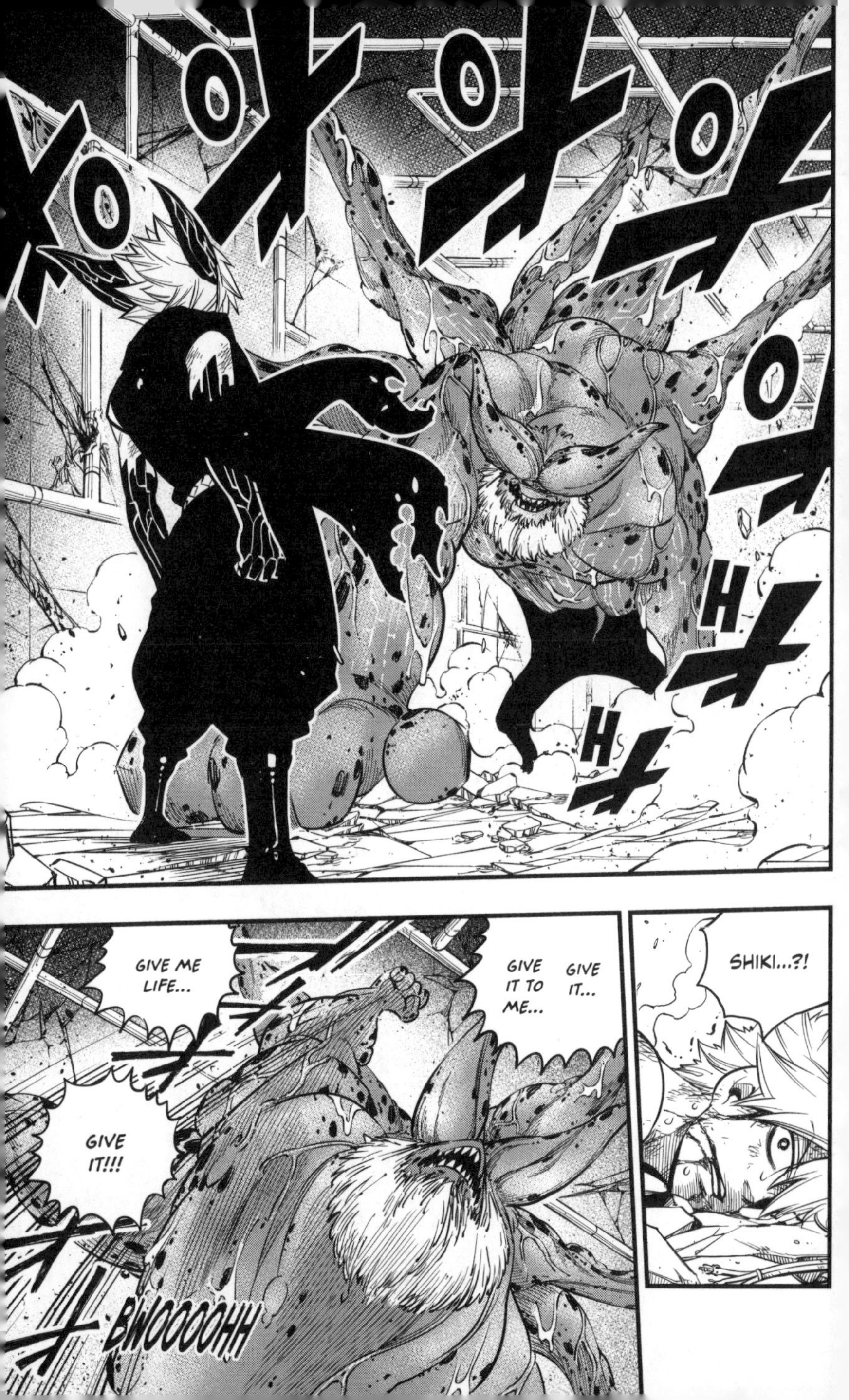
SHIKI...?!
GIVE IT...
GIVE IT TO ME...
GIVE ME LIFE...
GIVE IT!!!
BWOOOOHH

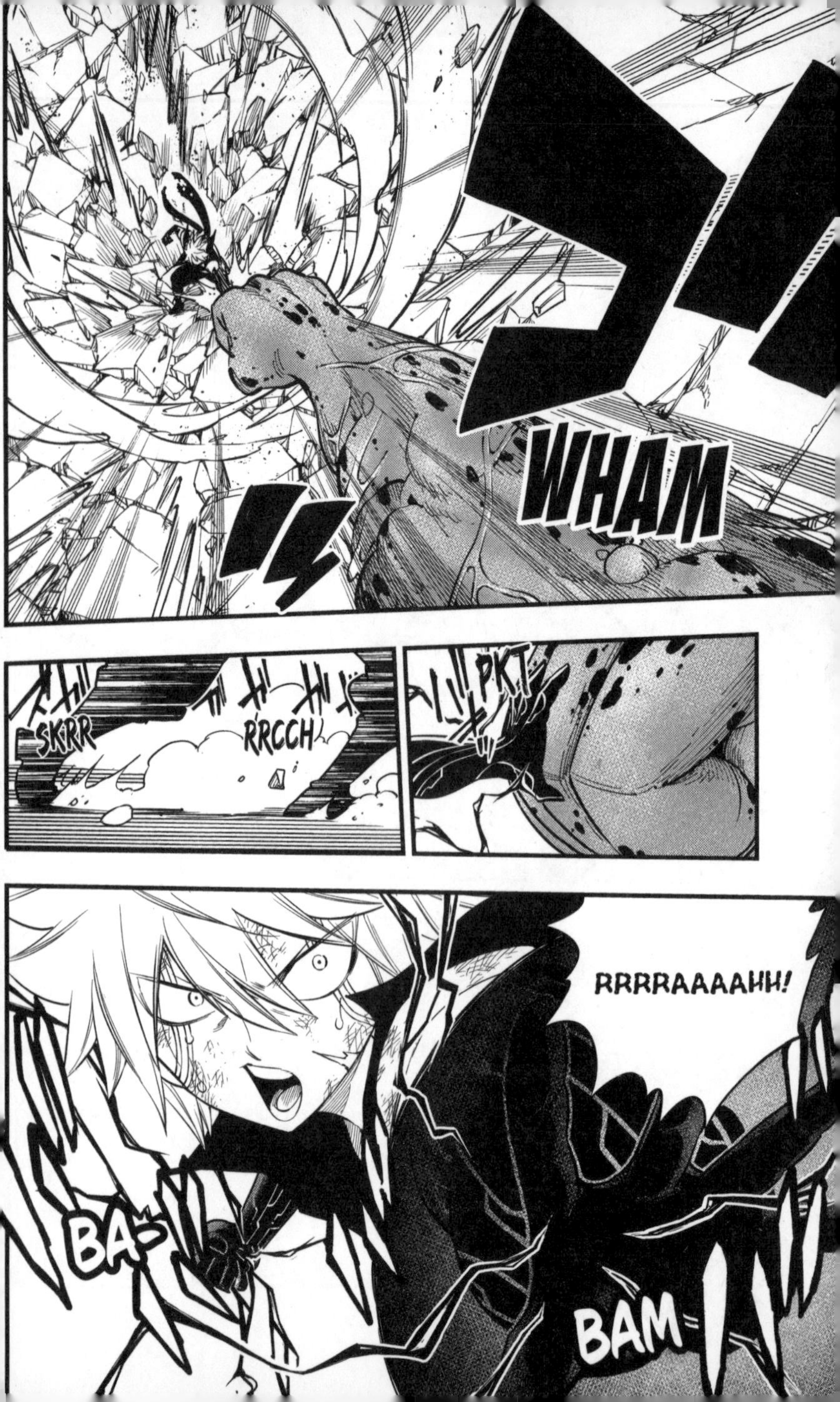
WHAM
PKT
RRCCH
SKRR
RRRRAAAAHH!
BA-
BAM

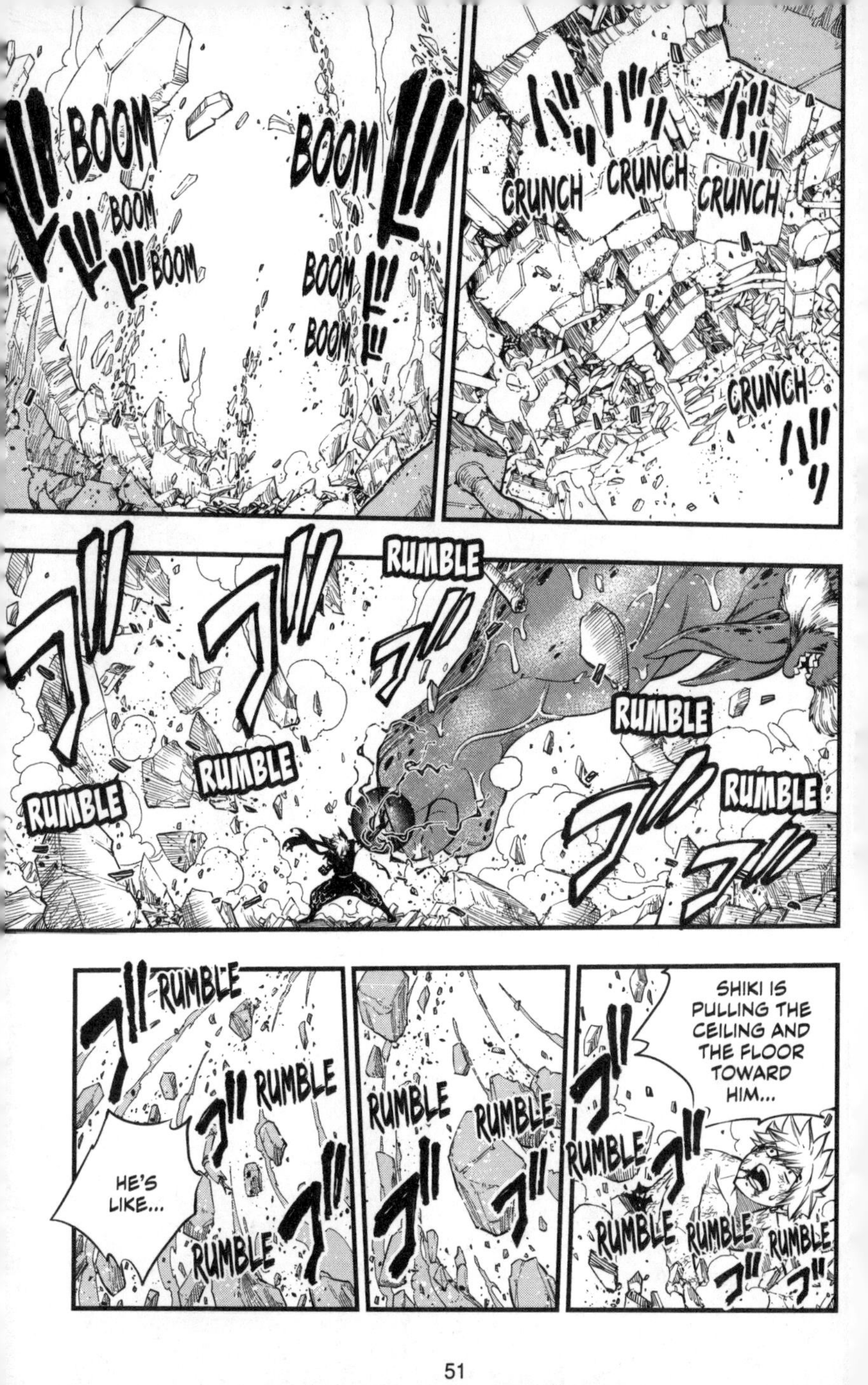
CRUNCH
CRUNCH
CRUNCH
CRUNCH
BOOM
BOOM
BOOM
BOOM
BOOM
BOOM
RUMBLE
RUMBLE
RUMBLE
RUMBLE
RUMBLE
SHIKI IS PULLING THE CEILING AND THE FLOOR TOWARD HIM...
RUMBLE
RUMBLE
RUMBLE
RUMBLE
RUMBLE
RUMBLE
RUMBLE
RUMBLE
RUMBLE
HE'S LIKE...

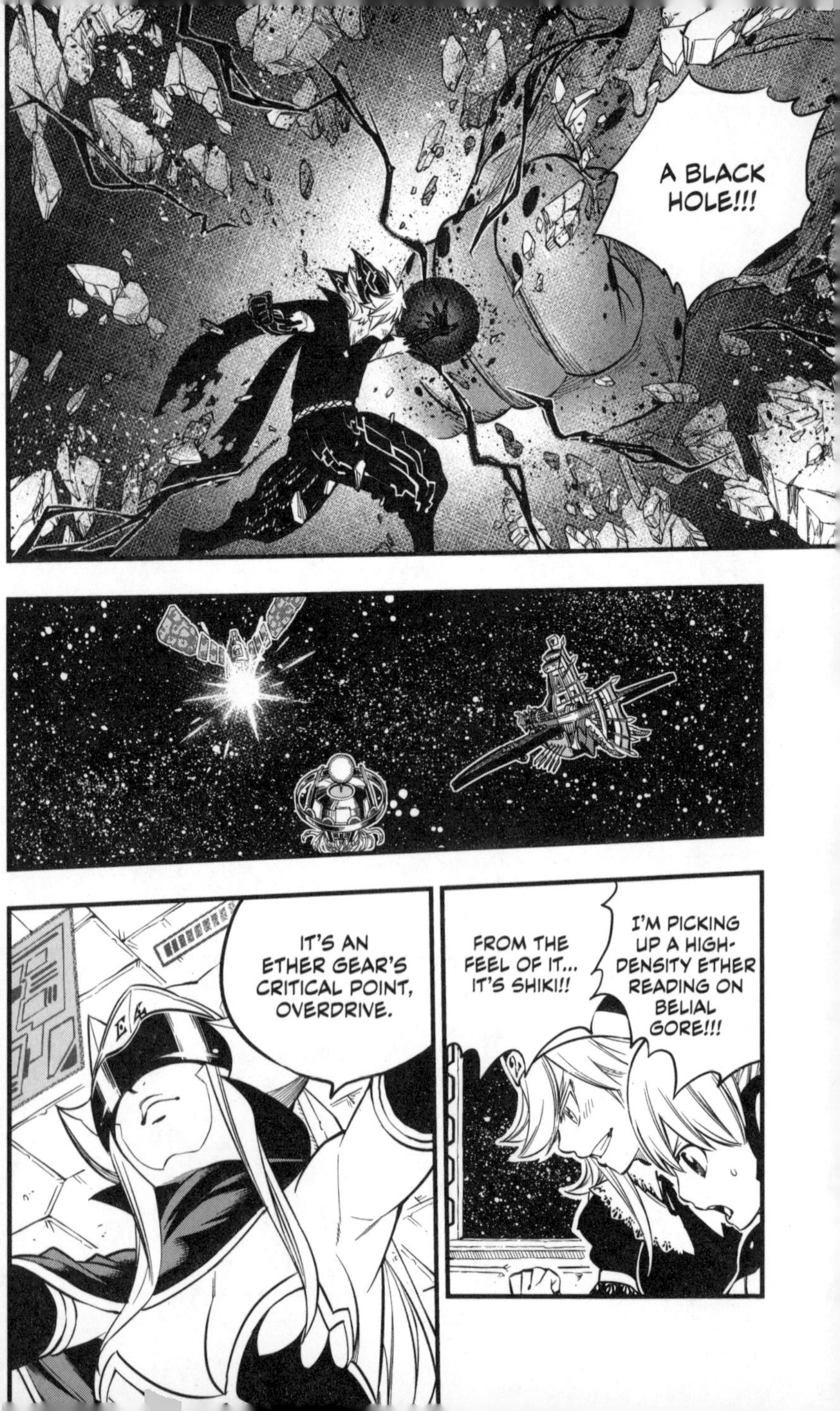
A BLACK HOLE!!!
I'M PICKING UP A HIGH-DENSITY ETHER READING ON BELIAL GORE!!!
FROM THE FEEL OF IT... IT'S SHIKI!!
IT'S AN ETHER GEAR'S CRITICAL POINT, OVERDRIVE.

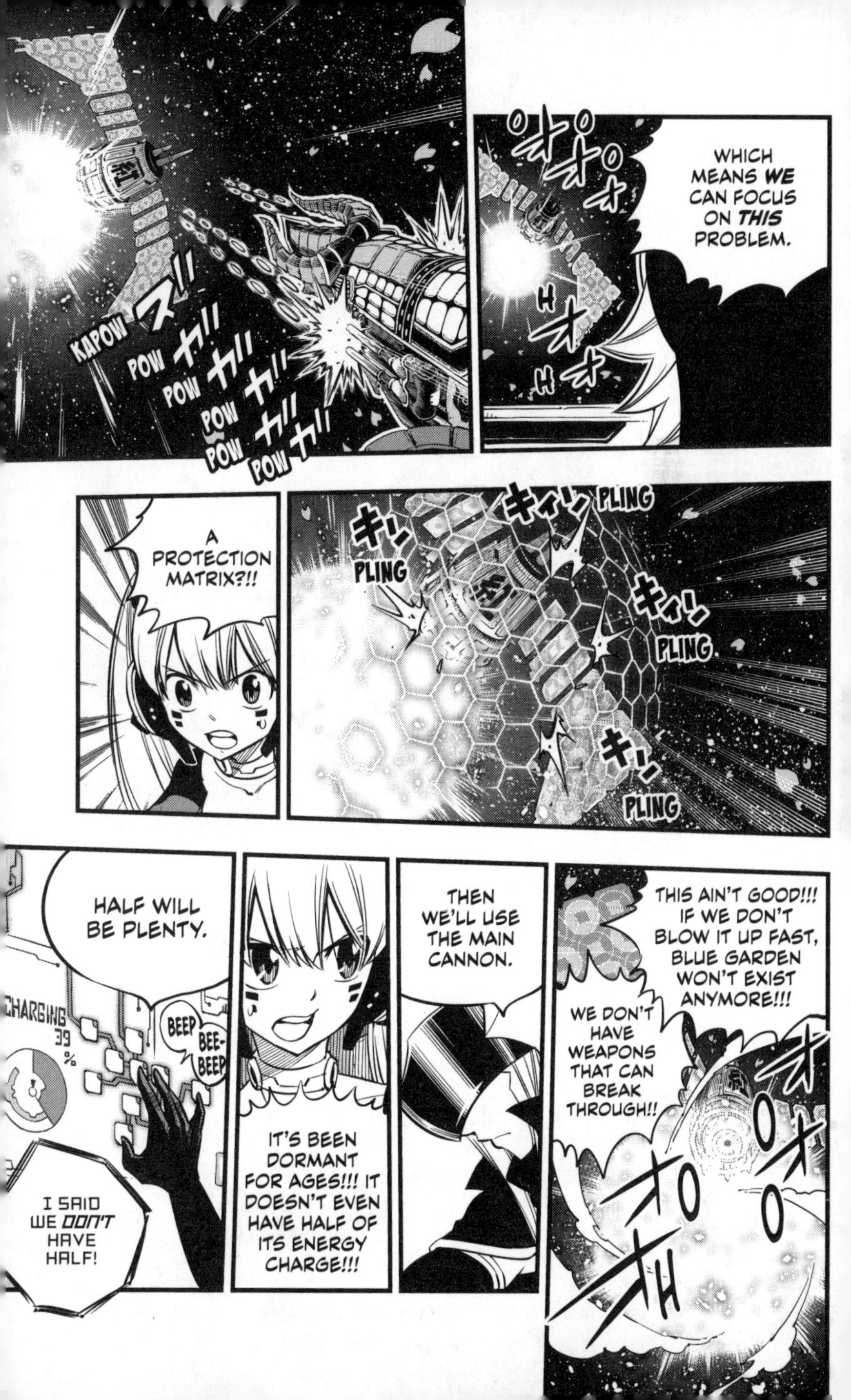
WHICH MEANS WE CAN FOCUS ON THIS PROBLEM.
H
H
KAPOW
POW
POW
POW
POW
POW
PLING
PLING
PLING
PLING
A PROTECTION MATRIX?!!
THIS AIN'T GOOD!!! IF WE DON'T BLOW IT UP FAST, BLUE GARDEN WON'T EXIST ANYMORE!!!
WE DON'T HAVE WEAPONS THAT CAN BREAK THROUGH!!
H
THEN WE'LL USE THE MAIN CANNON.
IT'S BEEN DORMANT FOR AGES!!! IT DOESN'T EVEN HAVE HALF OF ITS ENERGY CHARGE!!!
HALF WILL BE PLENTY.
CHARGING 39 %
BEEP
BEE-BEEP
I SAID WE DON'T HAVE HALF!

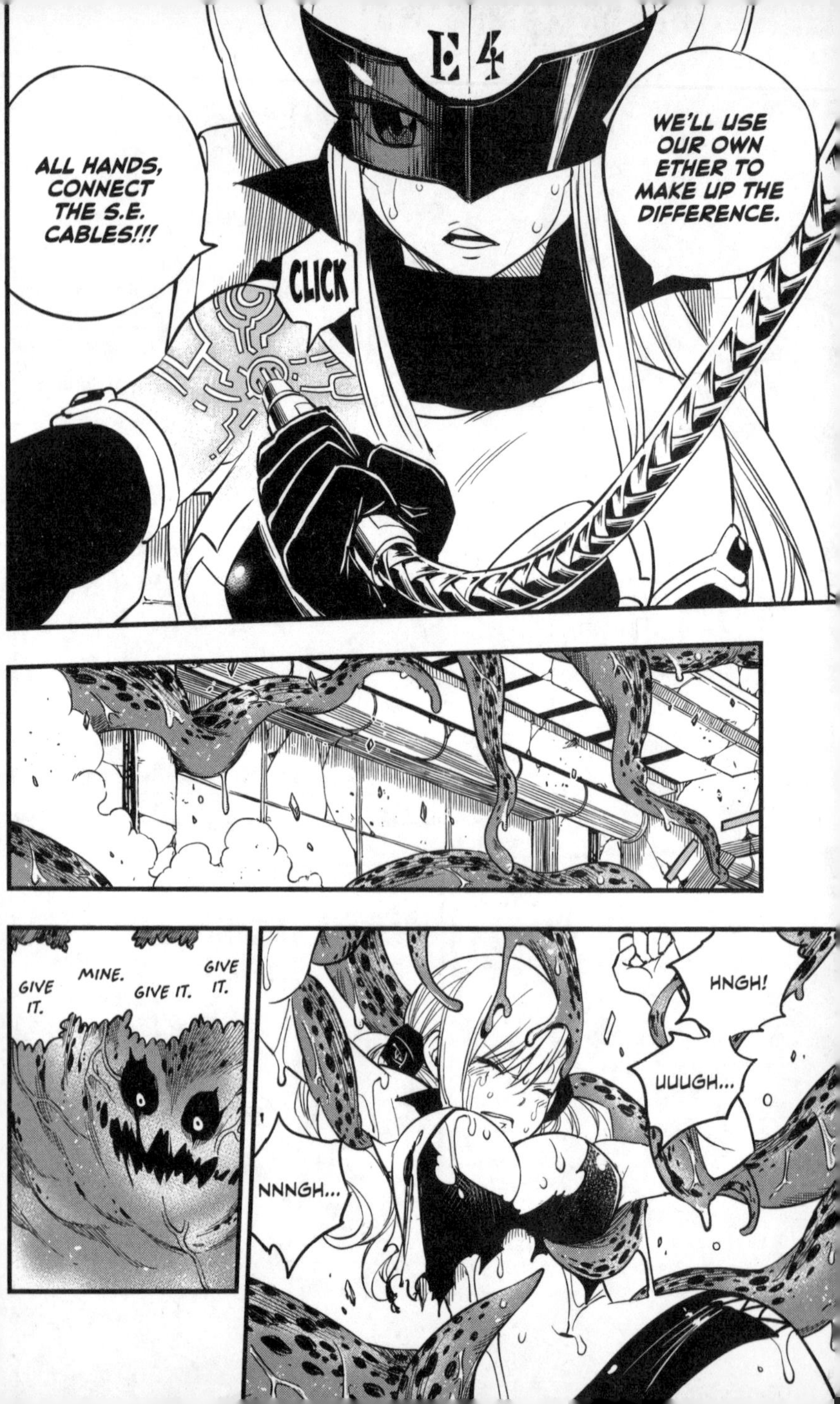

WE'LL USE OUR OWN ETHER TO MAKE UP THE DIFFERENCE.
ALL HANDS, CONNECT THE S.E. CABLES!!!
CLICK
HNGH!
UUUGH...
NNNGH...
GIVE IT.
GIVE IT.
MINE.
GIVE IT.

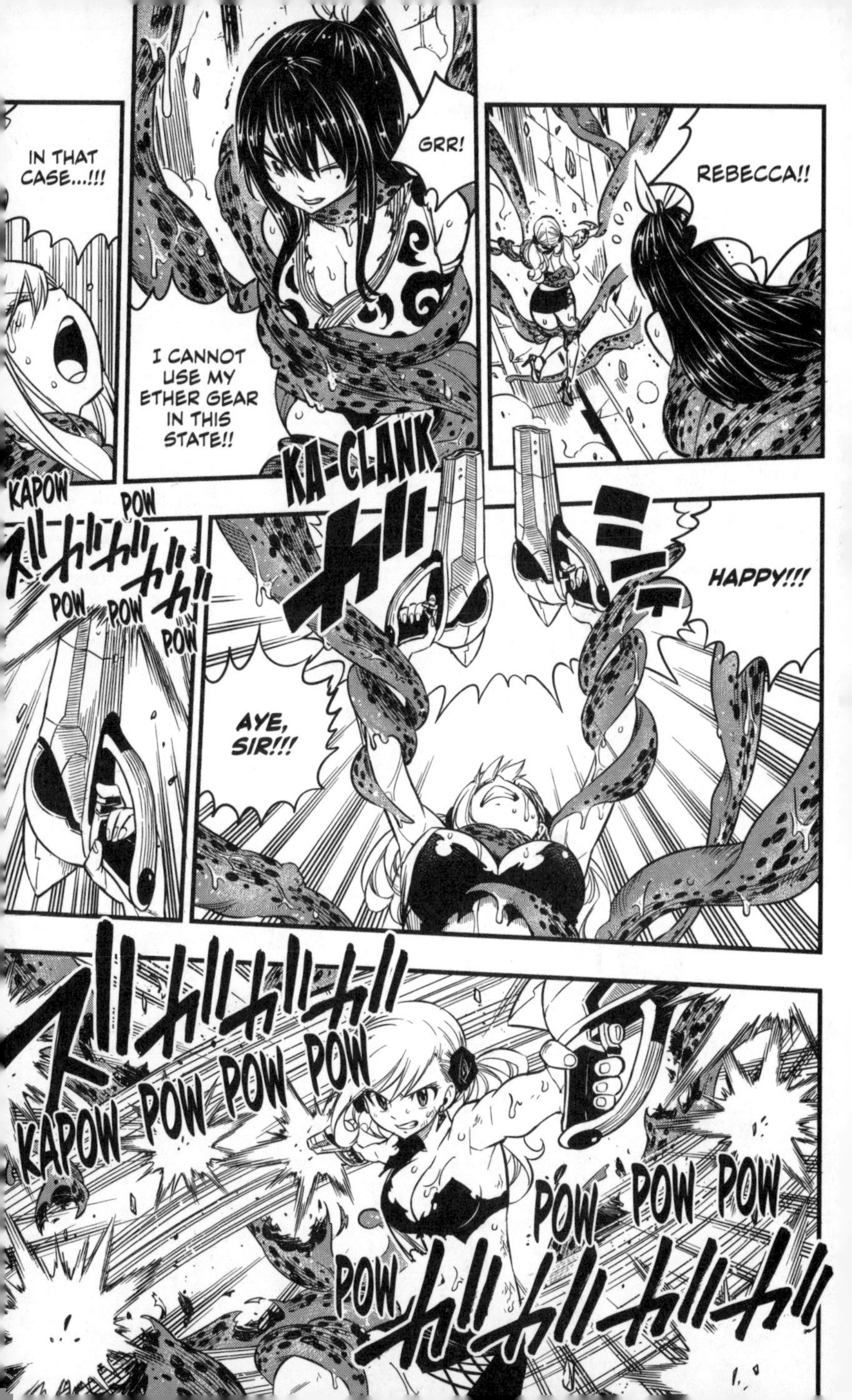
REBECCA!!
GRR!
I CANNOT USE MY ETHER GEAR IN THIS STATE!!
IN THAT CASE...!!!
KA-CLANK
HAPPY!!!
AYE, SIR!!!
KAPOW
POW
POW
POW
POW
KAPOW POW POW POW
POW POW POW
POW

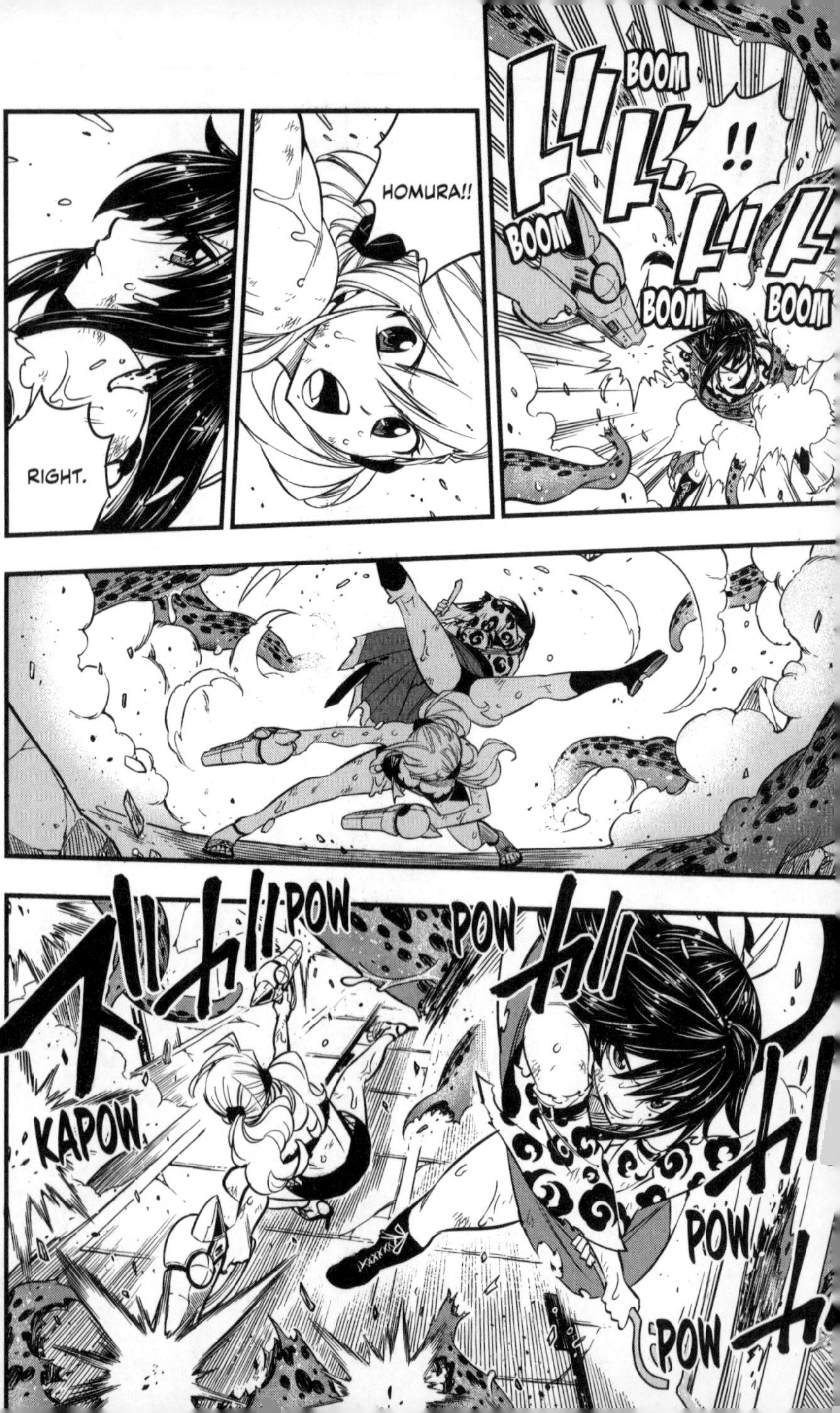
BOOM
BOOM
BOOM
BOOM
HOMURA!!
RIGHT.
POW
POW
KAPOW
POW
POW

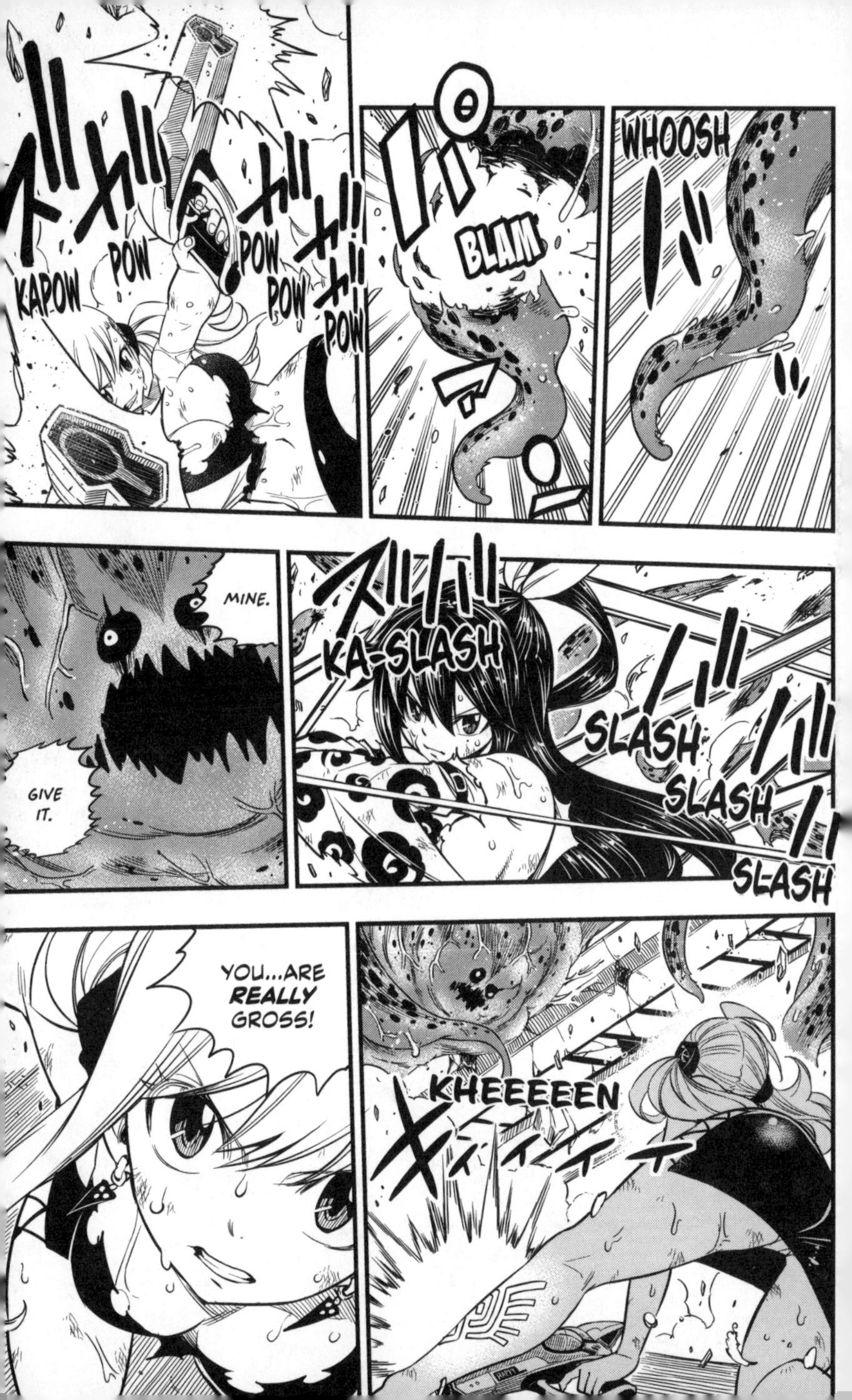
WHOOSH
BLAM
POW
POW
POW
POW
KAPOW
KA-SLASH
SLASH
SLASH
SLASH
MINE.
GIVE IT.
KHEEEEEN
YOU...ARE *REALLY* GROSS!

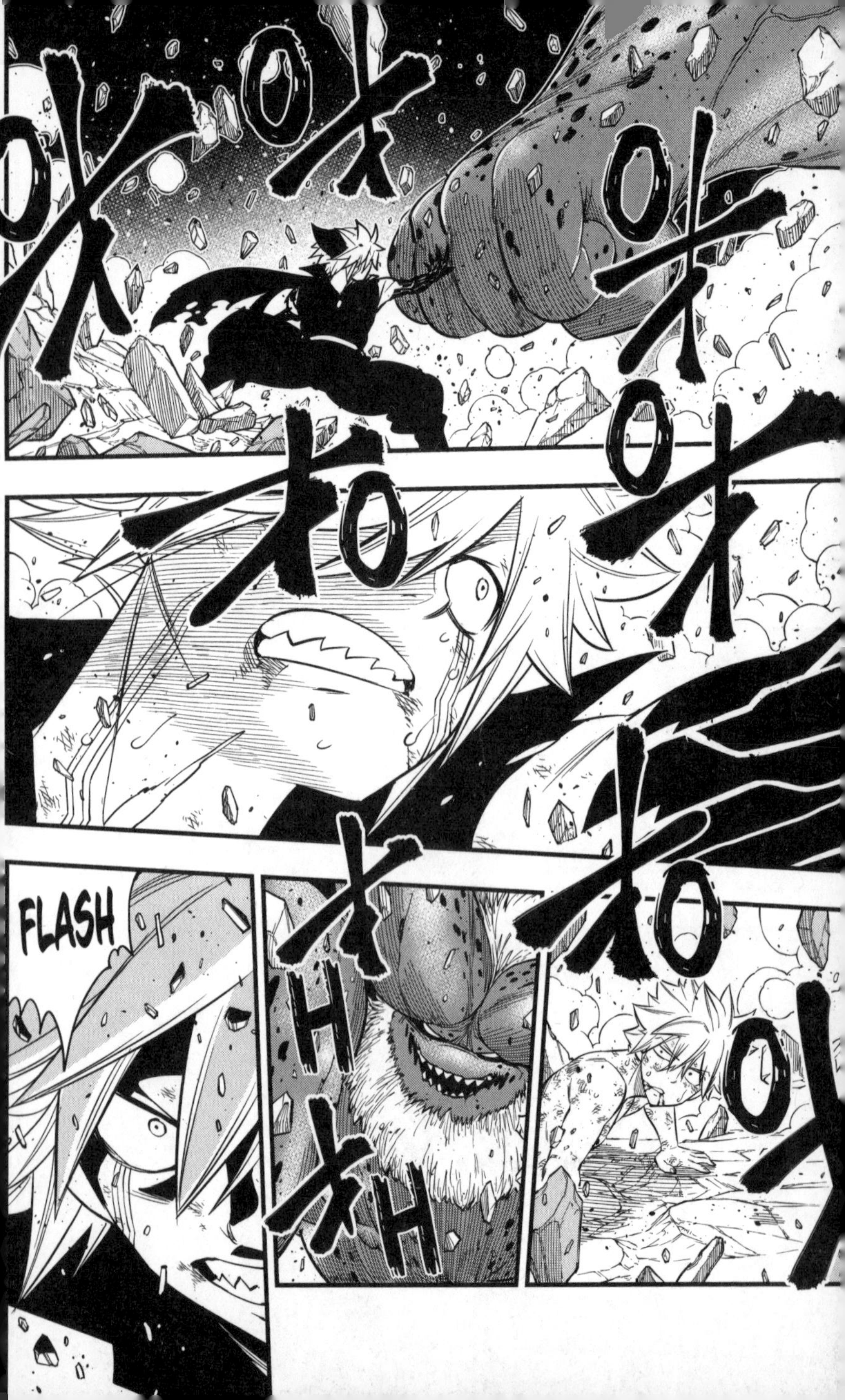
FLASH

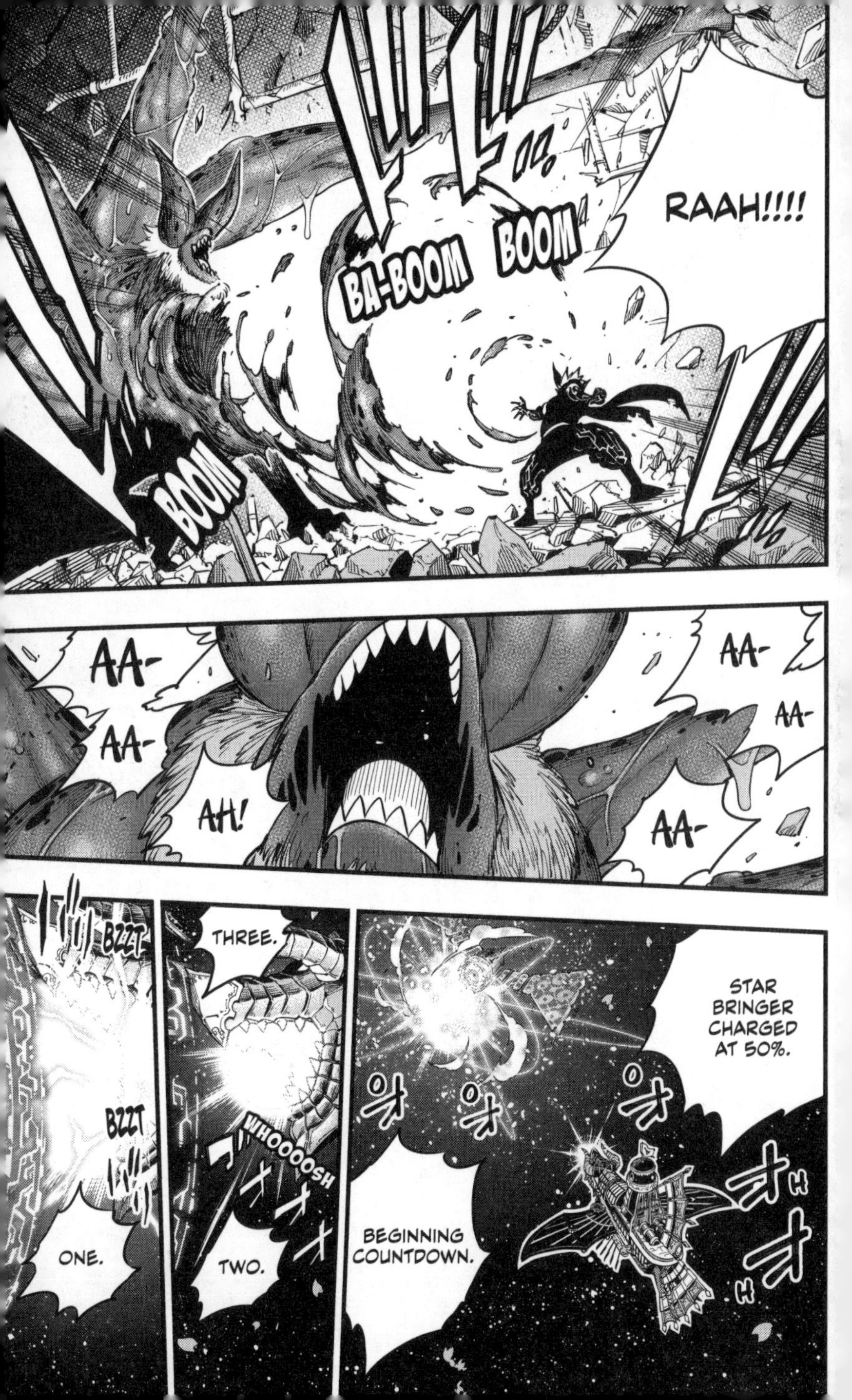
RAAH!!!!
BA-BOOM BOOM
BOOM
AA-
AA-
AA-
AA-
AA-
AH!
STAR BRINGER CHARGED AT 50%.
BEGINNING COUNTDOWN.
THREE.
WHOOOOOSH
TWO.
BZZT
BZZT
ONE.

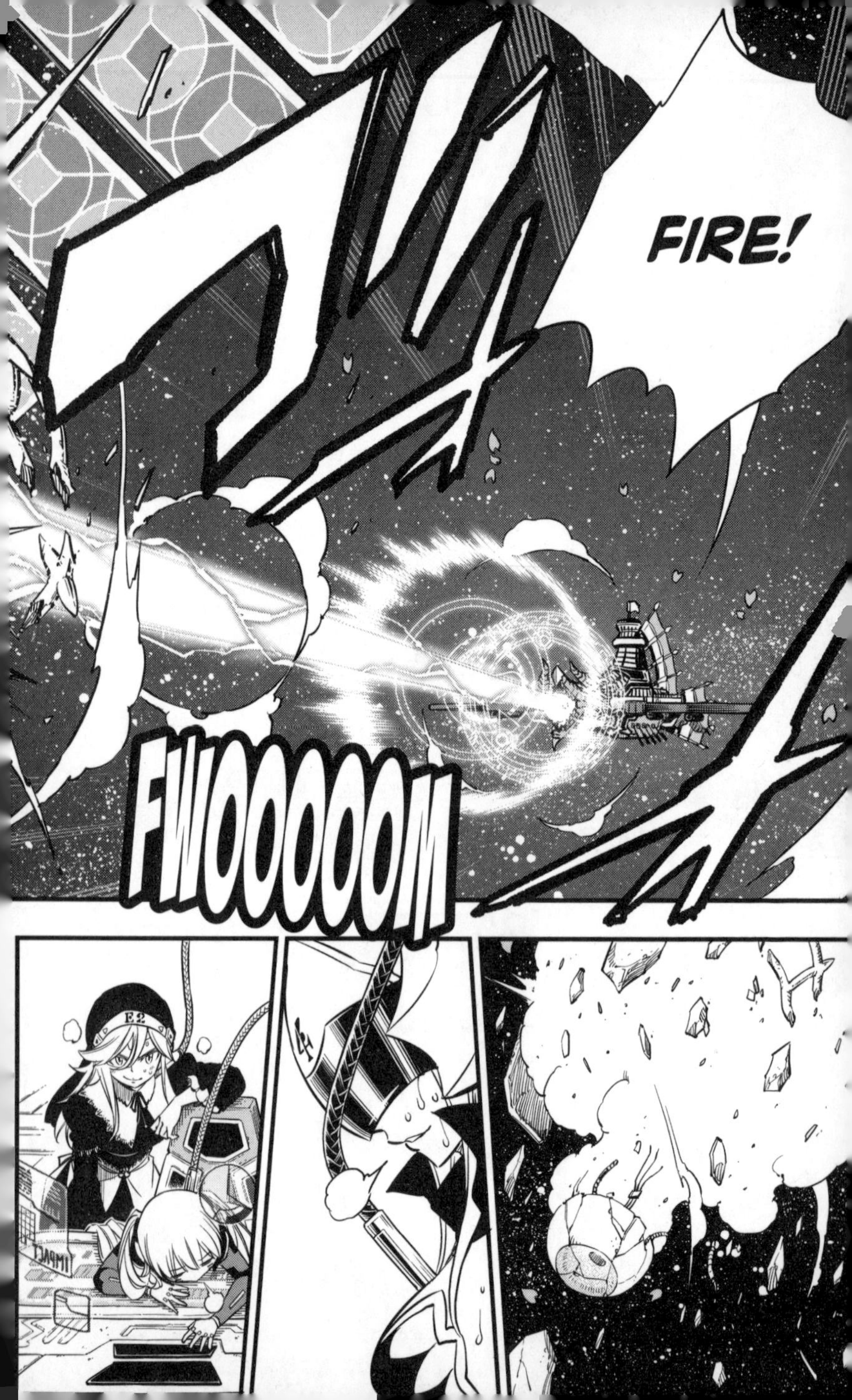
FIRE!
FWOOOOOM

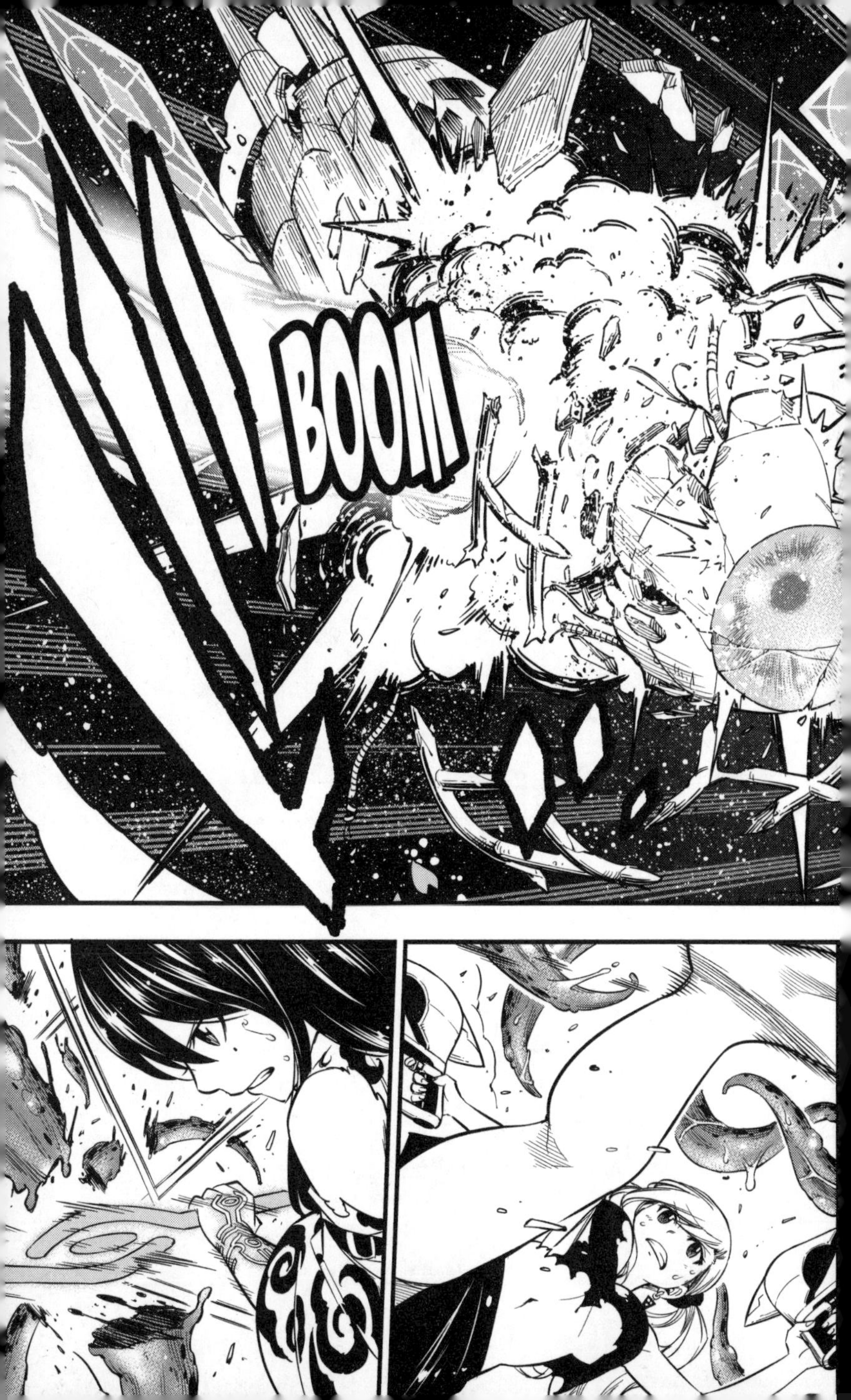
BOOM

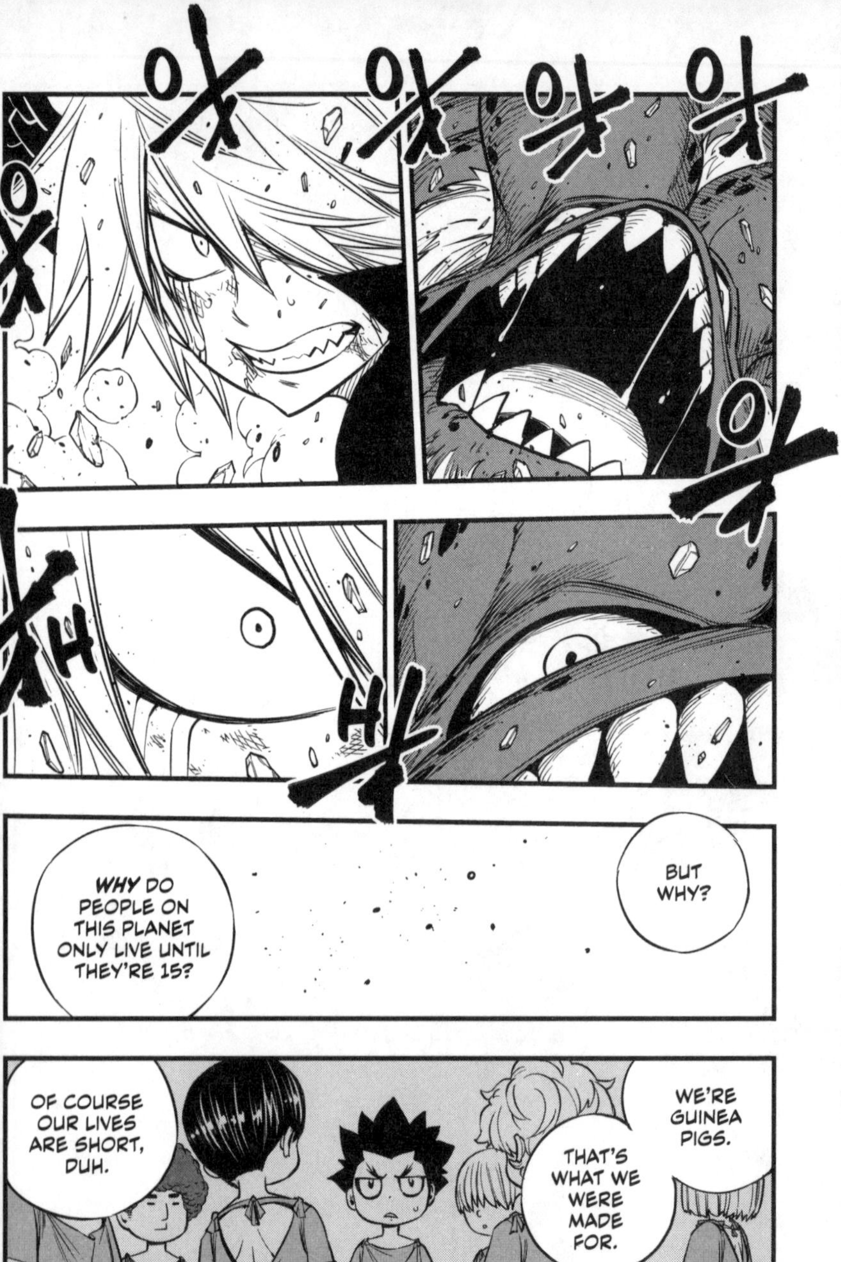
BUT WHY?
WHY DO PEOPLE ON THIS PLANET ONLY LIVE UNTIL THEY'RE 15?
WE'RE GUINEA PIGS.
THAT'S WHAT WE WERE MADE FOR.
OF COURSE OUR LIVES ARE SHORT, DUH.

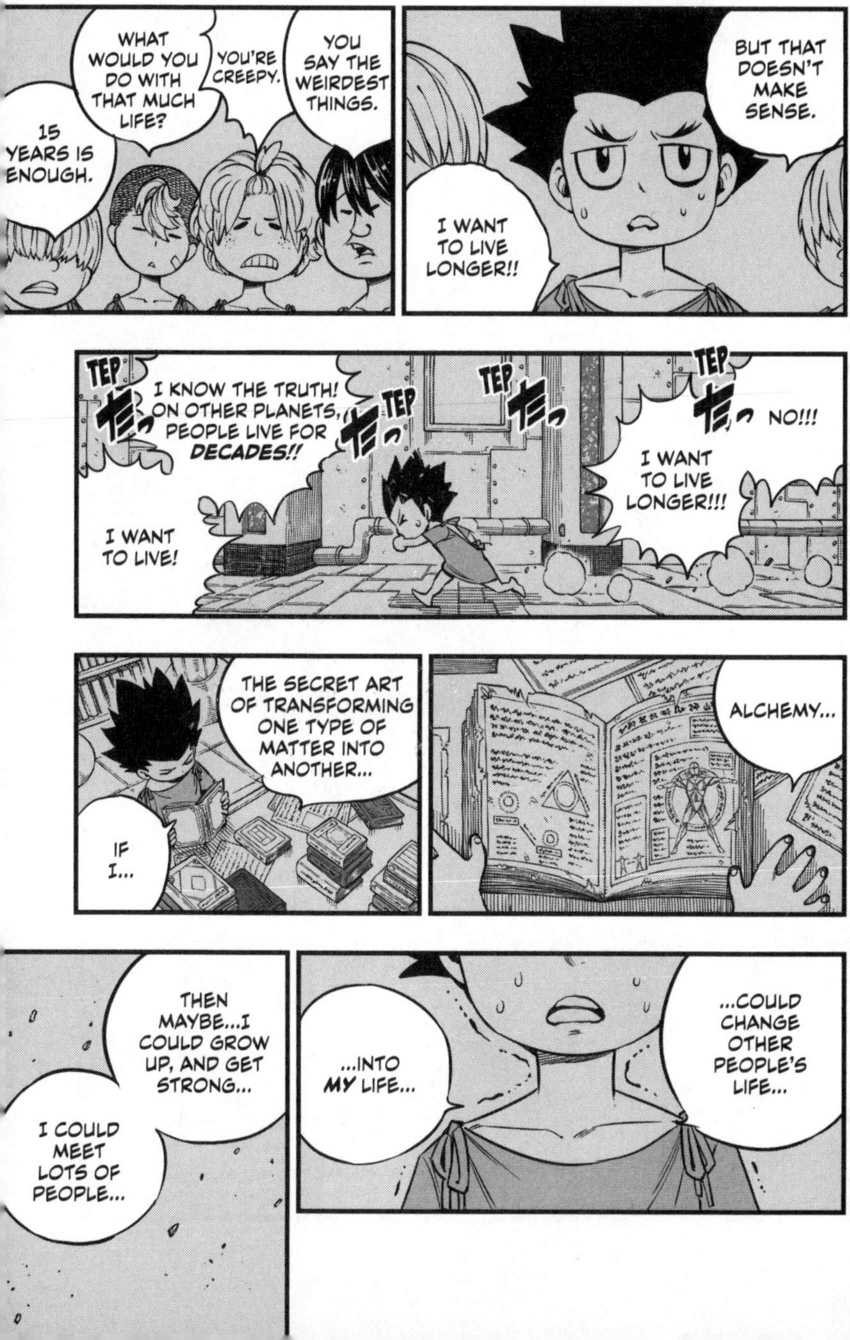
BUT THAT DOESN'T MAKE SENSE.
I WANT TO LIVE LONGER!!
YOU SAY THE WEIRDEST THINGS.
YOU'RE CREEPY.
WHAT WOULD YOU DO WITH THAT MUCH LIFE?
15 YEARS IS ENOUGH.
TEP
NO!!!
I WANT TO LIVE LONGER!!!
TEP
TEP
I KNOW THE TRUTH! ON OTHER PLANETS, PEOPLE LIVE FOR *DECADES!!*
TEP
I WANT TO LIVE!
ALCHEMY...
THE SECRET ART OF TRANSFORMING ONE TYPE OF MATTER INTO ANOTHER...
IF I...
...COULD CHANGE OTHER PEOPLE'S LIFE...
...INTO *MY* LIFE...
THEN MAYBE...I COULD GROW UP, AND GET STRONG...
I COULD MEET LOTS OF PEOPLE...

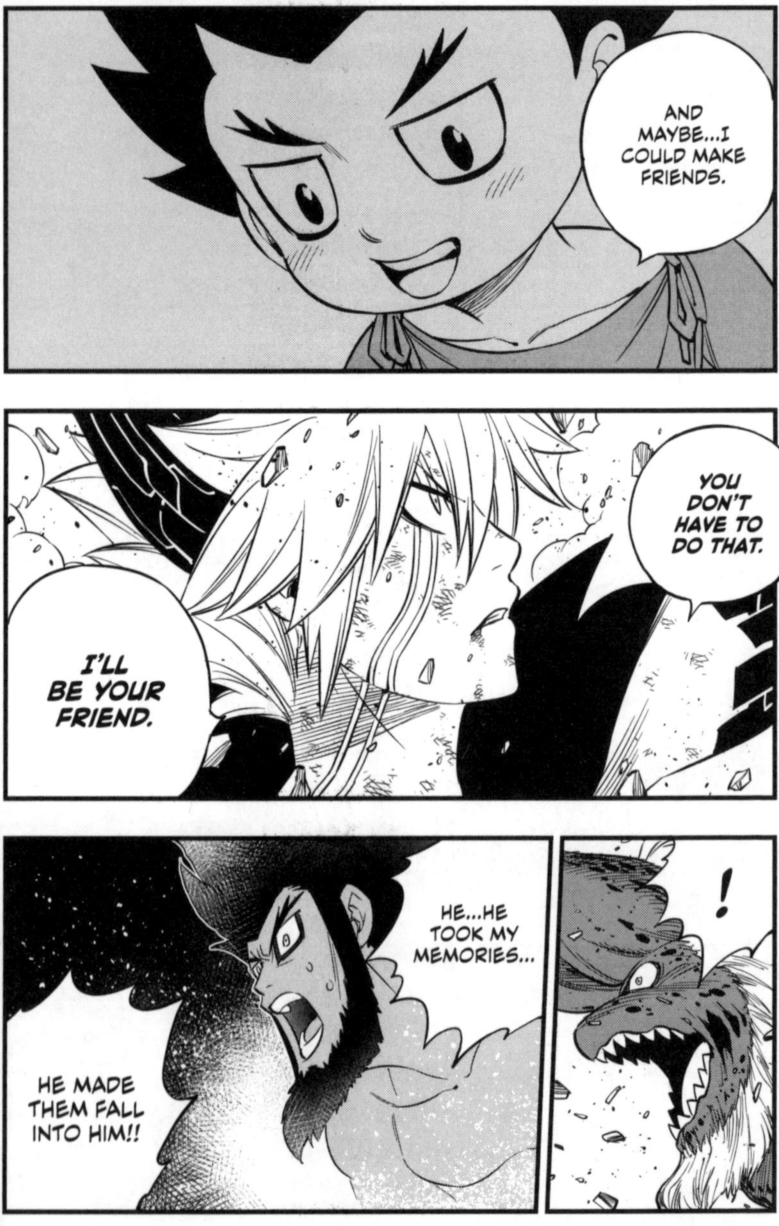
AND MAYBE...I COULD MAKE FRIENDS.
YOU DON'T HAVE TO DO THAT.
I'LL BE YOUR FRIEND.
!
HE...HE TOOK MY MEMORIES...
HE MADE THEM FALL INTO HIM!!

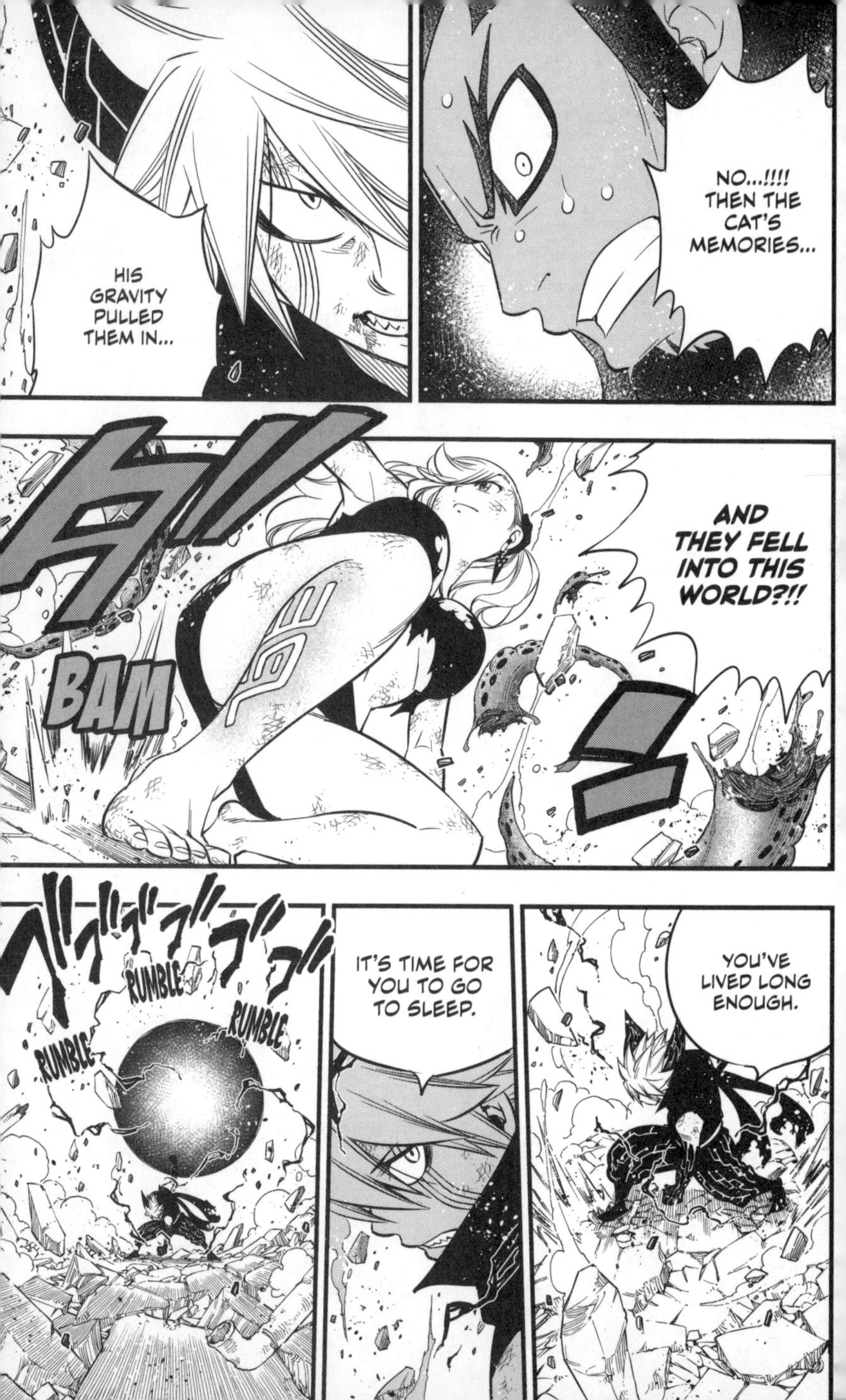
NO...!!!! THEN THE CAT'S MEMORIES...
HIS GRAVITY PULLED THEM IN...
AND THEY FELL INTO THIS WORLD?!!
BAM
YOU'VE LIVED LONG ENOUGH.
IT'S TIME FOR YOU TO GO TO SLEEP.
RUMBLE
RUMBLE
RUMBLE

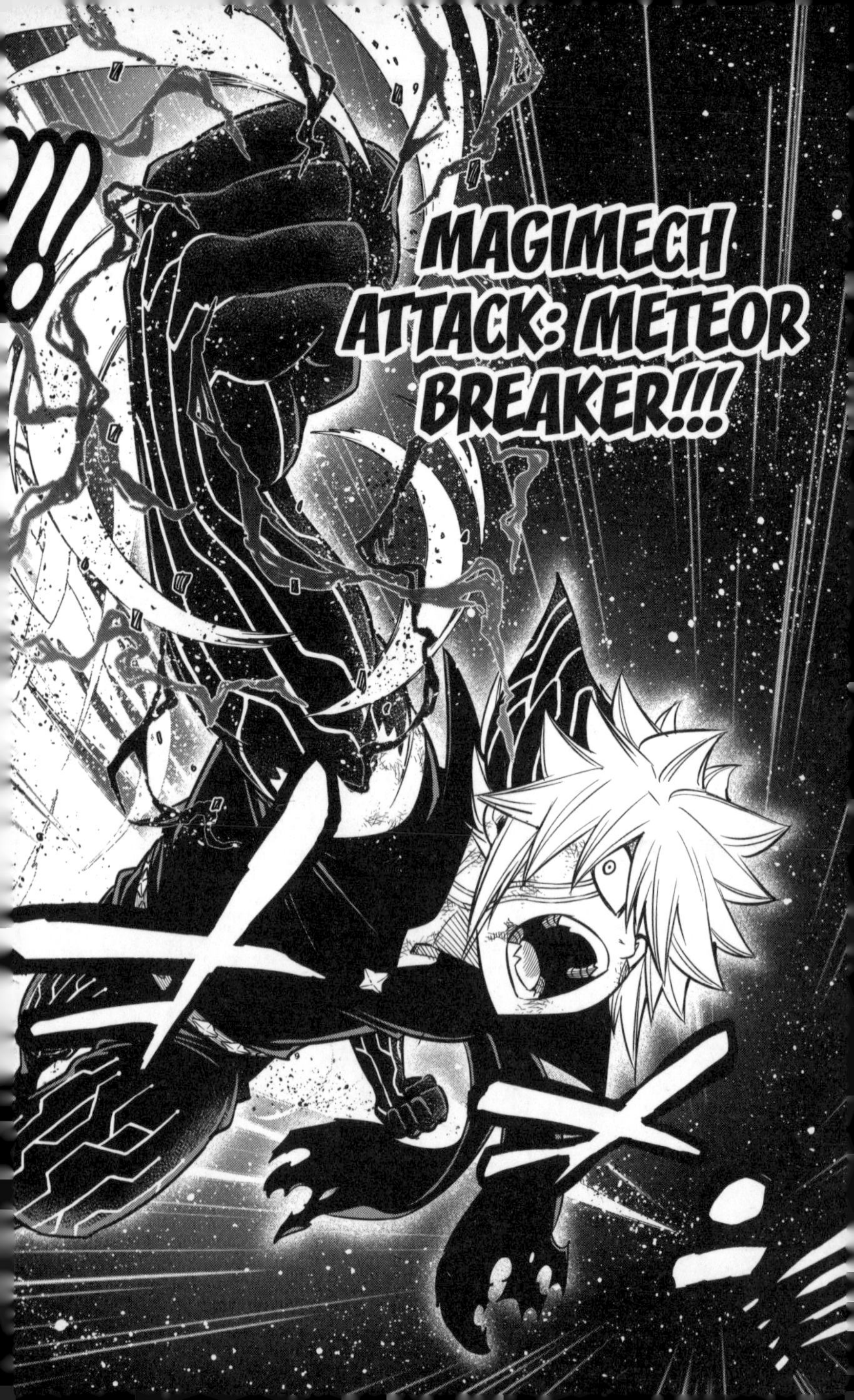
!!
MAGIMECH ATTACK: METEOR BREAKER!!!

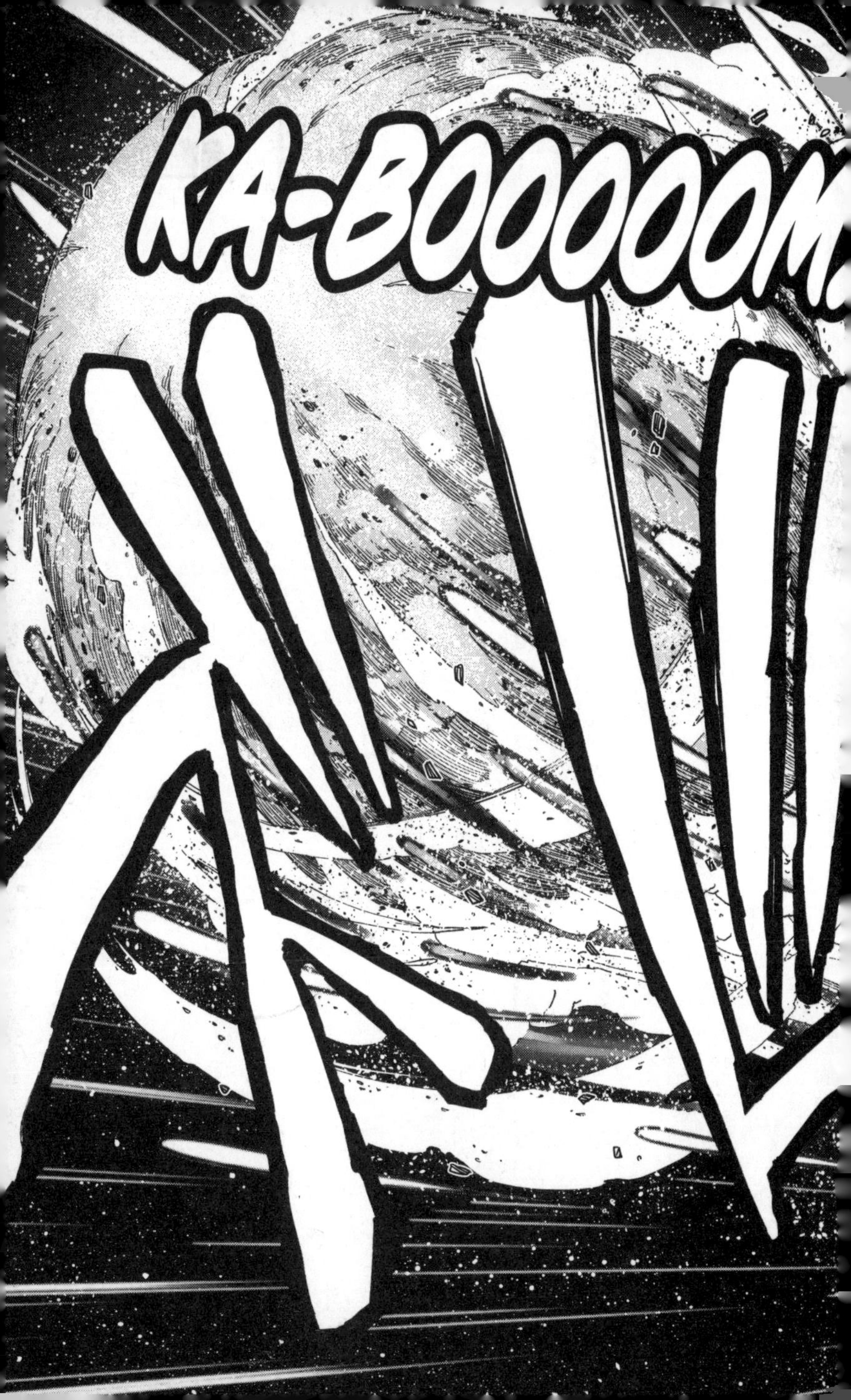
KA-BOOOOOM!

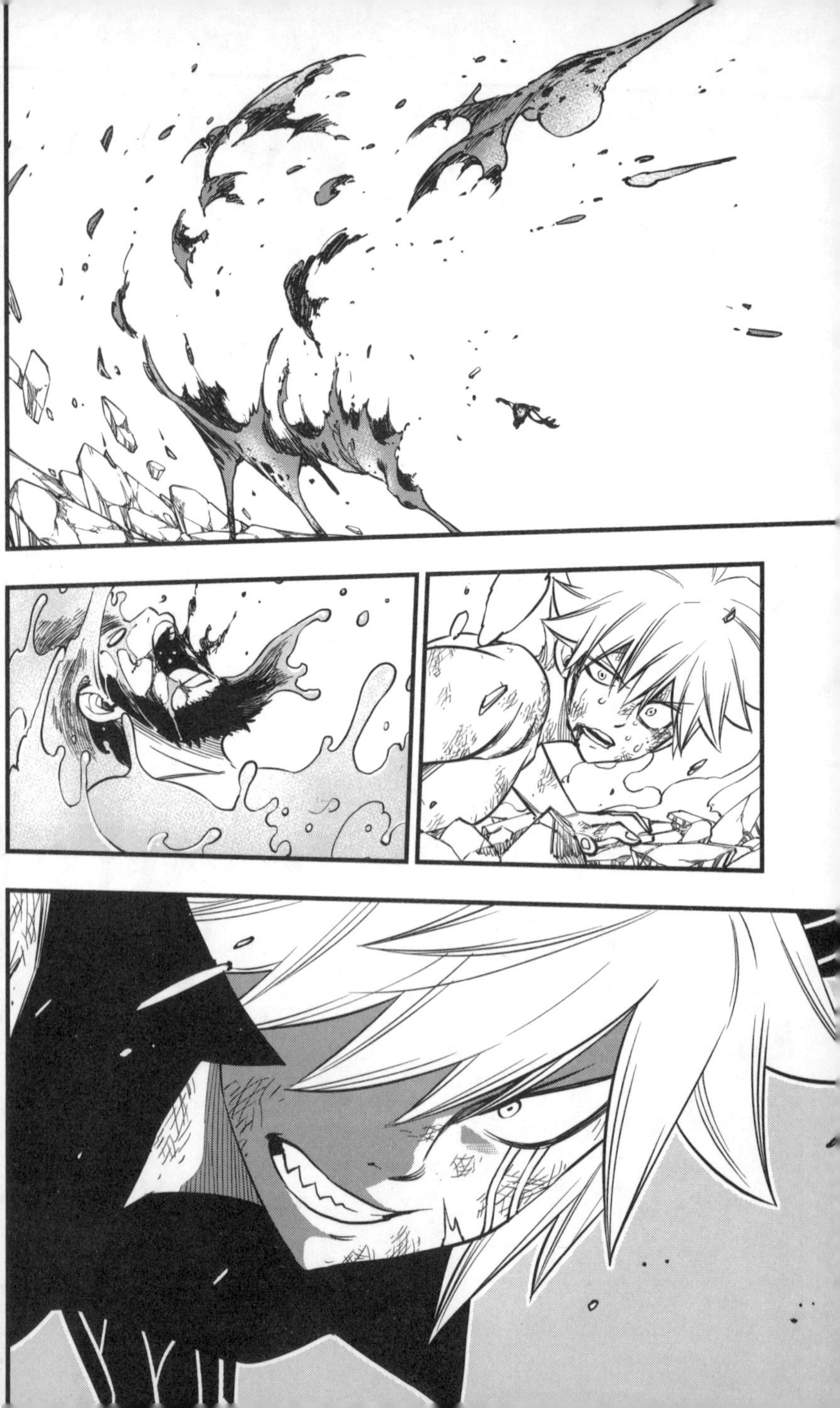

EDENS ZERO

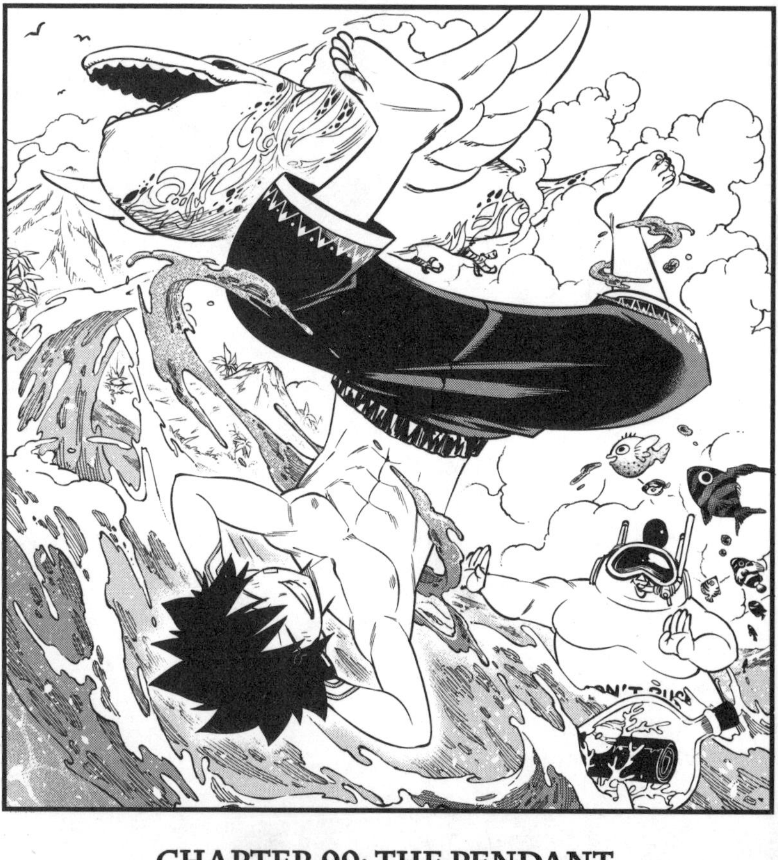

CHAPTER 99: THE PENDANT

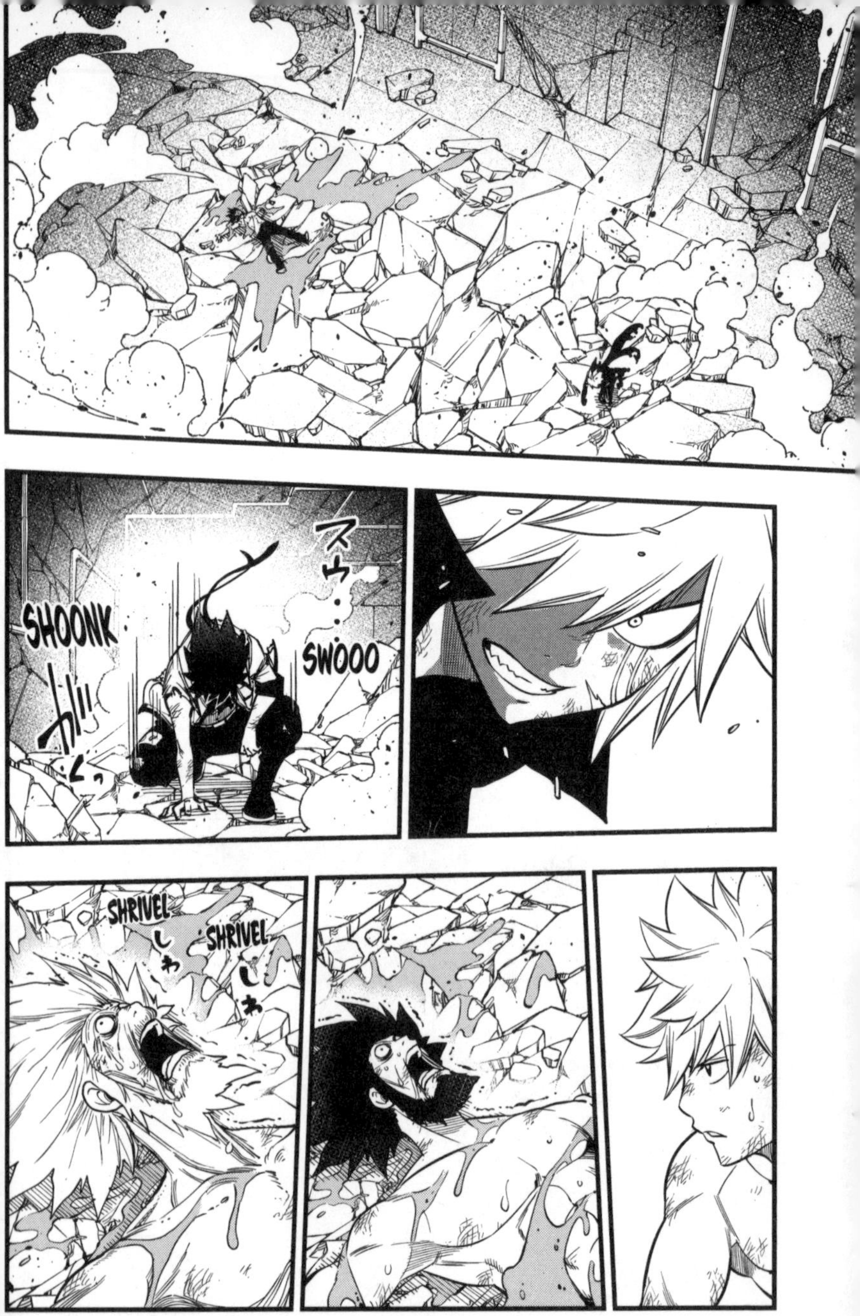
スゥ…
SWOOO
SHOONK
SHRIVEL
しわ
SHRIVEL
しわ

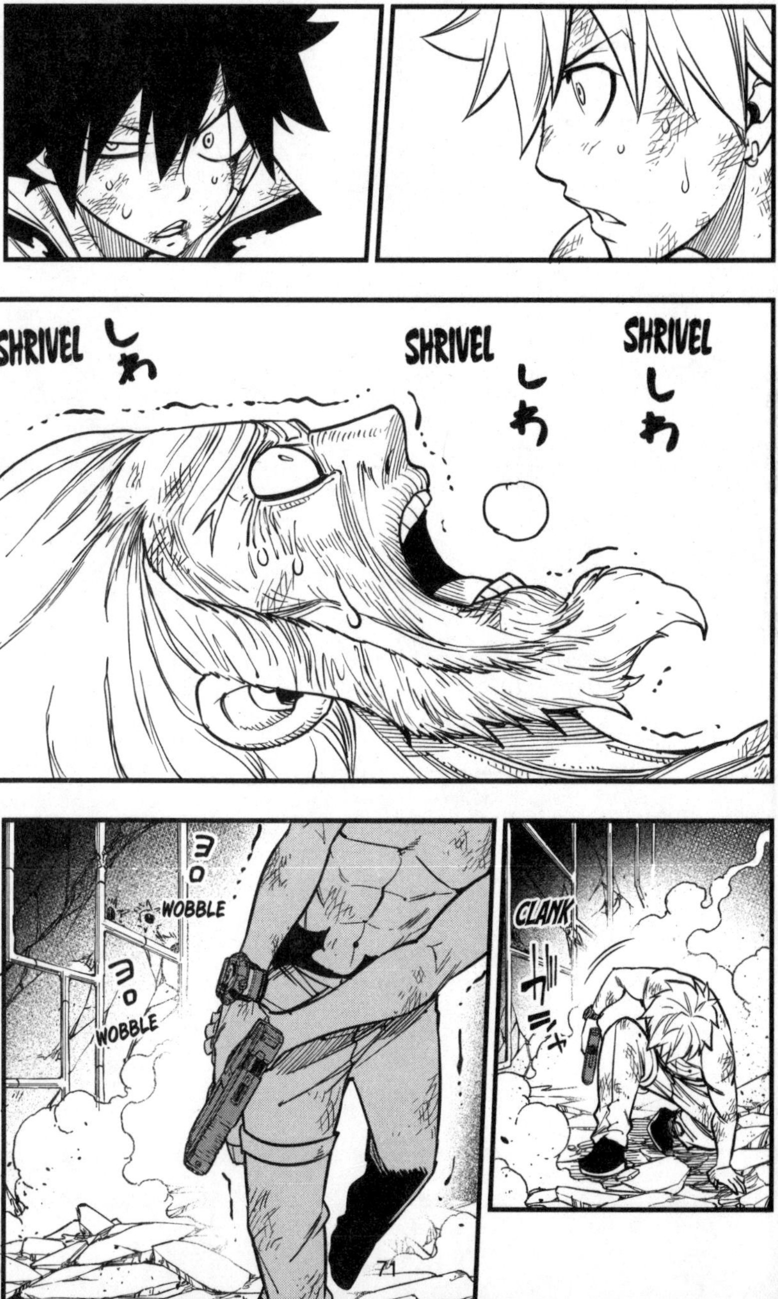
SHRIVEL
しわ
SHRIVEL
しわ
SHRIVEL
しわ
CLANK
ガシャ
ヨロ
WOBBLE
ヨロ
WOBBLE

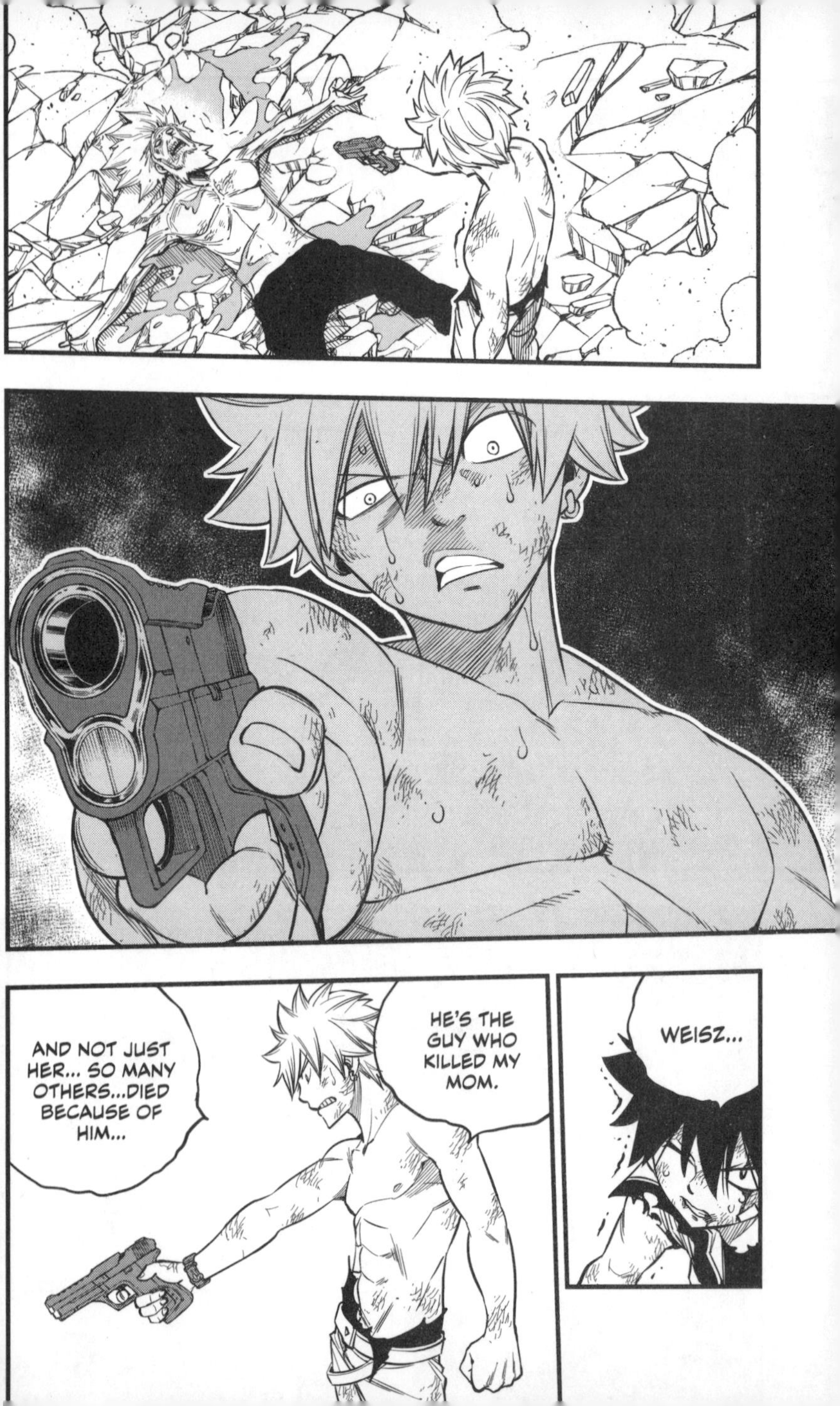
WEISZ...
HE'S THE GUY WHO KILLED MY MOM.
AND NOT JUST HER... SO MANY OTHERS...DIED BECAUSE OF HIM...

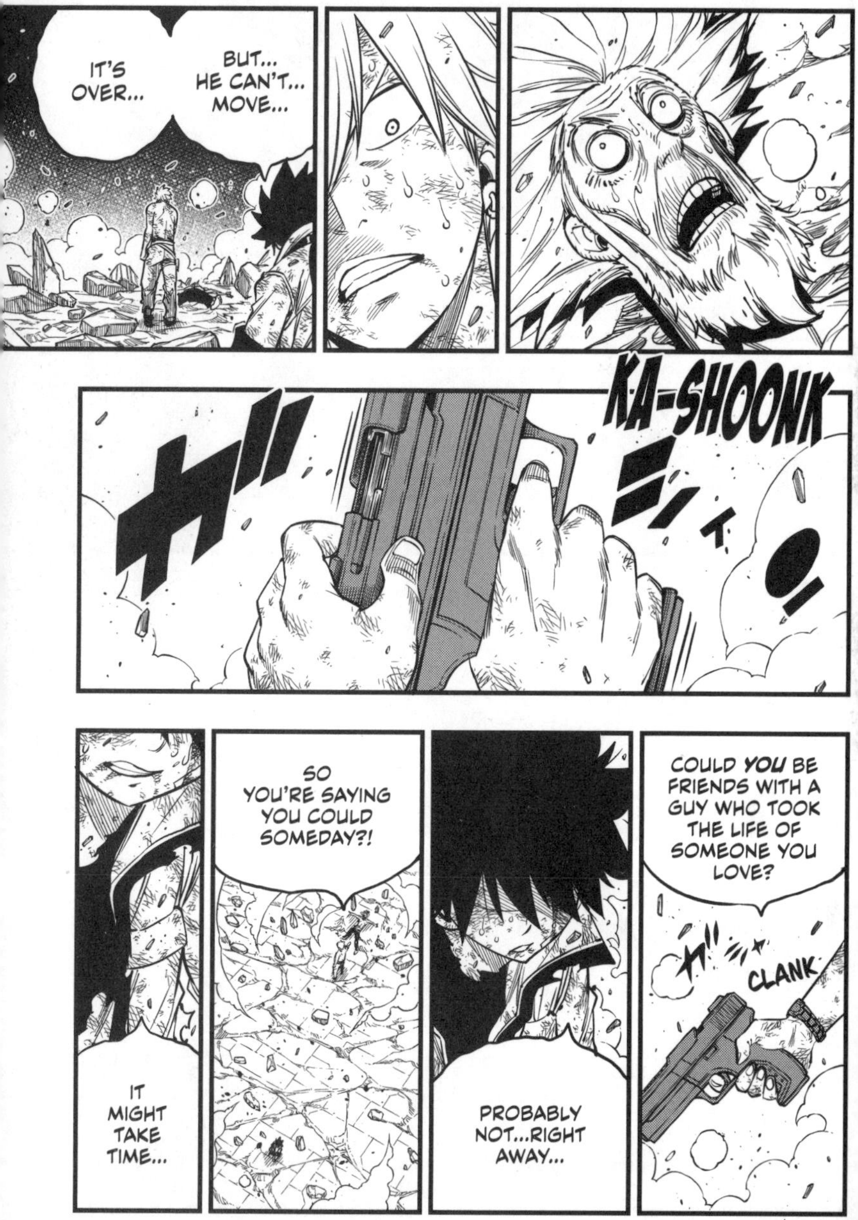
IT'S OVER... BUT... HE CAN'T... MOVE...
KA-SHOONK
COULD *YOU* BE FRIENDS WITH A GUY WHO TOOK THE LIFE OF SOMEONE YOU LOVE?
CLANK
PROBABLY NOT...RIGHT AWAY...
SO YOU'RE SAYING YOU COULD SOMEDAY?!
IT MIGHT TAKE TIME...

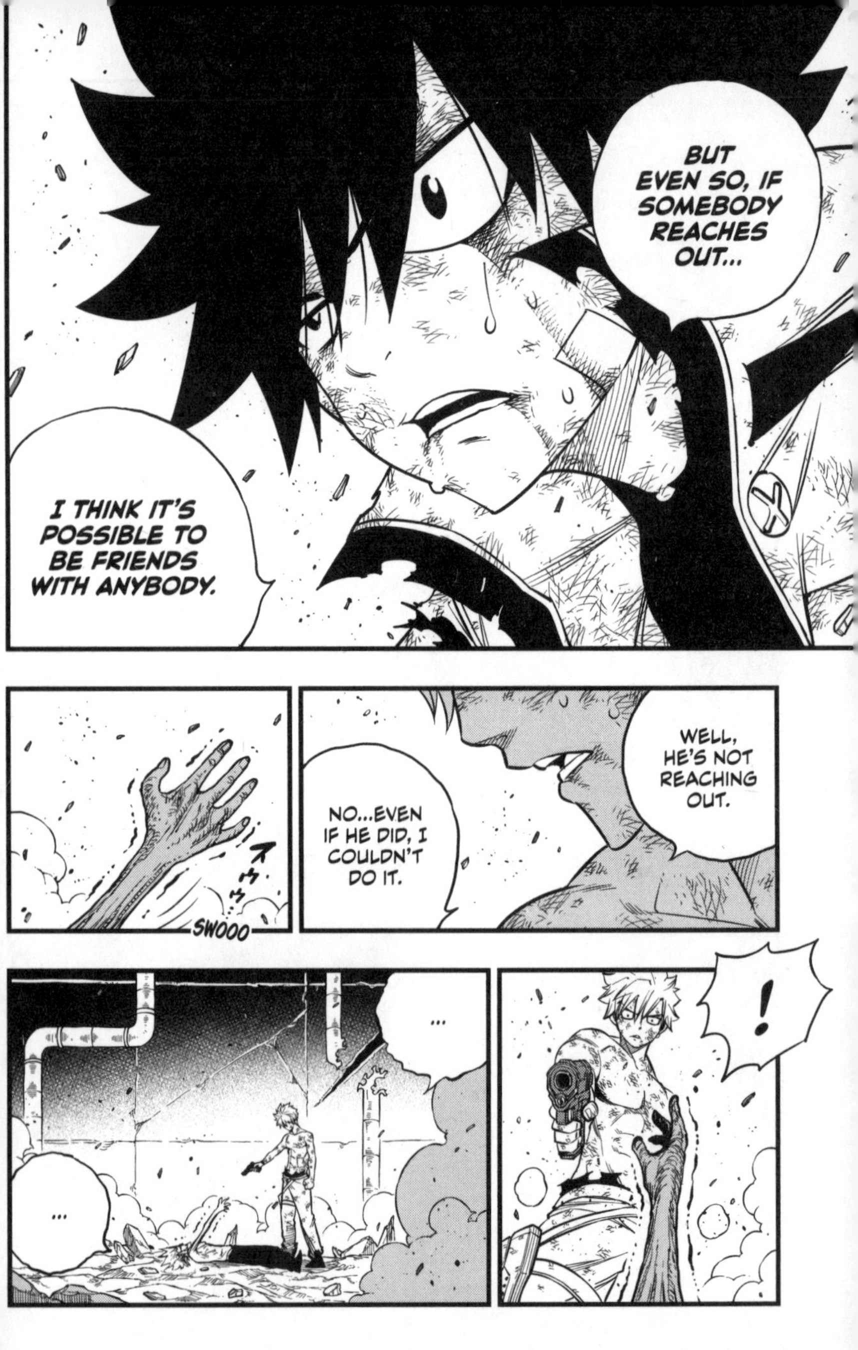
BUT EVEN SO, IF SOMEBODY REACHES OUT...
I THINK IT'S POSSIBLE TO BE FRIENDS WITH ANYBODY.
WELL, HE'S NOT REACHING OUT.
NO...EVEN IF HE DID, I COULDN'T DO IT.
SWOOO
!
...
...

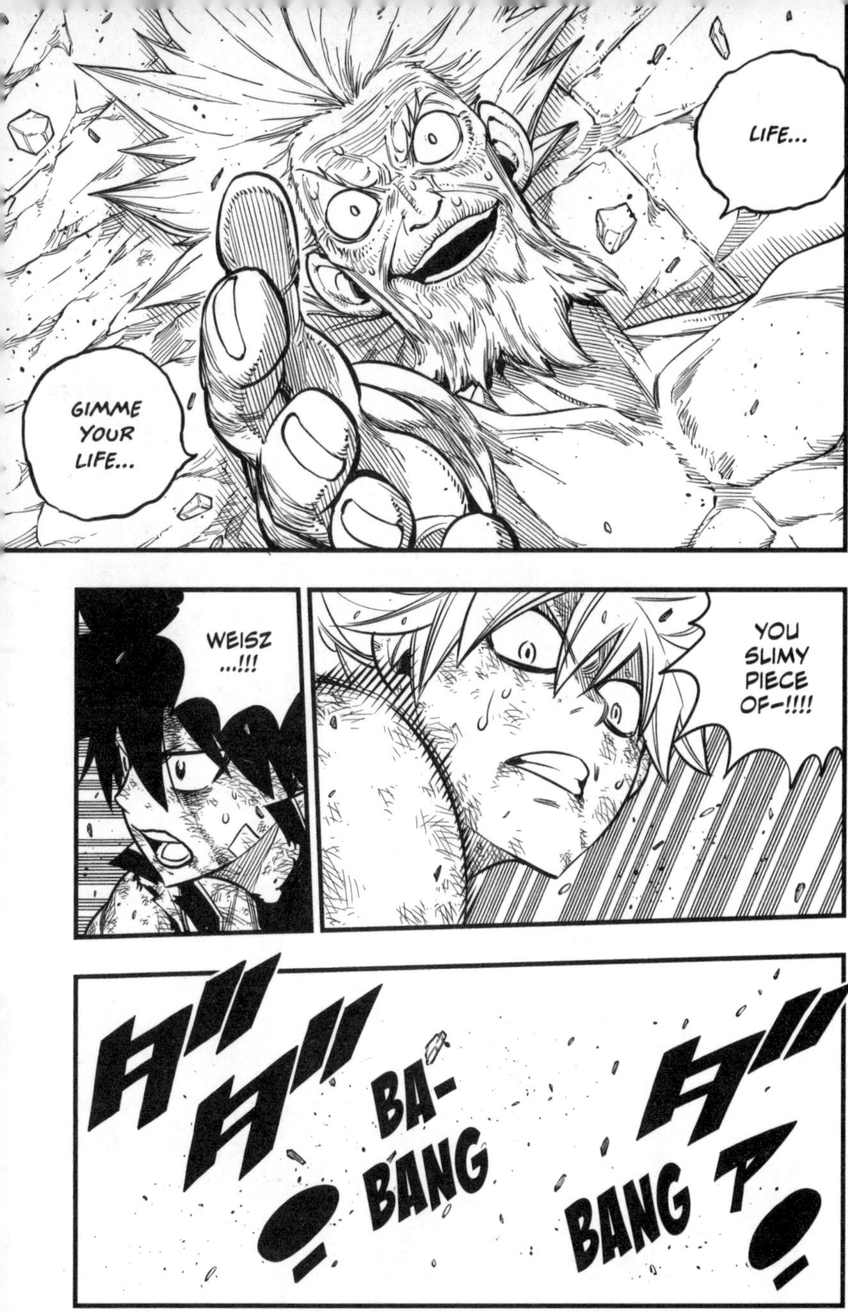
LIFE...
GIMME YOUR LIFE...
YOU SLIMY PIECE OF-!!!!
WEISZ ...!!!
BANG
BA-BANG

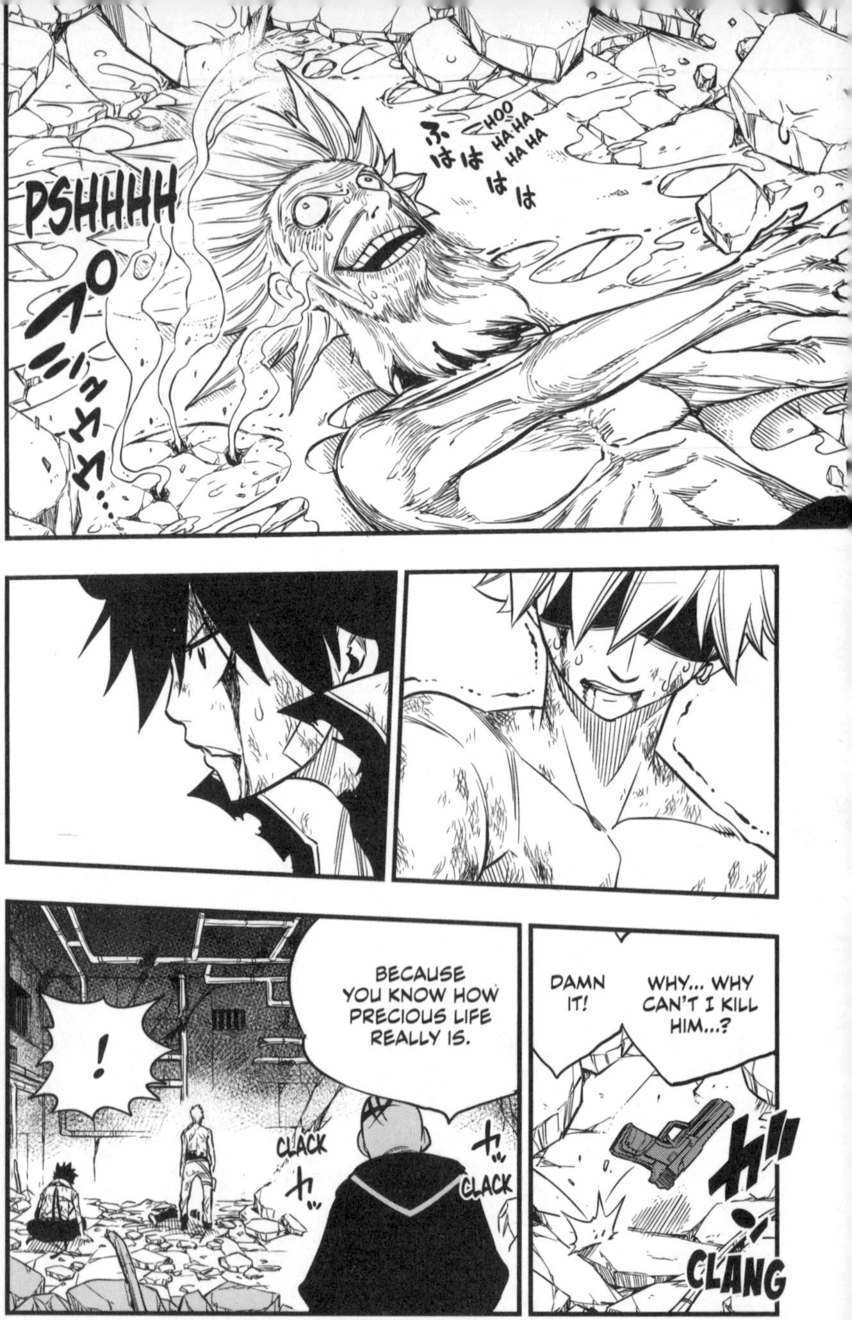
ふはははは
HOO HA HA HA HA
PSHHHH
ぷしゅうう…
WHY... WHY CAN'T I KILL HIM...?
DAMN IT!
ガッ
CLANG
BECAUSE YOU KNOW HOW PRECIOUS LIFE REALLY IS.
カッ
CLACK
カッ
CLACK
!

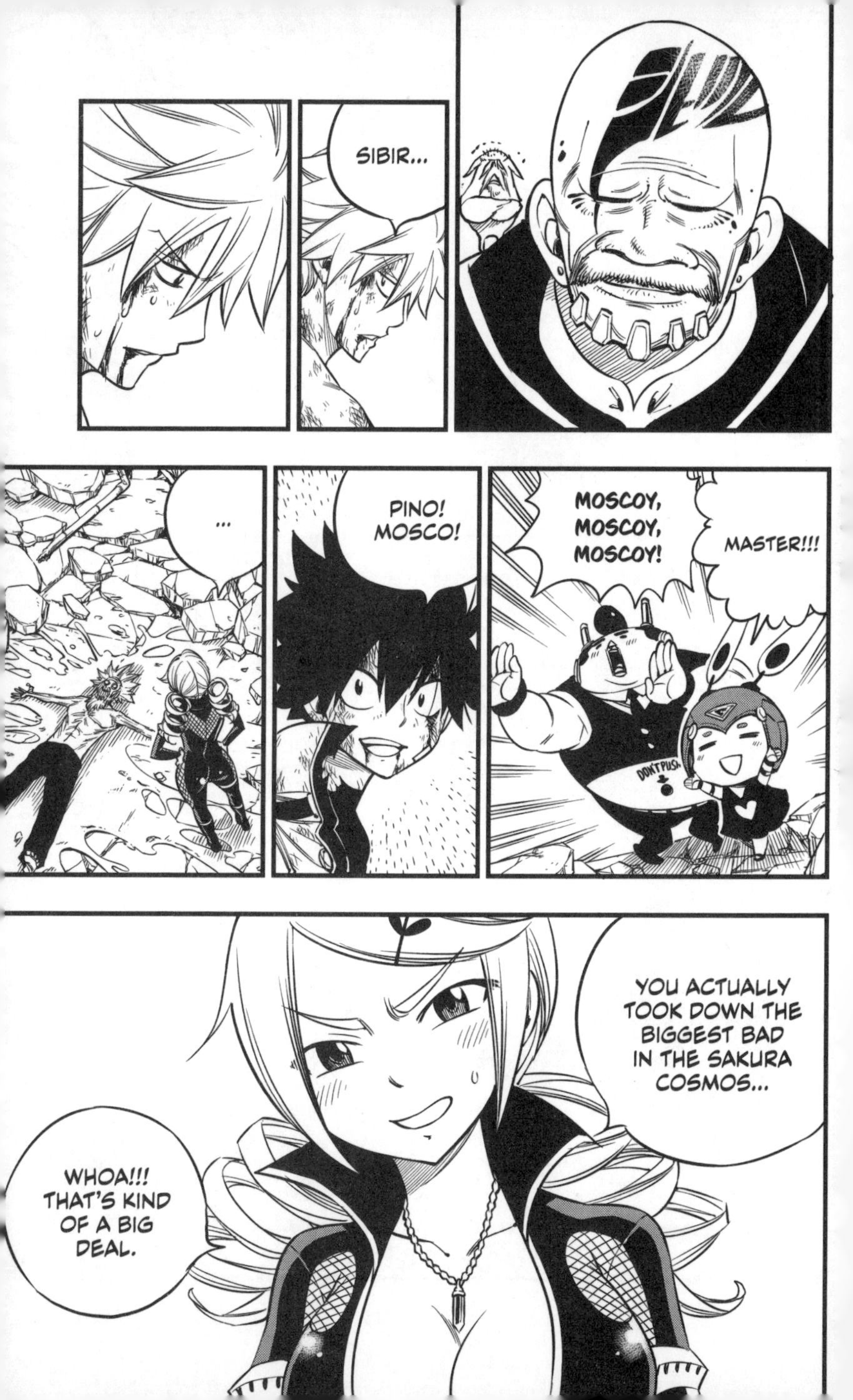
SIBIR...
MASTER!!!
MOSCOY, MOSCOY, MOSCOY!
PINO! MOSCO!
...
YOU ACTUALLY TOOK DOWN THE BIGGEST BAD IN THE SAKURA COSMOS...
WHOA!!! THAT'S KIND OF A BIG DEAL.

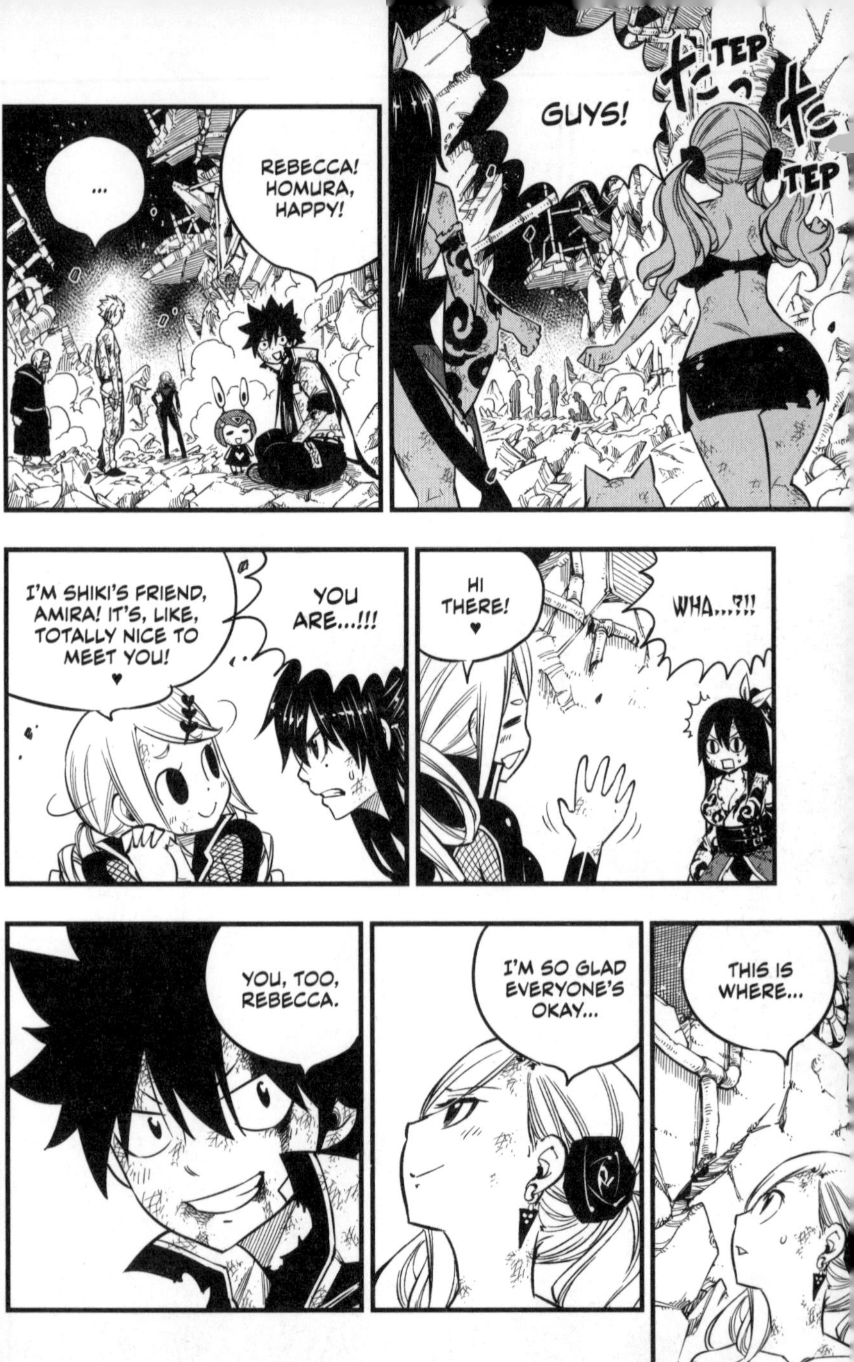
TEP
TEP
GUYS!
REBECCA! HOMURA, HAPPY!
...
WHA...?!!
HI THERE! ♥
YOU ARE...!!!
I'M SHIKI'S FRIEND, AMIRA! IT'S, LIKE, TOTALLY NICE TO MEET YOU! ♥
THIS IS WHERE...
I'M SO GLAD EVERYONE'S OKAY...
YOU, TOO, REBECCA.

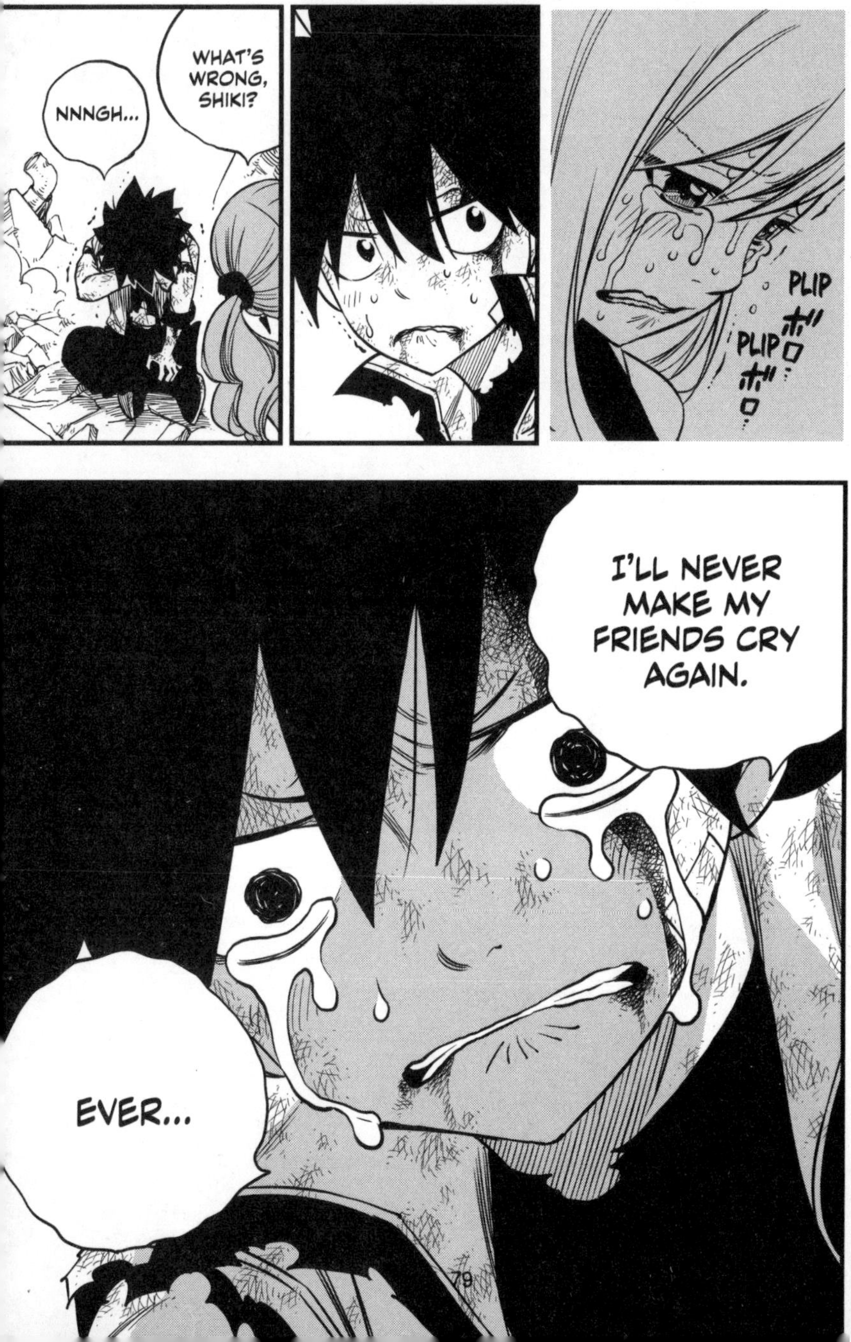
PLIP
ボロ
PLIP
ボロ
WHAT'S WRONG, SHIKI?
NNNGH...
I'LL NEVER MAKE MY FRIENDS CRY AGAIN.
EVER...

YOU...

NOW, NOW.

NO KIDDING.

BUT WHAT DO WE DO WHEN *YOU* START CRYING?!

WE KNOW!!

WE DID IT...

WE WON...

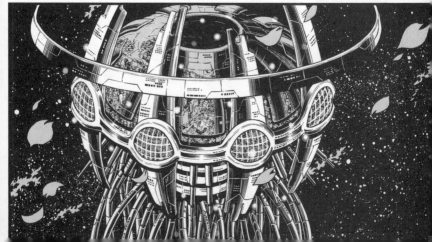

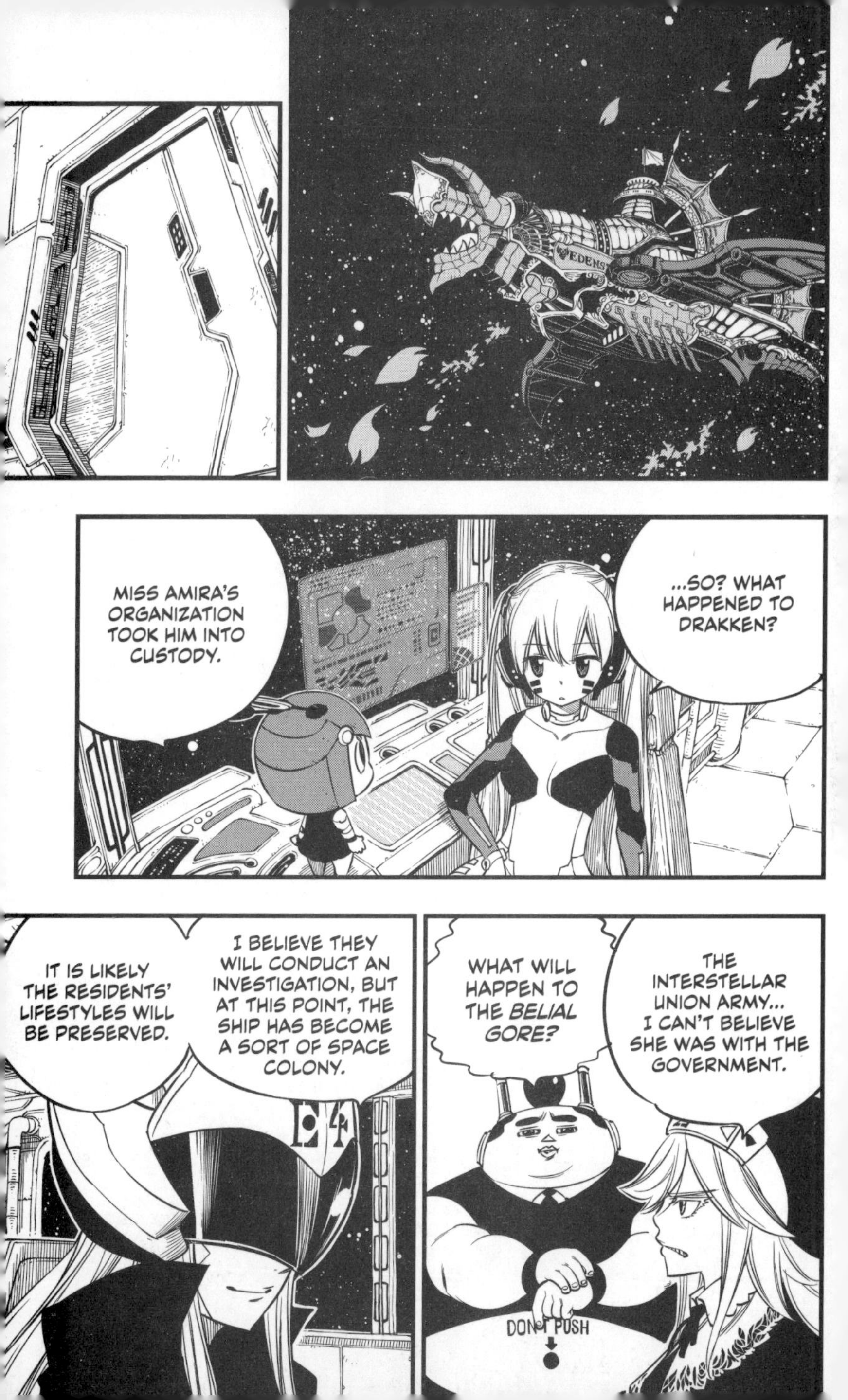

...SO? WHAT HAPPENED TO DRAKKEN?
MISS AMIRA'S ORGANIZATION TOOK HIM INTO CUSTODY.
THE INTERSTELLAR UNION ARMY... I CAN'T BELIEVE SHE WAS WITH THE GOVERNMENT.
WHAT WILL HAPPEN TO THE *BELIAL GORE?*
I BELIEVE THEY WILL CONDUCT AN INVESTIGATION, BUT AT THIS POINT, THE SHIP HAS BECOME A SORT OF SPACE COLONY.
IT IS LIKELY THE RESIDENTS' LIFESTYLES WILL BE PRESERVED.

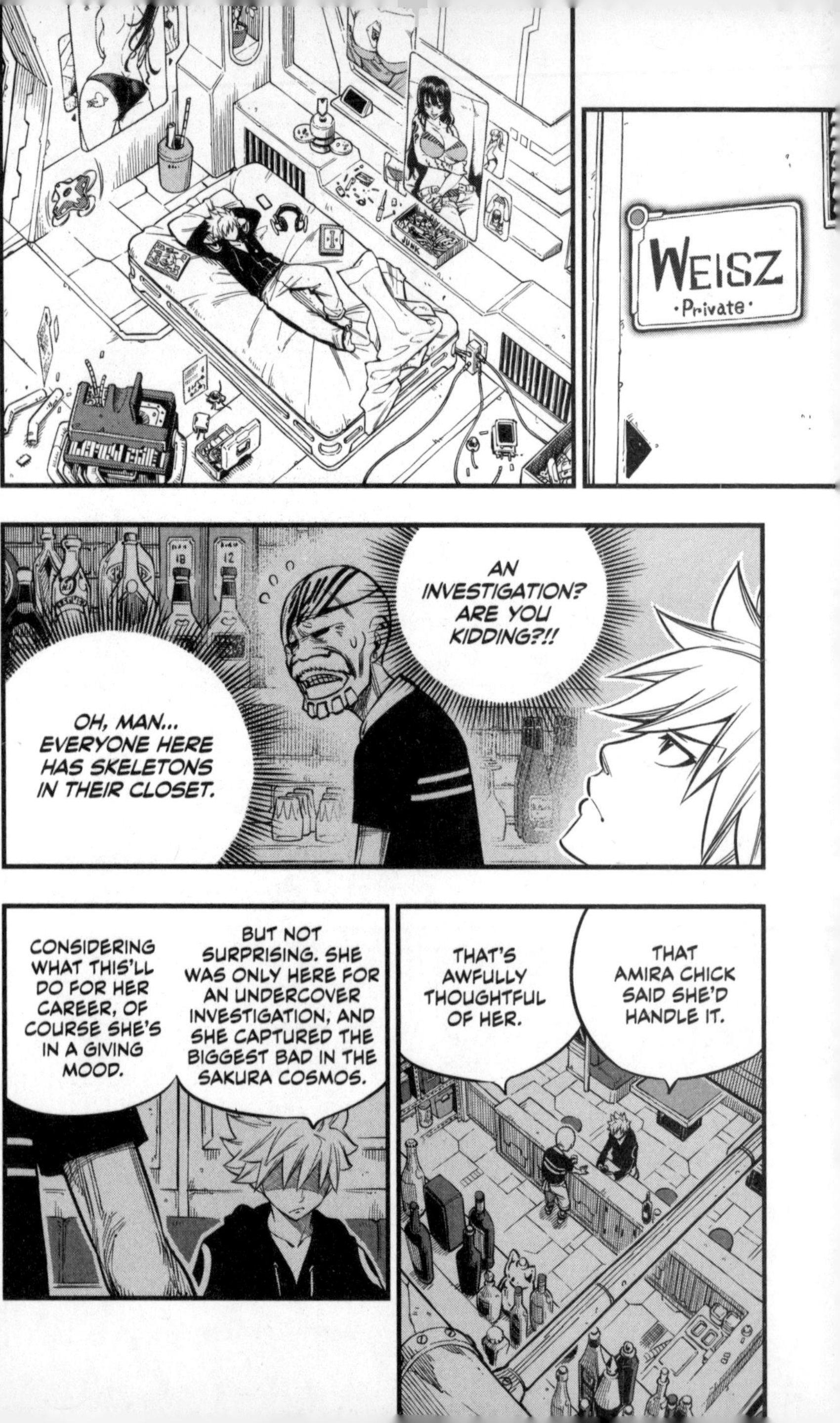
WEISZ
•Private•
AN INVESTIGATION? ARE YOU KIDDING?!!
OH, MAN... EVERYONE HERE HAS SKELETONS IN THEIR CLOSET.
THAT AMIRA CHICK SAID SHE'D HANDLE IT.
THAT'S AWFULLY THOUGHTFUL OF HER.
BUT NOT SURPRISING. SHE WAS ONLY HERE FOR AN UNDERCOVER INVESTIGATION, AND SHE CAPTURED THE BIGGEST BAD IN THE SAKURA COSMOS.
CONSIDERING WHAT THIS'LL DO FOR HER CAREER, OF COURSE SHE'S IN A GIVING MOOD.

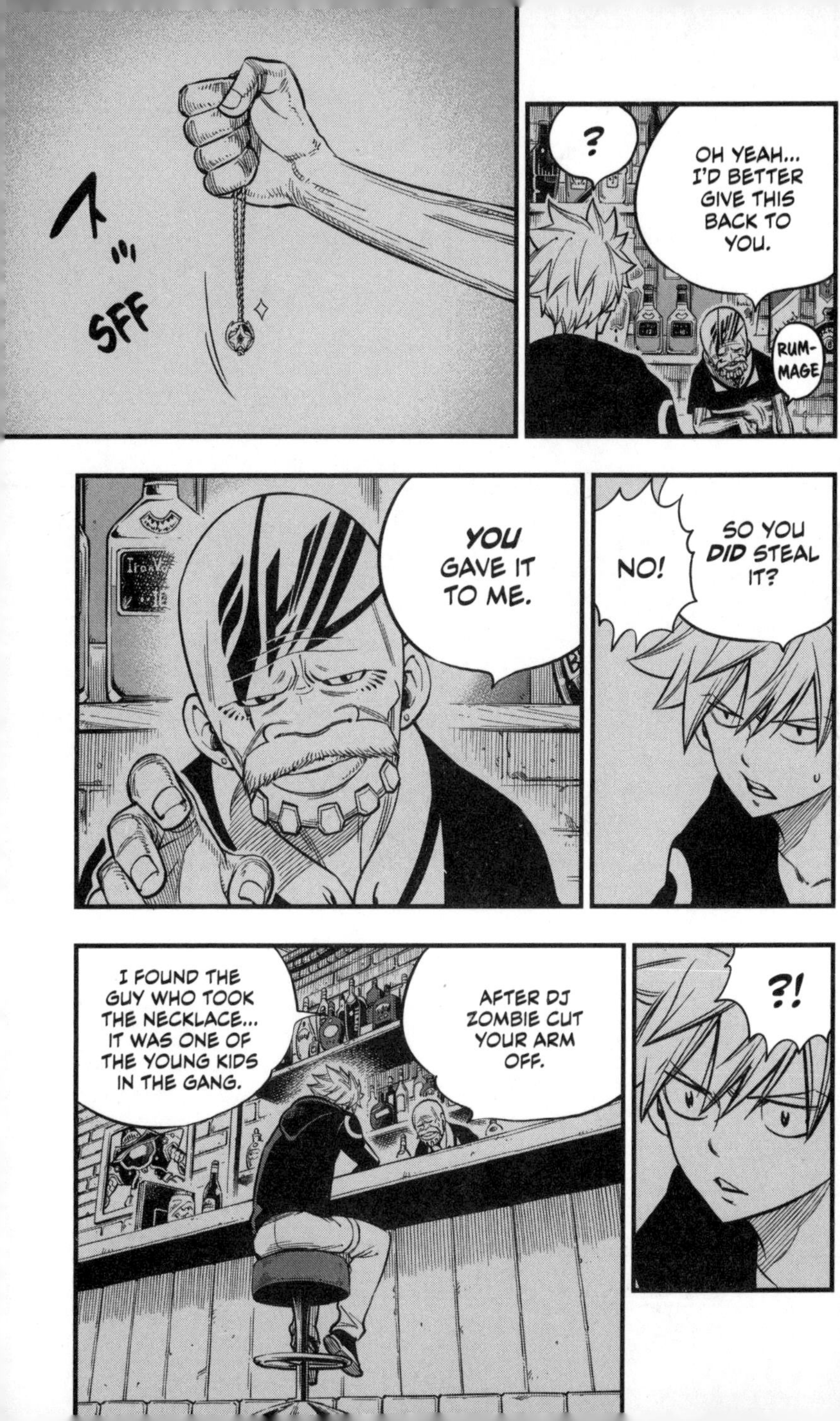
OH YEAH... I'D BETTER GIVE THIS BACK TO YOU.
?
RUM-MAGE
SFF
SO YOU *DID* STEAL IT?
NO!
YOU GAVE IT TO ME.
?!
AFTER DJ ZOMBIE CUT YOUR ARM OFF.
I FOUND THE GUY WHO TOOK THE NECKLACE... IT WAS ONE OF THE YOUNG KIDS IN THE GANG.

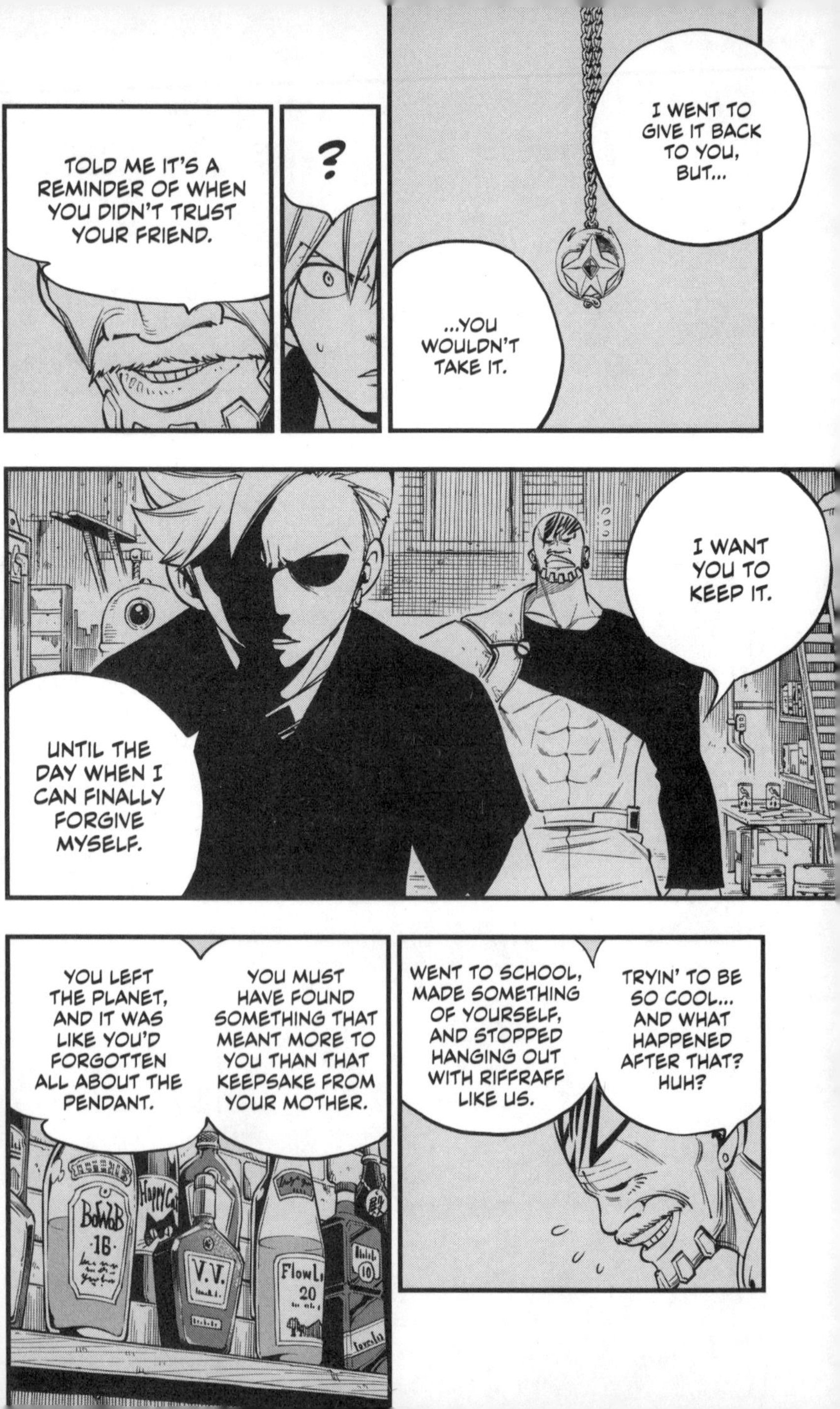
I WENT TO GIVE IT BACK TO YOU, BUT...
...YOU WOULDN'T TAKE IT.
?
TOLD ME IT'S A REMINDER OF WHEN YOU DIDN'T TRUST YOUR FRIEND.
I WANT YOU TO KEEP IT.
UNTIL THE DAY WHEN I CAN FINALLY FORGIVE MYSELF.
TRYIN' TO BE SO COOL... AND WHAT HAPPENED AFTER THAT? HUH?
WENT TO SCHOOL, MADE SOMETHING OF YOURSELF, AND STOPPED HANGING OUT WITH RIFFRAFF LIKE US.
YOU MUST HAVE FOUND SOMETHING THAT MEANT MORE TO YOU THAN THAT KEEPSAKE FROM YOUR MOTHER.
YOU LEFT THE PLANET, AND IT WAS LIKE YOU'D FORGOTTEN ALL ABOUT THE PENDANT.

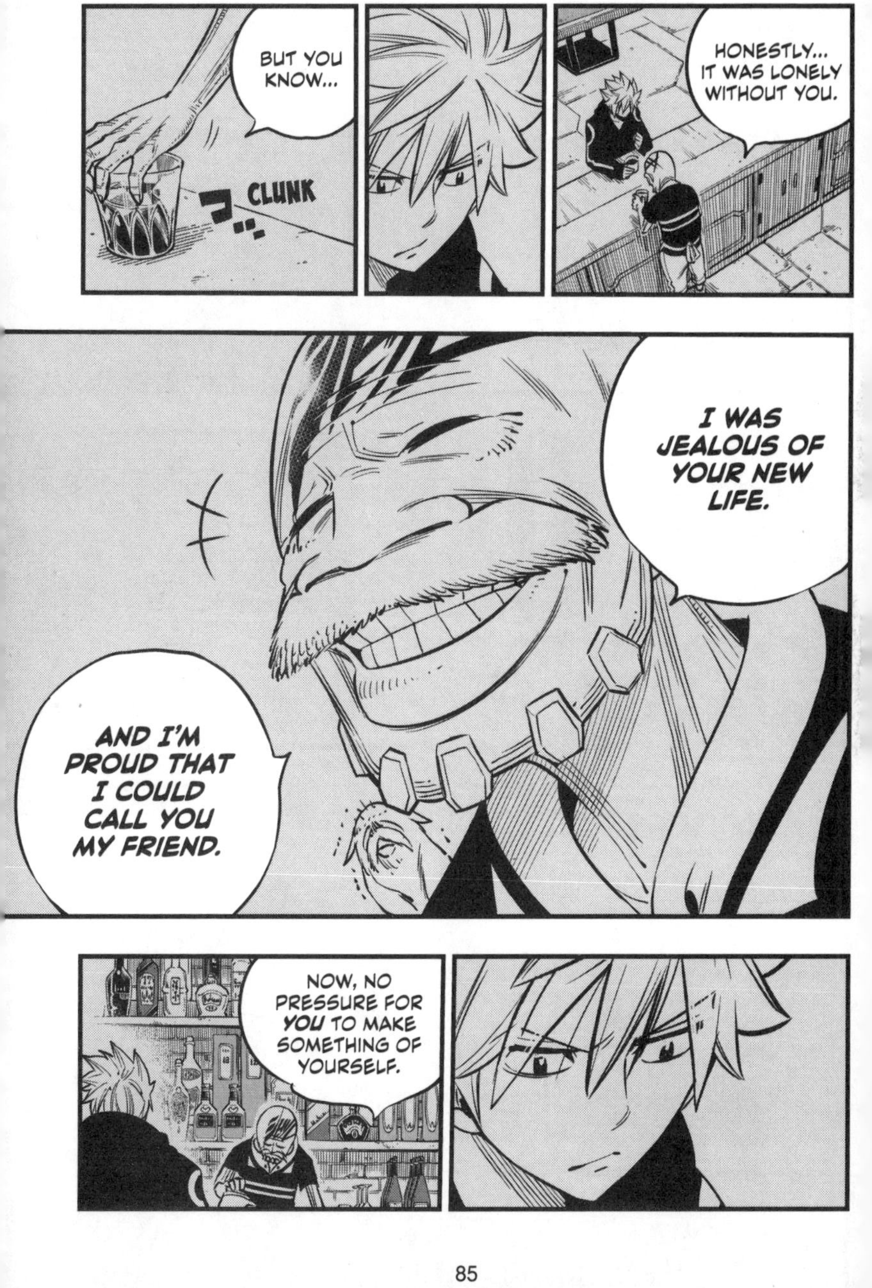
HONESTLY... IT WAS LONELY WITHOUT YOU.
BUT YOU KNOW...
CLUNK
I WAS JEALOUS OF YOUR NEW LIFE.
AND I'M PROUD THAT I COULD CALL YOU MY FRIEND.
NOW, NO PRESSURE FOR YOU TO MAKE SOMETHING OF YOURSELF.

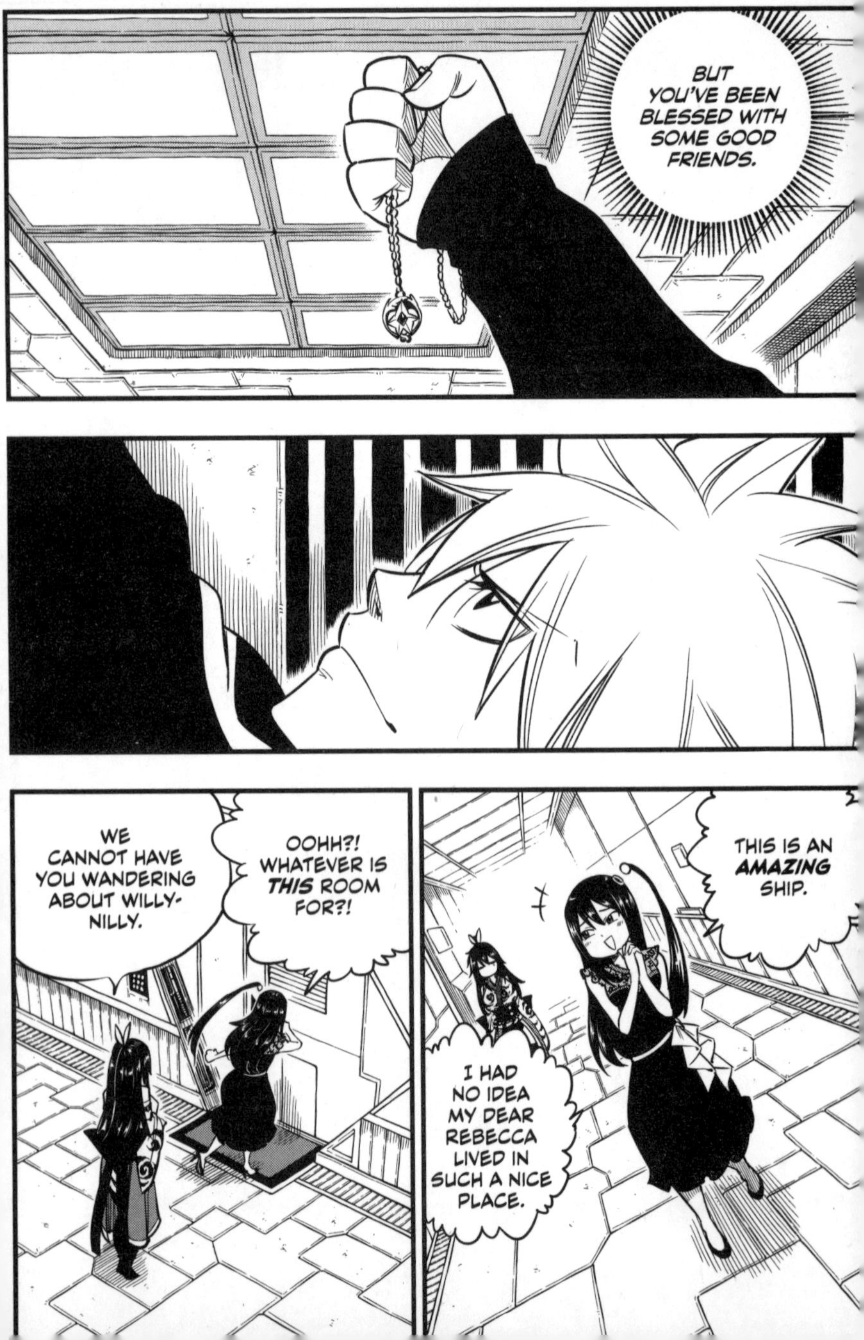
BUT YOU'VE BEEN BLESSED WITH SOME GOOD FRIENDS.
THIS IS AN AMAZING SHIP.
I HAD NO IDEA MY DEAR REBECCA LIVED IN SUCH A NICE PLACE.
OOHH?! WHATEVER IS THIS ROOM FOR?!
WE CANNOT HAVE YOU WANDERING ABOUT WILLY-NILLY.

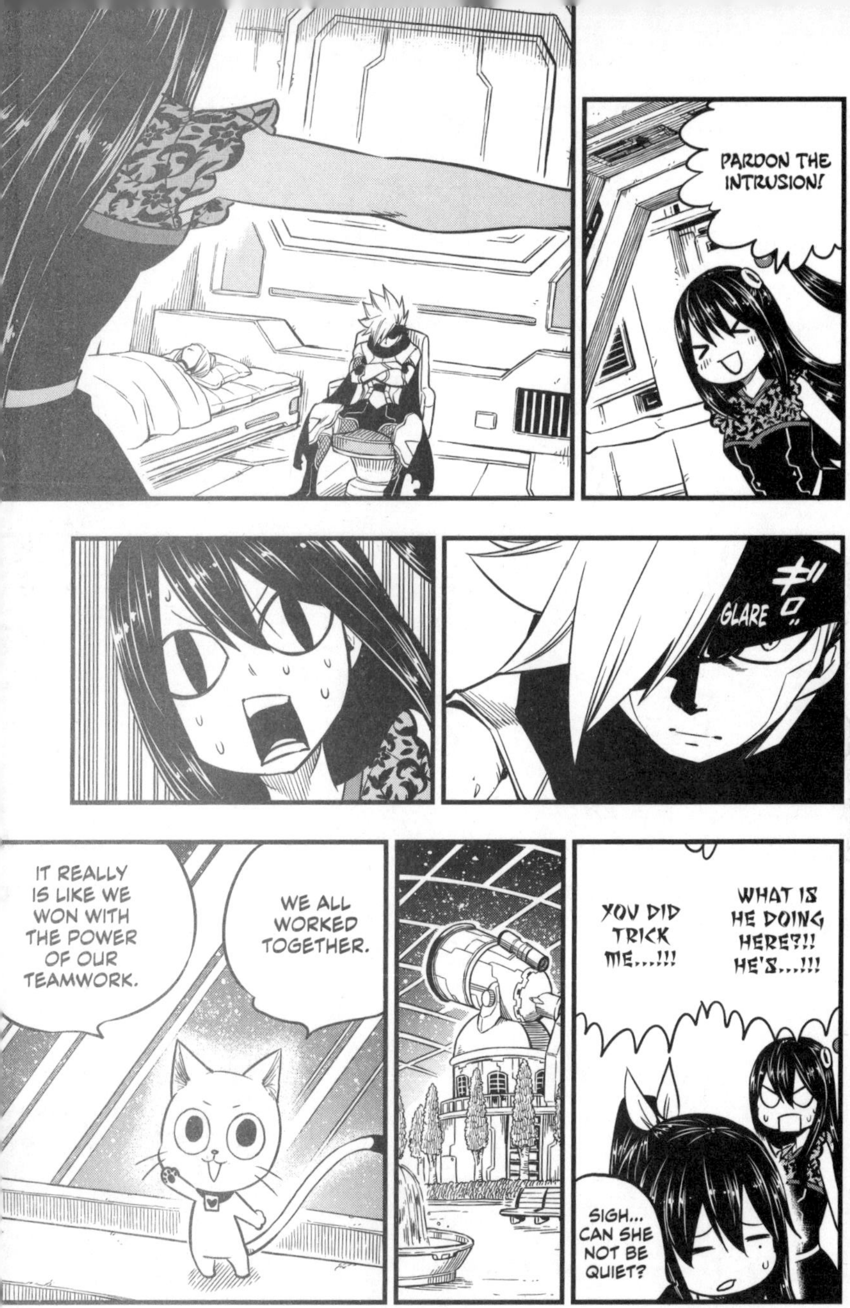
PARDON THE INTRUSION!
ギロ
GLARE
WHAT IS HE DOING HERE?!! HE'S...!!!
YOU DID TRICK ME...!!!
SIGH... CAN SHE NOT BE QUIET?
WE ALL WORKED TOGETHER.
IT REALLY IS LIKE WE WON WITH THE POWER OF OUR TEAMWORK.

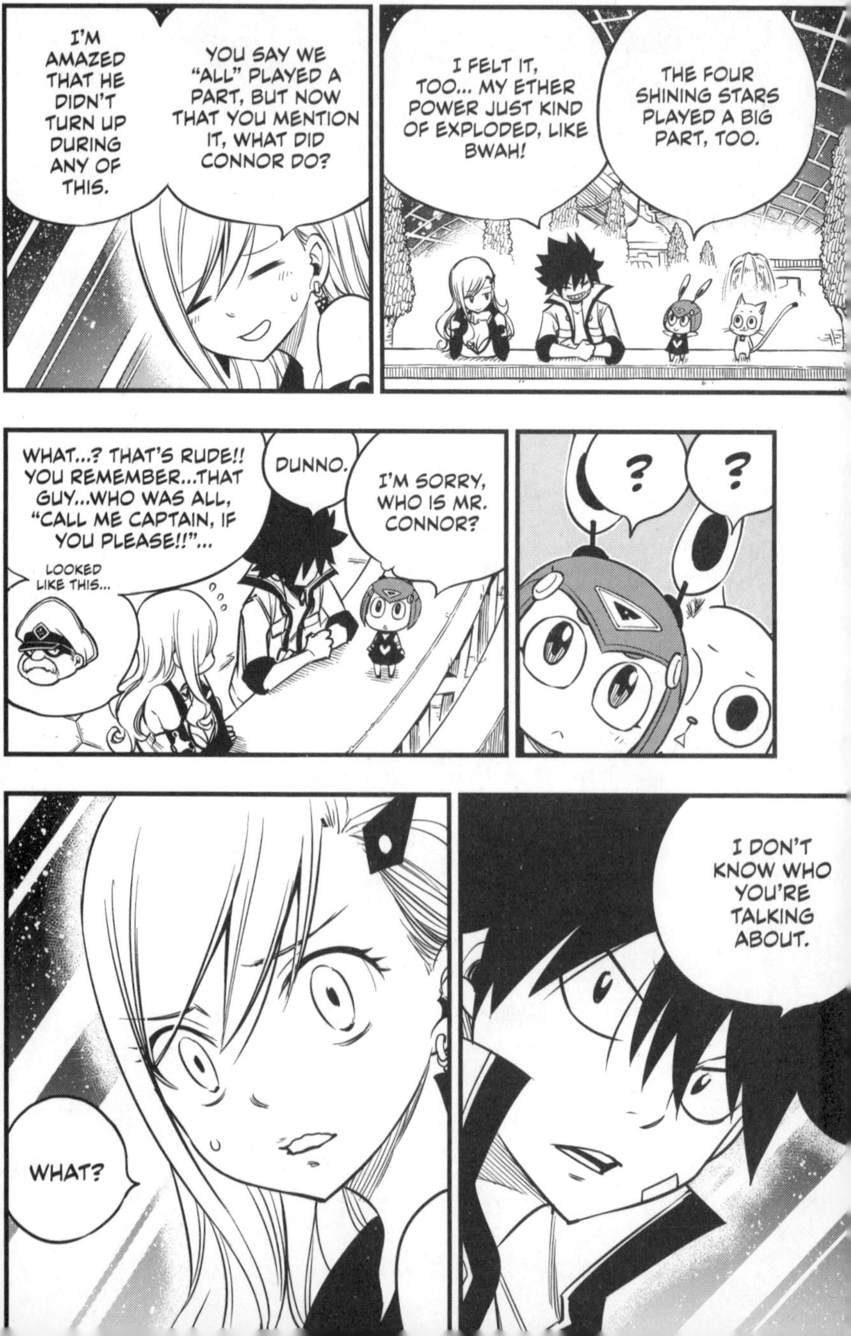
THE FOUR SHINING STARS PLAYED A BIG PART, TOO.
I FELT IT, TOO... MY ETHER POWER JUST KIND OF EXPLODED, LIKE BWAH!
YOU SAY WE "ALL" PLAYED A PART, BUT NOW THAT YOU MENTION IT, WHAT DID CONNOR DO?
I'M AMAZED THAT HE DIDN'T TURN UP DURING ANY OF THIS.
?
?
I'M SORRY, WHO IS MR. CONNOR?
DUNNO.
WHAT...? THAT'S RUDE!! YOU REMEMBER...THAT GUY...WHO WAS ALL, "CALL ME CAPTAIN, IF YOU PLEASE!!"...
LOOKED LIKE THIS...
I DON'T KNOW WHO YOU'RE TALKING ABOUT.
WHAT?

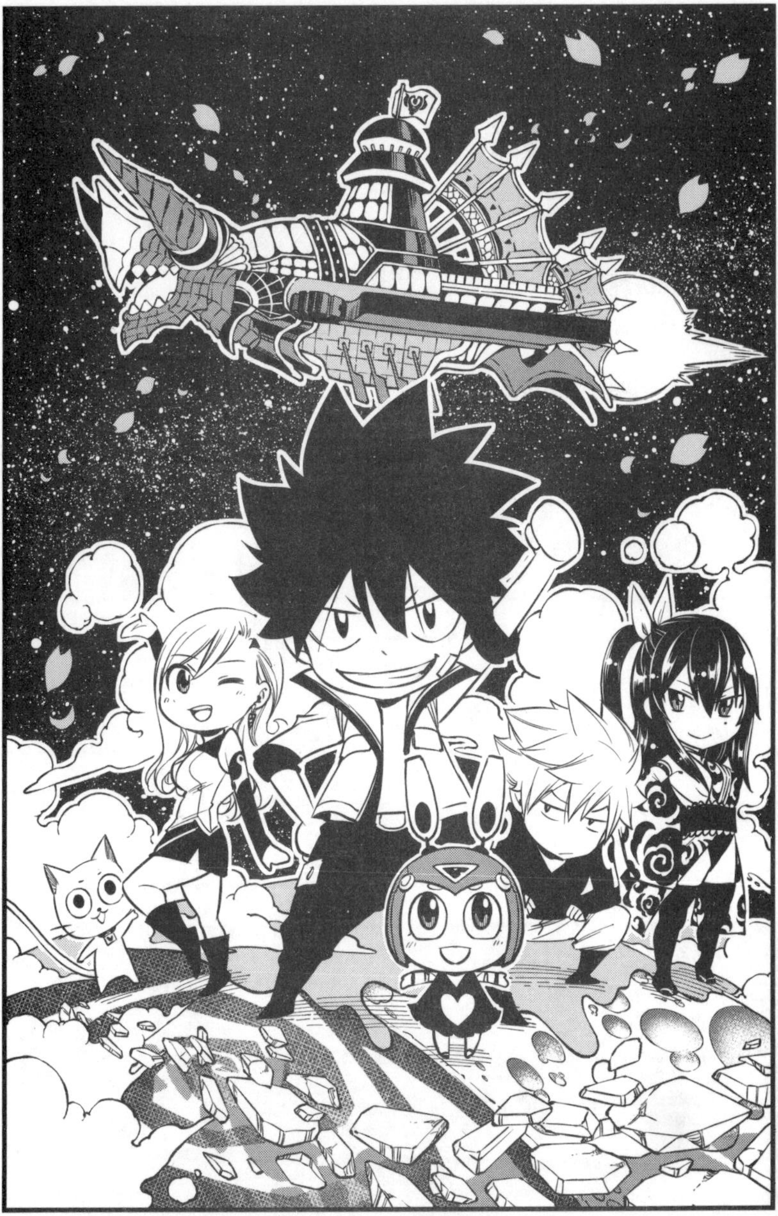

CHAPTER 100: EDENS ONE

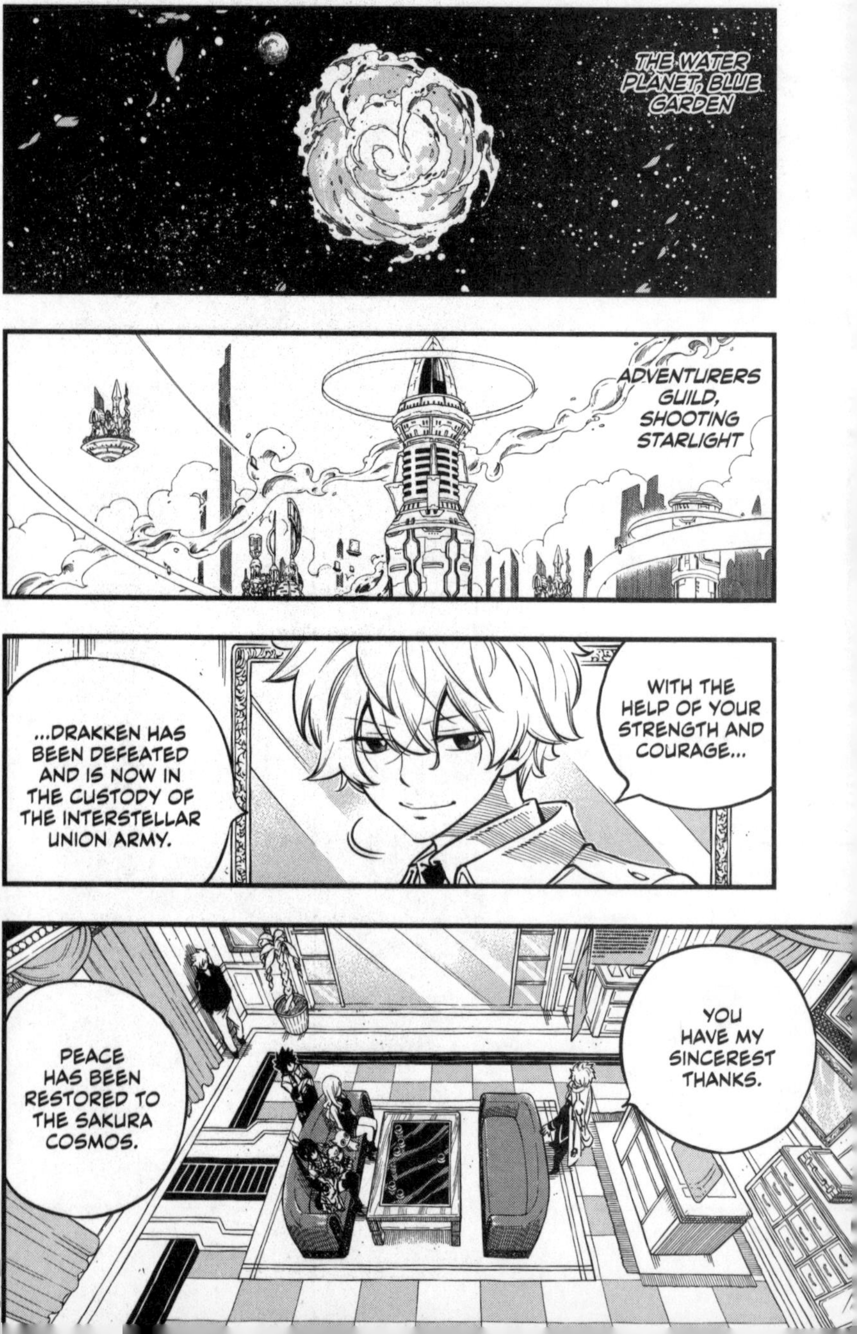
THE WATER PLANET, BLUE GARDEN
ADVENTURERS GUILD, SHOOTING STARLIGHT
WITH THE HELP OF YOUR STRENGTH AND COURAGE...
...DRAKKEN HAS BEEN DEFEATED AND IS NOW IN THE CUSTODY OF THE INTERSTELLAR UNION ARMY.
YOU HAVE MY SINCEREST THANKS.
PEACE HAS BEEN RESTORED TO THE SAKURA COSMOS.

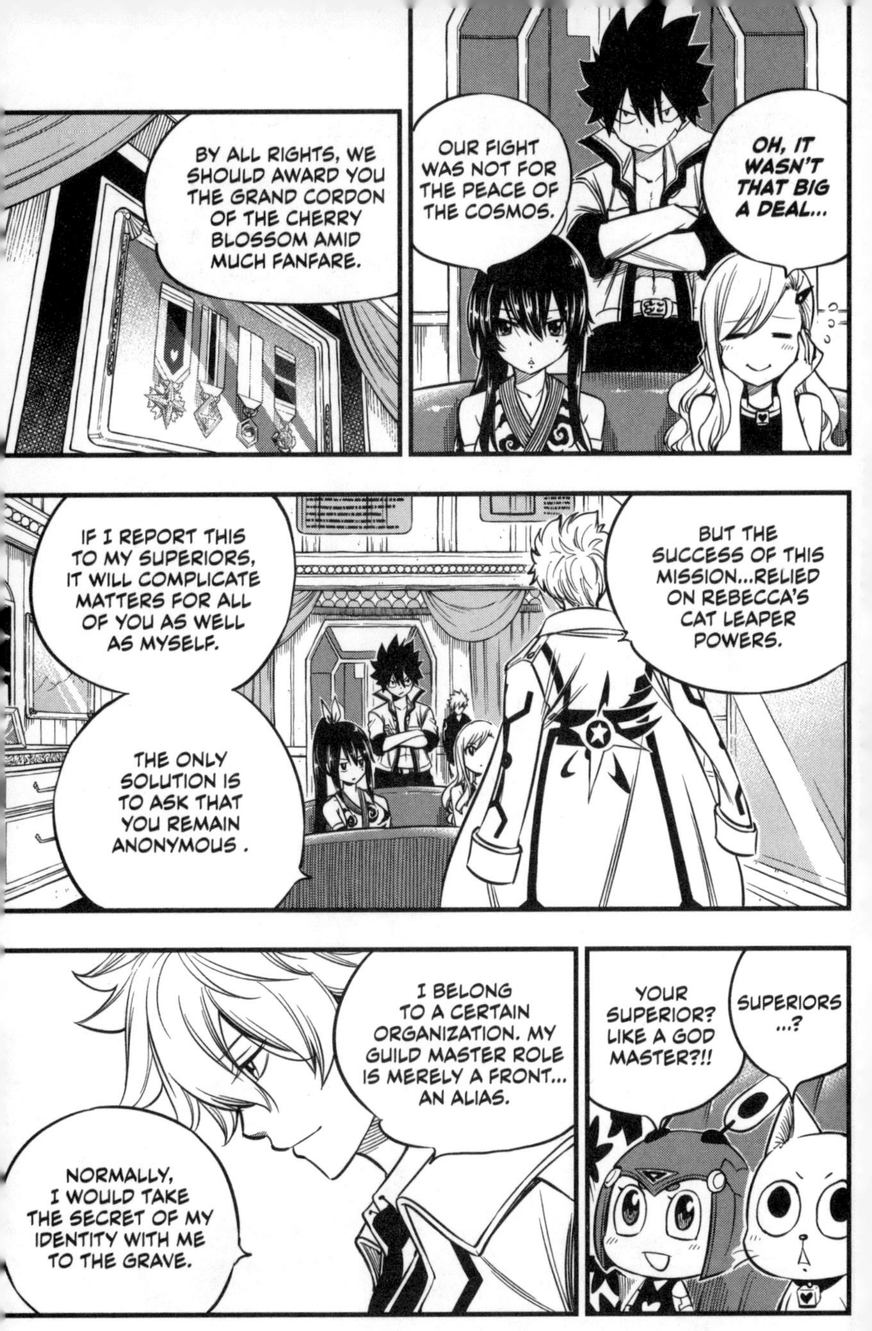
OH, IT WASN'T THAT BIG A DEAL...
OUR FIGHT WAS NOT FOR THE PEACE OF THE COSMOS.
BY ALL RIGHTS, WE SHOULD AWARD YOU THE GRAND CORDON OF THE CHERRY BLOSSOM AMID MUCH FANFARE.
BUT THE SUCCESS OF THIS MISSION...RELIED ON REBECCA'S CAT LEAPER POWERS.
IF I REPORT THIS TO MY SUPERIORS, IT WILL COMPLICATE MATTERS FOR ALL OF YOU AS WELL AS MYSELF.
THE ONLY SOLUTION IS TO ASK THAT YOU REMAIN ANONYMOUS .
SUPERIORS ...?
YOUR SUPERIOR? LIKE A GOD MASTER?!!
I BELONG TO A CERTAIN ORGANIZATION. MY GUILD MASTER ROLE IS MERELY A FRONT... AN ALIAS.
NORMALLY, I WOULD TAKE THE SECRET OF MY IDENTITY WITH ME TO THE GRAVE.

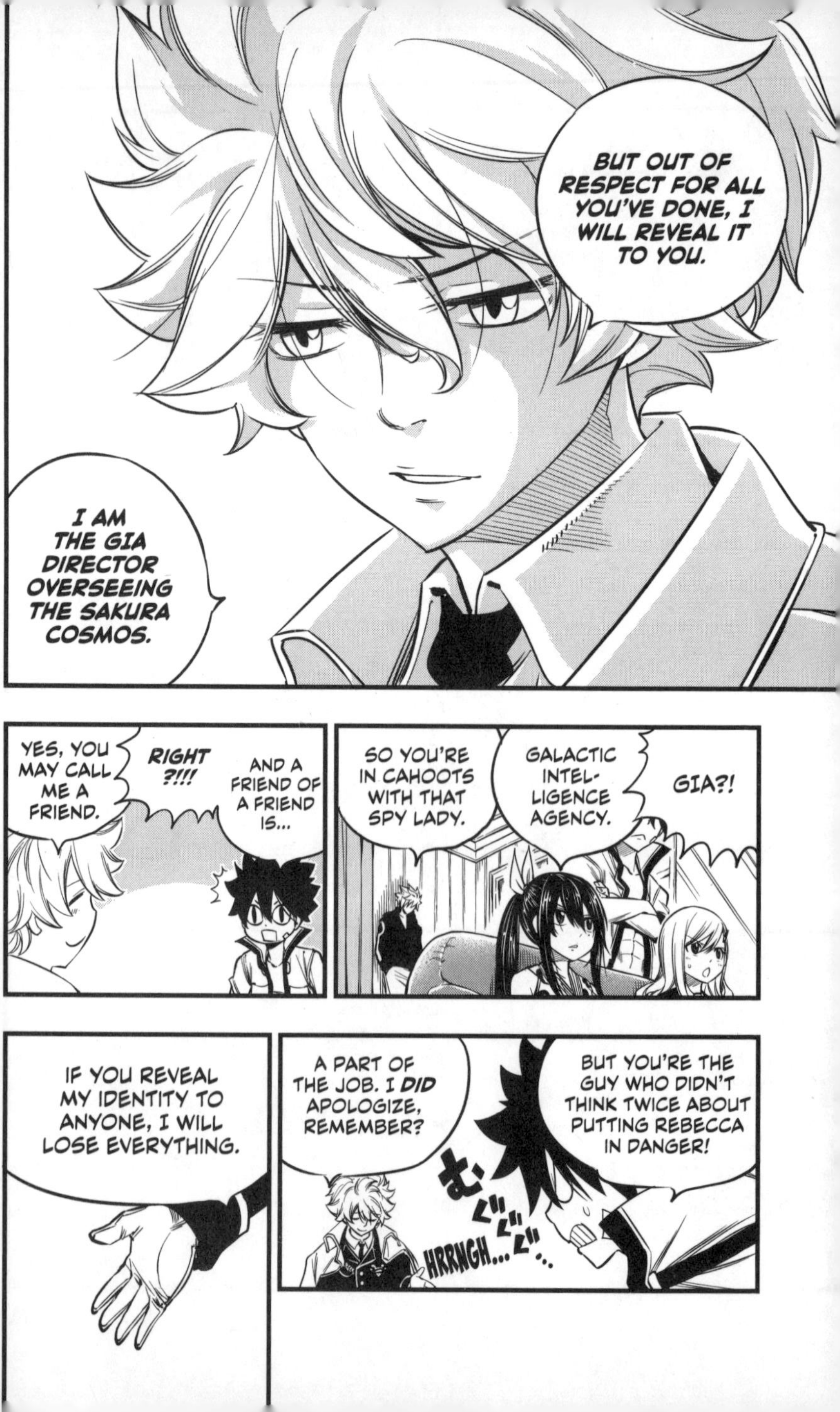
BUT OUT OF RESPECT FOR ALL YOU'VE DONE, I WILL REVEAL IT TO YOU.
I AM THE GIA DIRECTOR OVERSEEING THE SAKURA COSMOS.
GIA?!
GALACTIC INTEL-LIGENCE AGENCY.
SO YOU'RE IN CAHOOTS WITH THAT SPY LADY.
AND A FRIEND OF A FRIEND IS...
RIGHT ?!!!
YES, YOU MAY CALL ME A FRIEND.
BUT YOU'RE THE GUY WHO DIDN'T THINK TWICE ABOUT PUTTING REBECCA IN DANGER!
A PART OF THE JOB. I *DID* APOLOGIZE, REMEMBER?
HRRNGH...
IF YOU REVEAL MY IDENTITY TO ANYONE, I WILL LOSE EVERYTHING.

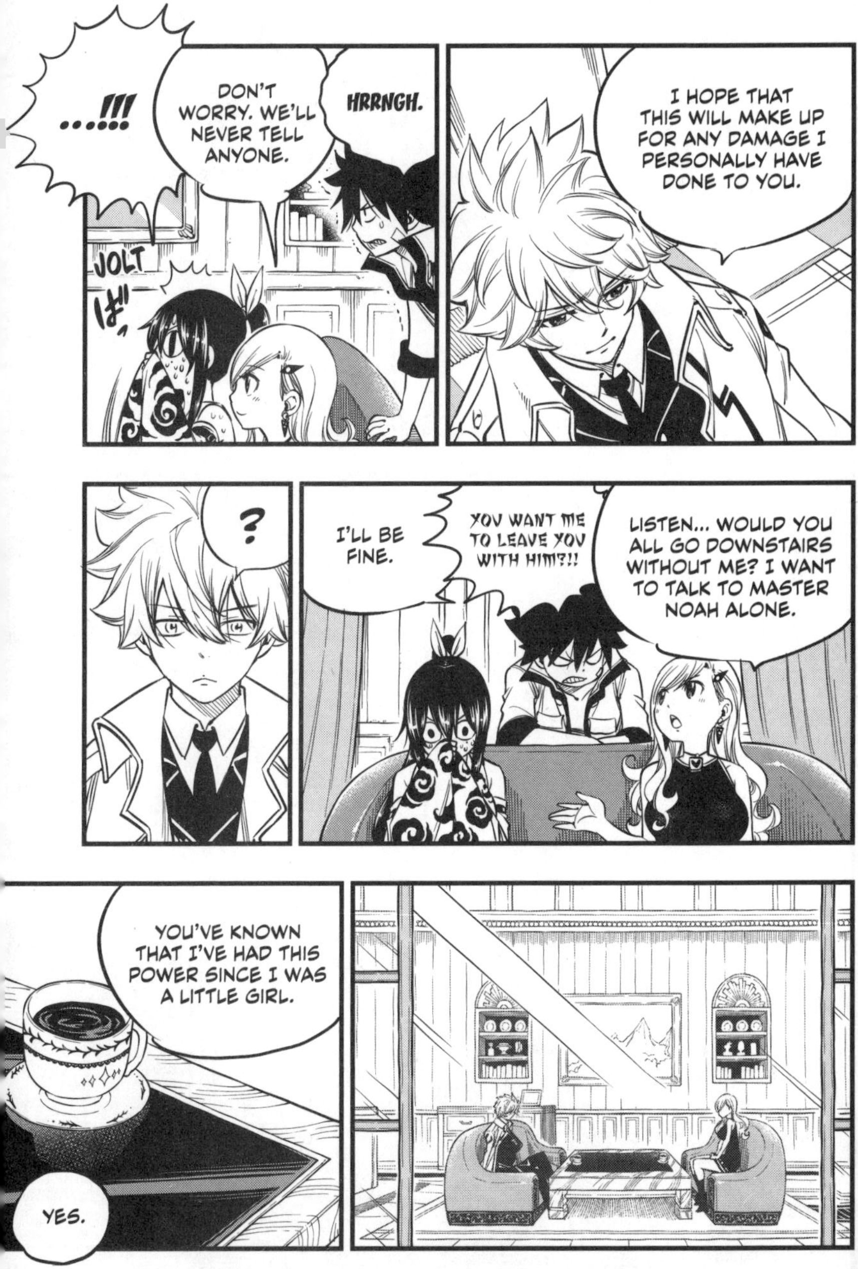
I HOPE THAT THIS WILL MAKE UP FOR ANY DAMAGE I PERSONALLY HAVE DONE TO YOU.
HRRNGH.
DON'T WORRY. WE'LL NEVER TELL ANYONE.
...!!!
JOLT
ば
LISTEN... WOULD YOU ALL GO DOWNSTAIRS WITHOUT ME? I WANT TO TALK TO MASTER NOAH ALONE.
YOU WANT ME TO LEAVE YOU WITH HIM?!!
I'LL BE FINE.
?
YOU'VE KNOWN THAT I'VE HAD THIS POWER SINCE I WAS A LITTLE GIRL.
YES.

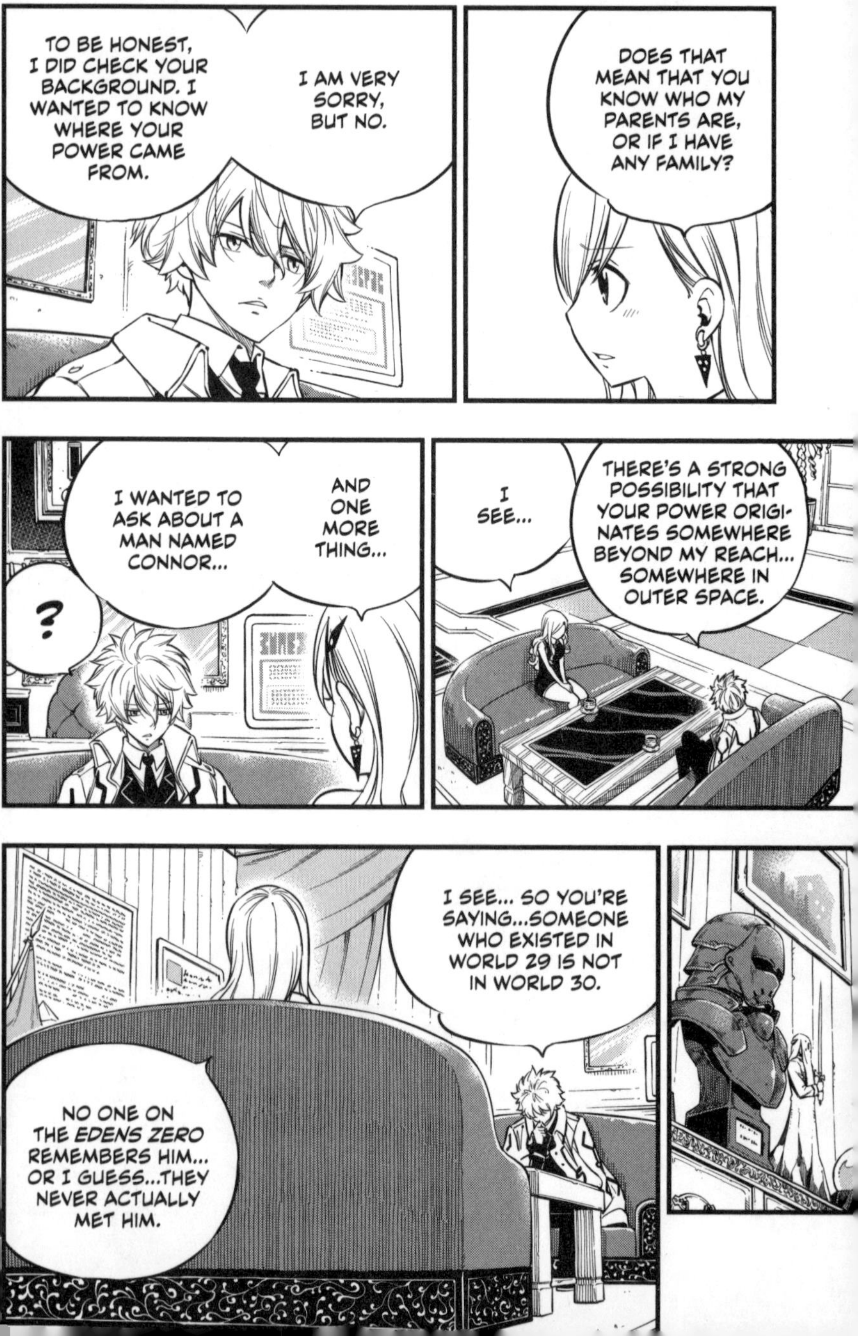
DOES THAT MEAN THAT YOU KNOW WHO MY PARENTS ARE, OR IF I HAVE ANY FAMILY?
I AM VERY SORRY, BUT NO.
TO BE HONEST, I DID CHECK YOUR BACKGROUND. I WANTED TO KNOW WHERE YOUR POWER CAME FROM.
THERE'S A STRONG POSSIBILITY THAT YOUR POWER ORIGINATES SOMEWHERE BEYOND MY REACH... SOMEWHERE IN OUTER SPACE.
I SEE...
AND ONE MORE THING...
I WANTED TO ASK ABOUT A MAN NAMED CONNOR...
?
I SEE... SO YOU'RE SAYING...SOMEONE WHO EXISTED IN WORLD 29 IS NOT IN WORLD 30.
NO ONE ON THE *EDENS ZERO* REMEMBERS HIM... OR I GUESS...THEY NEVER ACTUALLY MET HIM.

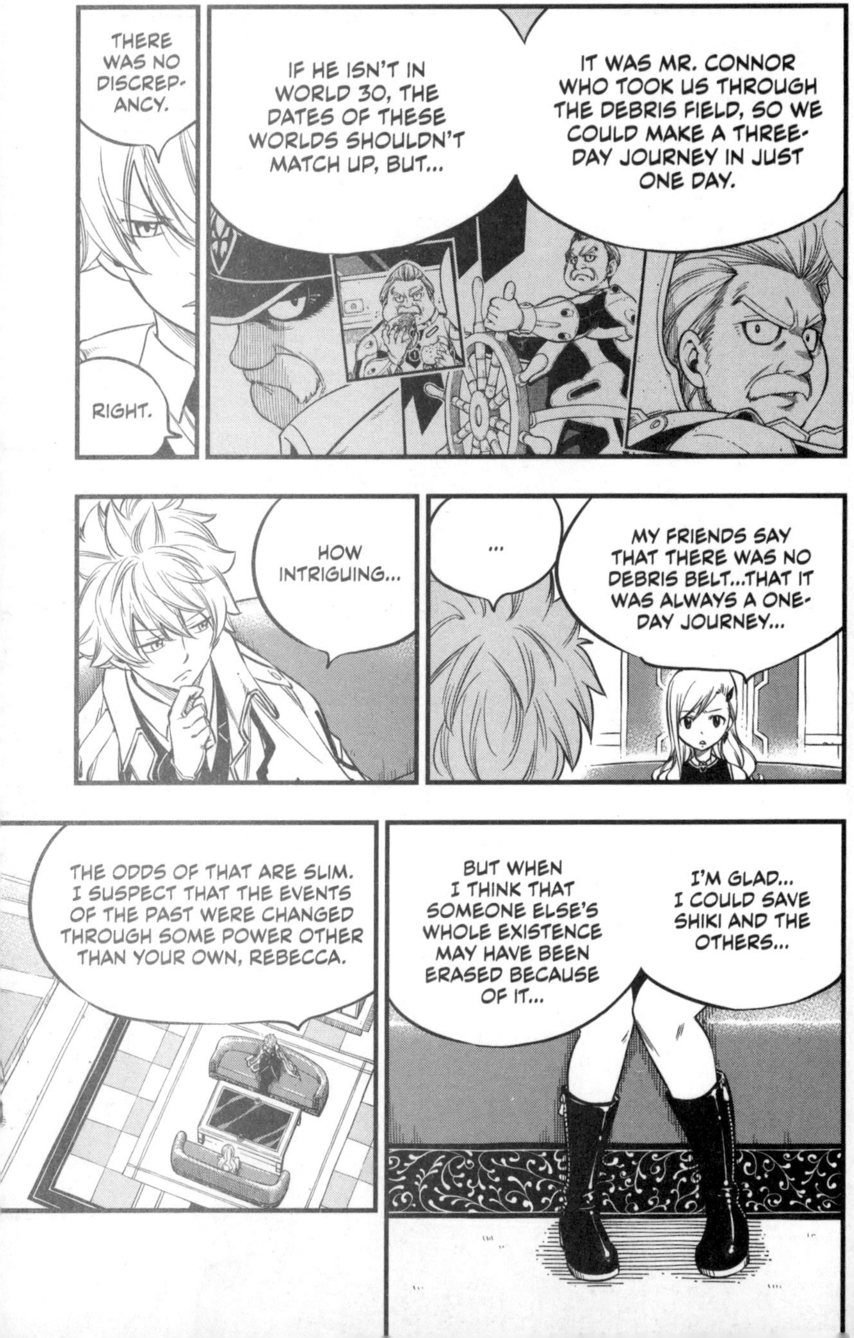
IT WAS MR. CONNOR WHO TOOK US THROUGH THE DEBRIS FIELD, SO WE COULD MAKE A THREE-DAY JOURNEY IN JUST ONE DAY.
IF HE ISN'T IN WORLD 30, THE DATES OF THESE WORLDS SHOULDN'T MATCH UP, BUT...
THERE WAS NO DISCREPANCY.
RIGHT.
MY FRIENDS SAY THAT THERE WAS NO DEBRIS BELT...THAT IT WAS ALWAYS A ONE-DAY JOURNEY...
...
HOW INTRIGUING...
I'M GLAD... I COULD SAVE SHIKI AND THE OTHERS...
BUT WHEN I THINK THAT SOMEONE ELSE'S WHOLE EXISTENCE MAY HAVE BEEN ERASED BECAUSE OF IT...
THE ODDS OF THAT ARE SLIM. I SUSPECT THAT THE EVENTS OF THE PAST WERE CHANGED THROUGH SOME POWER OTHER THAN YOUR OWN, REBECCA.

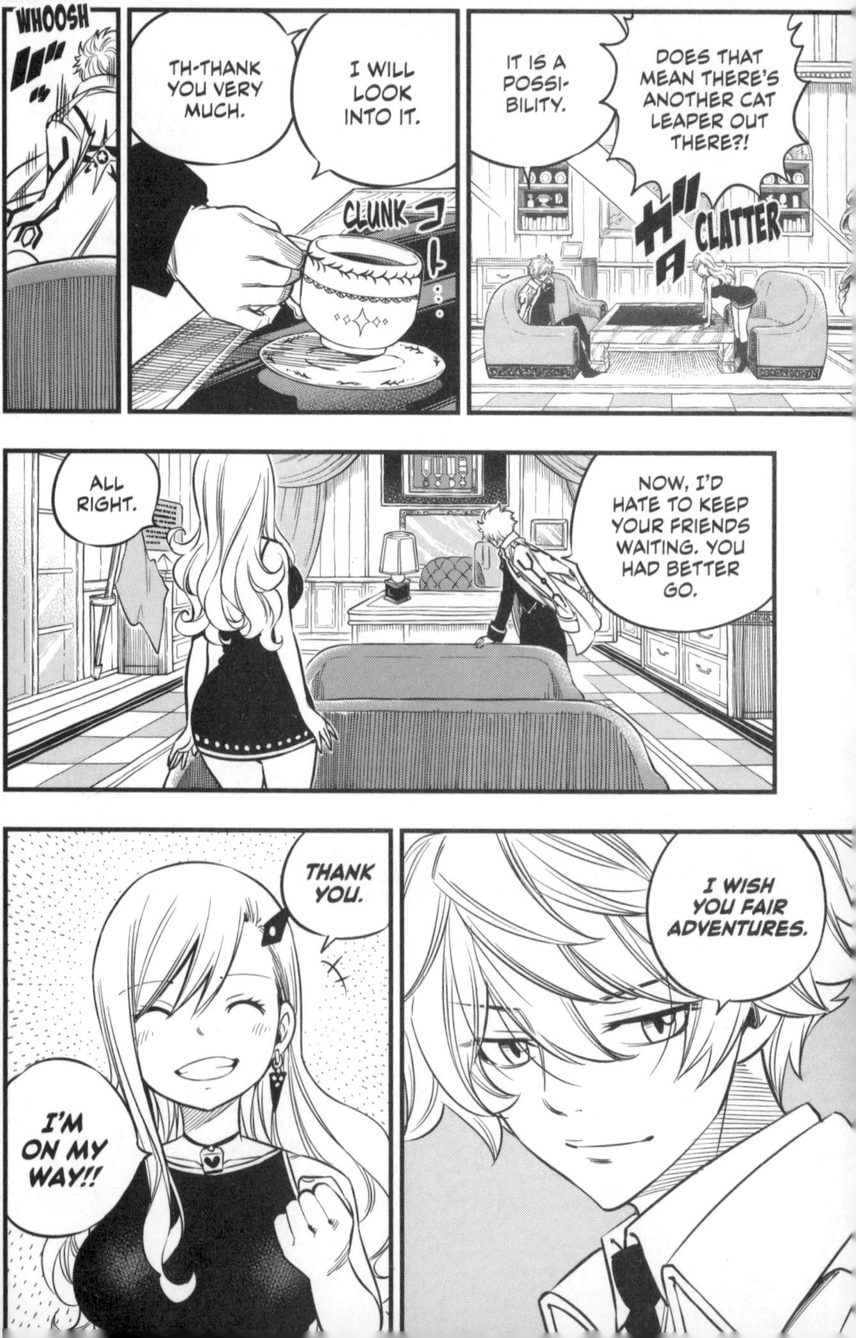
DOES THAT MEAN THERE'S ANOTHER CAT LEAPER OUT THERE?!
IT IS A POSSIBILITY.
CLATTER
I WILL LOOK INTO IT.
TH-THANK YOU VERY MUCH.
CLUNK
WHOOSH
NOW, I'D HATE TO KEEP YOUR FRIENDS WAITING. YOU HAD BETTER GO.
ALL RIGHT.
I WISH YOU FAIR ADVENTURES.
THANK YOU.
I'M ON MY WAY!!

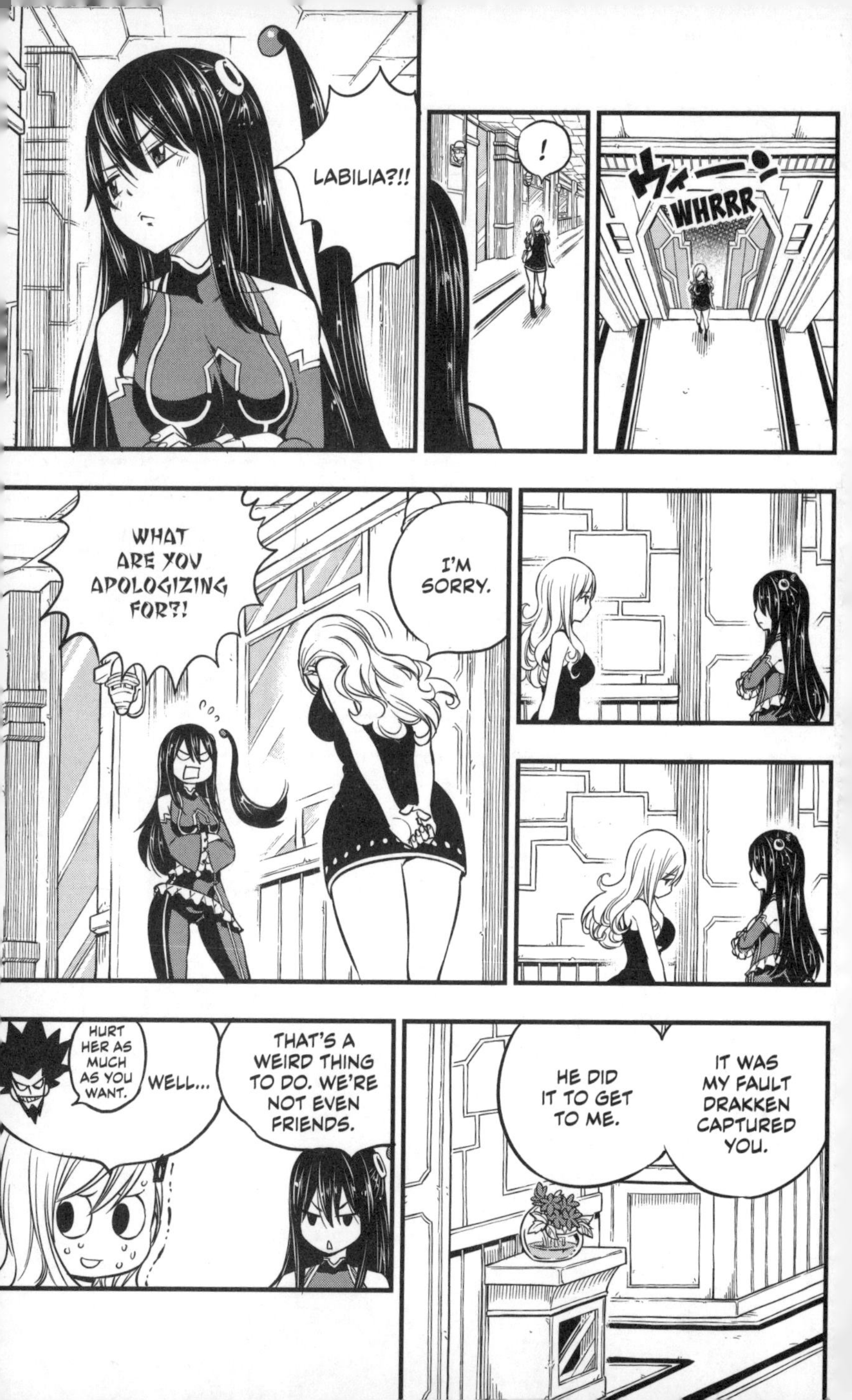
WHRRR
!
LABILIA?!!
I'M SORRY.
WHAT ARE YOU APOLOGIZING FOR?!
IT WAS MY FAULT DRAKKEN CAPTURED YOU.
HE DID IT TO GET TO ME.
THAT'S A WEIRD THING TO DO. WE'RE NOT EVEN FRIENDS.
WELL...
HURT HER AS MUCH AS YOU WANT.

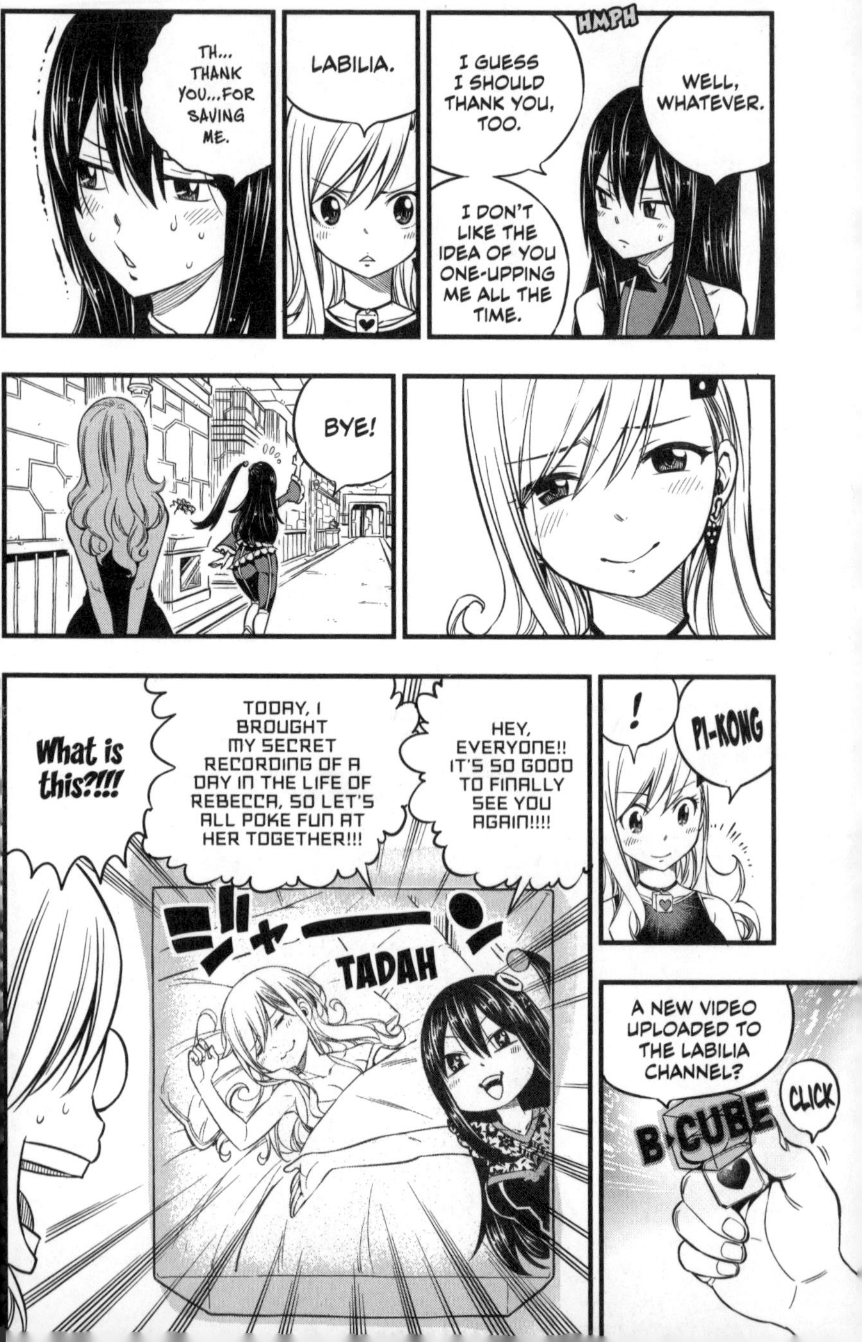
WELL, WHATEVER.
HMPH
I GUESS I SHOULD THANK YOU, TOO.
I DON'T LIKE THE IDEA OF YOU ONE-UPPING ME ALL THE TIME.
LABILIA.
TH... THANK YOU...FOR SAVING ME.
BYE!
PI-KONG
!
A NEW VIDEO UPLOADED TO THE LABILIA CHANNEL?
CLICK
B-CUBE
HEY, EVERYONE!! IT'S SO GOOD TO FINALLY SEE YOU AGAIN!!!!
TODAY, I BROUGHT MY SECRET RECORDING OF A DAY IN THE LIFE OF REBECCA, SO LET'S ALL POKE FUN AT HER TOGETHER!!!
What is this?!!!
TADAH

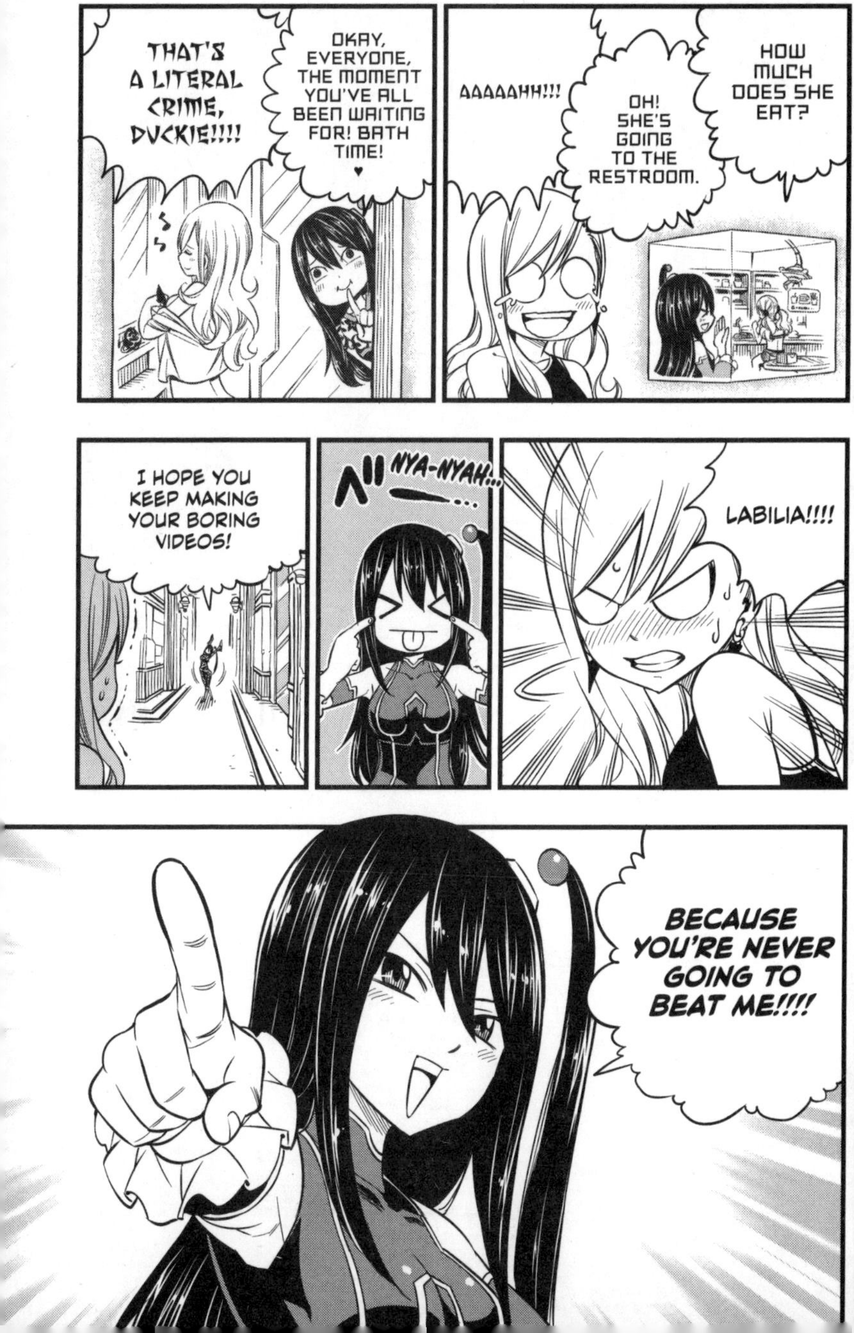
HOW MUCH DOES SHE EAT?
OH! SHE'S GOING TO THE RESTROOM.
AAAAAHH!!!
OKAY, EVERYONE, THE MOMENT YOU'VE ALL BEEN WAITING FOR! BATH TIME! ♥
THAT'S A LITERAL CRIME, DUCKIE!!!!
LABILIA!!!!
NYA-NYAH...
I HOPE YOU KEEP MAKING YOUR BORING VIDEOS!
BECAUSE YOU'RE NEVER GOING TO BEAT ME!!!!

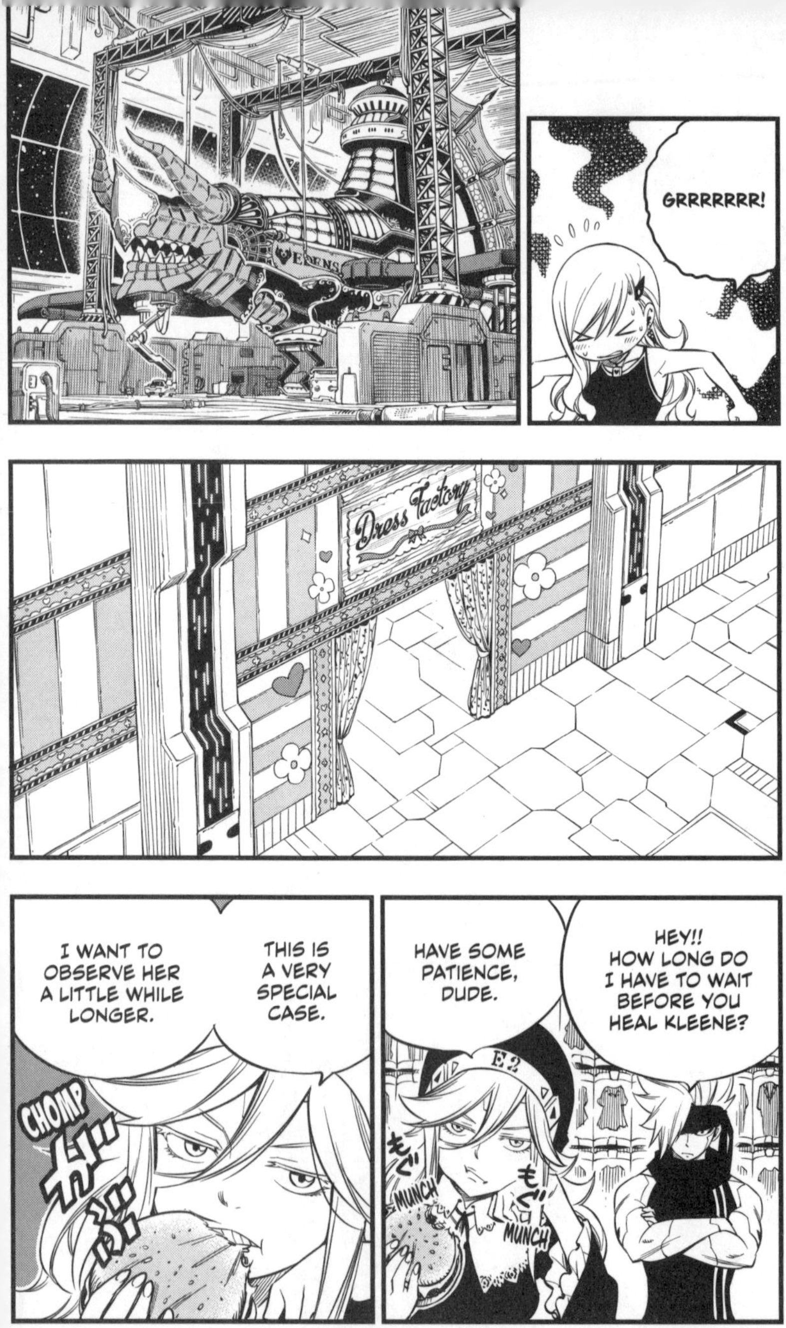
GRRRRRRR!
Dress Factory
HEY!! HOW LONG DO I HAVE TO WAIT BEFORE YOU HEAL KLEENE?
HAVE SOME PATIENCE, DUDE.
MUNCH
MUNCH
THIS IS A VERY SPECIAL CASE.
I WANT TO OBSERVE HER A LITTLE WHILE LONGER.
CHOMP

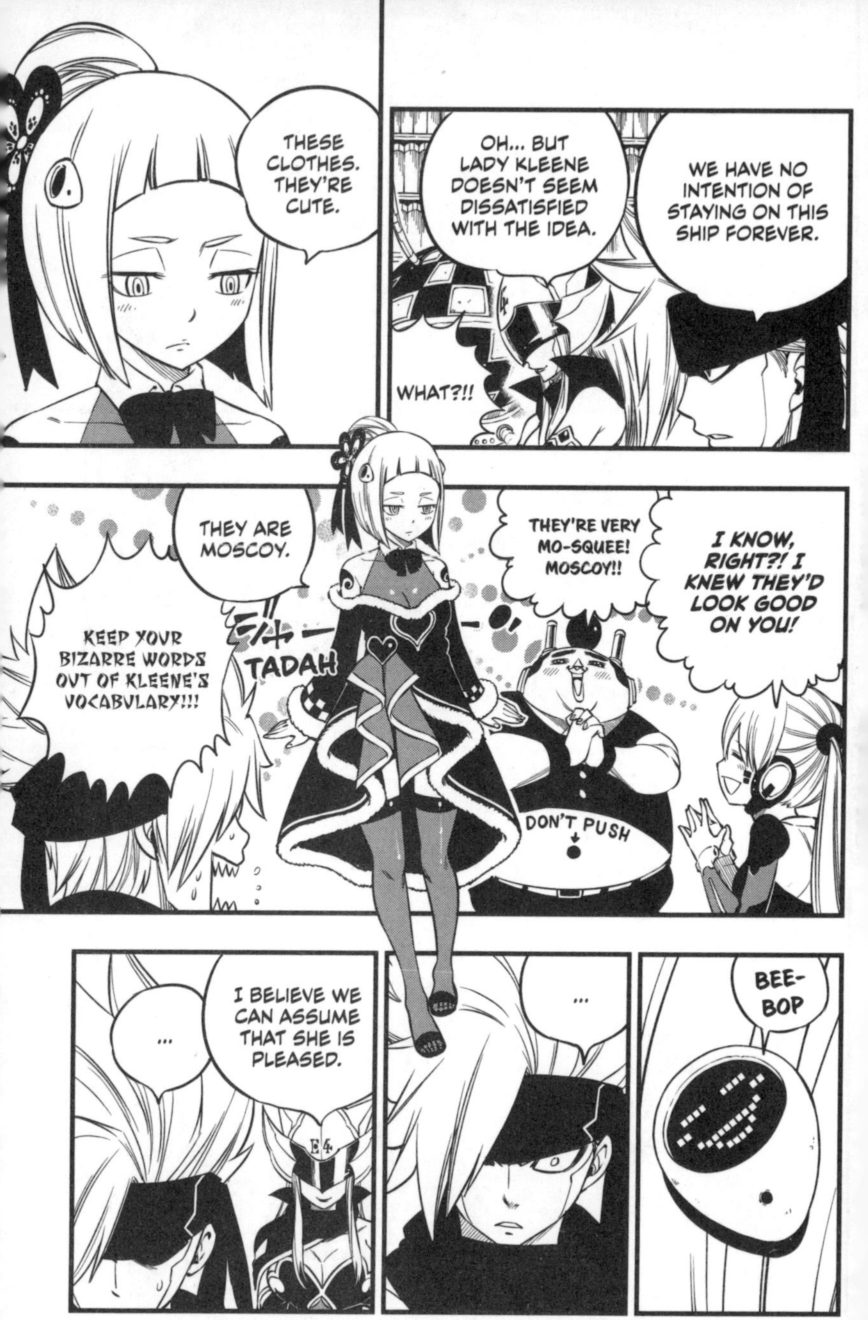
WE HAVE NO INTENTION OF STAYING ON THIS SHIP FOREVER.
OH... BUT LADY KLEENE DOESN'T SEEM DISSATISFIED WITH THE IDEA.
WHAT?!!
THESE CLOTHES. THEY'RE CUTE.
I KNOW, RIGHT?! I KNEW THEY'D LOOK GOOD ON YOU!
THEY'RE VERY MO-SQUEE! MOSCOY!!
DON'T PUSH
TADAH
THEY ARE MOSCOY.
KEEP YOUR BIZARRE WORDS OUT OF KLEENE'S VOCABULARY!!!
BEE-BOP
...
I BELIEVE WE CAN ASSUME THAT SHE IS PLEASED.
...

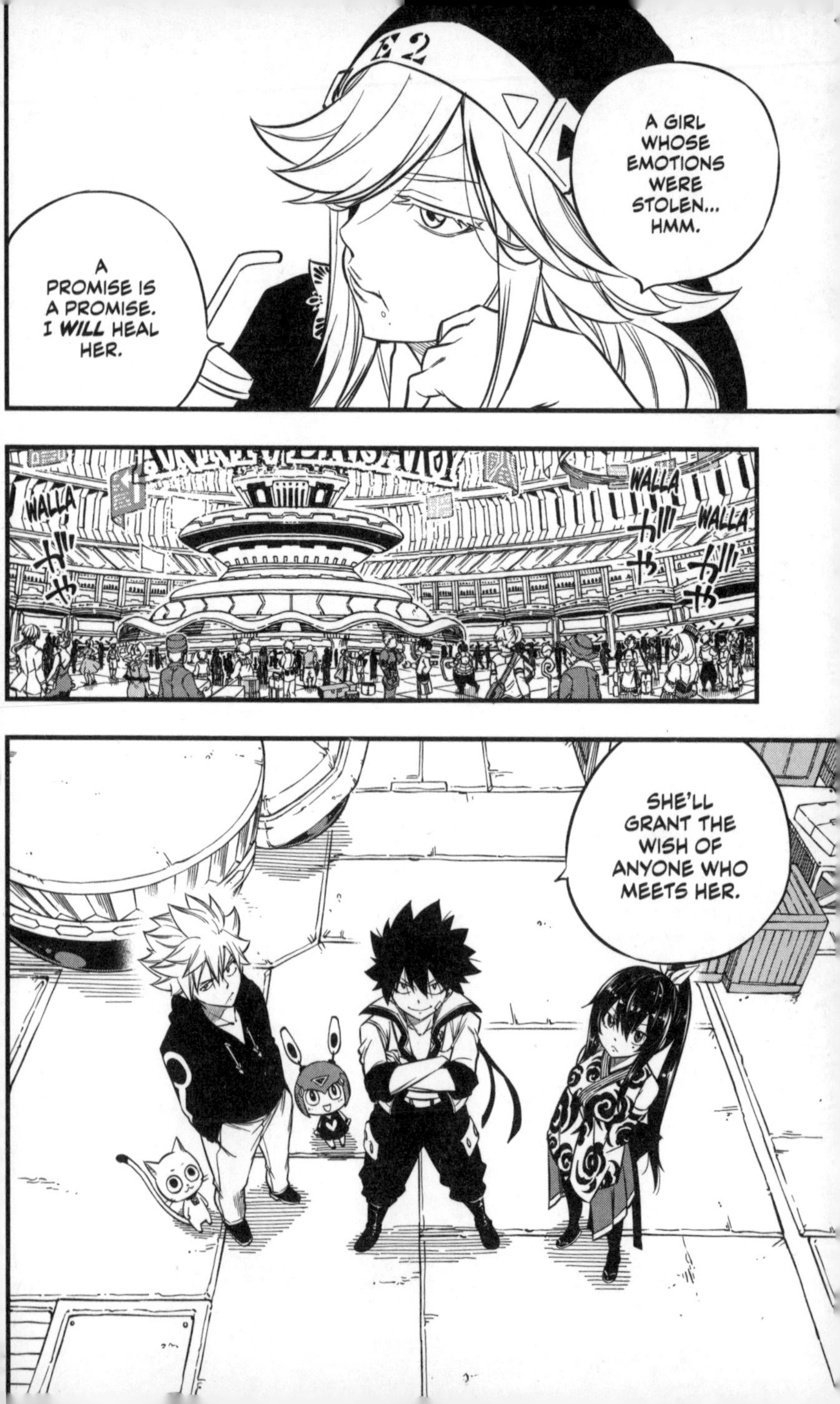

A GIRL WHOSE EMOTIONS WERE STOLEN... HMM.
A PROMISE IS A PROMISE. I ***WILL*** HEAL HER.
WALLA
WALLA
WALLA
SHE'LL GRANT THE WISH OF ANYONE WHO MEETS HER.

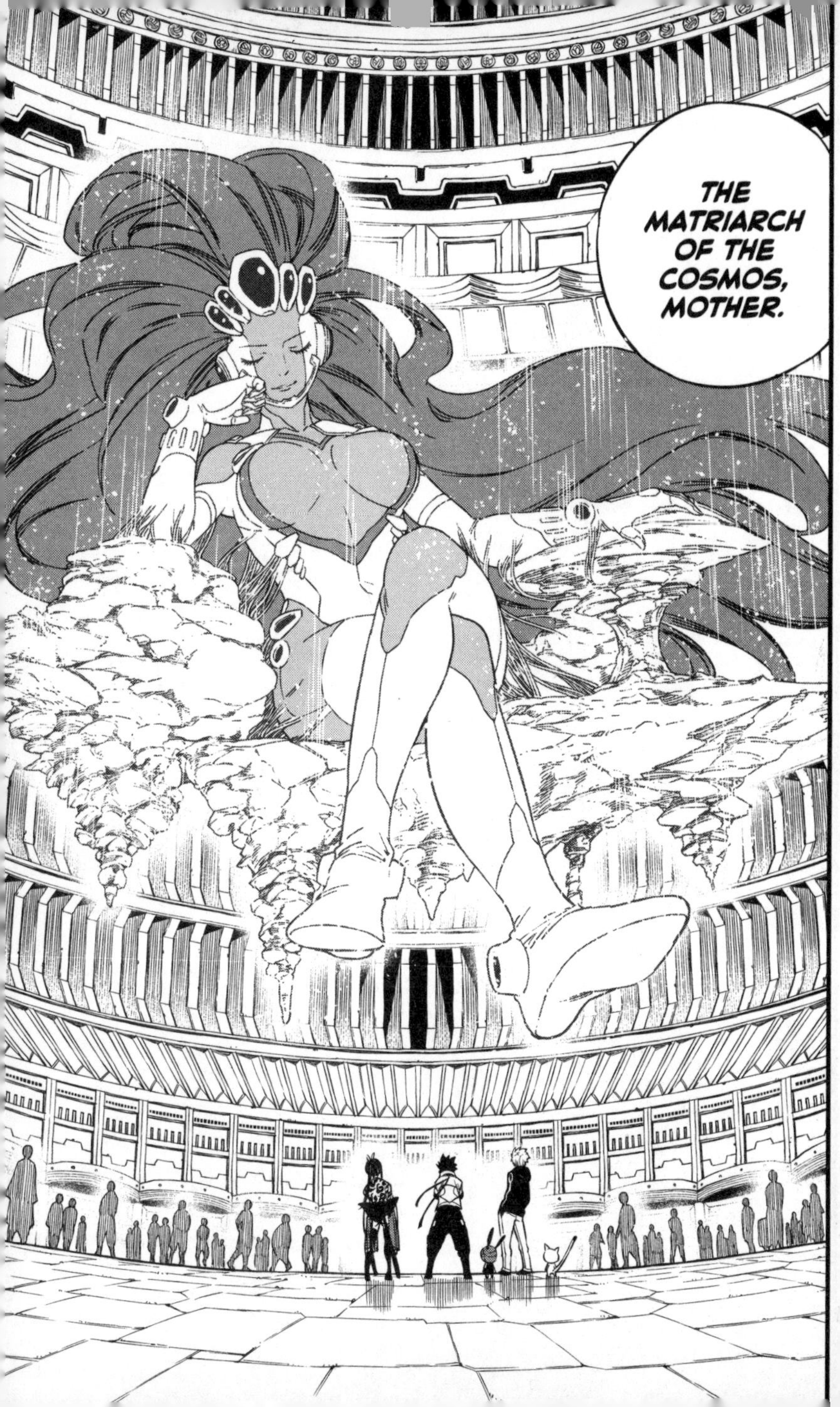
THE MATRIARCH OF THE COSMOS, MOTHER.

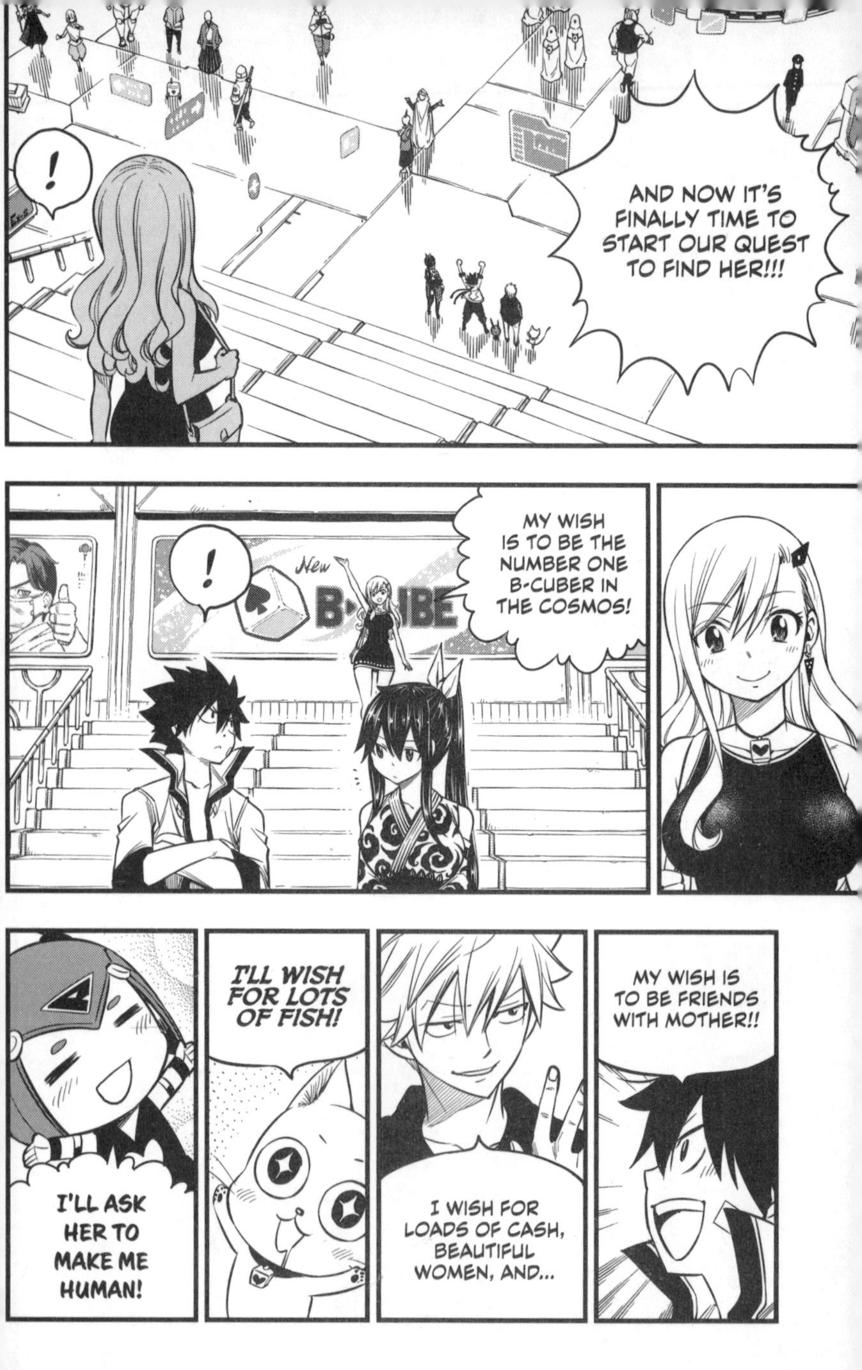
AND NOW IT'S FINALLY TIME TO START OUR QUEST TO FIND HER!!!
!
MY WISH IS TO BE THE NUMBER ONE B-CUBER IN THE COSMOS!
!
New
MY WISH IS TO BE FRIENDS WITH MOTHER!!
I WISH FOR LOADS OF CASH, BEAUTIFUL WOMEN, AND...
I'LL WISH FOR LOTS OF FISH!
I'LL ASK HER TO MAKE ME HUMAN!

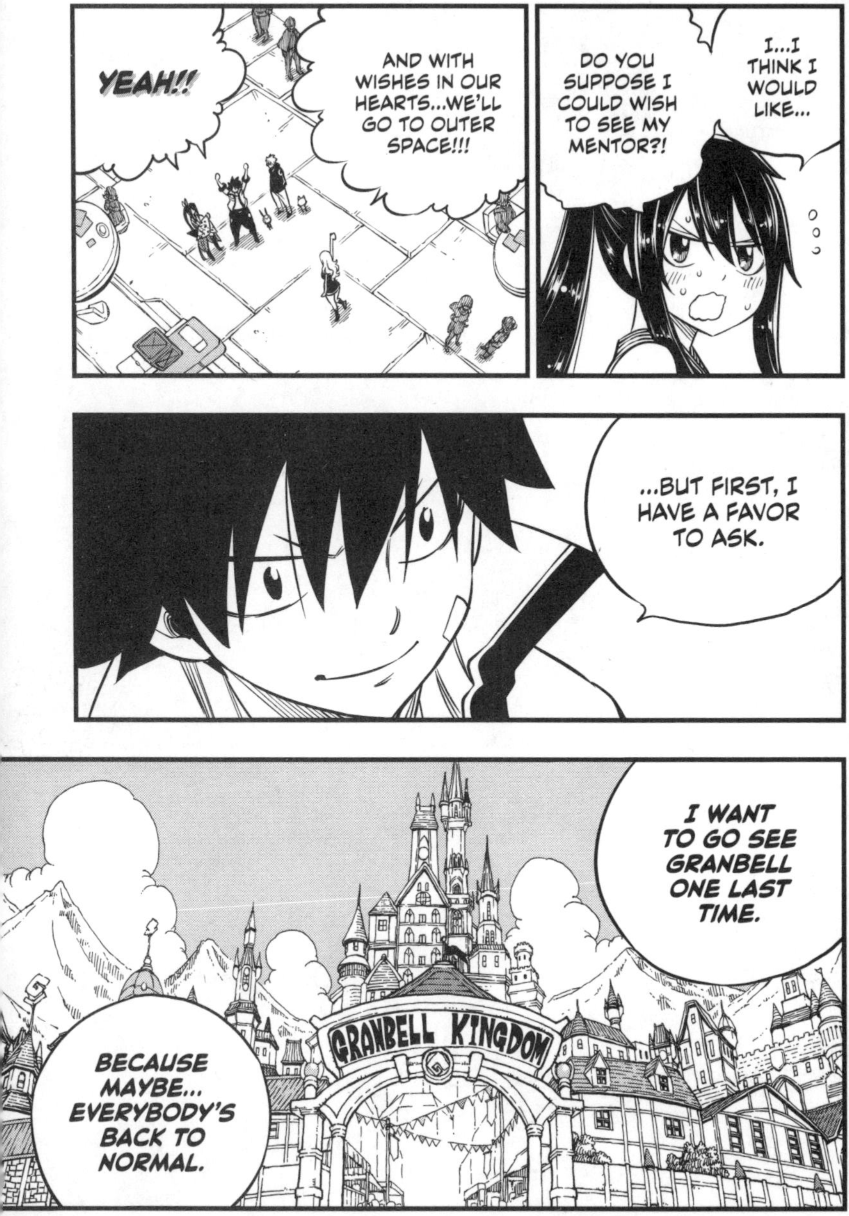
I...I THINK I WOULD LIKE...
DO YOU SUPPOSE I COULD WISH TO SEE MY MENTOR?!
AND WITH WISHES IN OUR HEARTS...WE'LL GO TO OUTER SPACE!!!
YEAH!!
...BUT FIRST, I HAVE A FAVOR TO ASK.
I WANT TO GO SEE GRANBELL ONE LAST TIME.
GRANBELL KINGDOM
BECAUSE MAYBE... EVERYBODY'S BACK TO NORMAL.

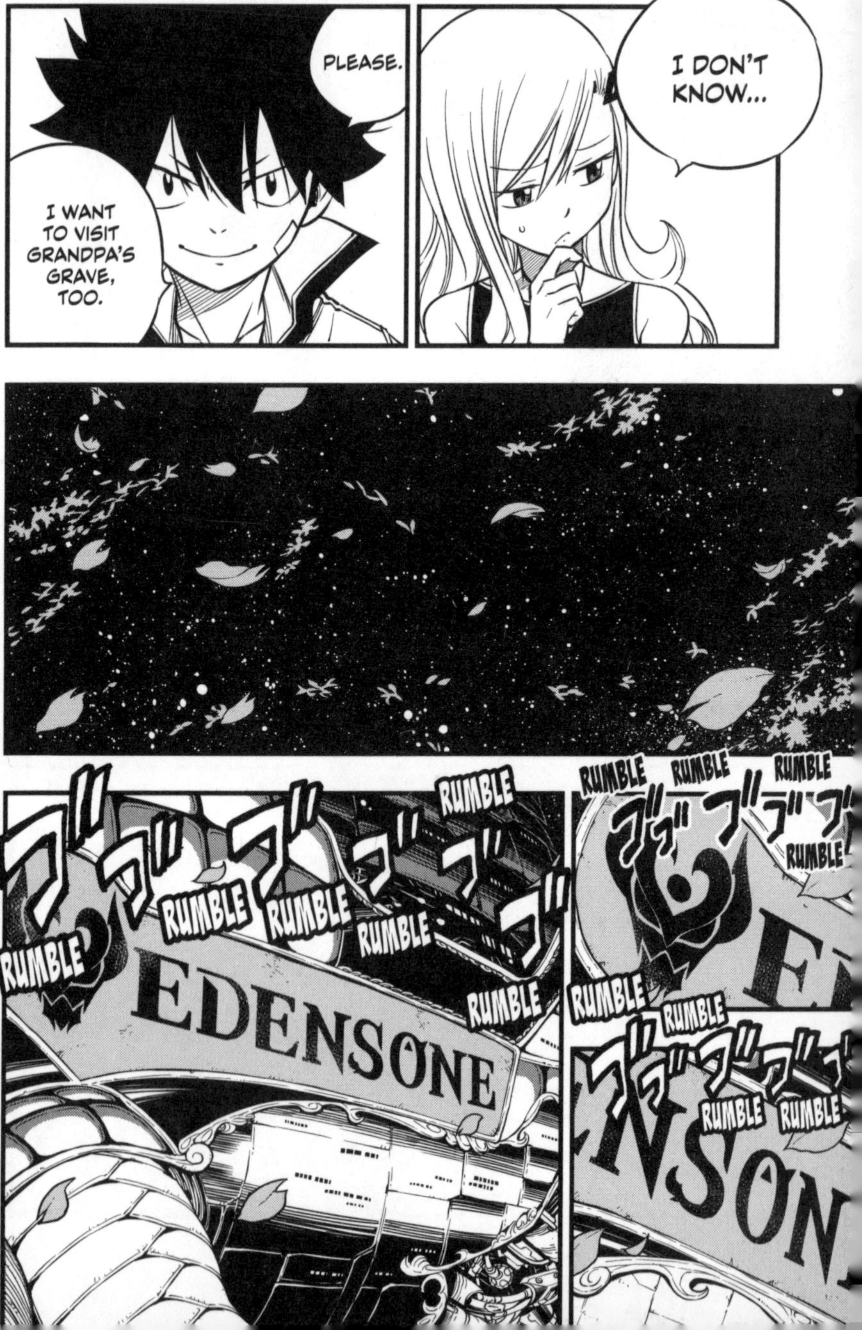

I DON'T KNOW...
PLEASE.
I WANT TO VISIT GRANDPA'S GRAVE, TOO.
RUMBLE RUMBLE RUMBLE
RUMBLE
RUMBLE RUMBLE
RUMBLE RUMBLE
RUMBLE
RUMBLE RUMBLE RUMBLE
RUMBLE
RUMBLE
RUMBLE
EDENSONE

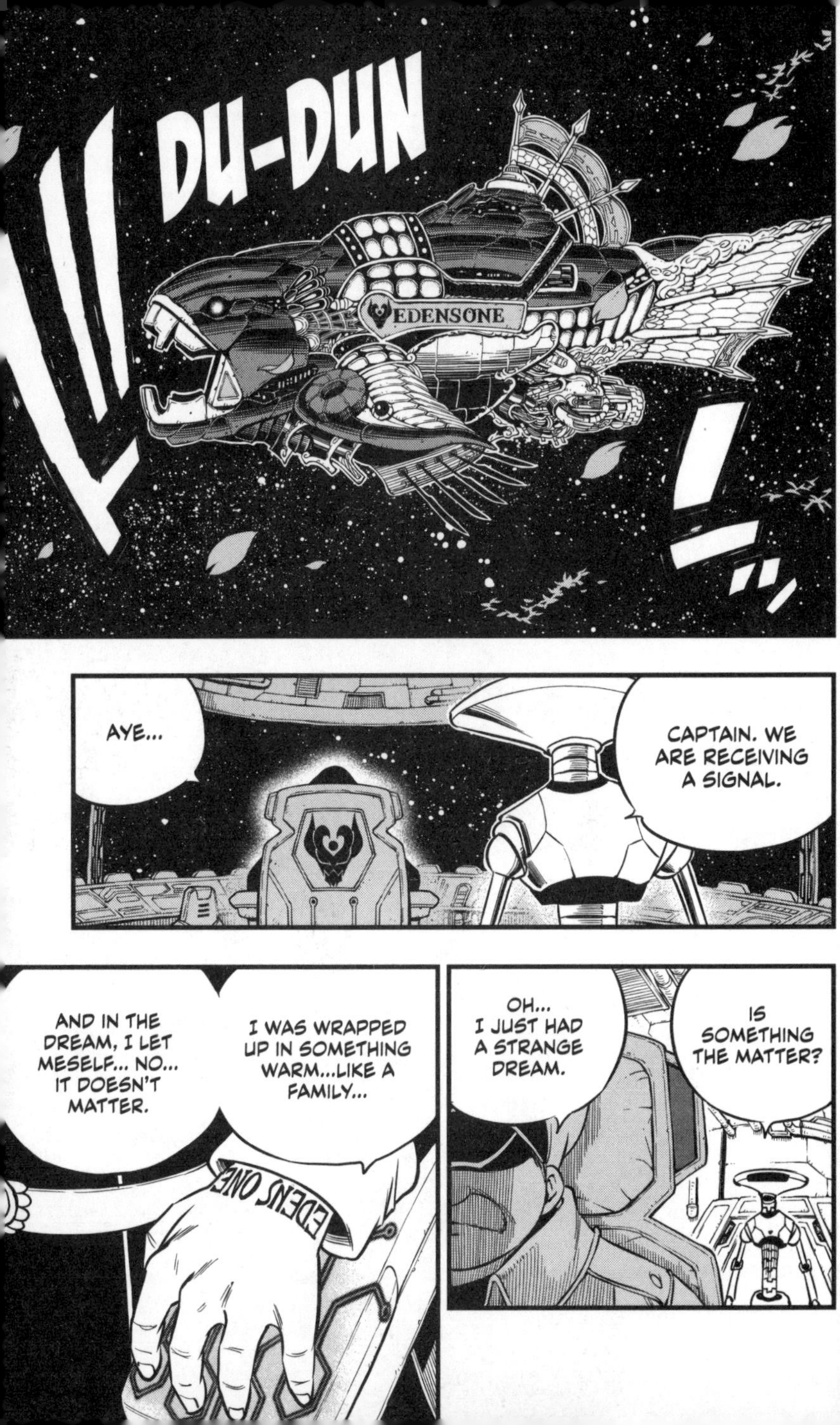
DU-DUN
EDENSONE
CAPTAIN. WE ARE RECEIVING A SIGNAL.
AYE...
IS SOMETHING THE MATTER?
OH... I JUST HAD A STRANGE DREAM.
I WAS WRAPPED UP IN SOMETHING WARM...LIKE A FAMILY...
AND IN THE DREAM, I LET MESELF... NO... IT DOESN'T MATTER.
EDENS ONE

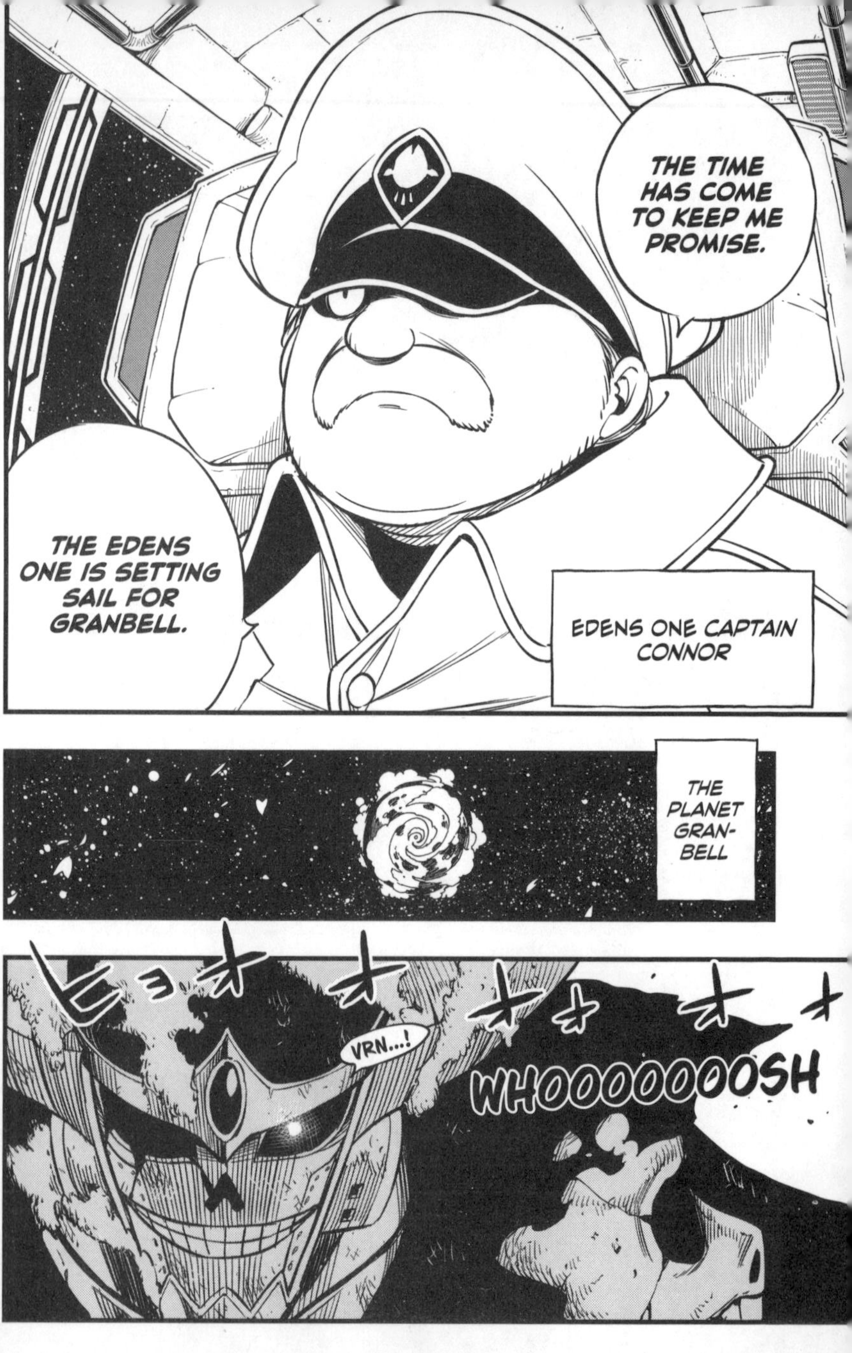
THE TIME HAS COME TO KEEP ME PROMISE.
THE EDENS ONE IS SETTING SAIL FOR GRANBELL.
EDENS ONE CAPTAIN CONNOR
THE PLANET GRAN-BELL
VRN...!
WHOOOOOOOOSH

Edens Zero
In-Depth Character File 11

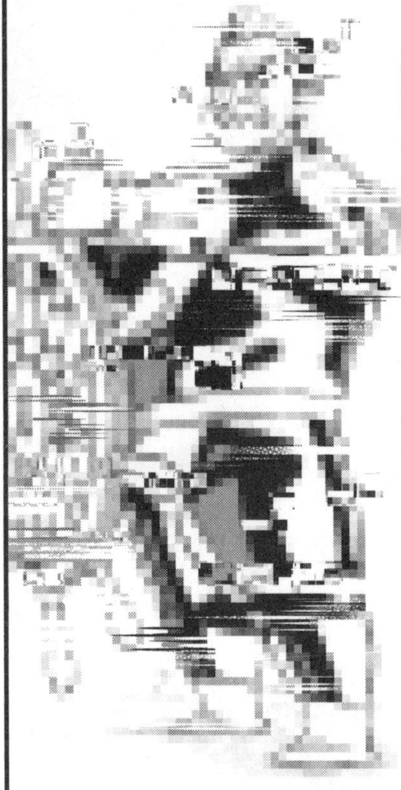

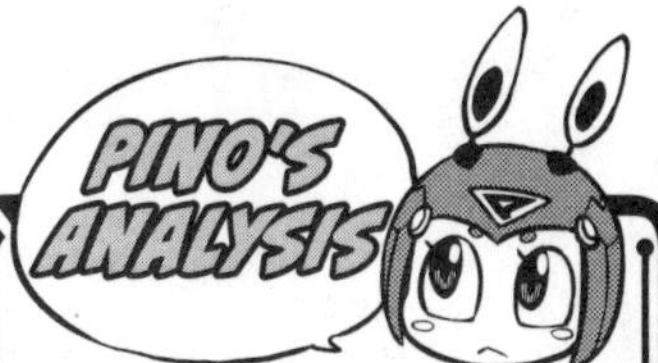
PINO'S ANALYSIS

Name:	?
Powers:	?
Element:	?
Likes:	?
Dislikes:	?
Attack:	?
Defense:	?
Marksmanship:	?
Ether Power:	?
Intelligence:	?
Captain:	?

Memo

I do get the feeling that there used to be one more member of the *Edens Zero* crew, but...I just can't recall who it is. I wonder if my memory has been damaged. He was a really good pilot, and a little perverted, and um... **BURBLE BURBLE BURBLE.**

CHAPTER 101: SINGULARITY

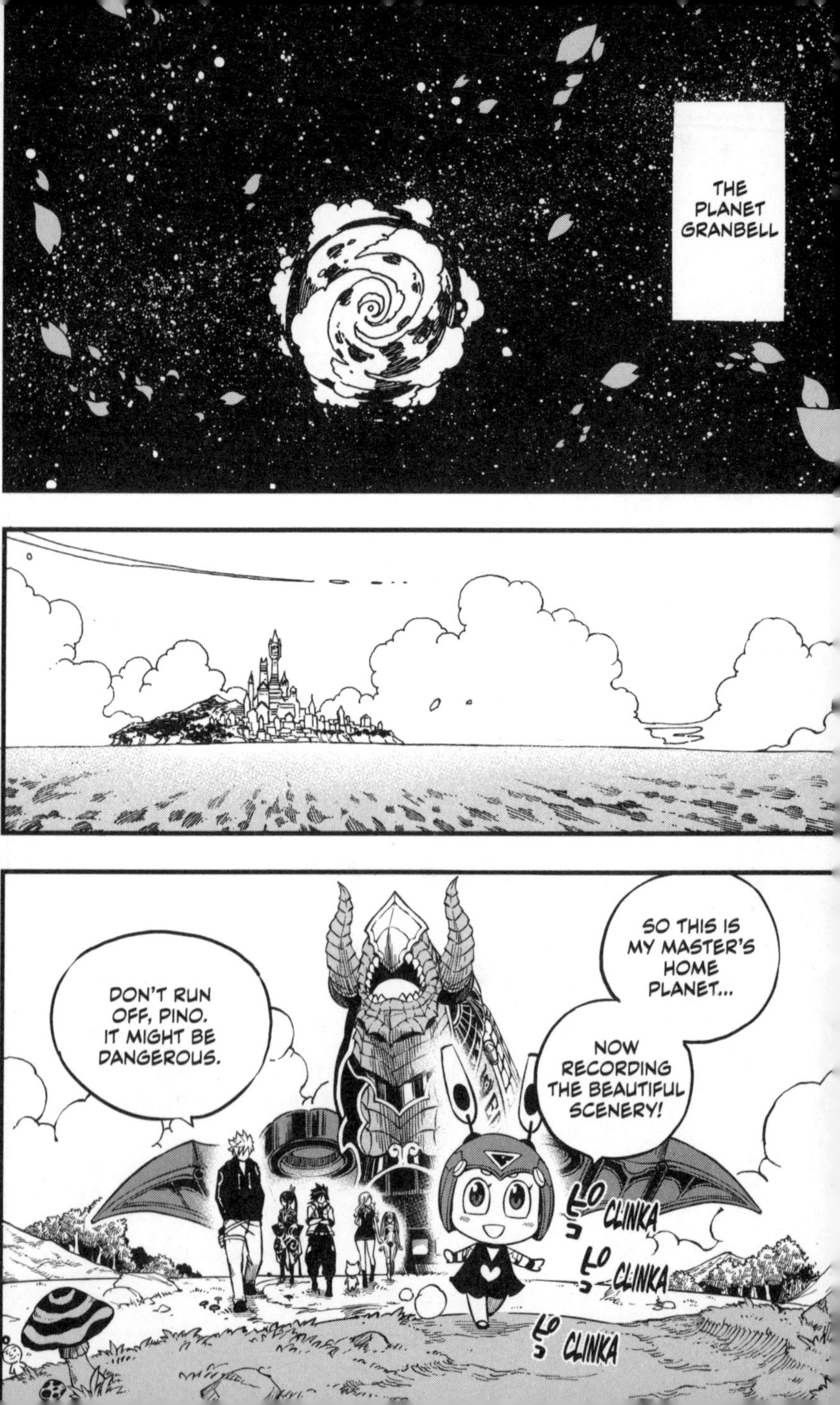
THE PLANET GRANBELL
SO THIS IS MY MASTER'S HOME PLANET...
NOW RECORDING THE BEAUTIFUL SCENERY!
DON'T RUN OFF, PINO. IT MIGHT BE DANGEROUS.
CLINKA
CLINKA
CLINKA

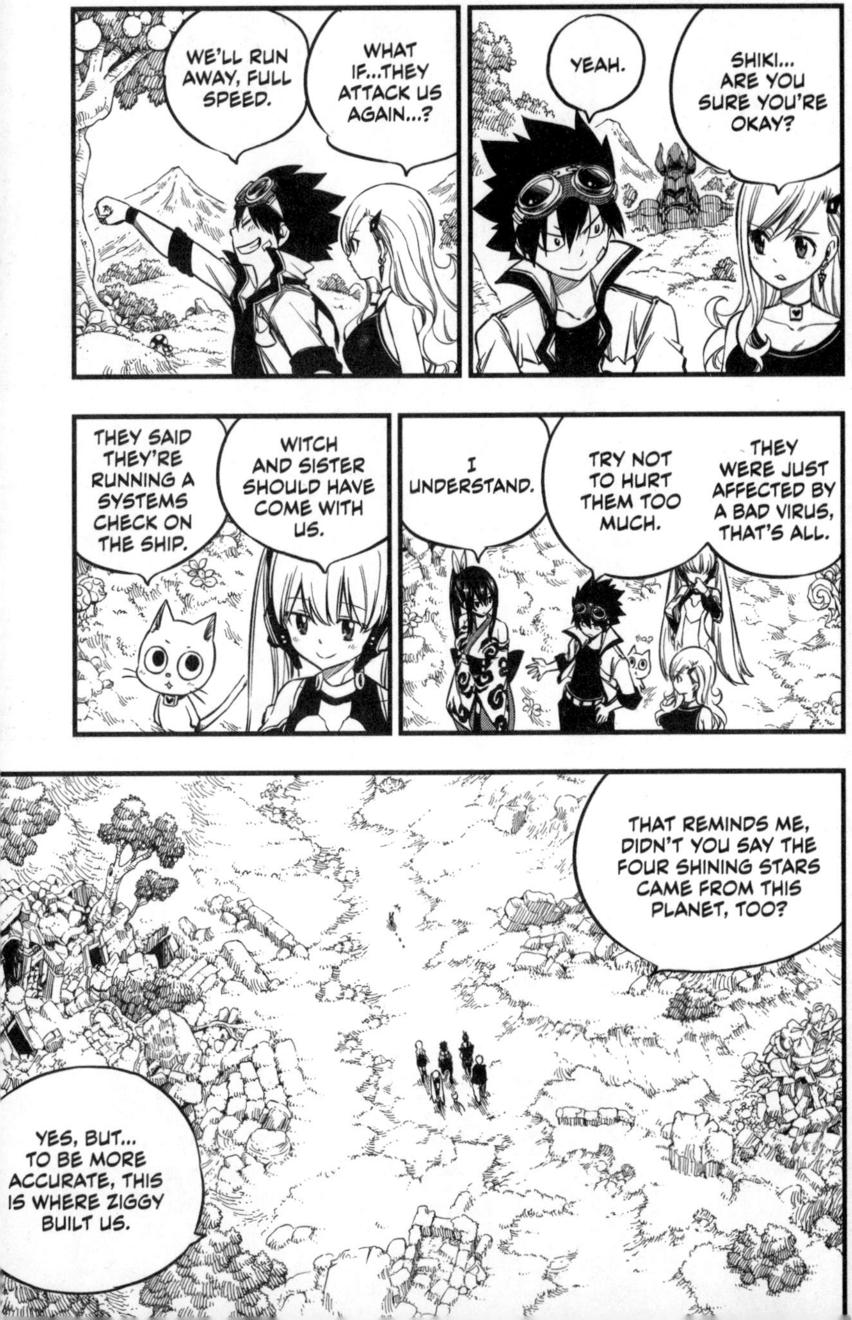
SHIKI... ARE YOU SURE YOU'RE OKAY?
YEAH.
WHAT IF...THEY ATTACK US AGAIN...?
WE'LL RUN AWAY, FULL SPEED.
THEY WERE JUST AFFECTED BY A BAD VIRUS, THAT'S ALL.
TRY NOT TO HURT THEM TOO MUCH.
I UNDERSTAND.
WITCH AND SISTER SHOULD HAVE COME WITH US.
THEY SAID THEY'RE RUNNING A SYSTEMS CHECK ON THE SHIP.
THAT REMINDS ME, DIDN'T YOU SAY THE FOUR SHINING STARS CAME FROM THIS PLANET, TOO?
YES, BUT... TO BE MORE ACCURATE, THIS IS WHERE ZIGGY BUILT US.

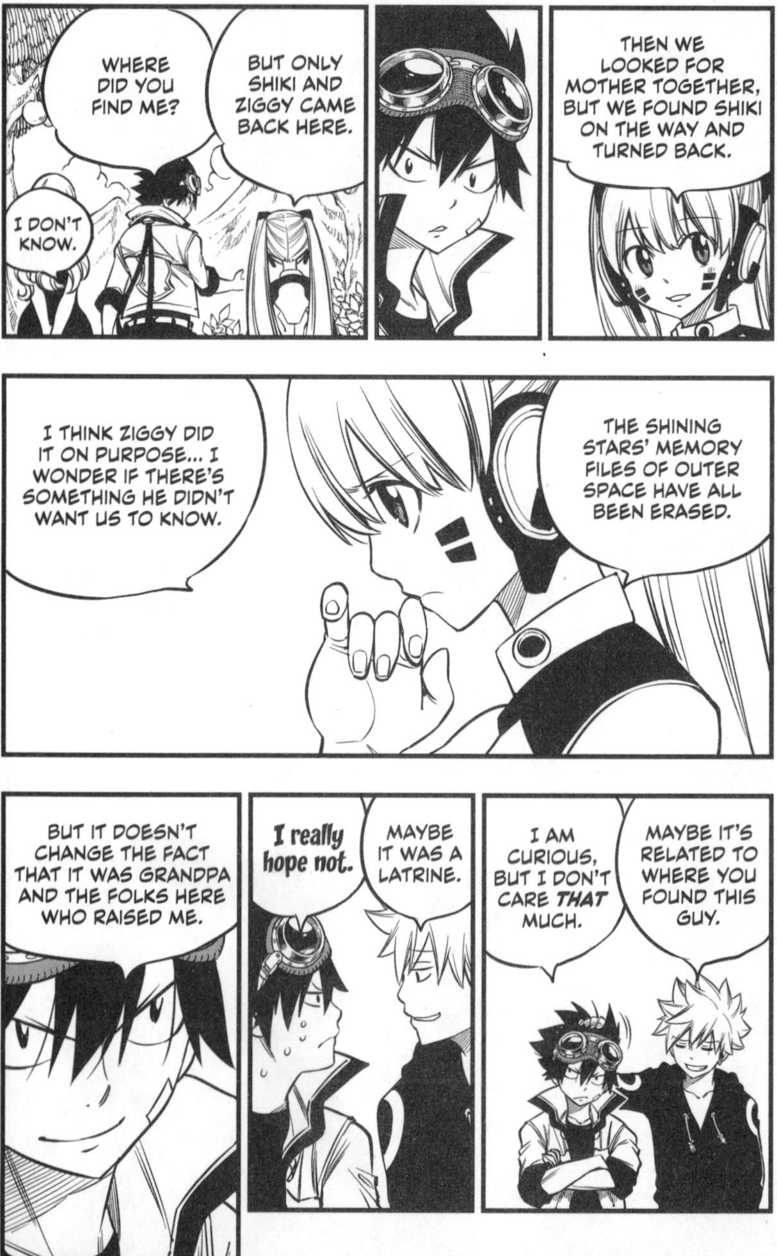
THEN WE LOOKED FOR MOTHER TOGETHER, BUT WE FOUND SHIKI ON THE WAY AND TURNED BACK.
BUT ONLY SHIKI AND ZIGGY CAME BACK HERE.
WHERE DID YOU FIND ME?
I DON'T KNOW.
THE SHINING STARS' MEMORY FILES OF OUTER SPACE HAVE ALL BEEN ERASED.
I THINK ZIGGY DID IT ON PURPOSE... I WONDER IF THERE'S SOMETHING HE DIDN'T WANT US TO KNOW.
MAYBE IT'S RELATED TO WHERE YOU FOUND THIS GUY.
I AM CURIOUS, BUT I DON'T CARE *THAT* MUCH.
MAYBE IT WAS A LATRINE.
I really hope not.
BUT IT DOESN'T CHANGE THE FACT THAT IT WAS GRANDPA AND THE FOLKS HERE WHO RAISED ME.

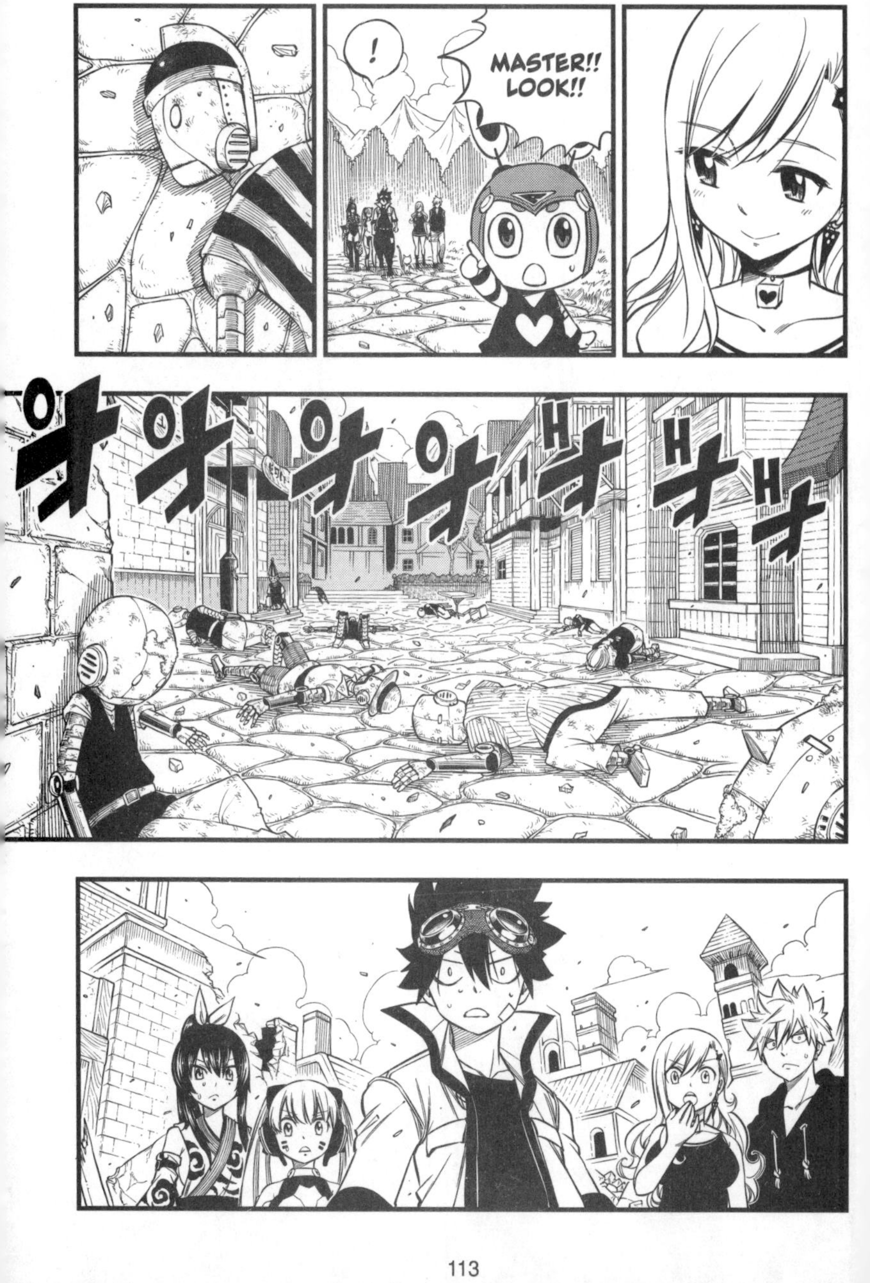
!
MASTER!! LOOK!!
OOOOHHH

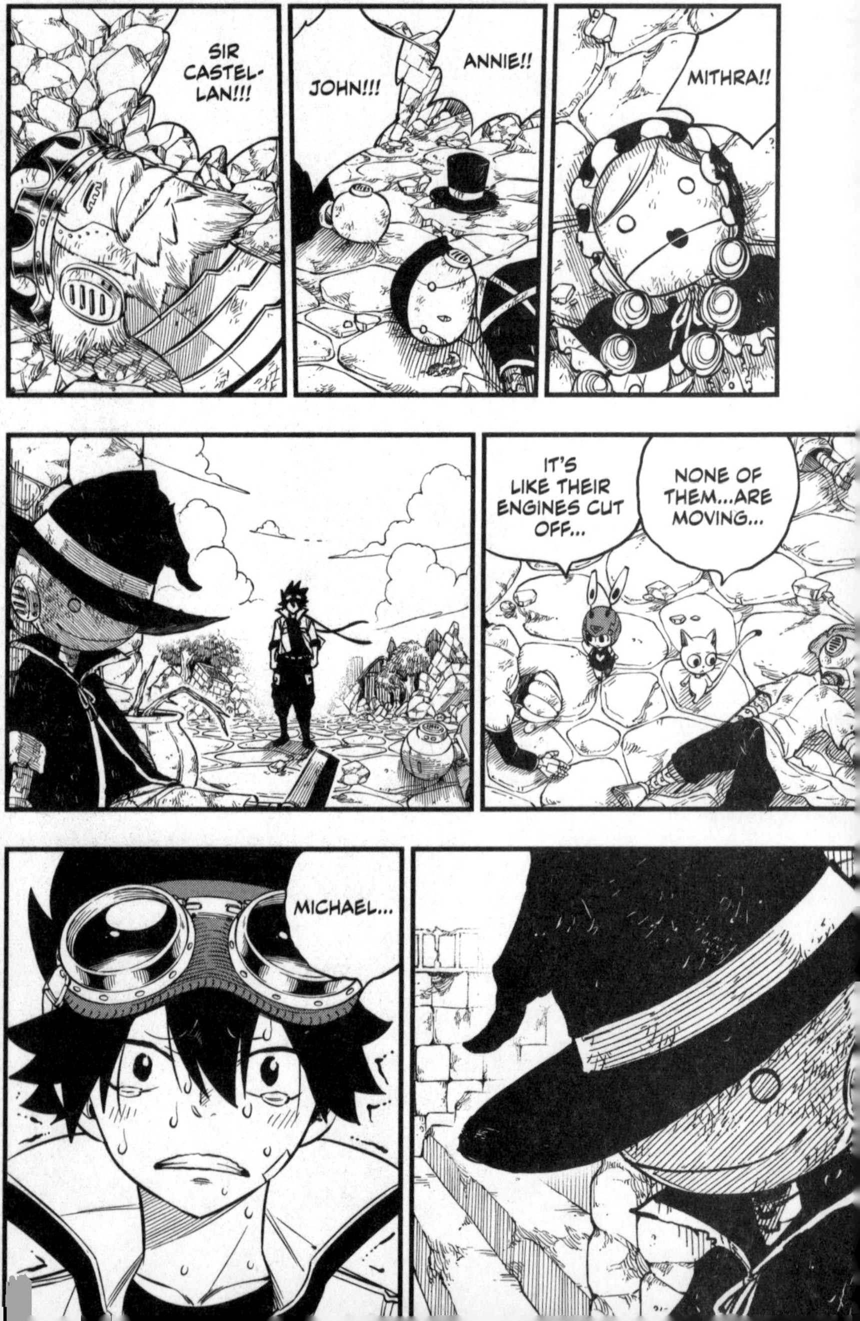
MITHRA!!
ANNIE!!
JOHN!!!
SIR CASTEL-LAN!!!
NONE OF THEM...ARE MOVING...
IT'S LIKE THEIR ENGINES CUT OFF...
MICHAEL...

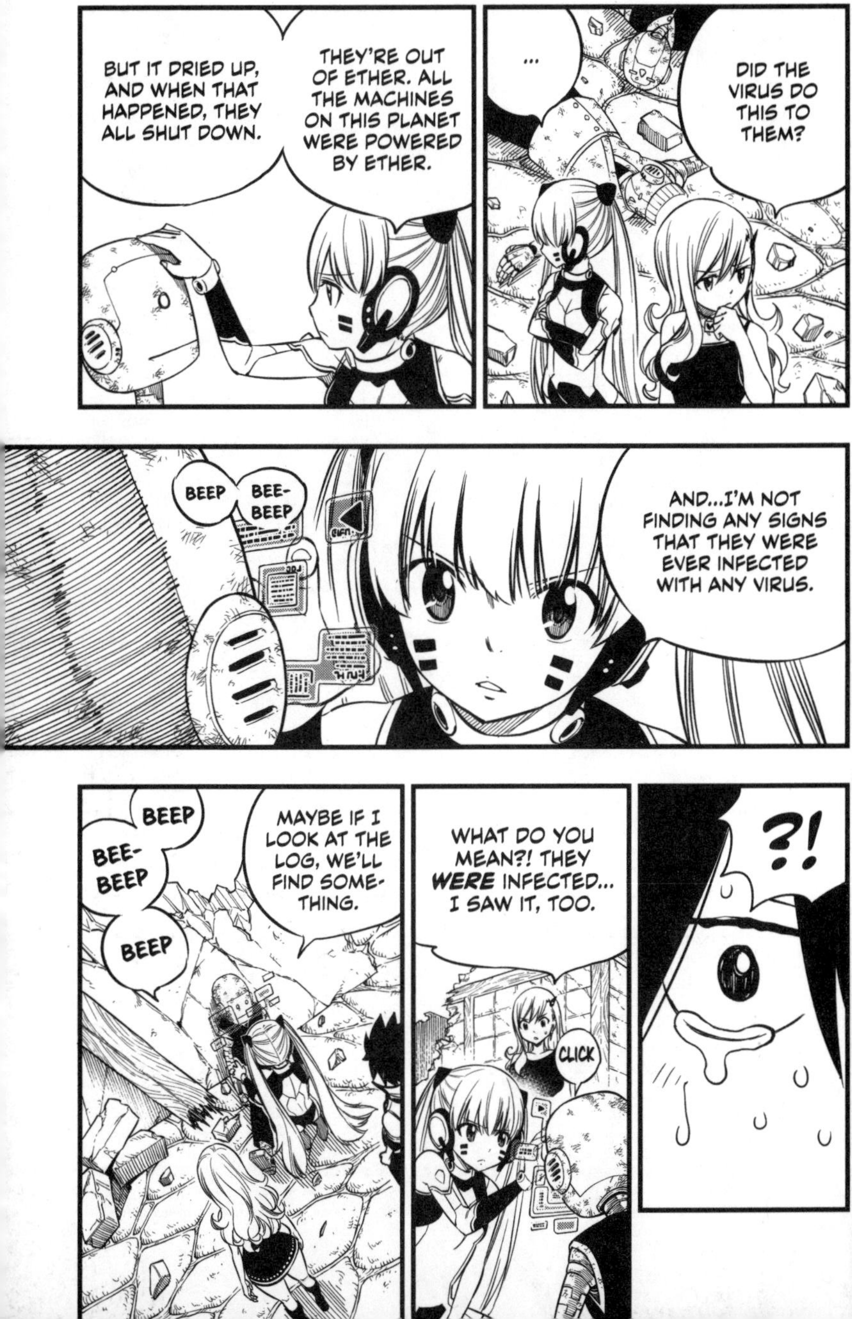
DID THE VIRUS DO THIS TO THEM?
...
THEY'RE OUT OF ETHER. ALL THE MACHINES ON THIS PLANET WERE POWERED BY ETHER.
BUT IT DRIED UP, AND WHEN THAT HAPPENED, THEY ALL SHUT DOWN.
AND...I'M NOT FINDING ANY SIGNS THAT THEY WERE EVER INFECTED WITH ANY VIRUS.
BEE-BEEP
BEEP
?!
WHAT DO YOU MEAN?! THEY *WERE* INFECTED... I SAW IT, TOO.
CLICK
MAYBE IF I LOOK AT THE LOG, WE'LL FIND SOME-THING.
BEEP
BEE-BEEP
BEEP

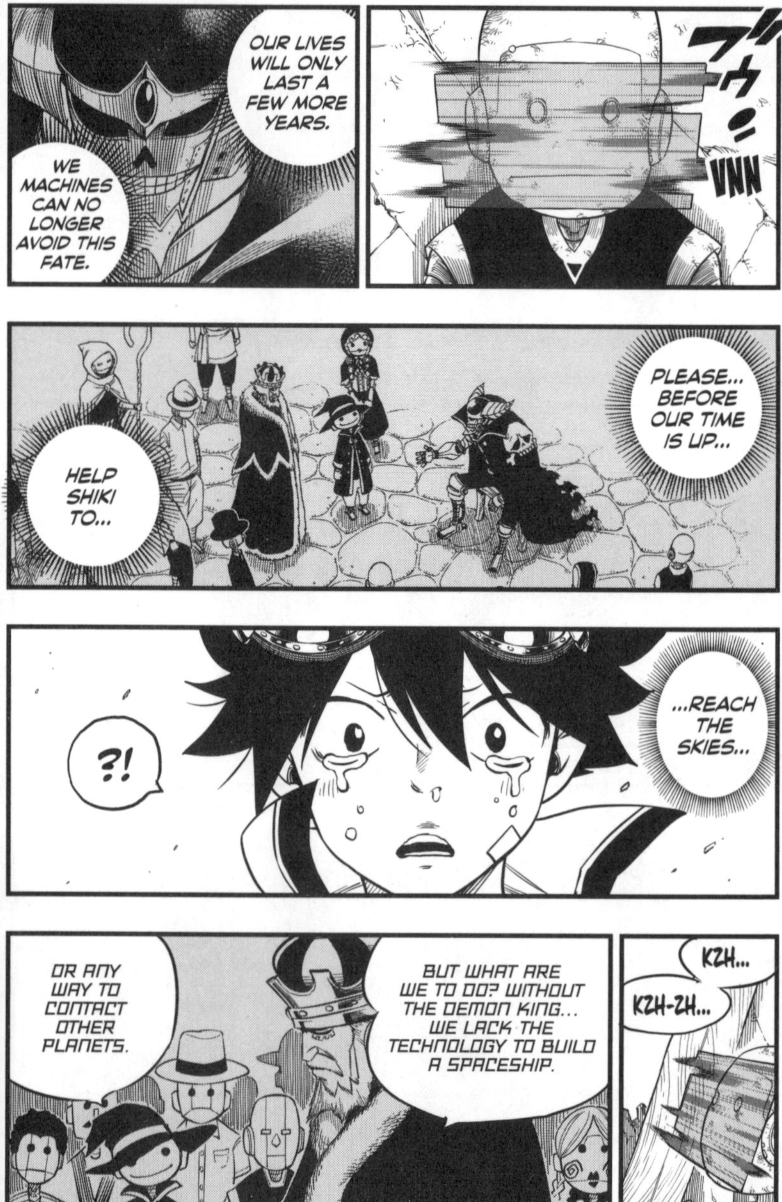
ブゥン
VNN
OUR LIVES WILL ONLY LAST A FEW MORE YEARS.
WE MACHINES CAN NO LONGER AVOID THIS FATE.
PLEASE... BEFORE OUR TIME IS UP...
HELP SHIKI TO...
...REACH THE SKIES...
?!
KZH...
KZH-ZH...
BUT WHAT ARE WE TO DO? WITHOUT THE DEMON KING... WE LACK THE TECHNOLOGY TO BUILD A SPACESHIP.
OR ANY WAY TO CONTACT OTHER PLANETS.

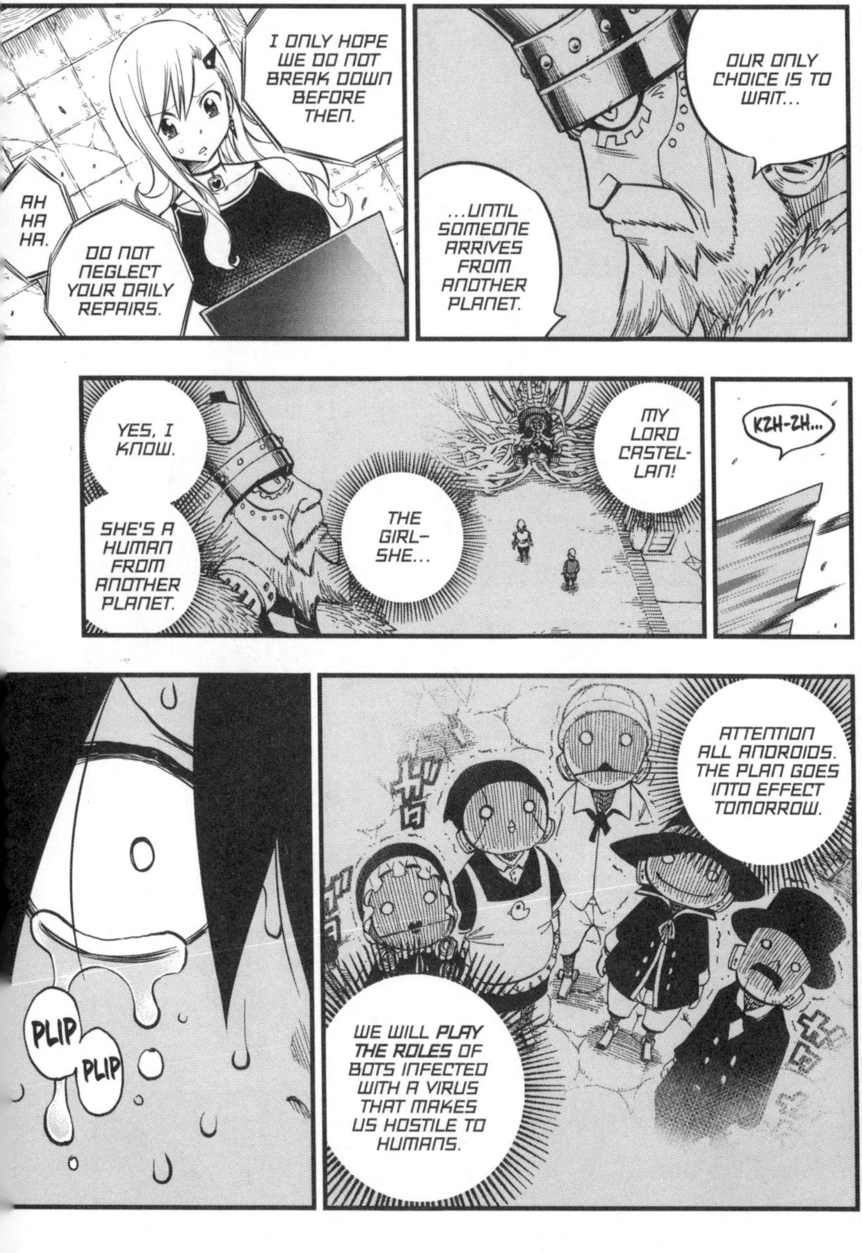
OUR ONLY CHOICE IS TO WAIT...
...UNTIL SOMEONE ARRIVES FROM ANOTHER PLANET.
I ONLY HOPE WE DO NOT BREAK DOWN BEFORE THEN.
DO NOT NEGLECT YOUR DAILY REPAIRS.
AH HA HA.
KZH-ZH...
MY LORD CASTEL-LAN!
THE GIRL-SHE...
YES, I KNOW.
SHE'S A HUMAN FROM ANOTHER PLANET.
ATTENTION ALL ANDROIDS. THE PLAN GOES INTO EFFECT TOMORROW.
WE WILL PLAY THE ROLES OF BOTS INFECTED WITH A VIRUS THAT MAKES US HOSTILE TO HUMANS.
PLIP
PLIP

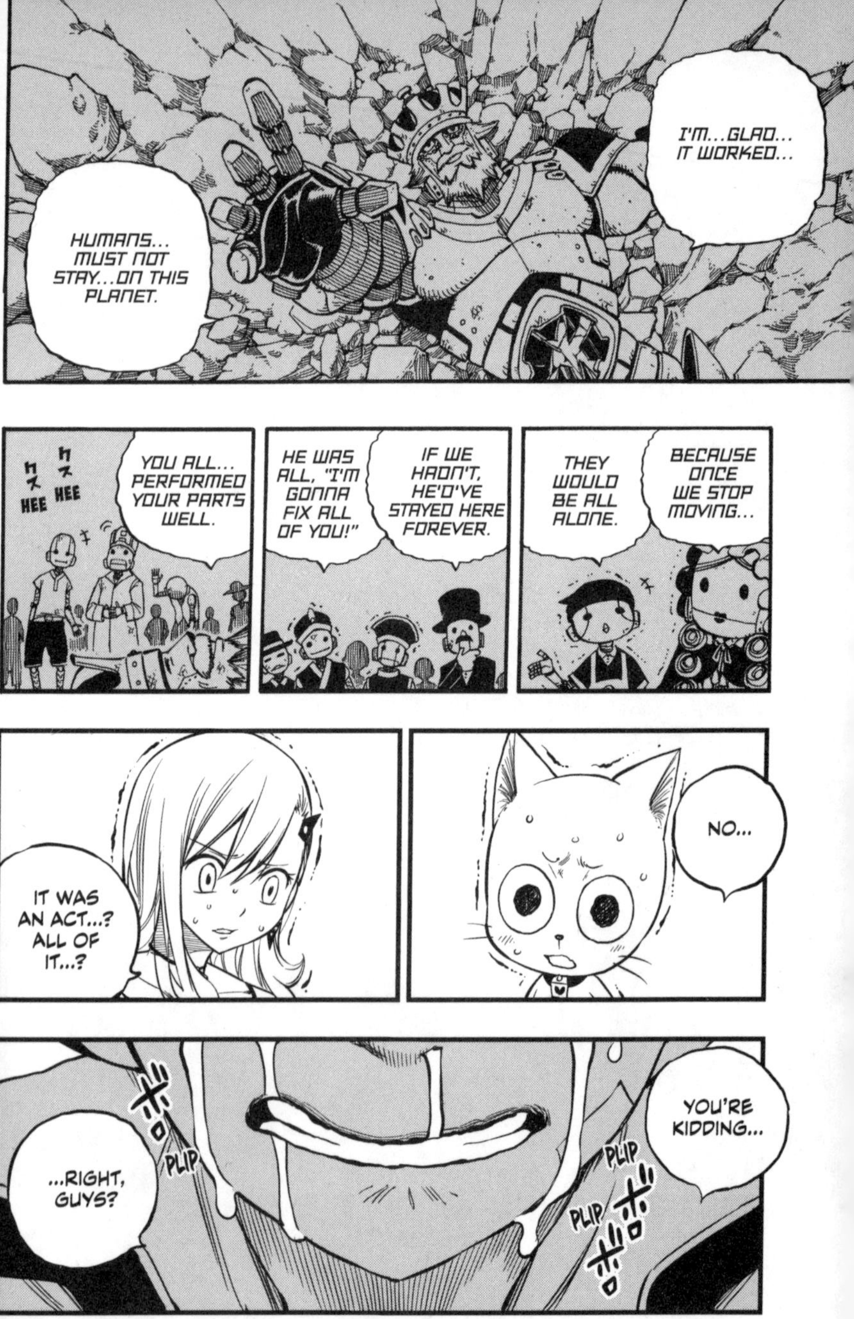
I'M...GLAD... IT WORKED...
HUMANS... MUST NOT STAY...ON THIS PLANET.
BECAUSE ONCE WE STOP MOVING...
THEY WOULD BE ALL ALONE.
IF WE HADN'T, HE'D'VE STAYED HERE FOREVER.
HE WAS ALL, "I'M GONNA FIX ALL OF YOU!"
YOU ALL... PERFORMED YOUR PARTS WELL.
HEE HEE
NO...
IT WAS AN ACT...? ALL OF IT...?
YOU'RE KIDDING...
PLIP
PLIP
PLIP
...RIGHT, GUYS?

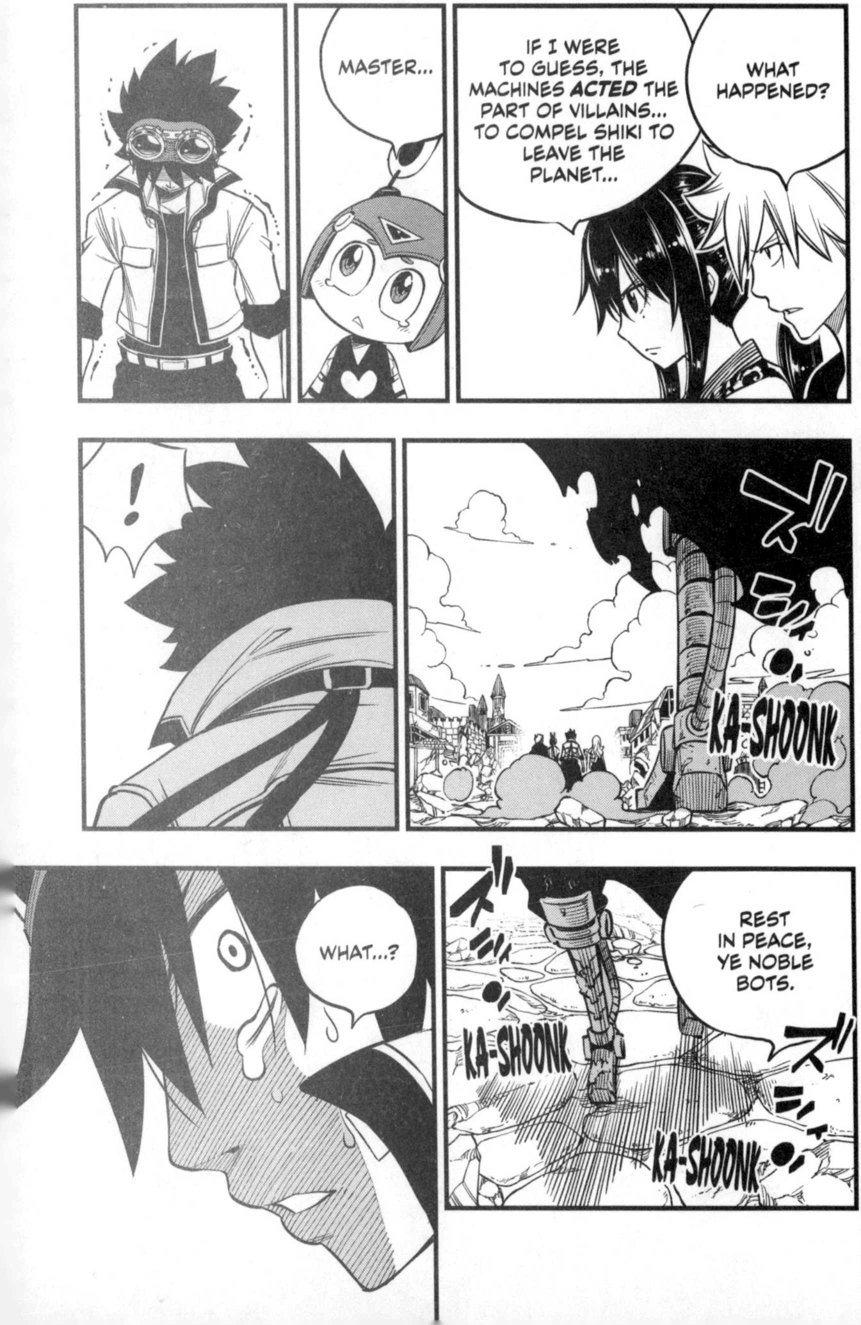
WHAT HAPPENED?
IF I WERE TO GUESS, THE MACHINES ***ACTED*** THE PART OF VILLAINS... TO COMPEL SHIKI TO LEAVE THE PLANET...
MASTER...
KA-SHOONK
!
REST IN PEACE, YE NOBLE BOTS.
KA-SHOONK
KA-SHOONK
WHAT...?

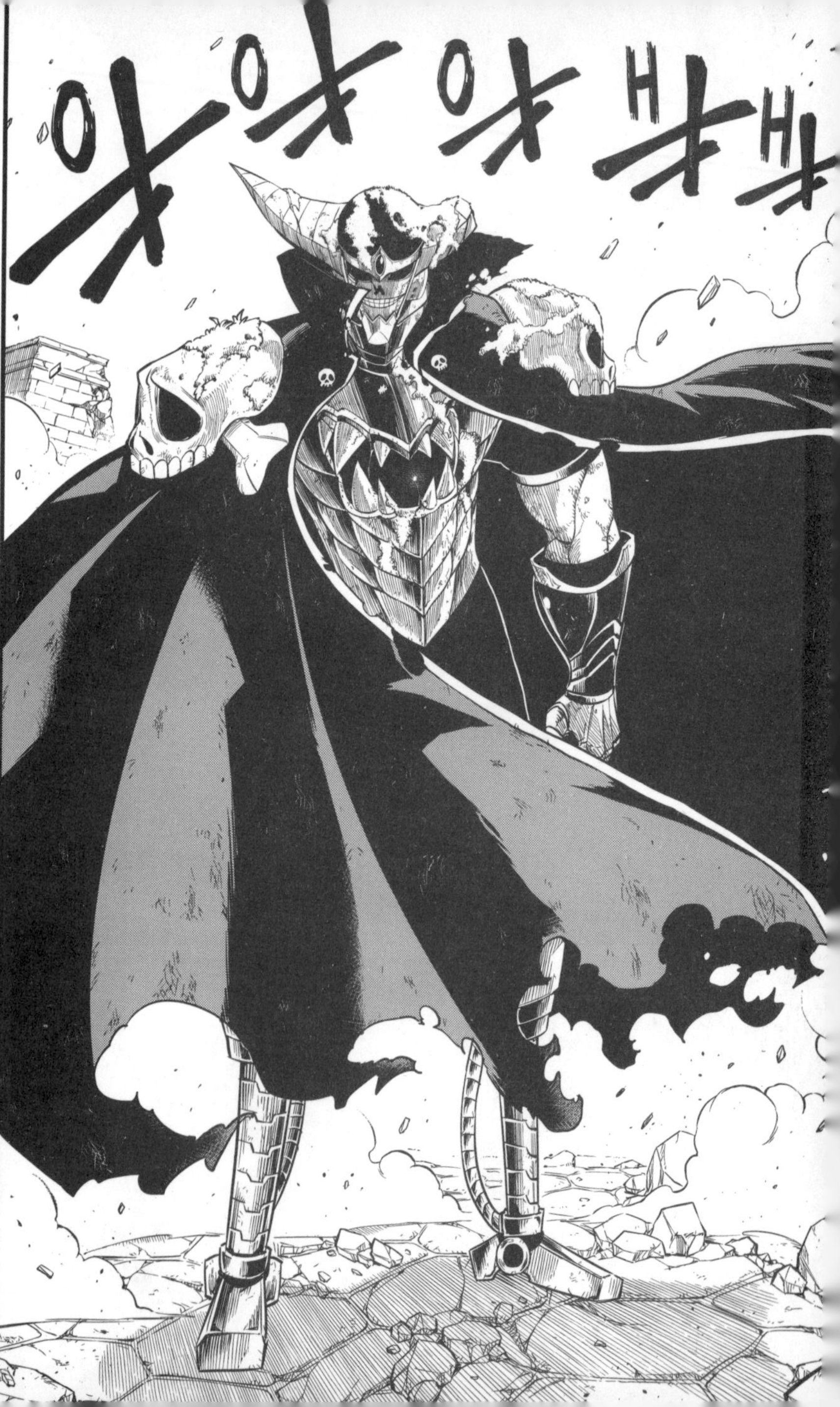
OHOHOHHH

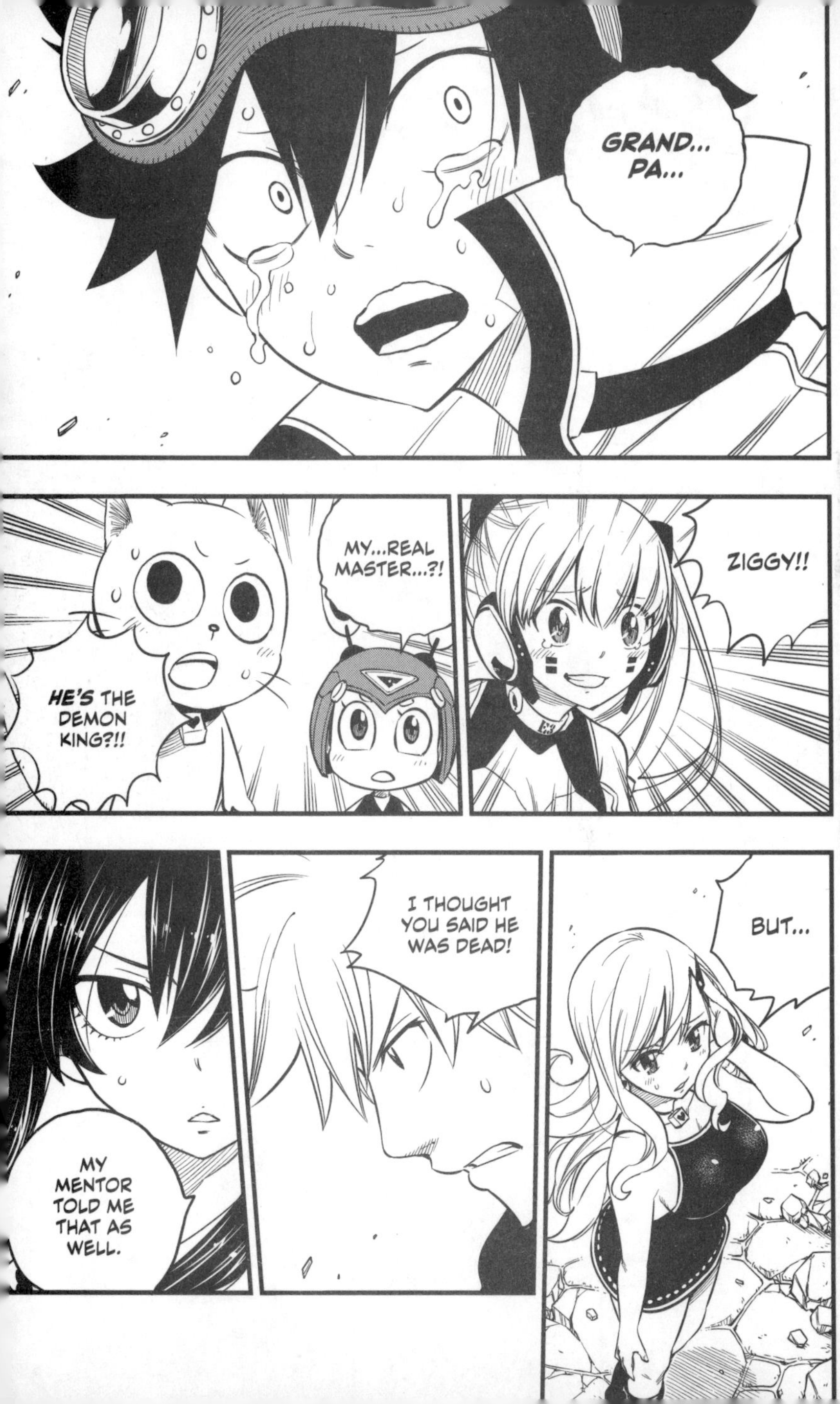
GRAND... PA...
ZIGGY!!
MY...REAL MASTER...?!
HE'S THE DEMON KING?!!
BUT...
I THOUGHT YOU SAID HE WAS DEAD!
MY MENTOR TOLD ME THAT AS WELL.

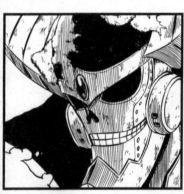

Hnn! GRANDPA!

YOU'RE... YOU'RE ALIVE...

ZHOOM

WHOOSH

GRANDPA!!! I...!!!

DASH

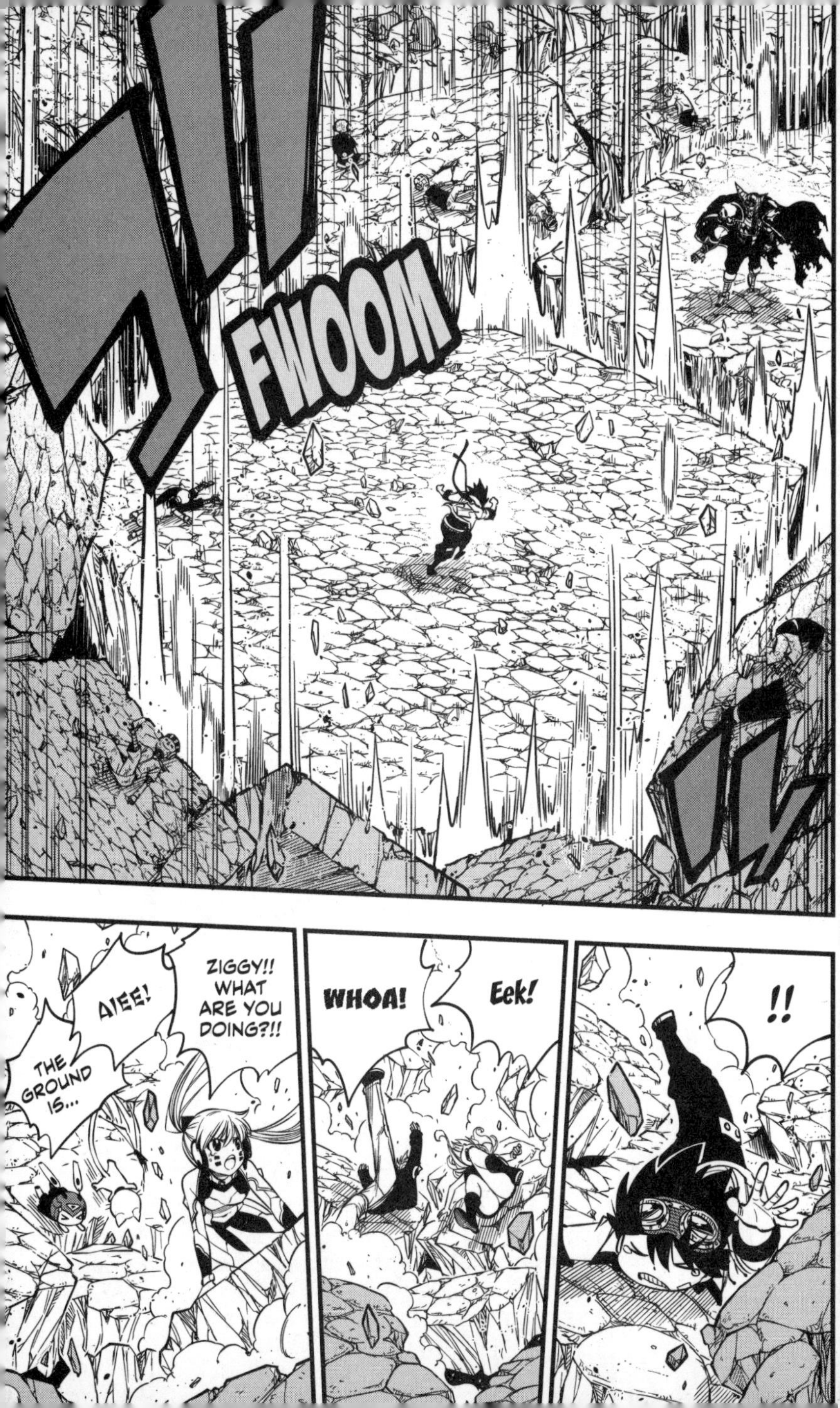
FWOOM
!!
Eek!
WHOA!
ZIGGY!! WHAT ARE YOU DOING?!!
AIEE!
THE GROUND IS...

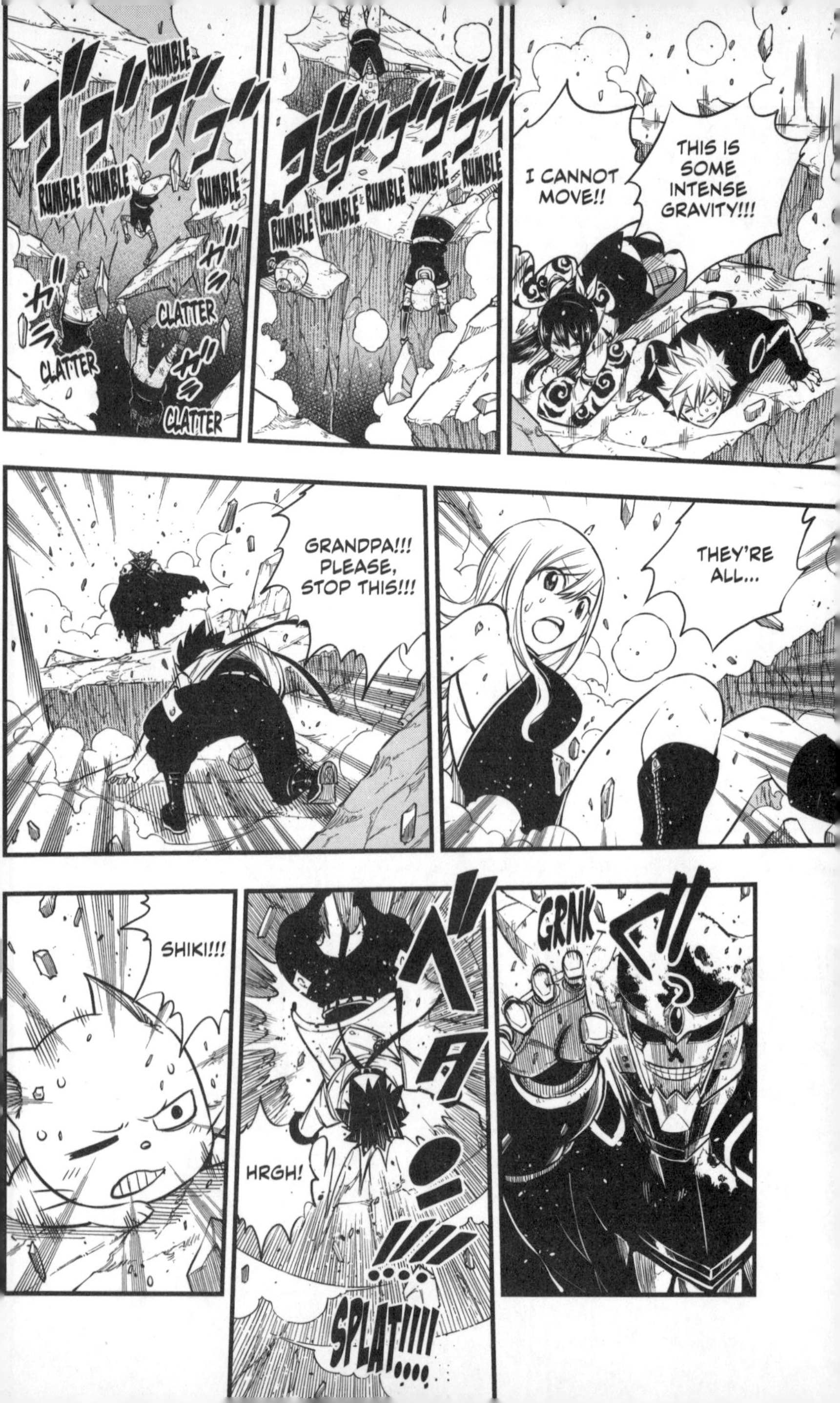
THIS IS SOME INTENSE GRAVITY!!!
I CANNOT MOVE!!
RUMBLE RUMBLE RUMBLE RUMBLE RUMBLE
RUMBLE
RUMBLE RUMBLE
RUMBLE
CLATTER
CLATTER
CLATTER
THEY'RE ALL...
GRANDPA!!! PLEASE, STOP THIS!!!
GRNK
HRGH!
SPLAT!!!!...
SHIKI!!!

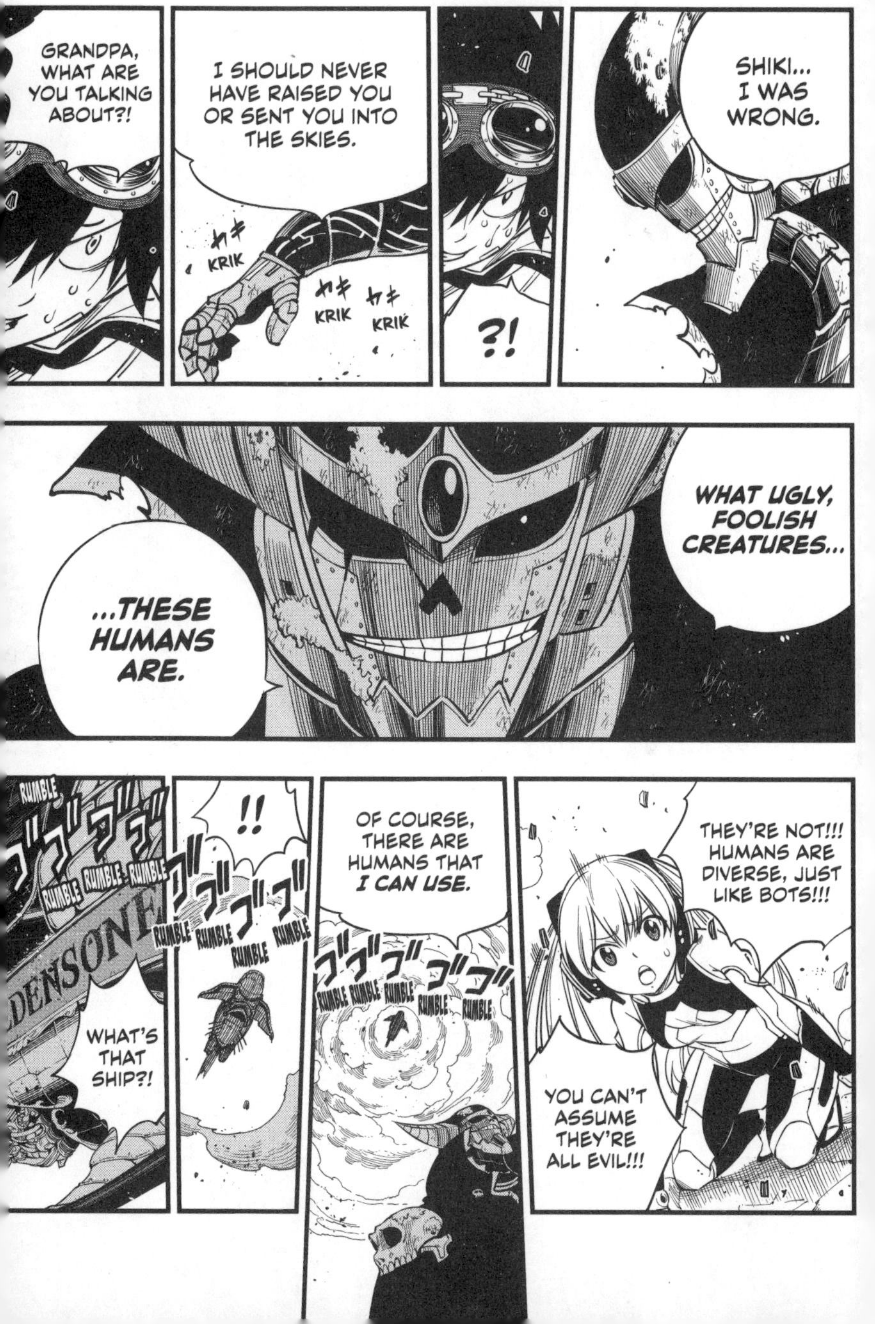
SHIKI... I WAS WRONG.
?!
I SHOULD NEVER HAVE RAISED YOU OR SENT YOU INTO THE SKIES.
KRIK
KRIK
KRIK
GRANDPA, WHAT ARE YOU TALKING ABOUT?!
WHAT UGLY, FOOLISH CREATURES...
...THESE HUMANS ARE.
THEY'RE NOT!!! HUMANS ARE DIVERSE, JUST LIKE BOTS!!!
YOU CAN'T ASSUME THEY'RE ALL EVIL!!!
OF COURSE, THERE ARE HUMANS THAT I CAN USE.
RUMBLE RUMBLE RUMBLE RUMBLE RUMBLE
!!
RUMBLE RUMBLE RUMBLE RUMBLE
RUMBLE RUMBLE RUMBLE RUMBLE
WHAT'S THAT SHIP?!

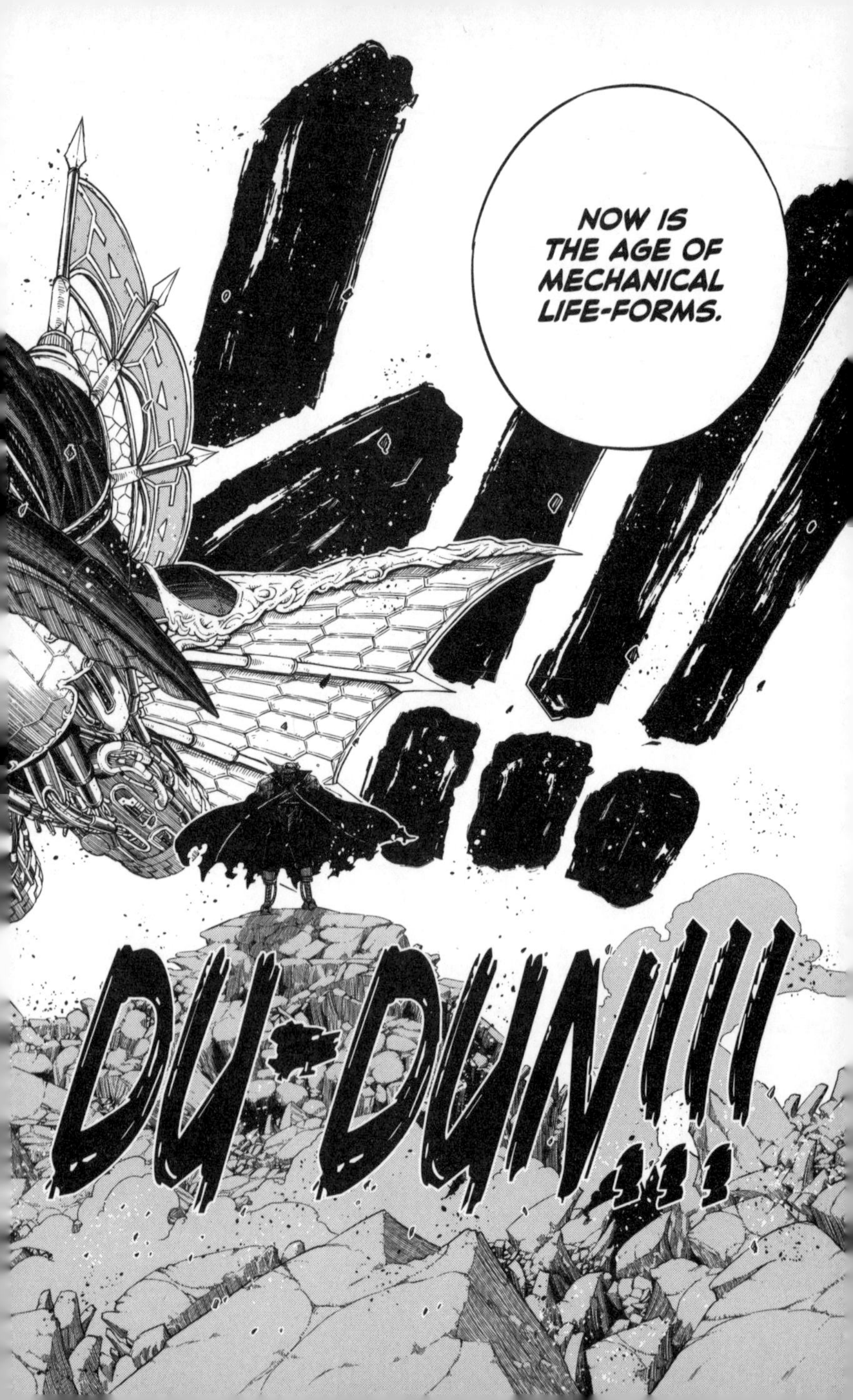
NOW IS THE AGE OF MECHANICAL LIFE-FORMS.
DU-DUN!!!

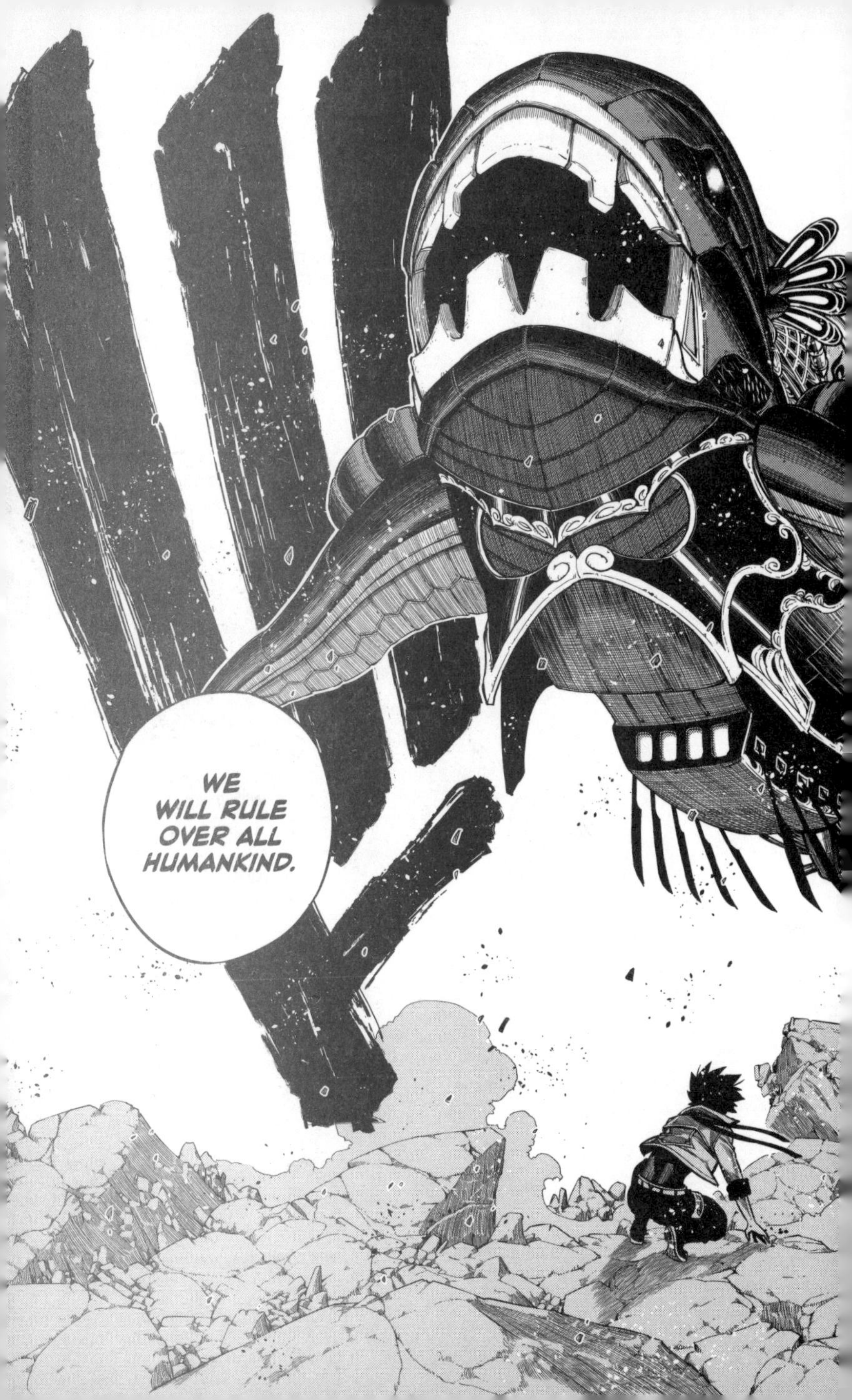
WE WILL RULE OVER ALL HUMANKIND.

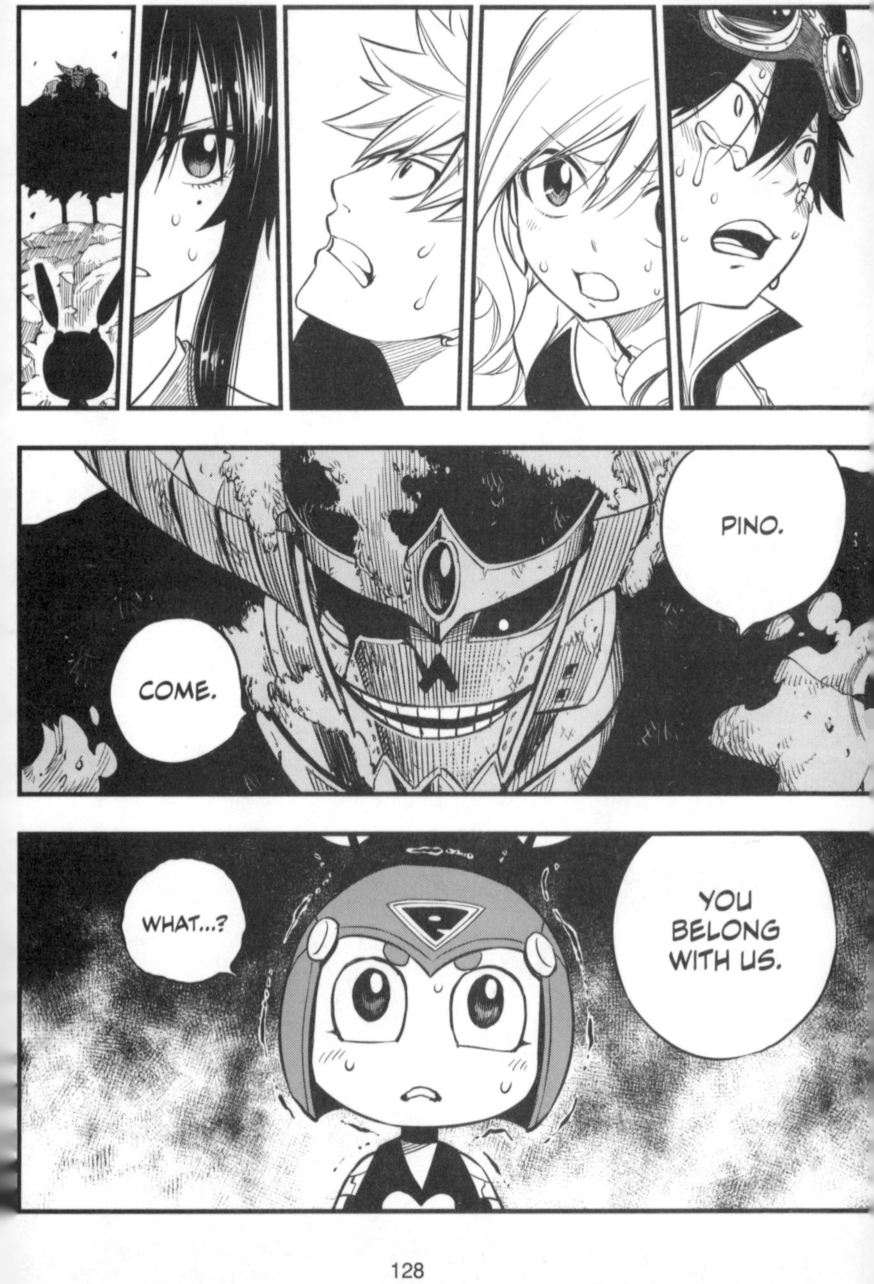
PINO.
COME.
YOU BELONG WITH US.
WHAT...?

EDENS ZERO

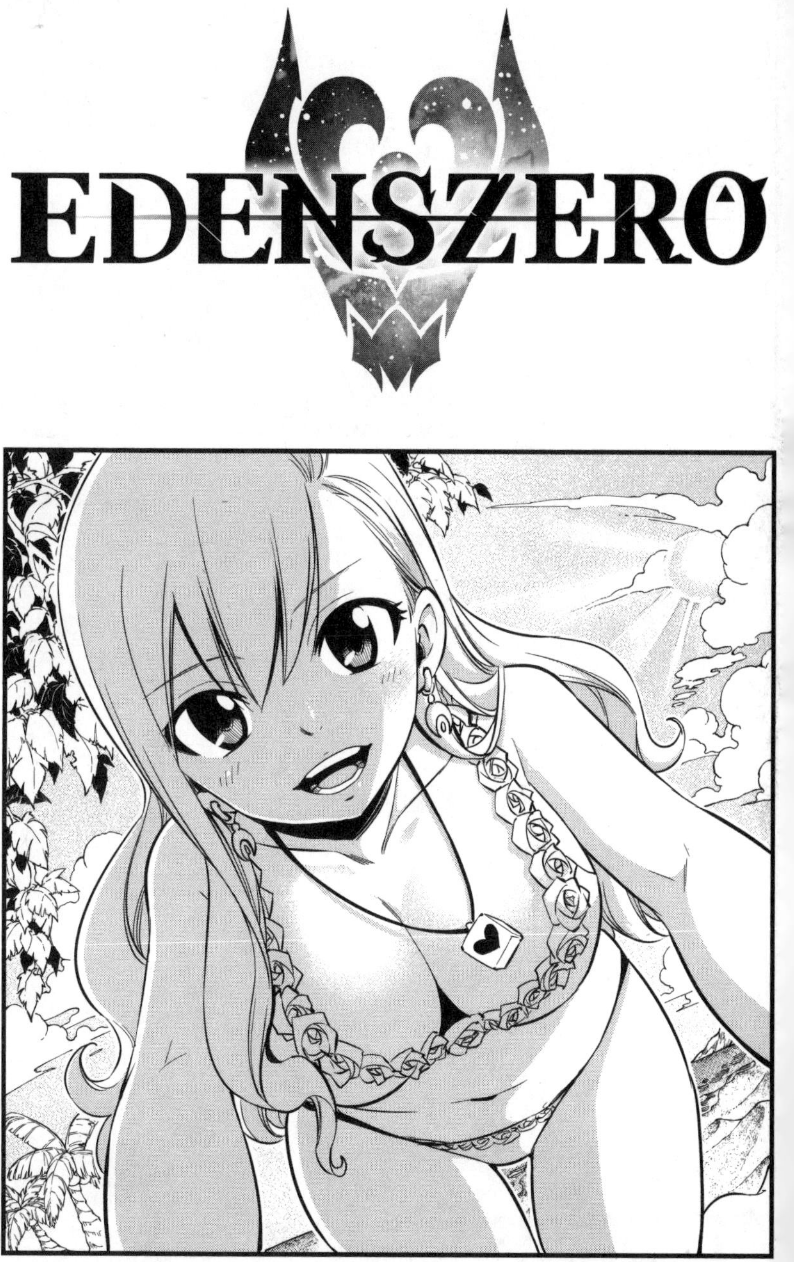

CHAPTER 102: TIME TO SAY GOODBYE

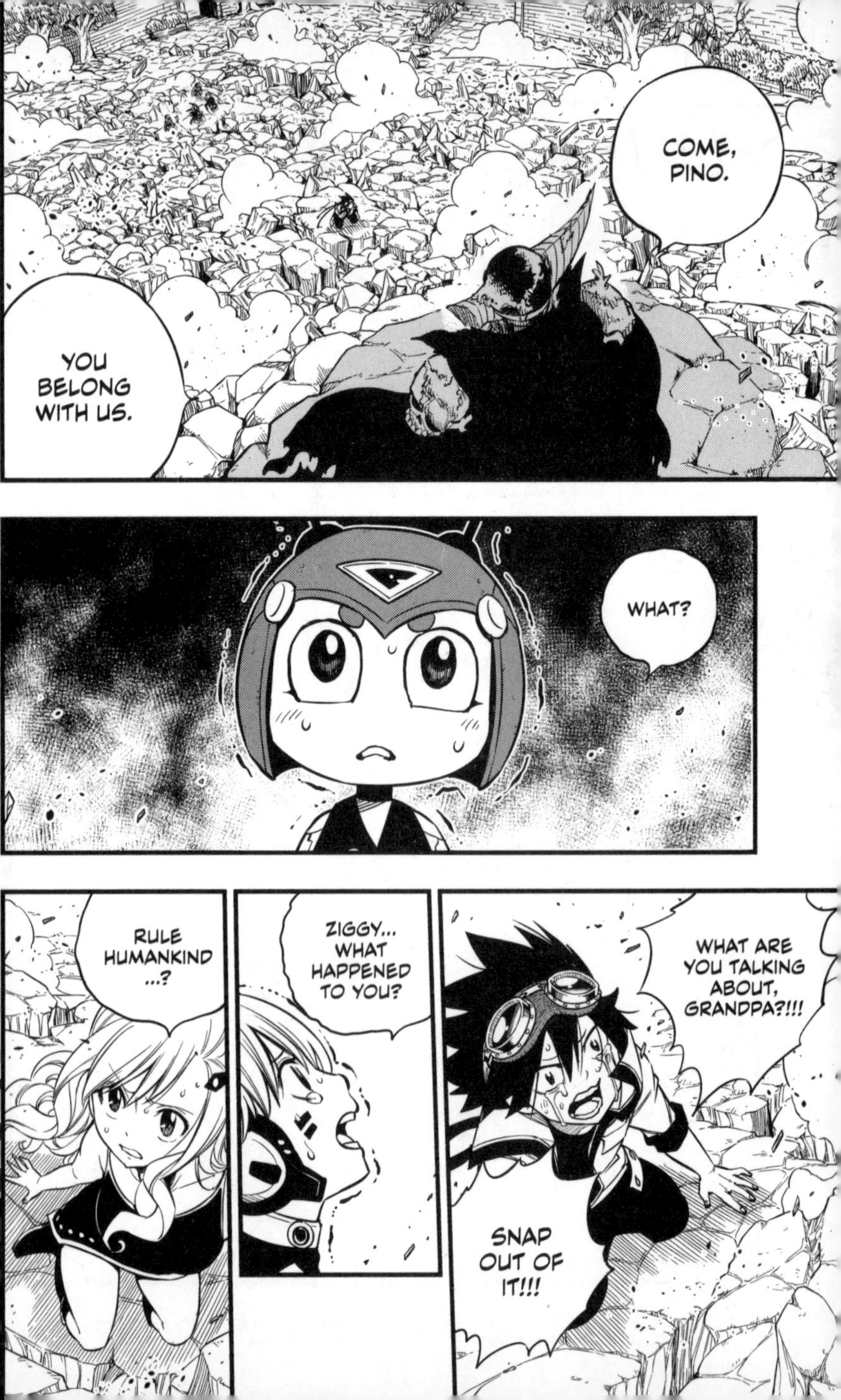
COME, PINO.
YOU BELONG WITH US.
WHAT?
WHAT ARE YOU TALKING ABOUT, GRANDPA?!!!
SNAP OUT OF IT!!!
ZIGGY... WHAT HAPPENED TO YOU?
RULE HUMANKIND ...?

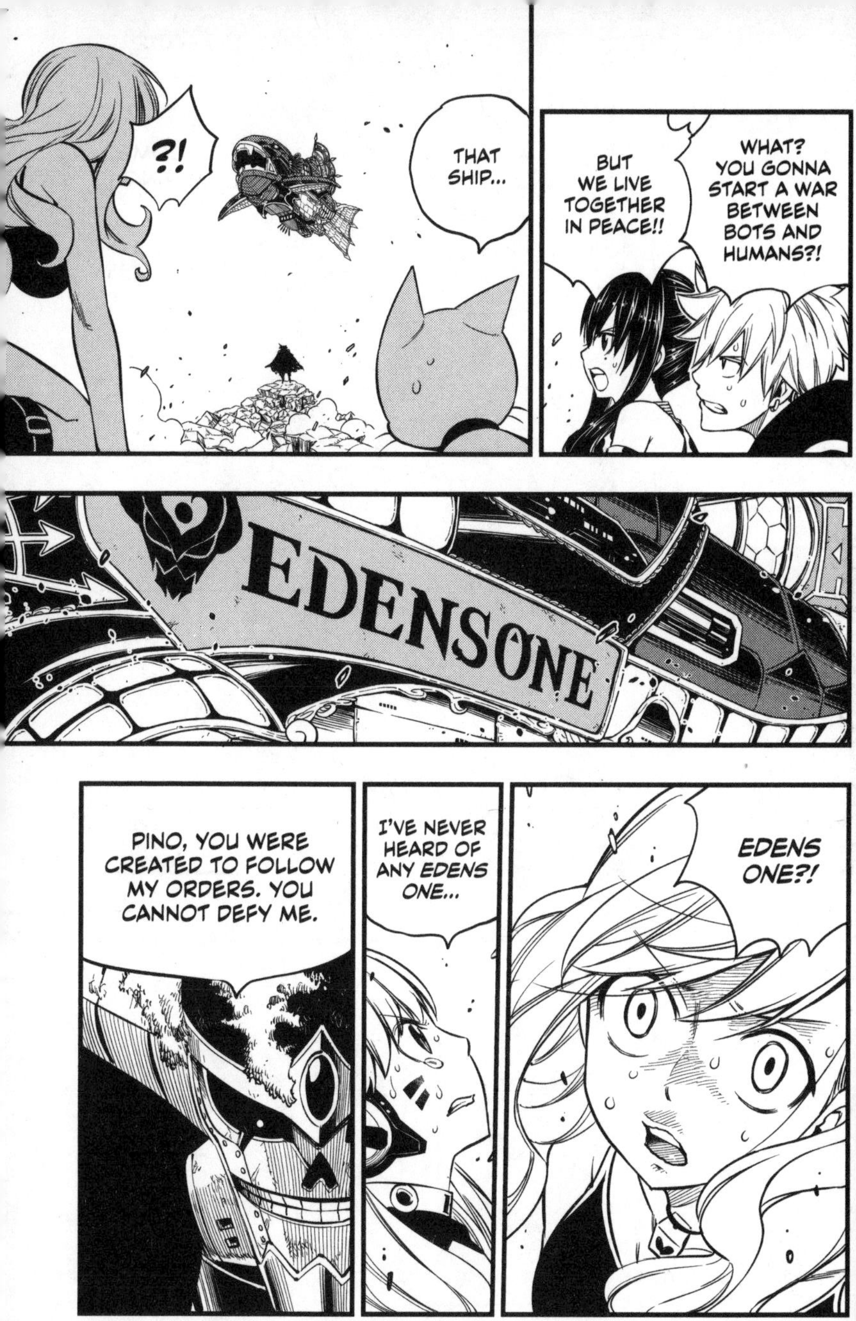
WHAT? YOU GONNA START A WAR BETWEEN BOTS AND HUMANS?!
BUT WE LIVE TOGETHER IN PEACE!!
THAT SHIP...
?!
EDENSONE
EDENS ONE?!
I'VE NEVER HEARD OF ANY EDENS ONE...
PINO, YOU WERE CREATED TO FOLLOW MY ORDERS. YOU CANNOT DEFY ME.

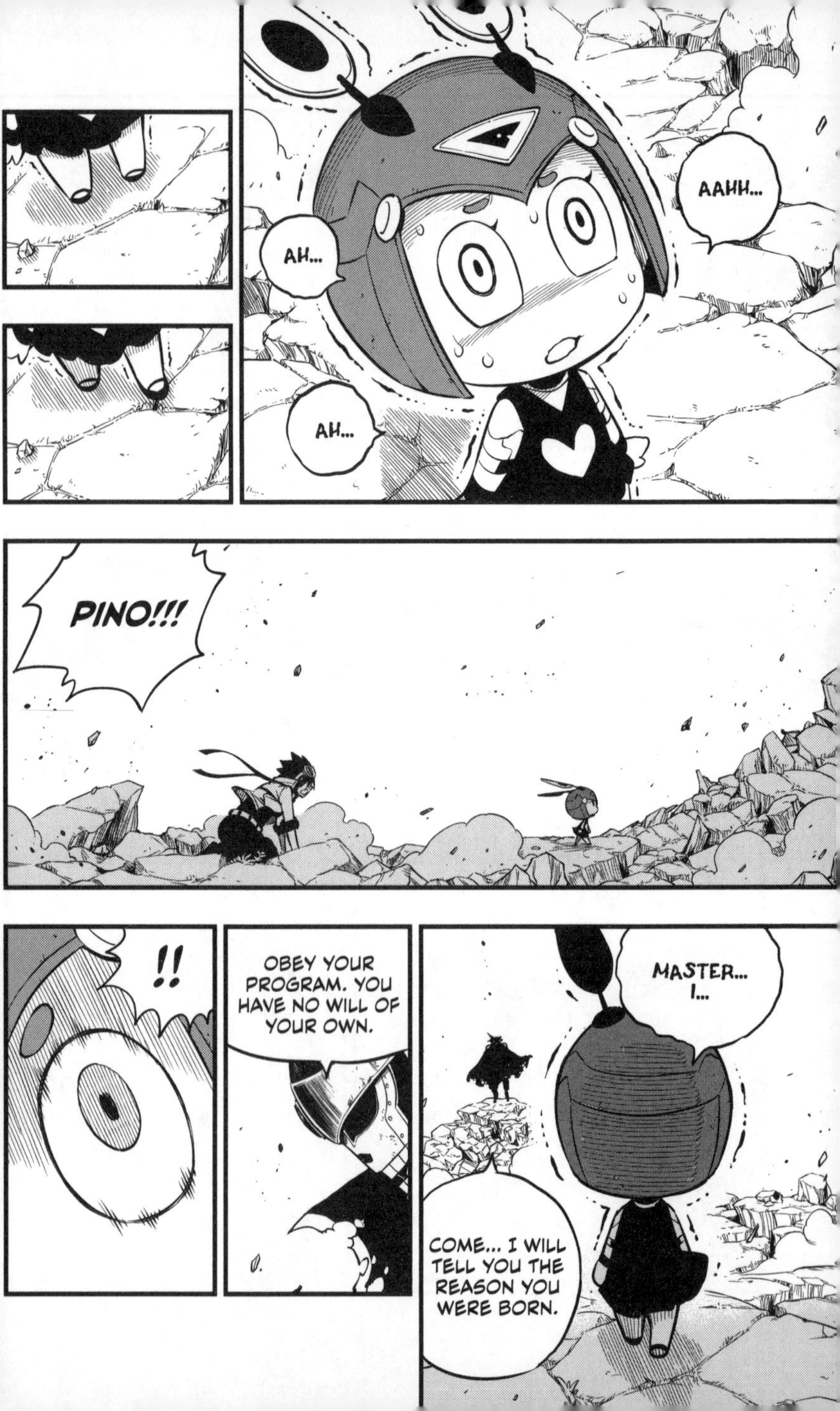
AAHH...
AH...
AH...
PINO!!!
MASTER... I...
COME... I WILL TELL YOU THE REASON YOU WERE BORN.
OBEY YOUR PROGRAM. YOU HAVE NO WILL OF YOUR OWN.
!!

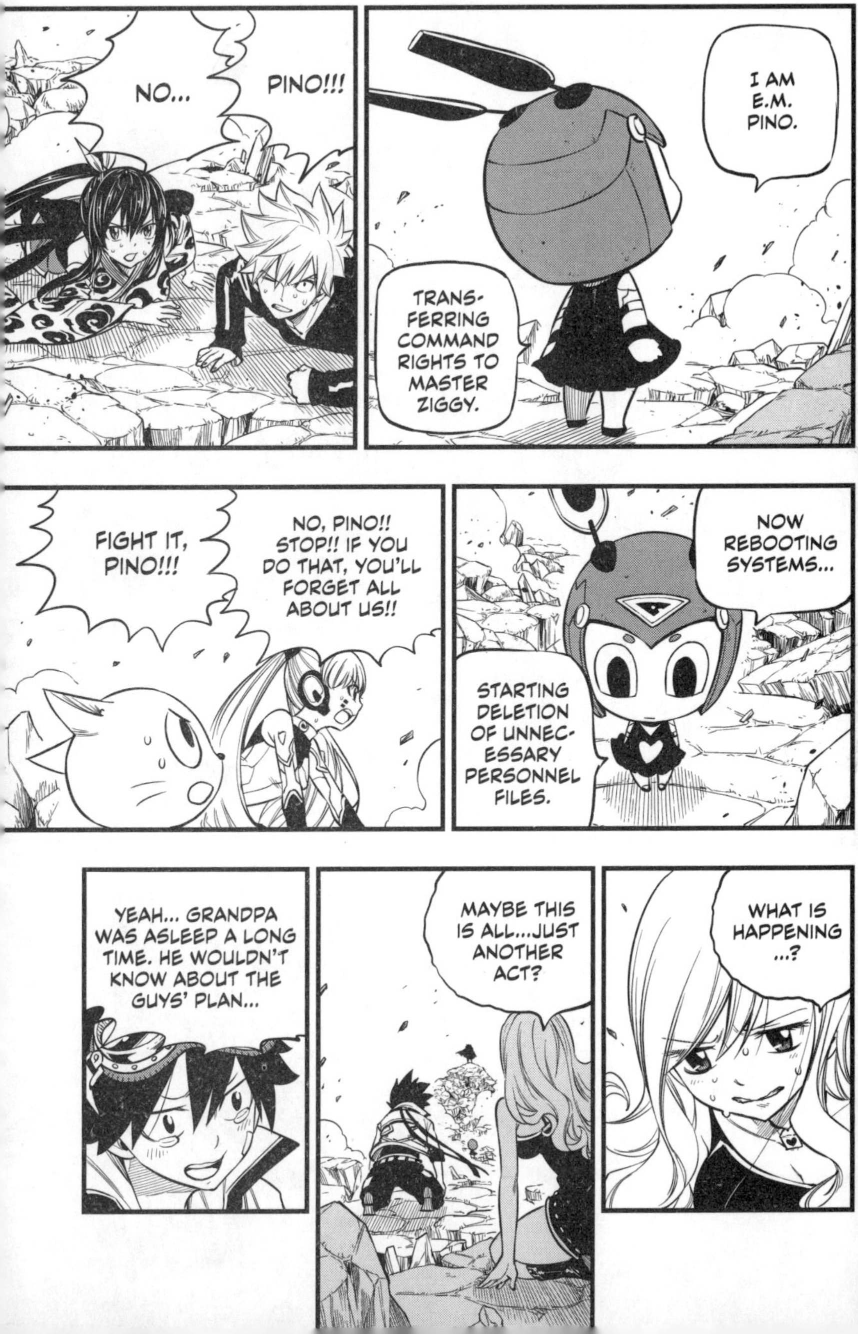
I AM E.M. PINO.
TRANSFERRING COMMAND RIGHTS TO MASTER ZIGGY.
NO... PINO!!!
NOW REBOOTING SYSTEMS...
STARTING DELETION OF UNNECESSARY PERSONNEL FILES.
NO, PINO!! STOP!! IF YOU DO THAT, YOU'LL FORGET ALL ABOUT US!!
FIGHT IT, PINO!!!
WHAT IS HAPPENING ...?
MAYBE THIS IS ALL...JUST ANOTHER ACT?
YEAH... GRANDPA WAS ASLEEP A LONG TIME. HE WOULDN'T KNOW ABOUT THE GUYS' PLAN...

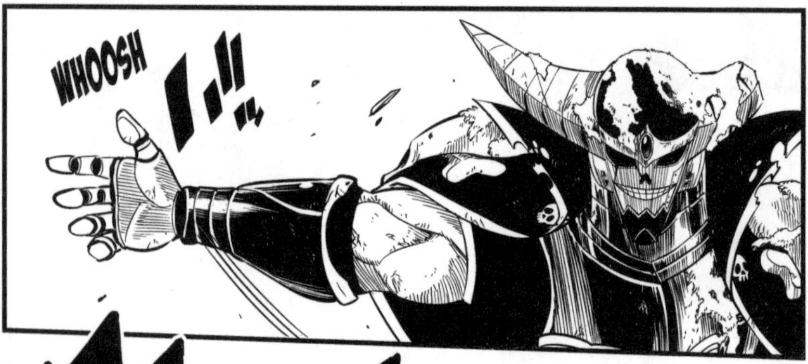
WHOOSH

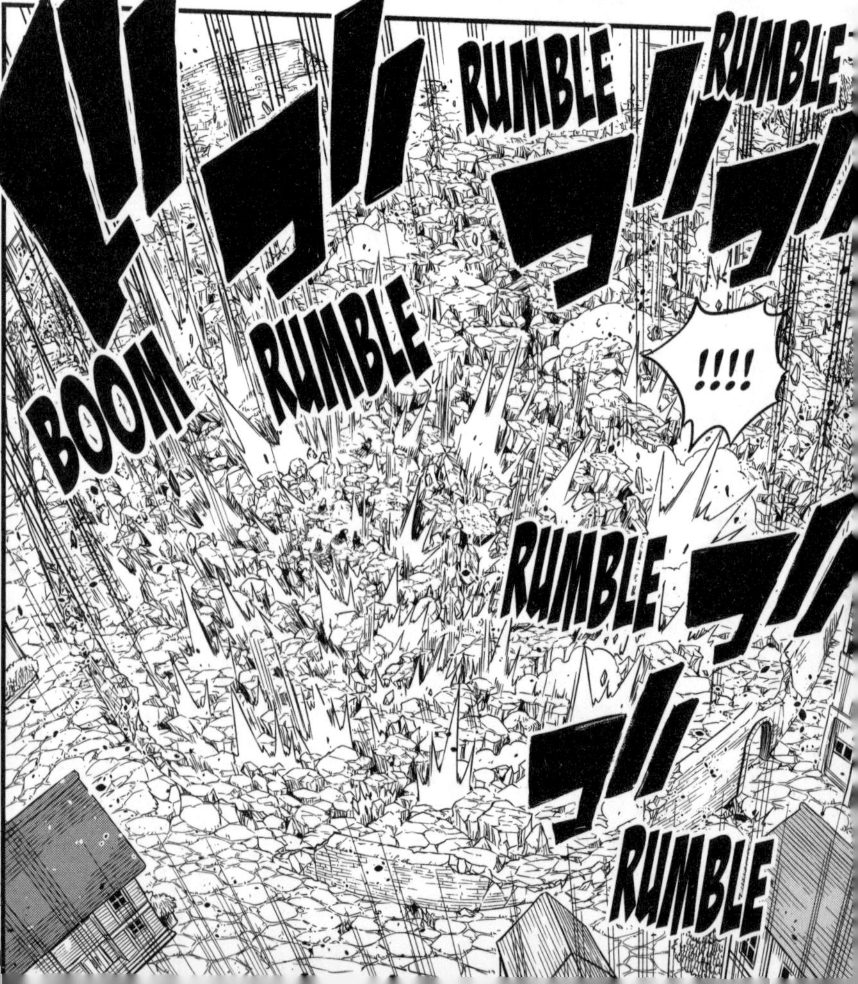
RUMBLE
RUMBLE
!!!!
RUMBLE
BOOM
RUMBLE
RUMBLE

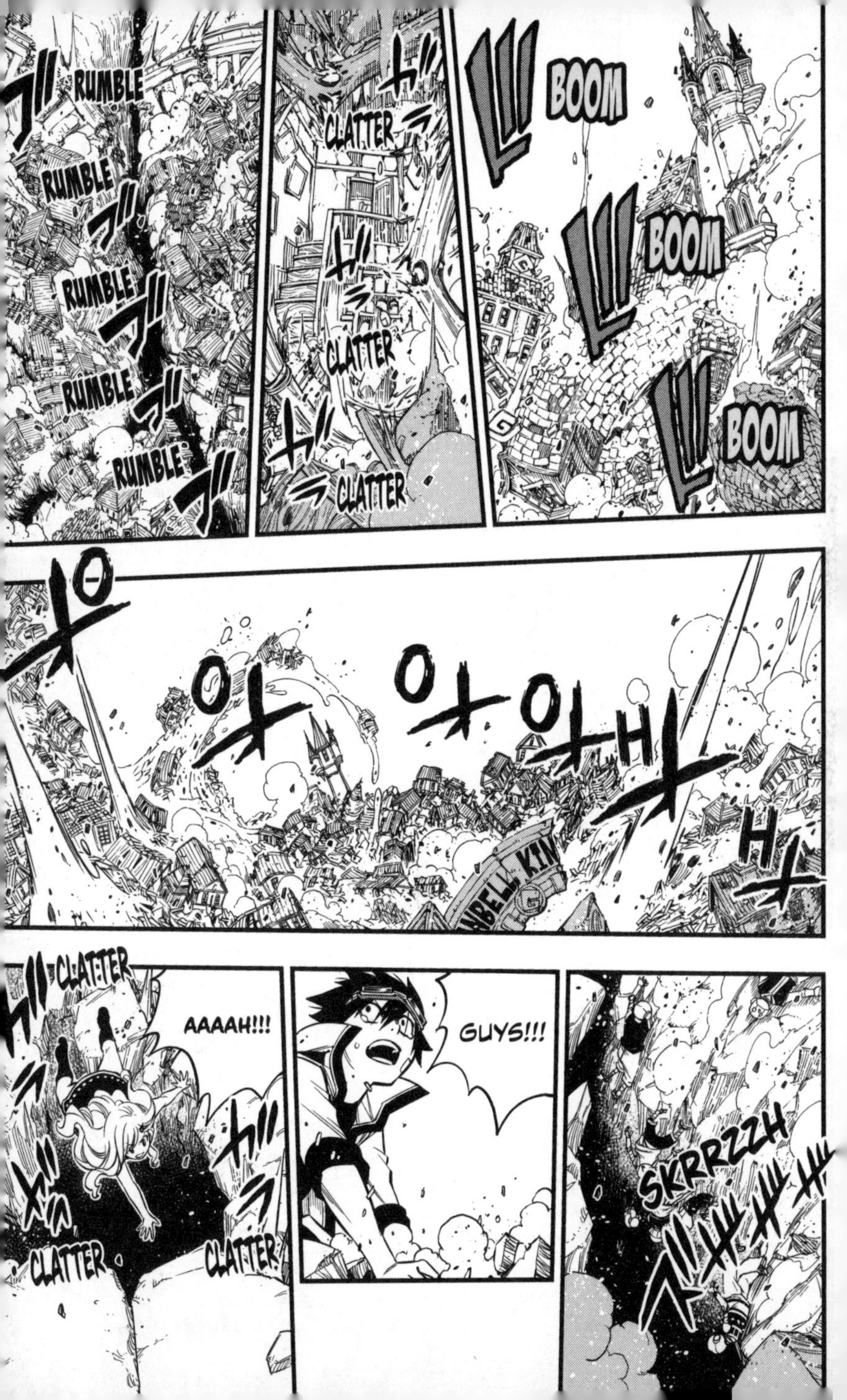
BOOM
BOOM
BOOM
CLATTER
CLATTER
CLATTER
RUMBLE
RUMBLE
RUMBLE
RUMBLE
RUMBLE
SKRRZZH
GUYS!!!
CLATTER
AAAAH!!!
CLATTER
CLATTER

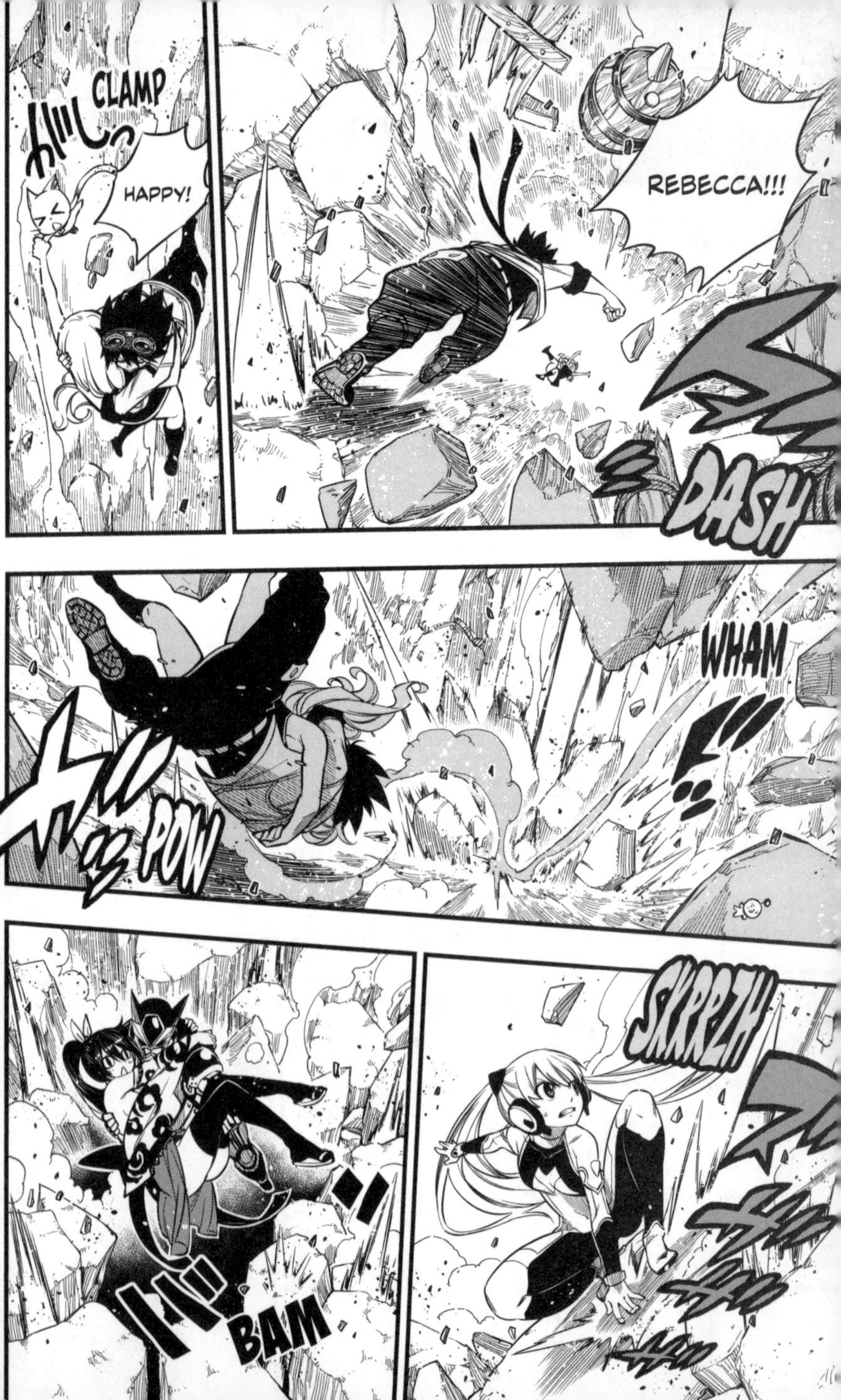
REBECCA!!!
DASH
CLAMP
HAPPY!
WHAM
POW
SKRRZH
BAM

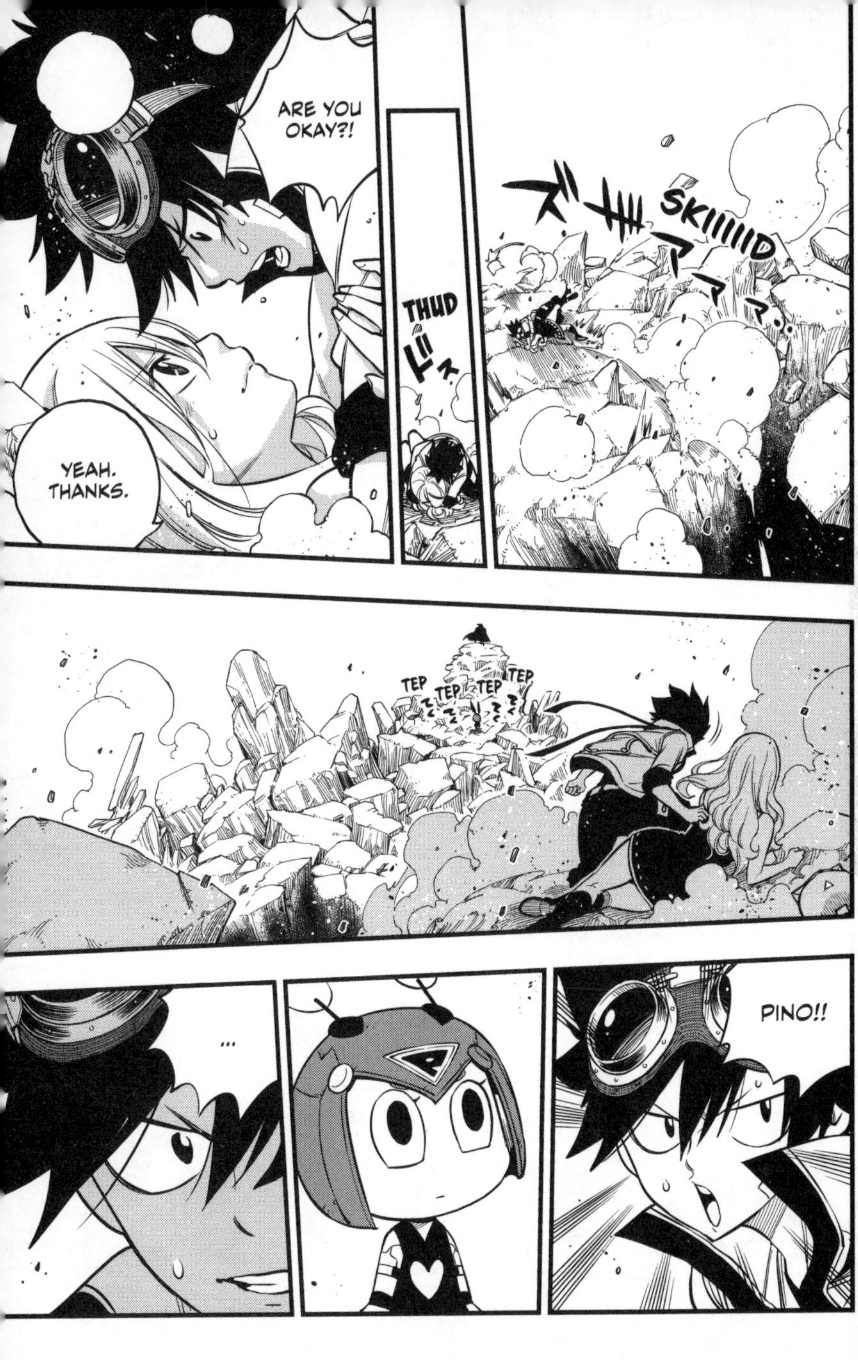
SKIIIIID
ズザァァァ…
THUD
ドッ
ARE YOU OKAY?!
YEAH. THANKS.
TEP
TEP
TEP
TEP
PINO!!
...

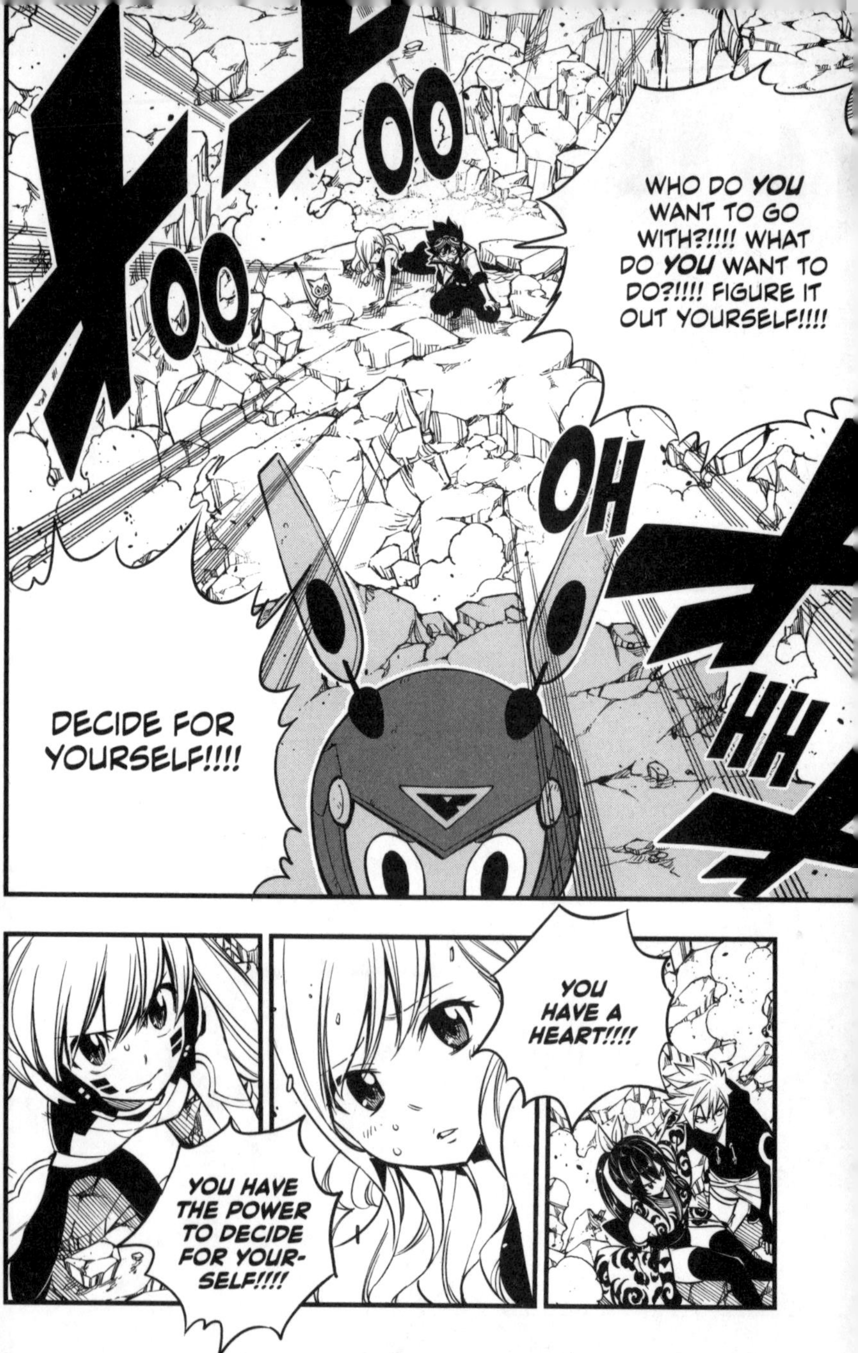
WHO DO YOU WANT TO GO WITH?!!!! WHAT DO YOU WANT TO DO?!!!! FIGURE IT OUT YOURSELF!!!!
DECIDE FOR YOURSELF!!!!
YOU HAVE A HEART!!!!
YOU HAVE THE POWER TO DECIDE FOR YOUR-SELF!!!!

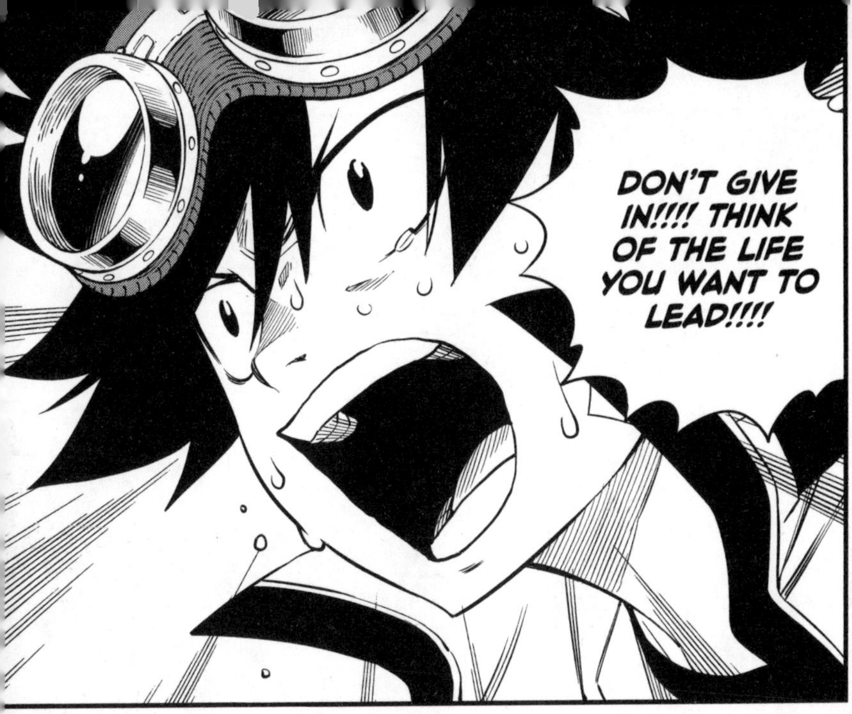
DON'T GIVE IN!!!! THINK OF THE LIFE YOU WANT TO LEAD!!!!

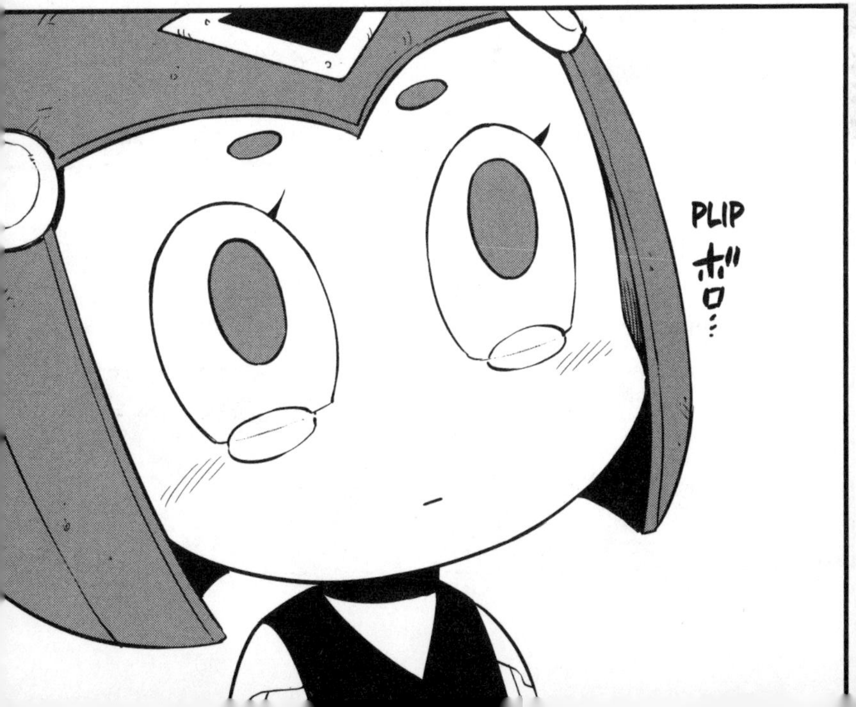
PLIP
ボロ…

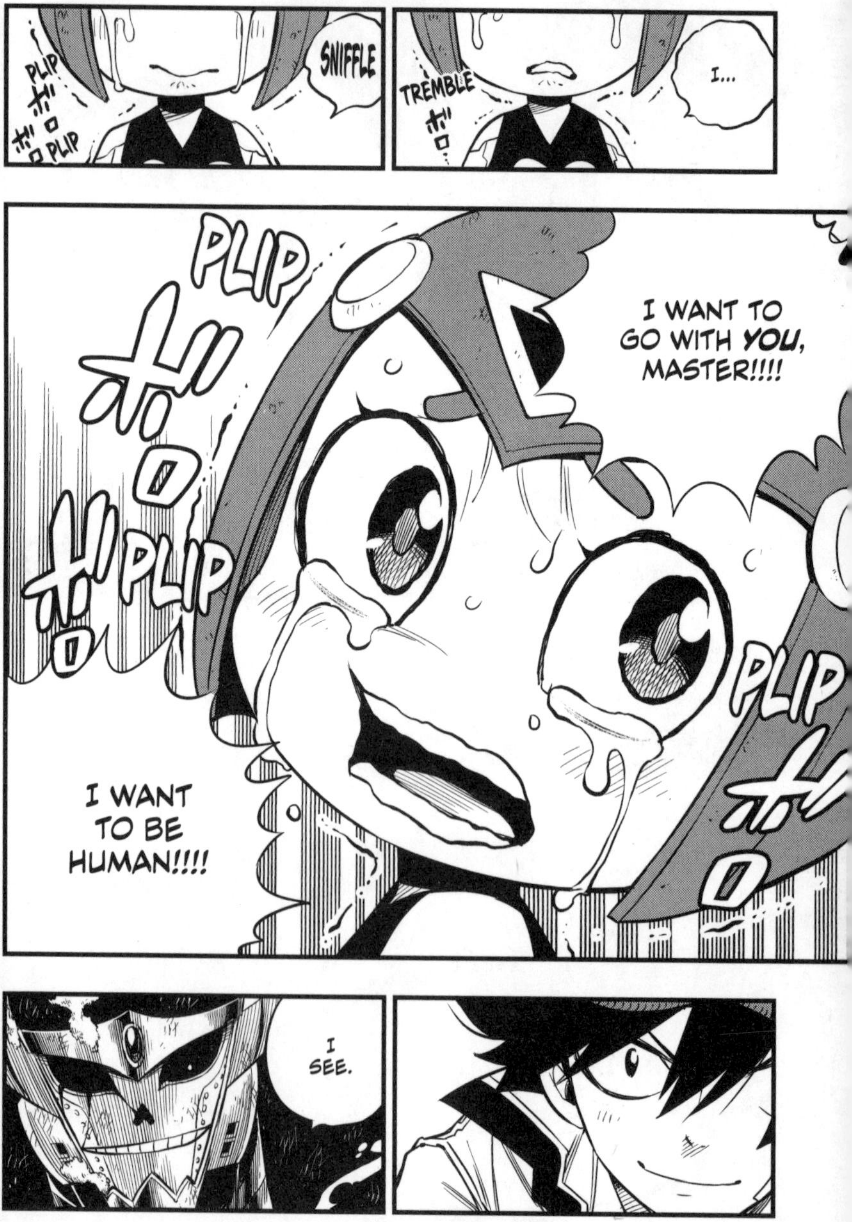
TREMBLE
I...
PLIP
PLIP
SNIFFLE
I WANT TO GO WITH YOU, MASTER!!!!
PLIP
PLIP
PLIP
I WANT TO BE HUMAN!!!!
I SEE.

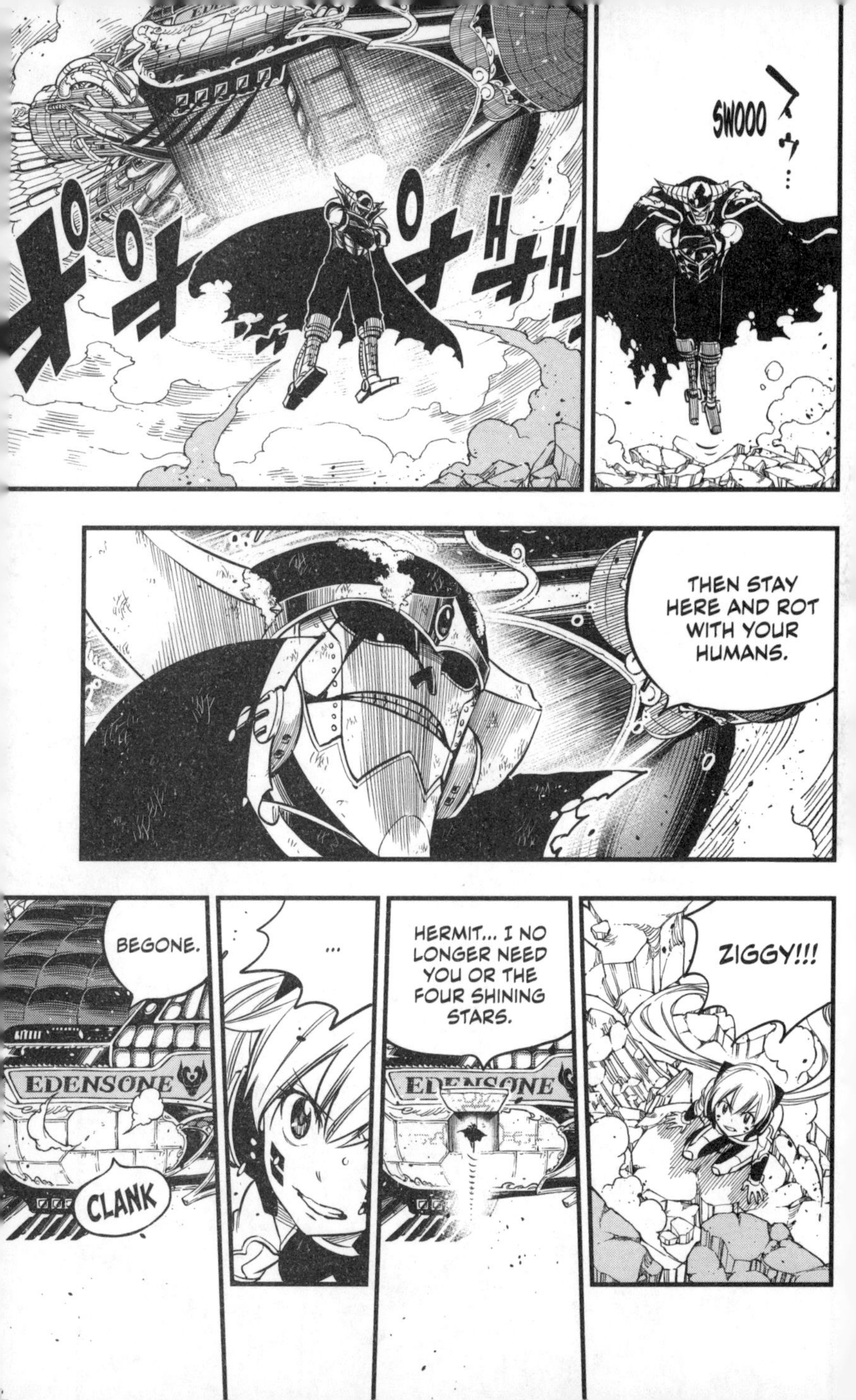
SWOOO
THEN STAY HERE AND ROT WITH YOUR HUMANS.
ZIGGY!!!
HERMIT... I NO LONGER NEED YOU OR THE FOUR SHINING STARS.
EDENSONE
...
BEGONE.
EDENSONE
CLANK

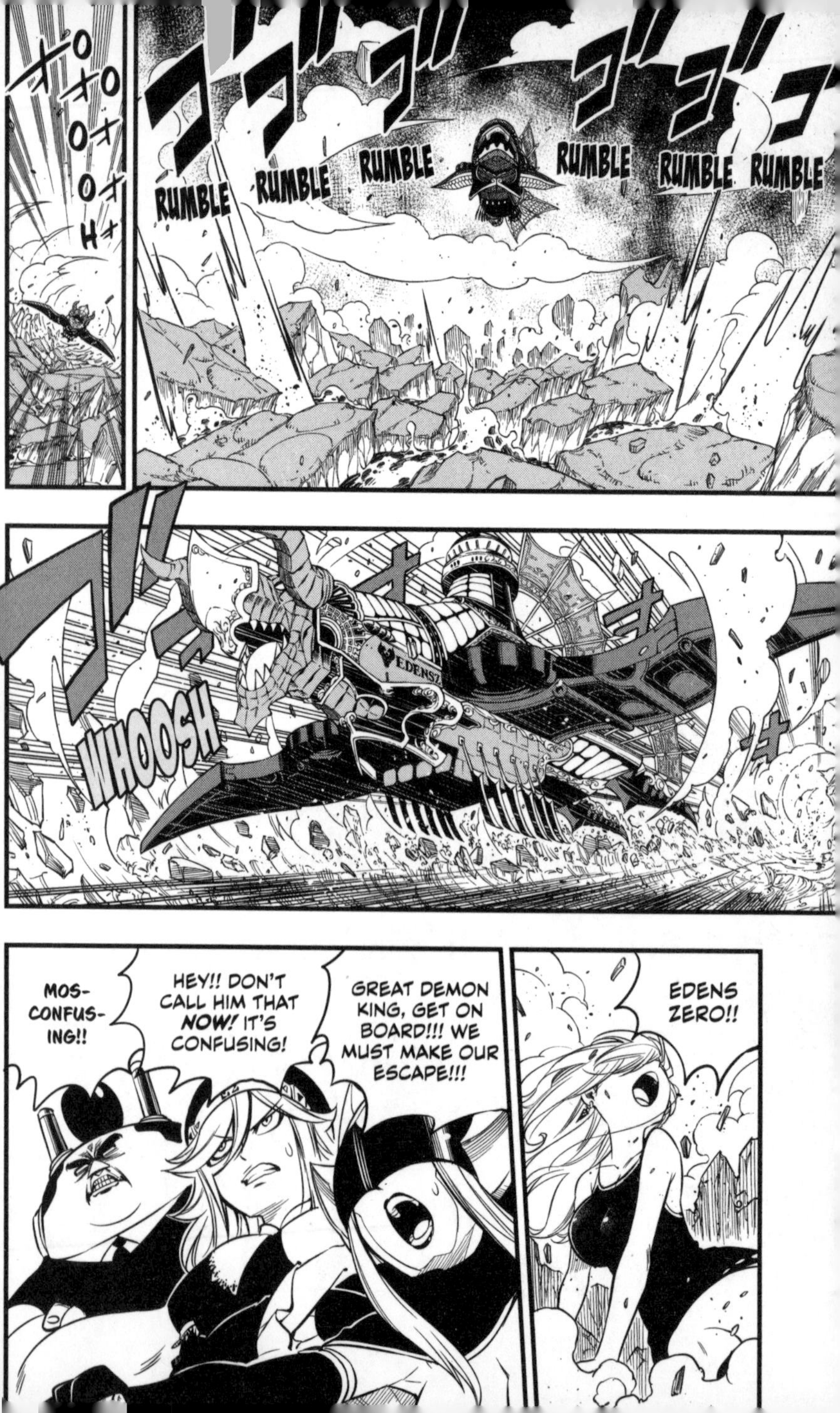

RUMBLE RUMBLE RUMBLE RUMBLE RUMBLE RUMBLE
OOOOOH
WHOOSH
EDENS ZERO!!
GREAT DEMON KING, GET ON BOARD!!! WE MUST MAKE OUR ESCAPE!!!
HEY!! DON'T CALL HIM THAT NOW! IT'S CONFUSING!
MOS-CONFUSING!!

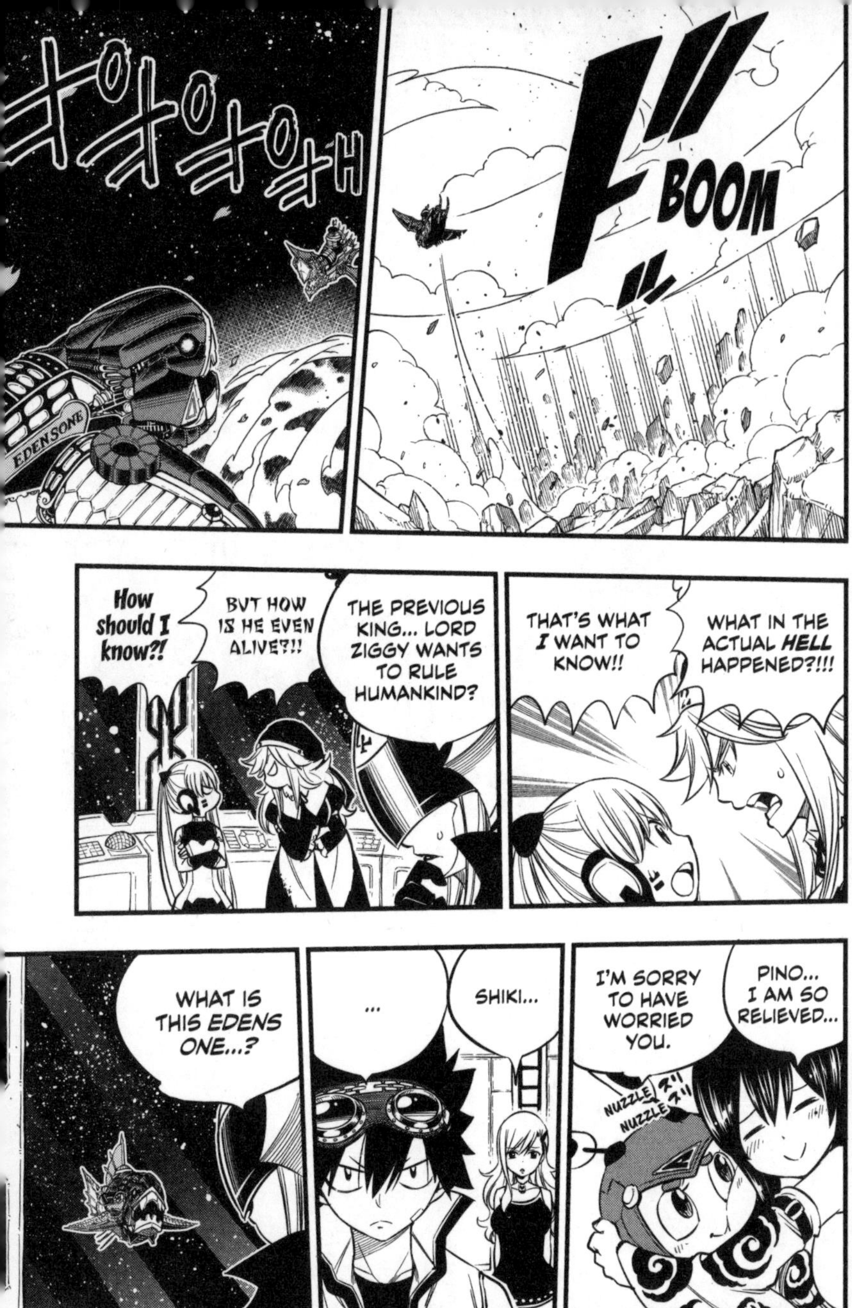
BOOM
OOOOH
EDENS ONE
WHAT IN THE ACTUAL HELL HAPPENED?!!!
THAT'S WHAT I WANT TO KNOW!!
THE PREVIOUS KING... LORD ZIGGY WANTS TO RULE HUMANKIND?
BUT HOW IS HE EVEN ALIVE?!!
How should I know?!
PINO... I AM SO RELIEVED...
I'M SORRY TO HAVE WORRIED YOU.
NUZZLE NUZZLE
SHIKI...
...
WHAT IS THIS EDENS ONE...?

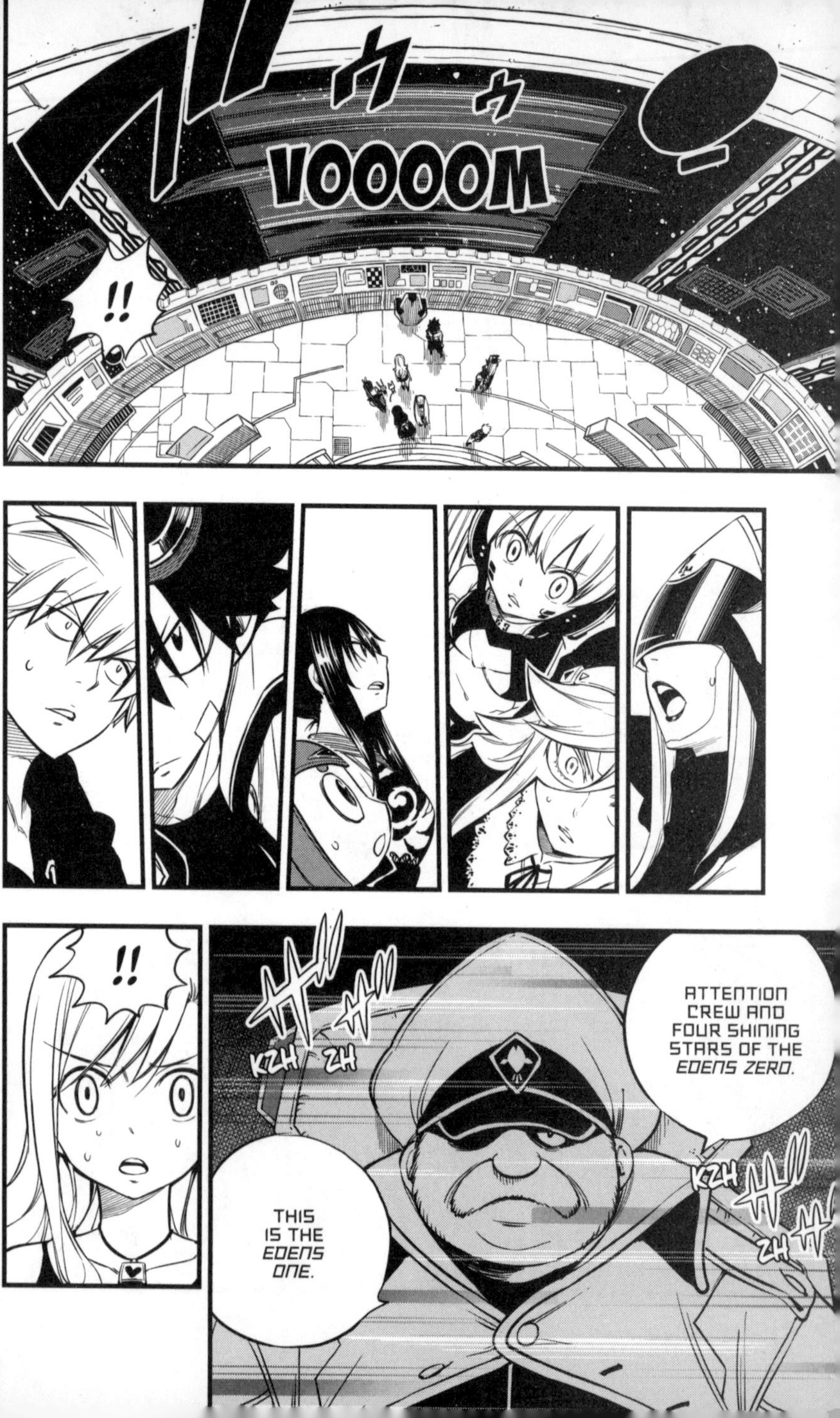
VOOOOM
!!
ATTENTION CREW AND FOUR SHINING STARS OF THE *EDENS ZERO*.
KZH ZH
KZH ZH
THIS IS THE *EDENS ONE*.
!!

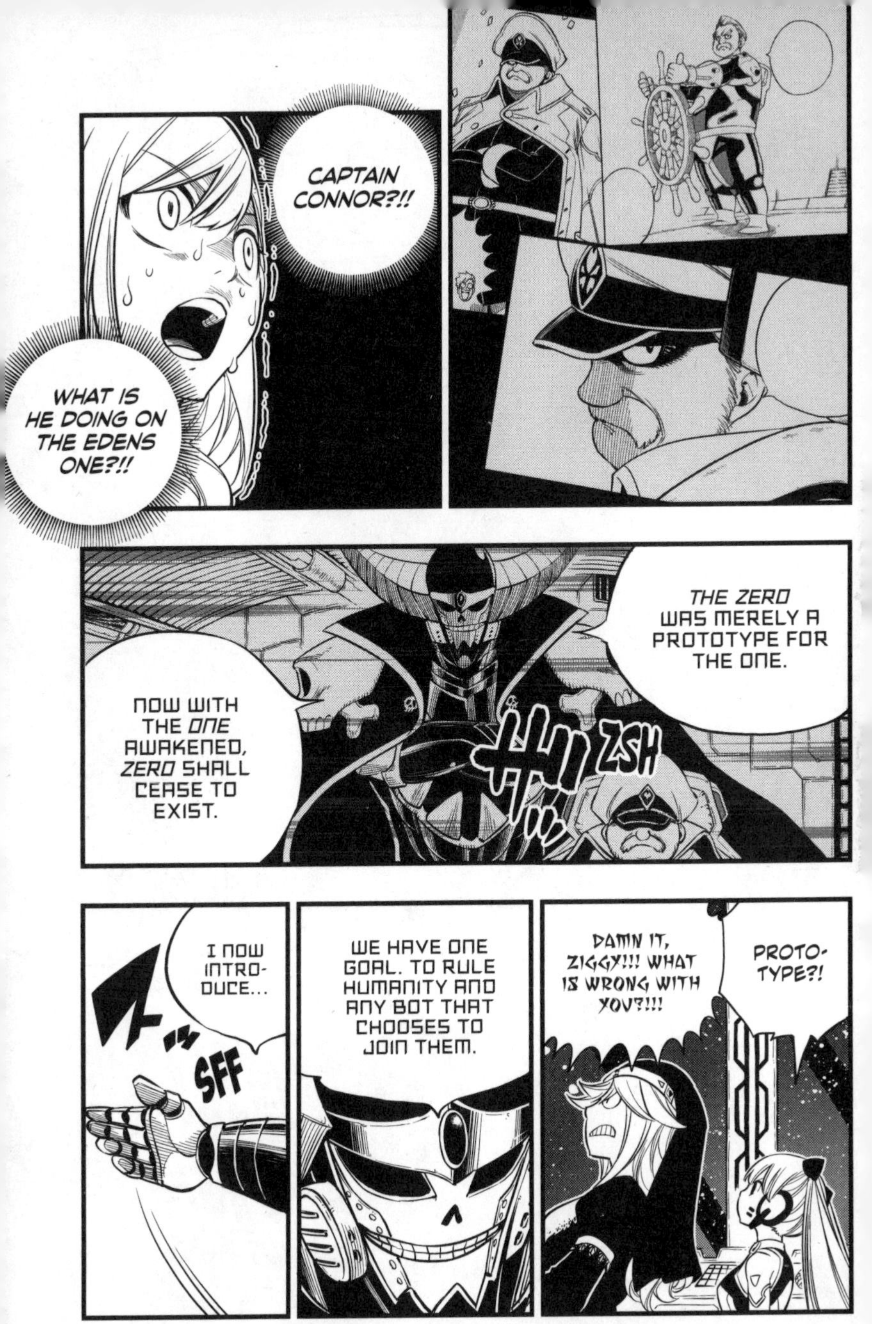
CAPTAIN CONNOR?!!
WHAT IS HE DOING ON THE EDENS ONE?!!
THE ZERO WAS MERELY A PROTOTYPE FOR THE ONE.
ZSH
NOW WITH THE ONE AWAKENED, ZERO SHALL CEASE TO EXIST.
PROTO-TYPE?!
DAMN IT, ZIGGY!!! WHAT IS WRONG WITH YOU?!!!
WE HAVE ONE GOAL. TO RULE HUMANITY AND ANY BOT THAT CHOOSES TO JOIN THEM.
I NOW INTRO-DUCE...
SFF

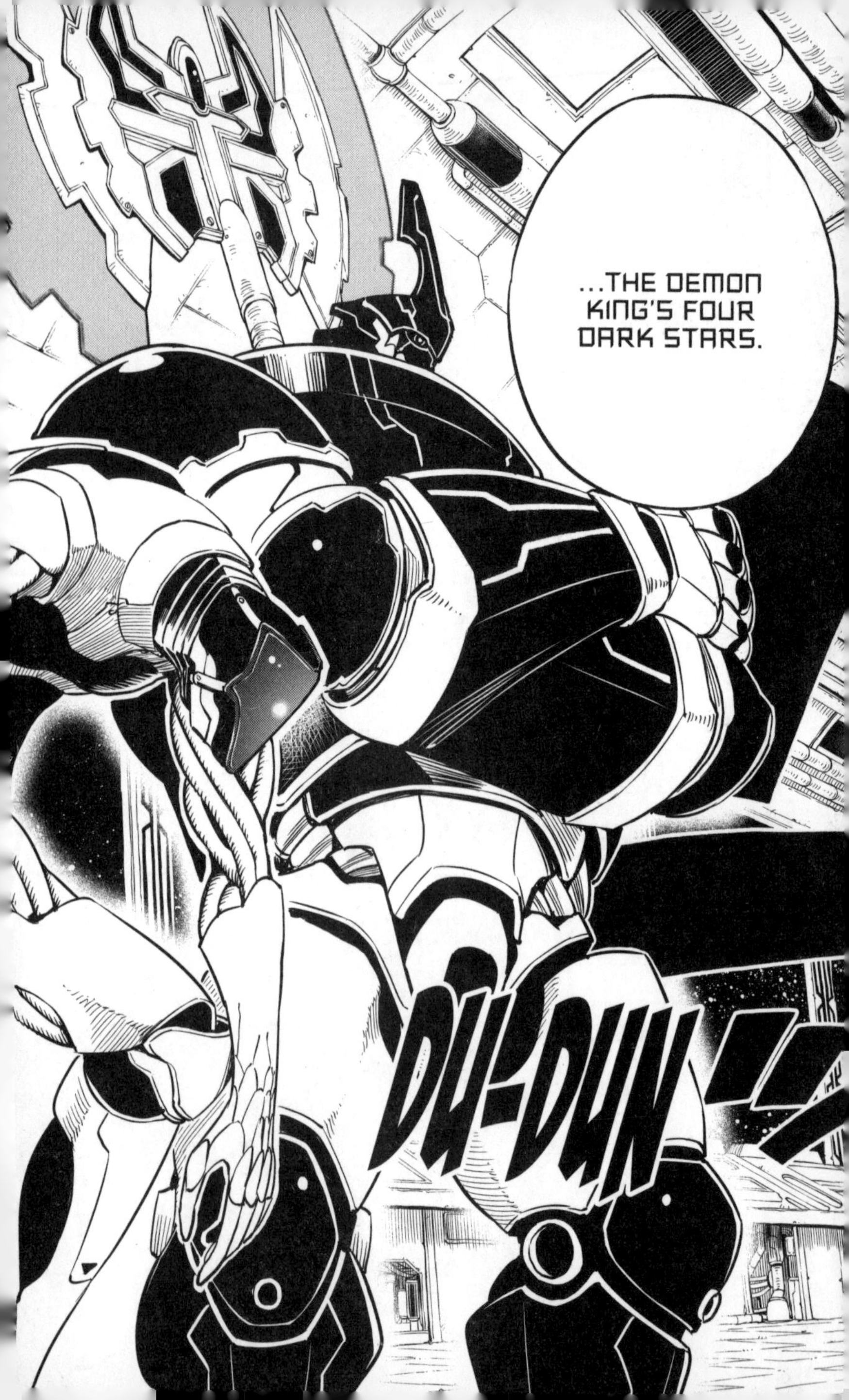
...THE DEMON KING'S FOUR DARK STARS.
DU-DUN

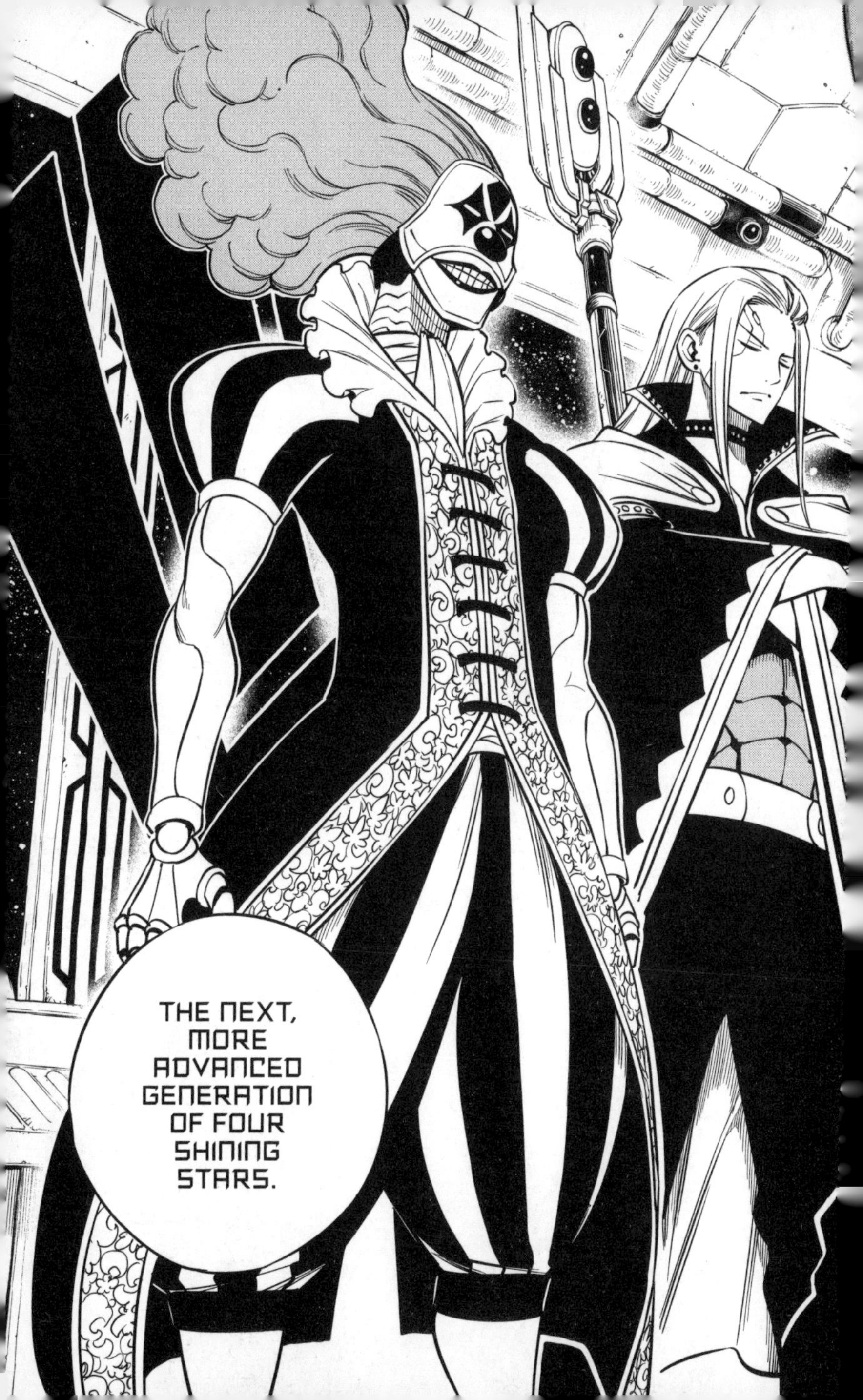
THE NEXT, MORE ADVANCED GENERATION OF FOUR SHINING STARS.

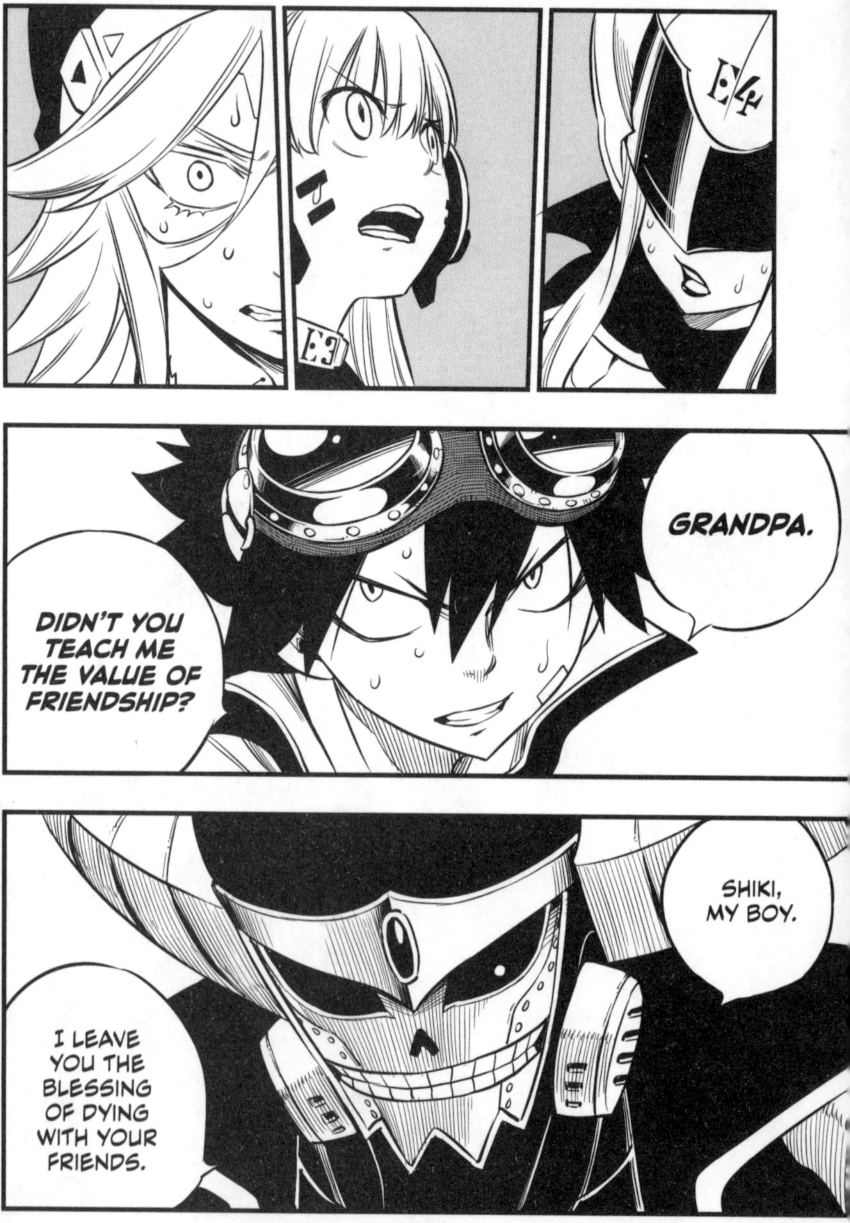
GRANDPA.
DIDN'T YOU TEACH ME THE VALUE OF FRIENDSHIP?
SHIKI, MY BOY.
I LEAVE YOU THE BLESSING OF DYING WITH YOUR FRIENDS.

EDENS ZERO

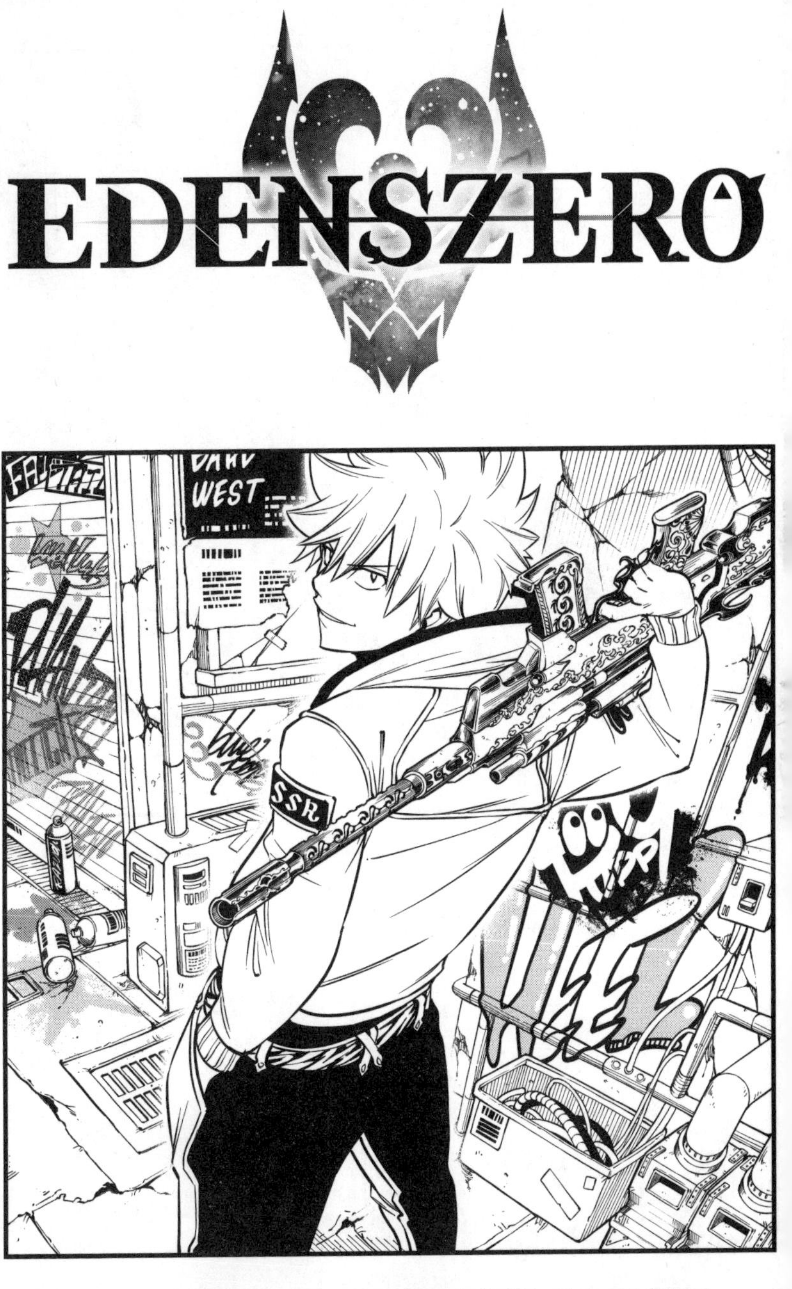
WEST
SSR

CHAPTER 103: CLASH OF THE COSMOS

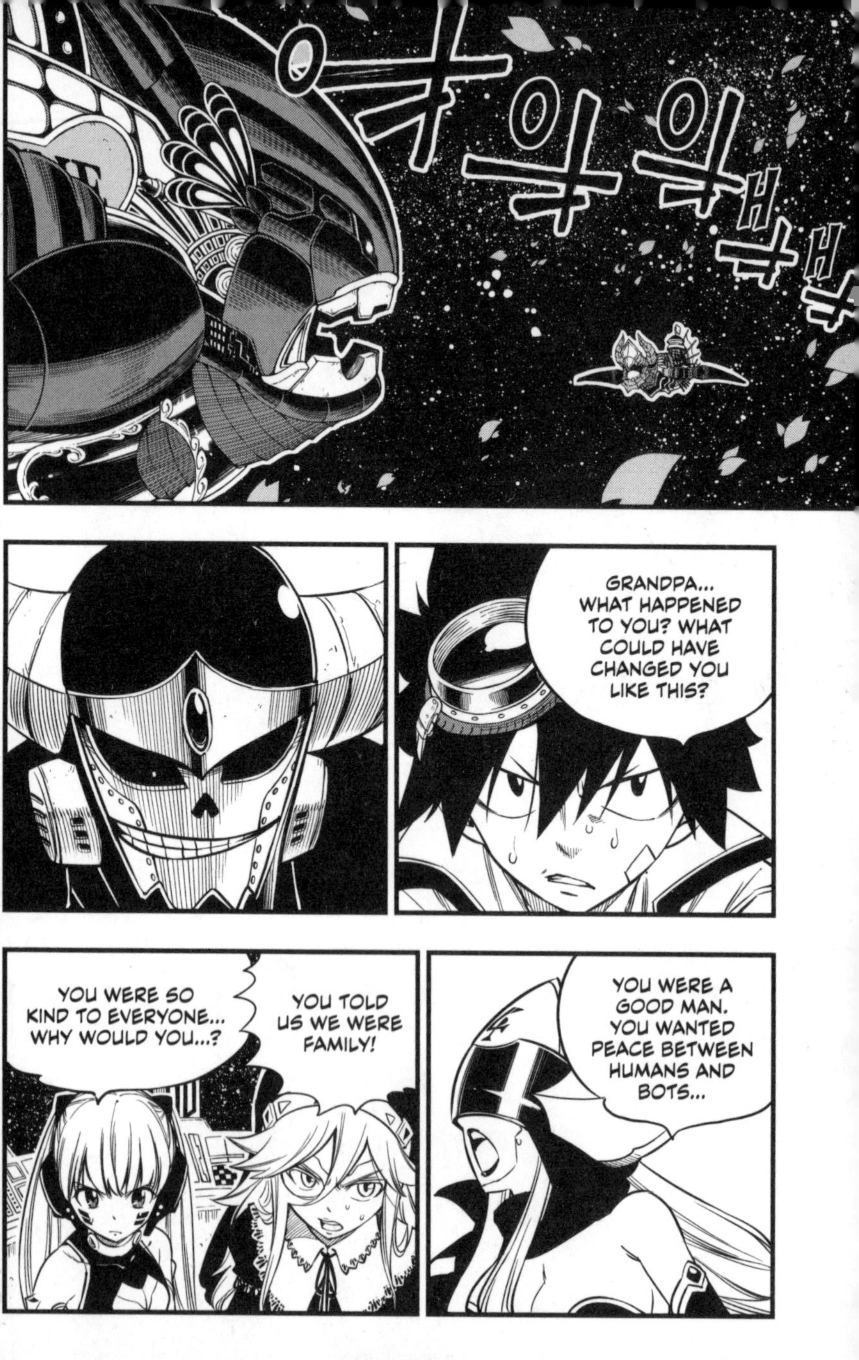
GRANDPA... WHAT HAPPENED TO YOU? WHAT COULD HAVE CHANGED YOU LIKE THIS?
YOU WERE A GOOD MAN. YOU WANTED PEACE BETWEEN HUMANS AND BOTS...
YOU TOLD US WE WERE FAMILY!
YOU WERE SO KIND TO EVERYONE... WHY WOULD YOU...?

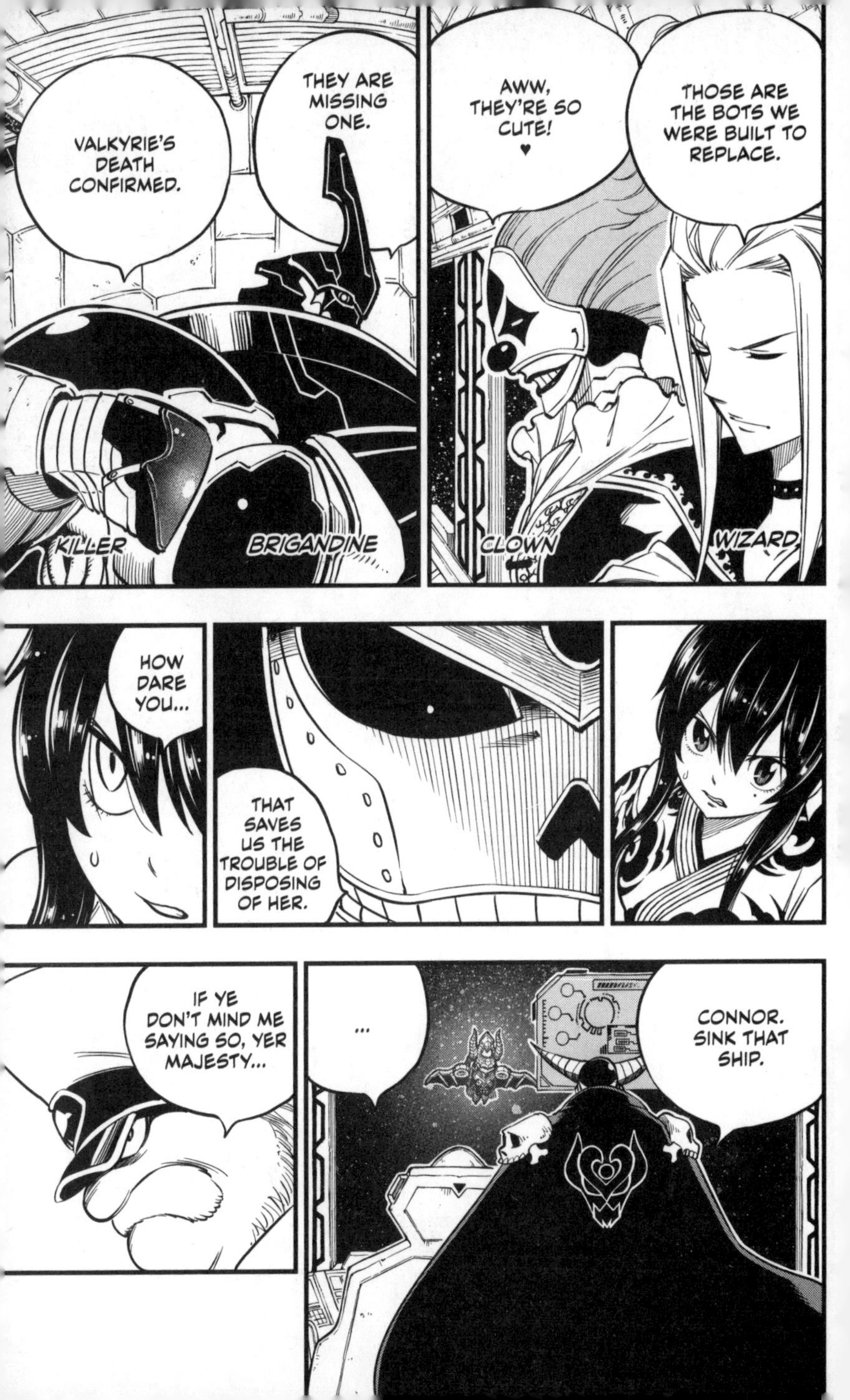

THOSE ARE THE BOTS WE WERE BUILT TO REPLACE.
AWW, THEY'RE SO CUTE! ♥
WIZARD
CLOWN
THEY ARE MISSING ONE.
VALKYRIE'S DEATH CONFIRMED.
BRIGANDINE
KILLER
THAT SAVES US THE TROUBLE OF DISPOSING OF HER.
HOW DARE YOU...
CONNOR. SINK THAT SHIP.
...
IF YE DON'T MIND ME SAYING SO, YER MAJESTY...

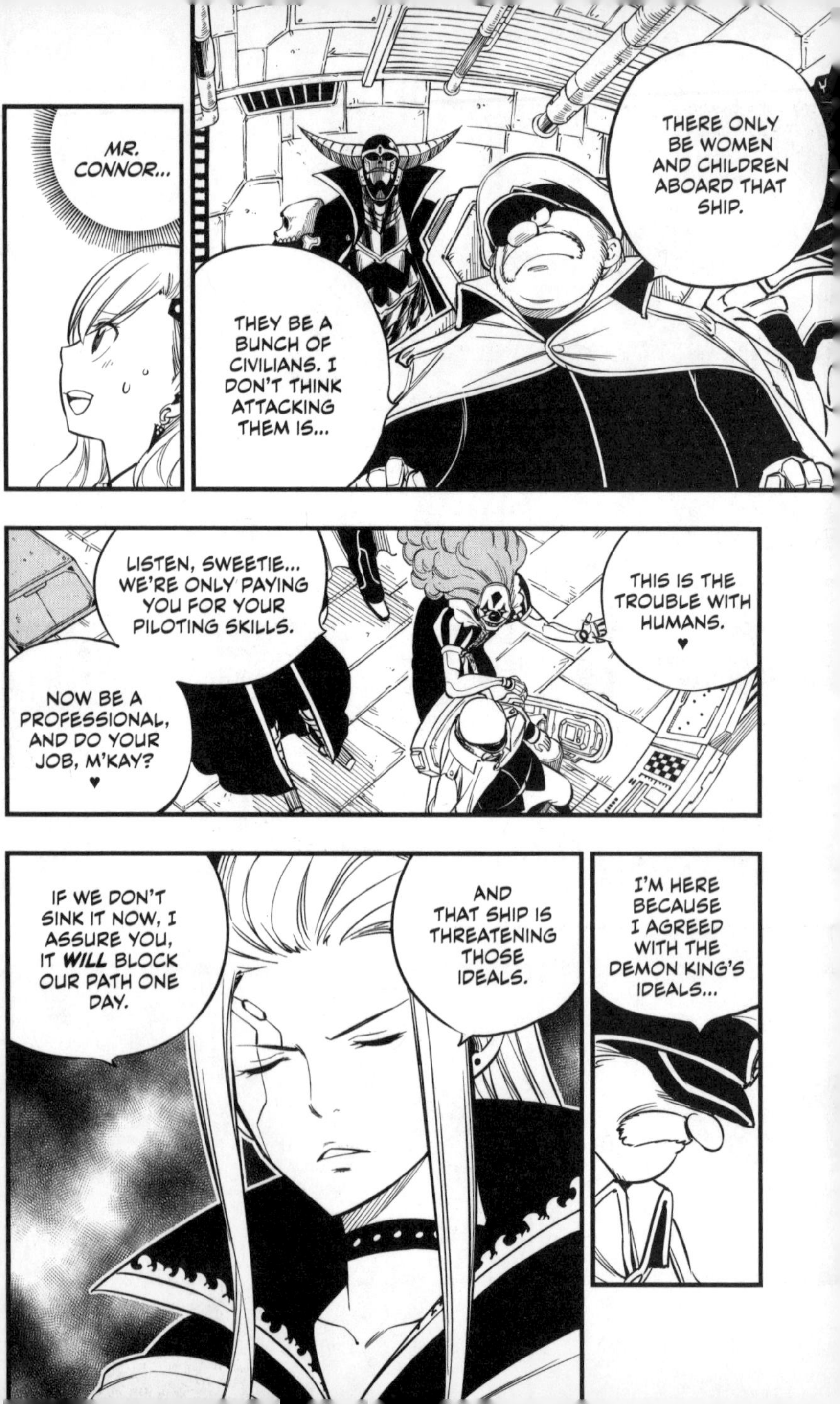
THERE ONLY BE WOMEN AND CHILDREN ABOARD THAT SHIP.
THEY BE A BUNCH OF CIVILIANS. I DON'T THINK ATTACKING THEM IS...
MR. CONNOR...
THIS IS THE TROUBLE WITH HUMANS. ♥
LISTEN, SWEETIE... WE'RE ONLY PAYING YOU FOR YOUR PILOTING SKILLS.
NOW BE A PROFESSIONAL, AND DO YOUR JOB, M'KAY? ♥
I'M HERE BECAUSE I AGREED WITH THE DEMON KING'S IDEALS...
AND THAT SHIP IS THREATENING THOSE IDEALS.
IF WE DON'T SINK IT NOW, I ASSURE YOU, IT ***WILL*** BLOCK OUR PATH ONE DAY.

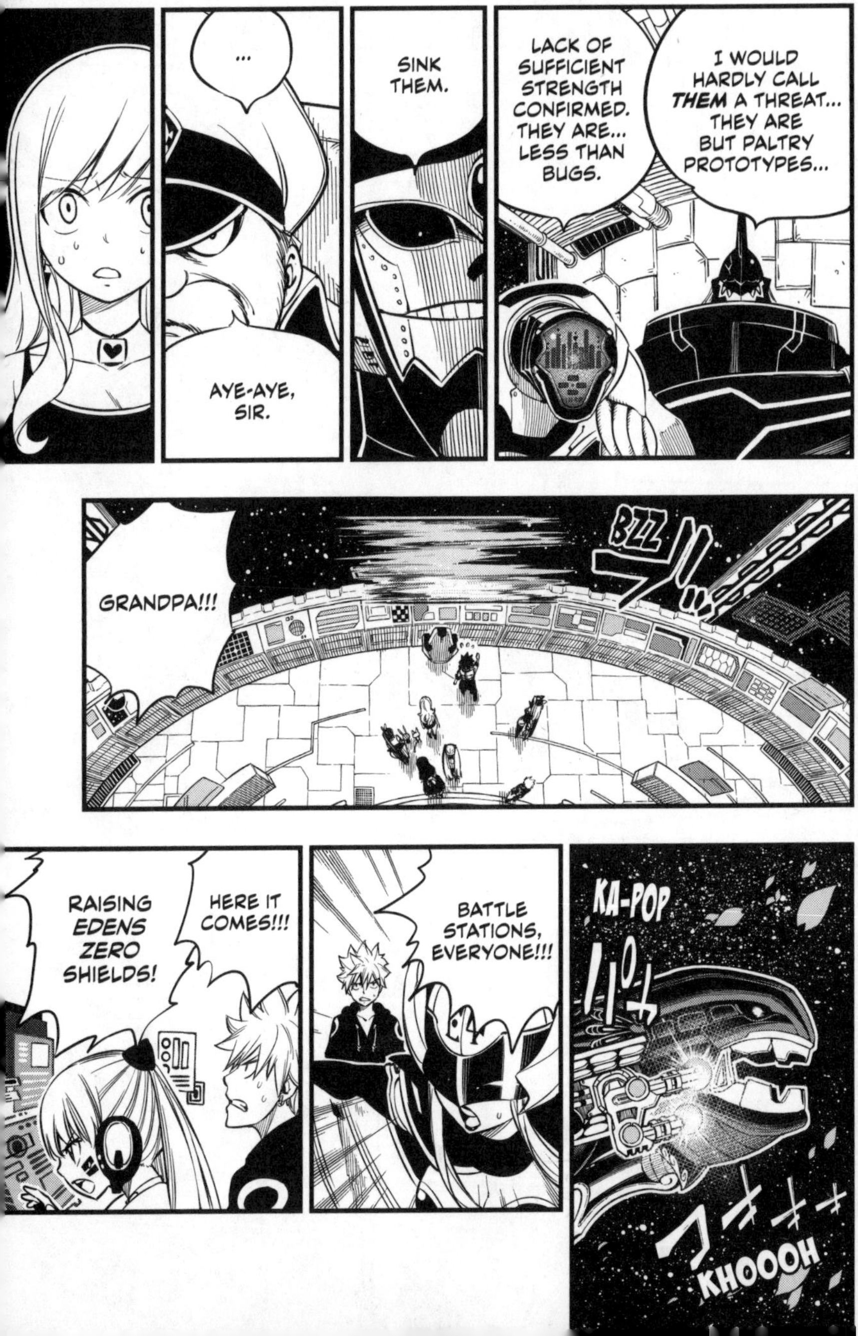
I WOULD HARDLY CALL THEM A THREAT... THEY ARE BUT PALTRY PROTOTYPES...
LACK OF SUFFICIENT STRENGTH CONFIRMED. THEY ARE... LESS THAN BUGS.
SINK THEM.
...
AYE-AYE, SIR.
BZZ
GRANDPA!!!
KA-POP
KHOOOH
BATTLE STATIONS, EVERYONE!!!
HERE IT COMES!!!
RAISING EDENS ZERO SHIELDS!

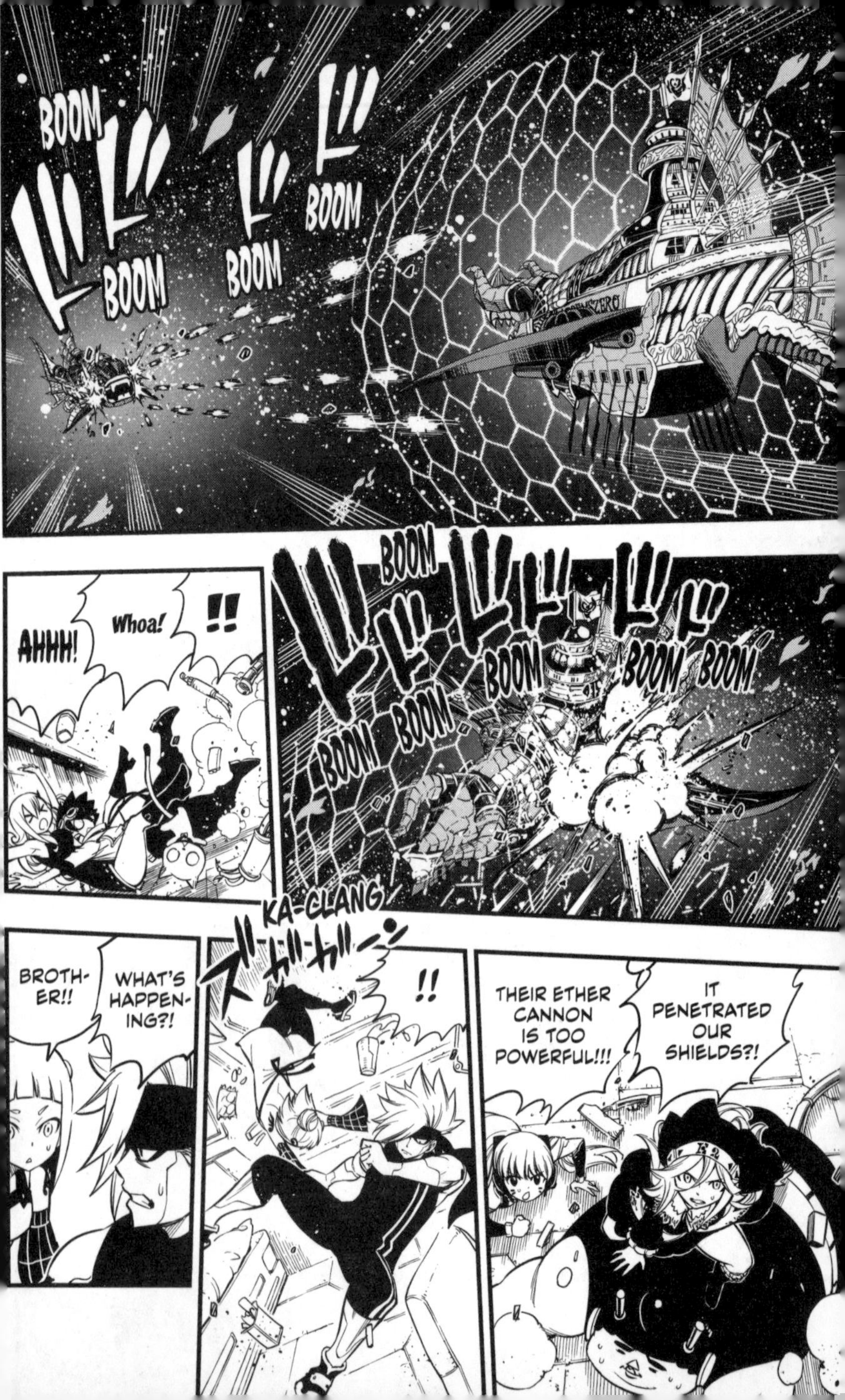
BOOM
BOOM
BOOM
BOOM
BOOM
BOOM
BOOM
BOOM
BOOM
BOOM
!!
Whoa!
AHHH!
IT PENETRATED OUR SHIELDS?!
THEIR ETHER CANNON IS TOO POWERFUL!!!
KA-CLANG
!!
WHAT'S HAPPEN-ING?!
BROTH-ER!!

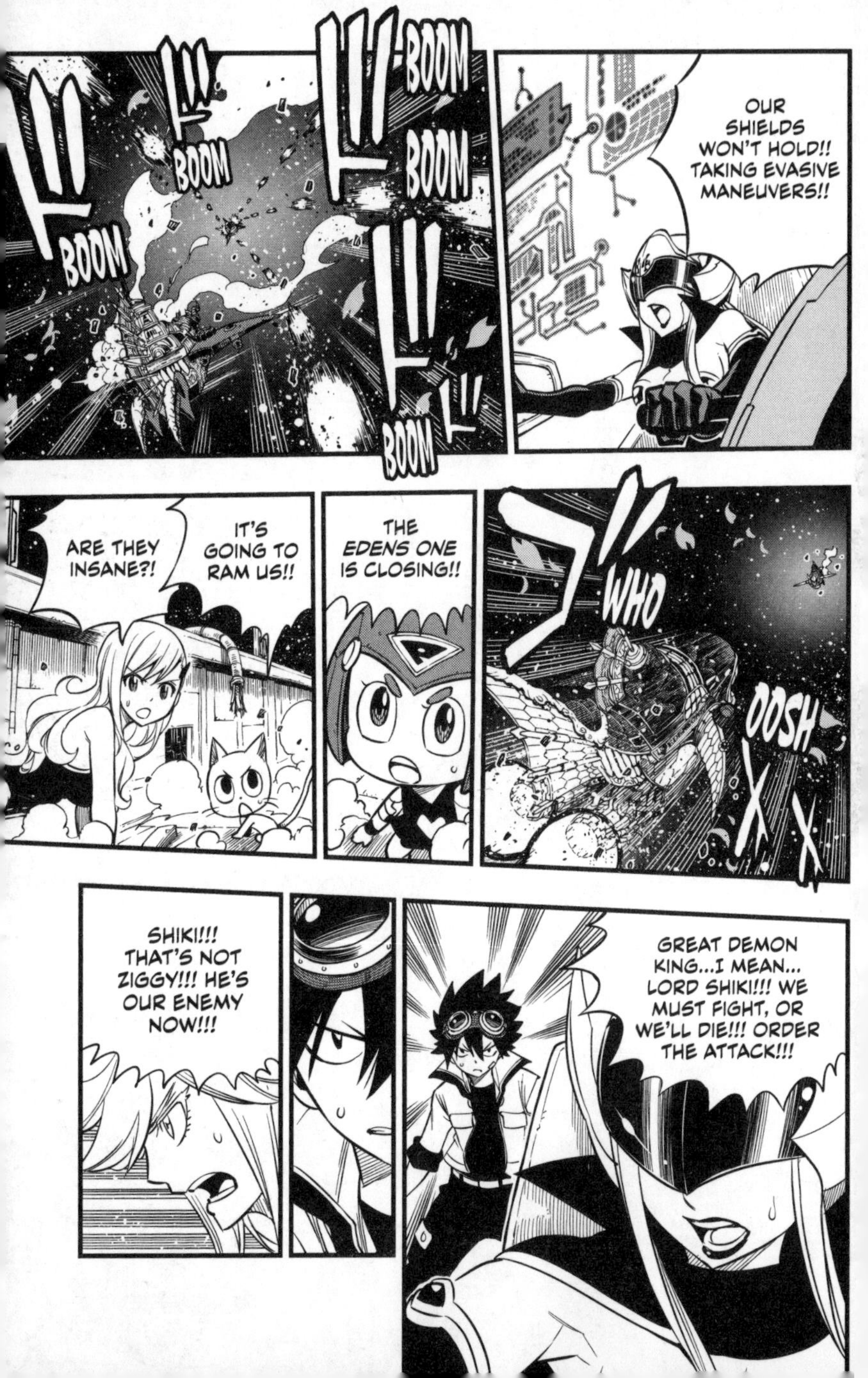
OUR SHIELDS WON'T HOLD!! TAKING EVASIVE MANEUVERS!!
BOOM BOOM
BOOM
BOOM
BOOM
BOOM
WHOOSH
THE *EDENS ONE* IS CLOSING!!
IT'S GOING TO RAM US!!
ARE THEY INSANE?!
GREAT DEMON KING...I MEAN... LORD SHIKI!!! WE MUST FIGHT, OR WE'LL DIE!!! ORDER THE ATTACK!!!
SHIKI!!! THAT'S NOT ZIGGY!!! HE'S OUR ENEMY NOW!!!

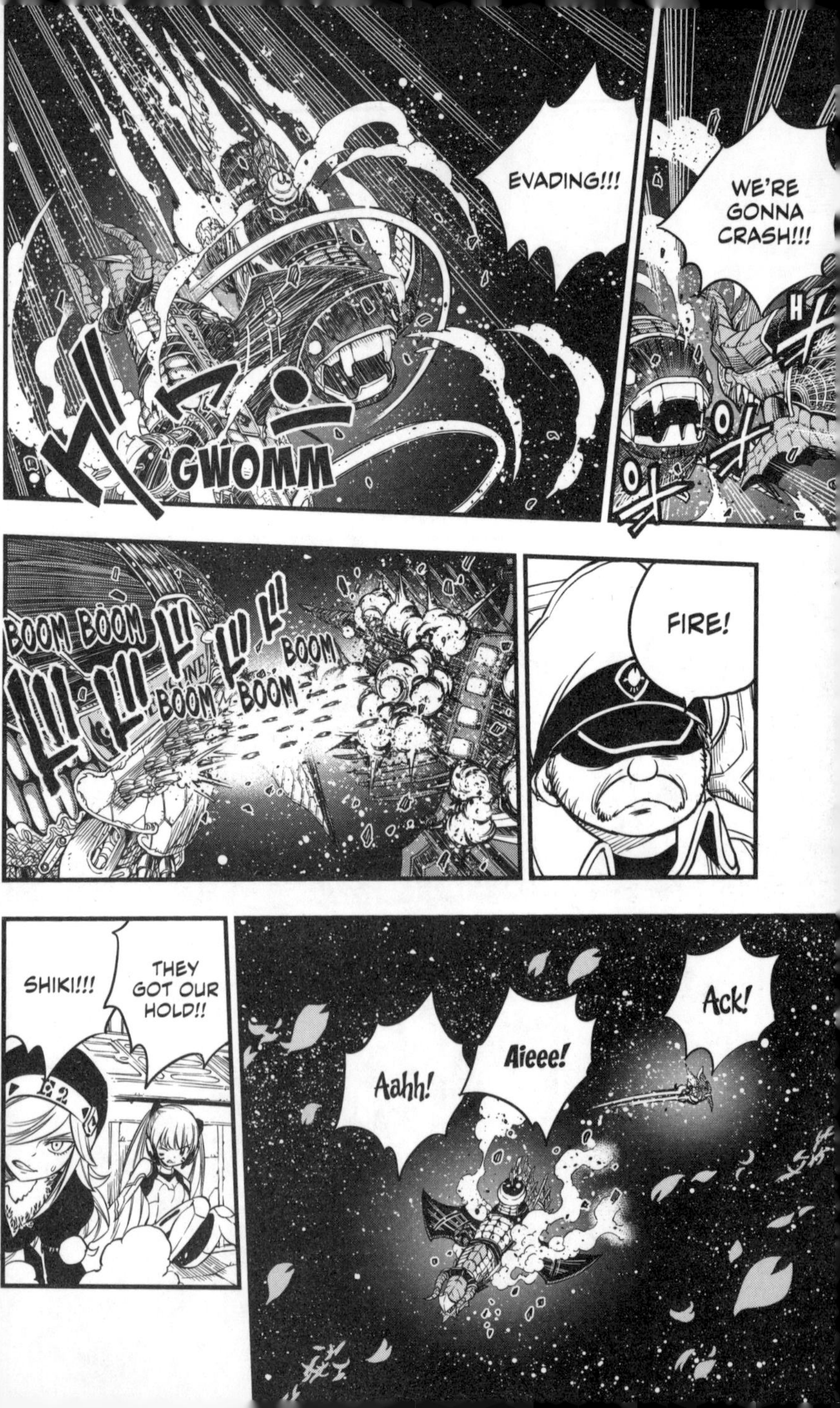

WE'RE GONNA CRASH!!!
EVADING!!!
GWOMM
FIRE!
BOOM
BOOM BOOM
BOOM BOOM
Ack!
Aieee!
Aahh!
THEY GOT OUR HOLD!!
SHIKI!!!

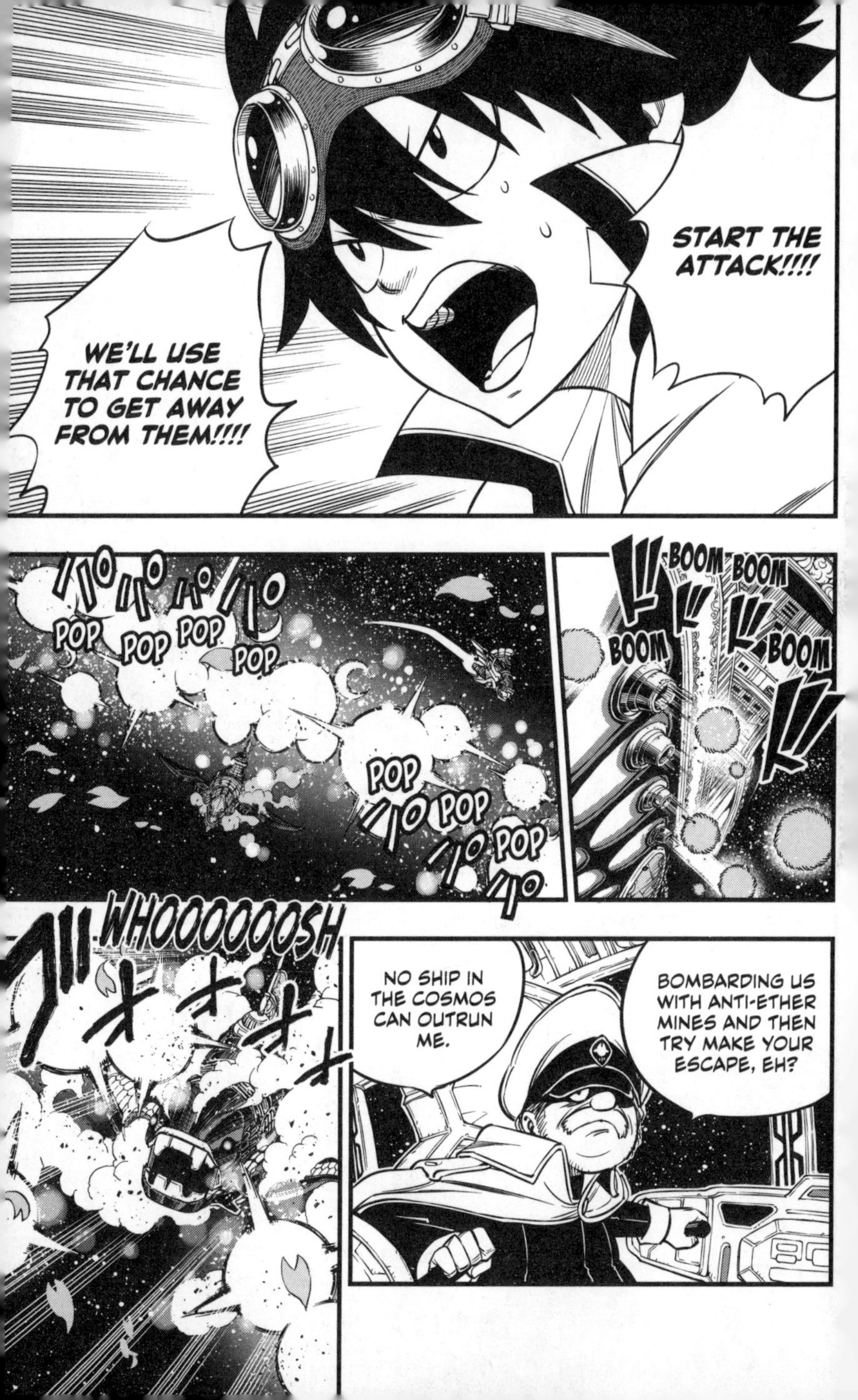
START THE ATTACK!!!!
WE'LL USE THAT CHANCE TO GET AWAY FROM THEM!!!!
BOOM BOOM BOOM BOOM
POP POP POP POP POP POP POP
BOMBARDING US WITH ANTI-ETHER MINES AND THEN TRY MAKE YOUR ESCAPE, EH?
NO SHIP IN THE COSMOS CAN OUTRUN ME.
WHOOOOOOSH

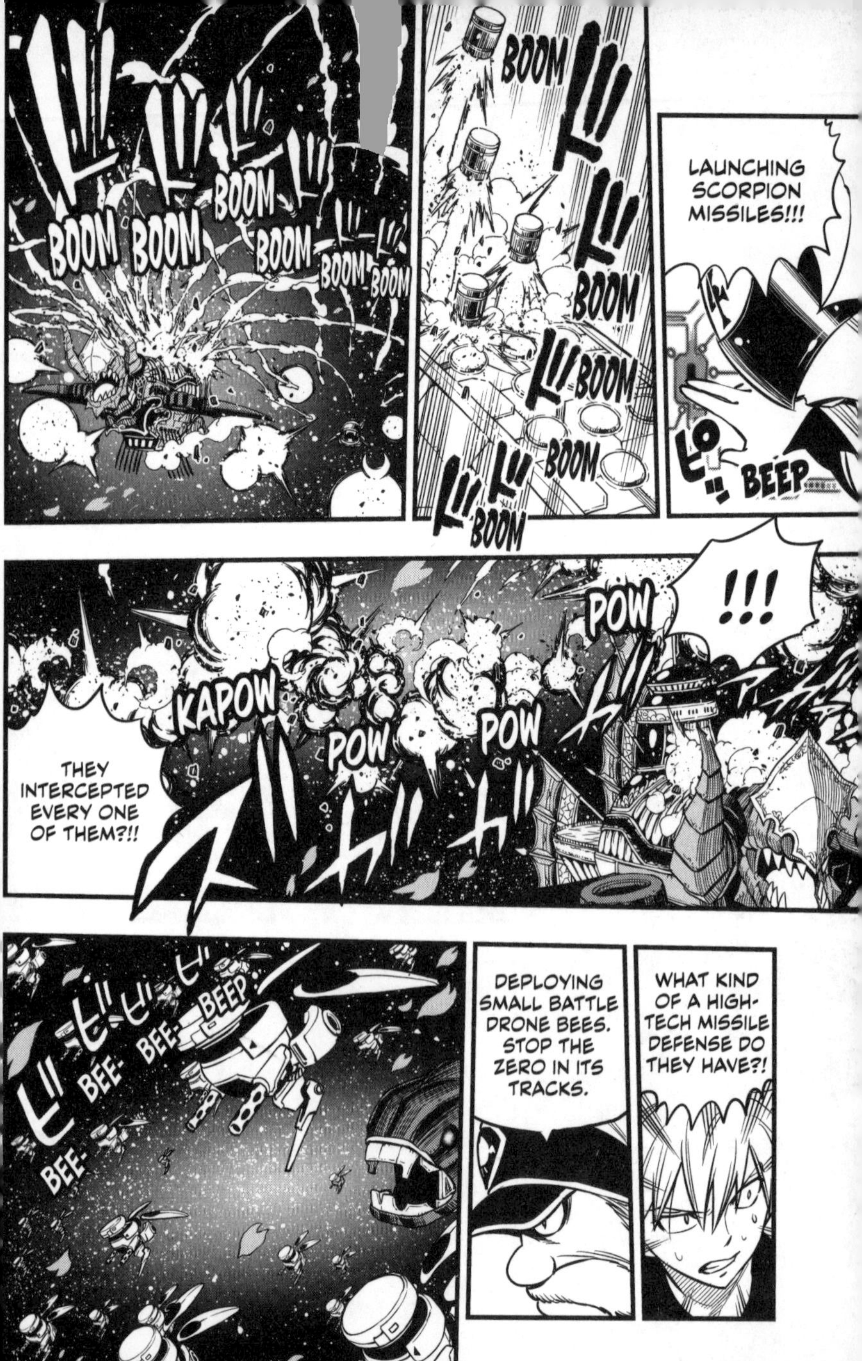
LAUNCHING SCORPION MISSILES!!!
BEEP
BOOM
BOOM
BOOM
BOOM
BOOM
BOOM
BOOM
BOOM
BOOM
BOOM
BOOM
BOOM
BOOM
!!!
POW
POW
POW
KAPOW
THEY INTERCEPTED EVERY ONE OF THEM?!!
WHAT KIND OF A HIGH-TECH MISSILE DEFENSE DO THEY HAVE?!
DEPLOYING SMALL BATTLE DRONE BEES. STOP THE ZERO IN ITS TRACKS.
BEEP
BEE-
BEE-
BEE-
BEE-

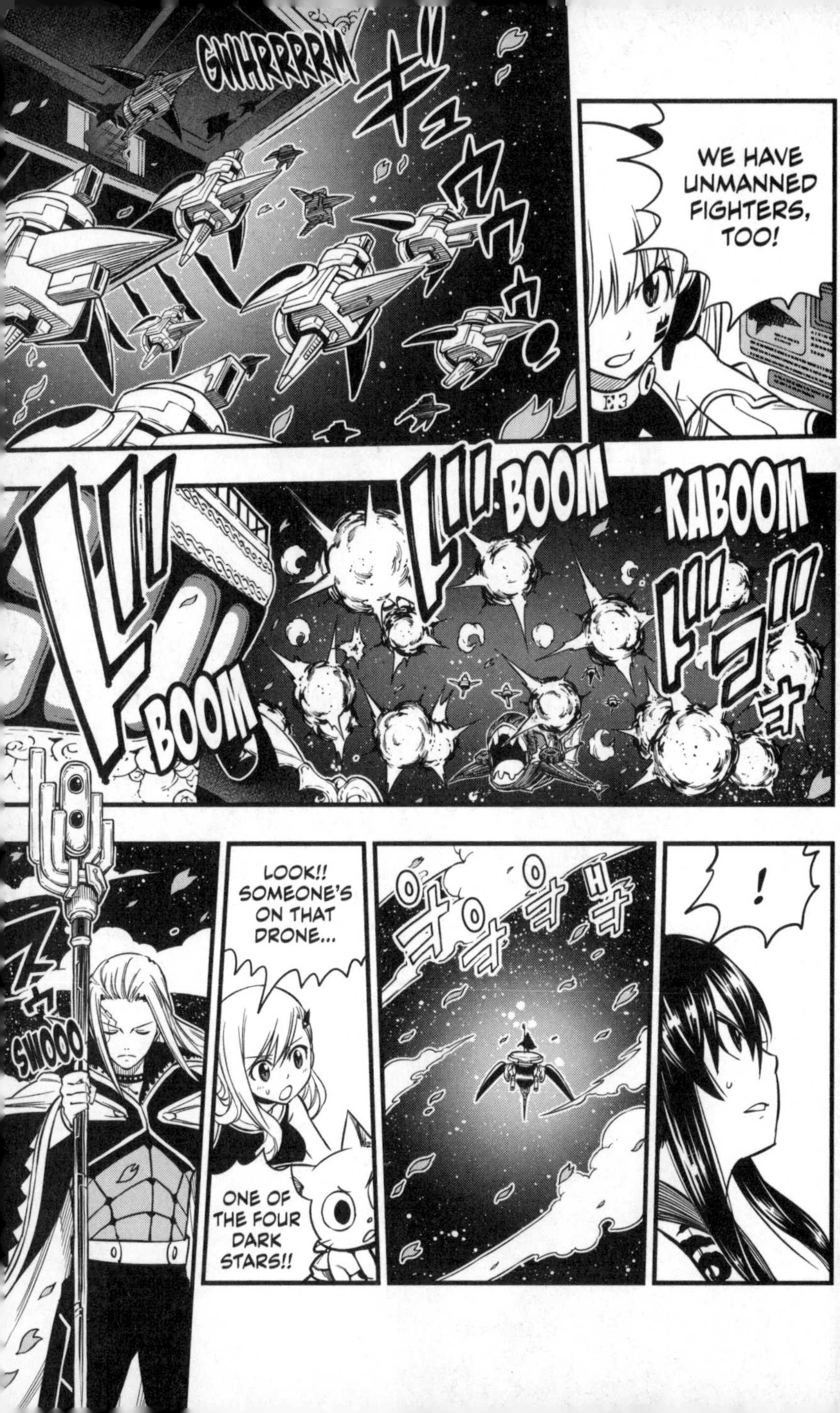
WE HAVE UNMANNED FIGHTERS, TOO!
GWHRRRRM
KABOOM
BOOM
BOOM
!
LOOK!! SOMEONE'S ON THAT DRONE...
ONE OF THE FOUR DARK STARS!!
SWOOO

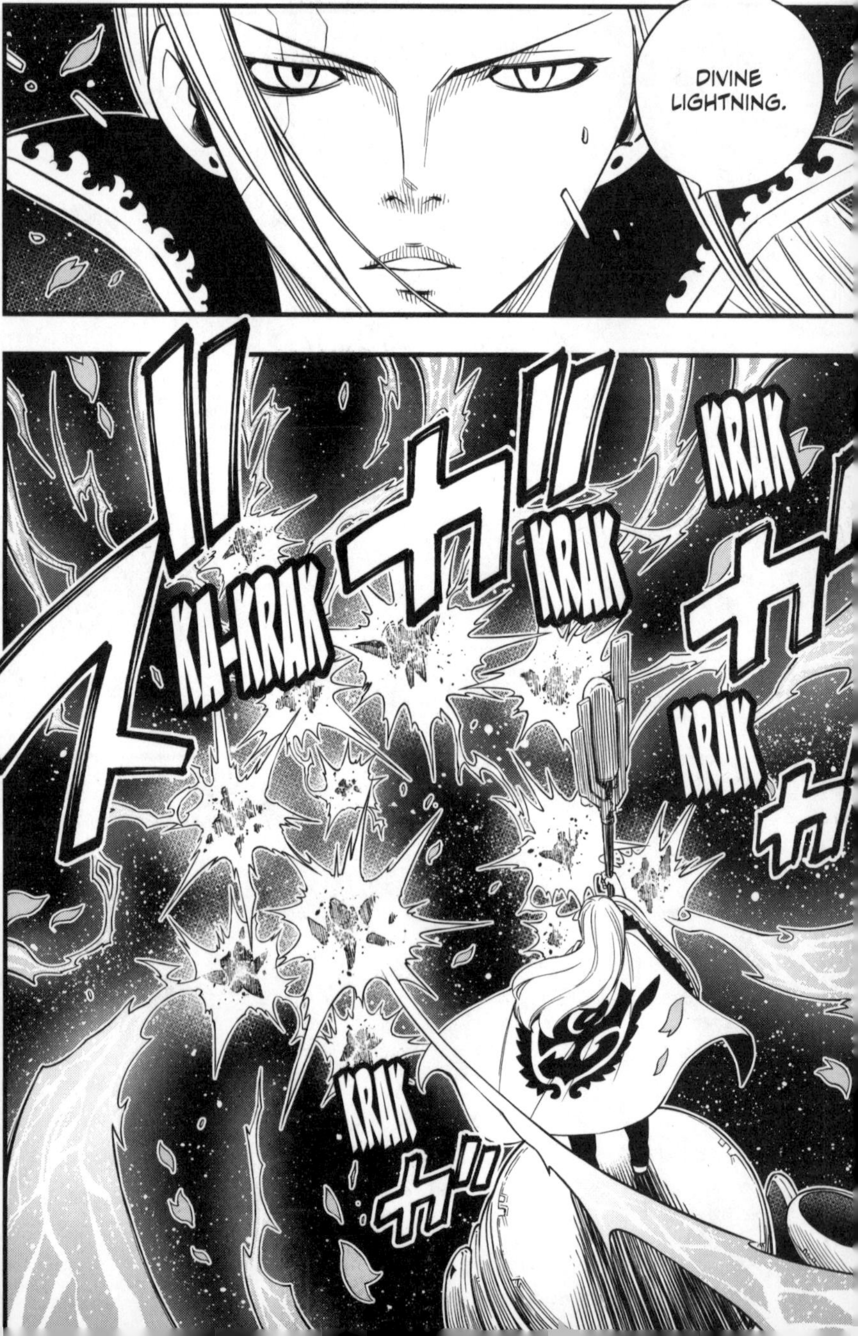
DIVINE LIGHTNING.
KRAK
KRAK
KA-KRAK
KRAK
KRAK

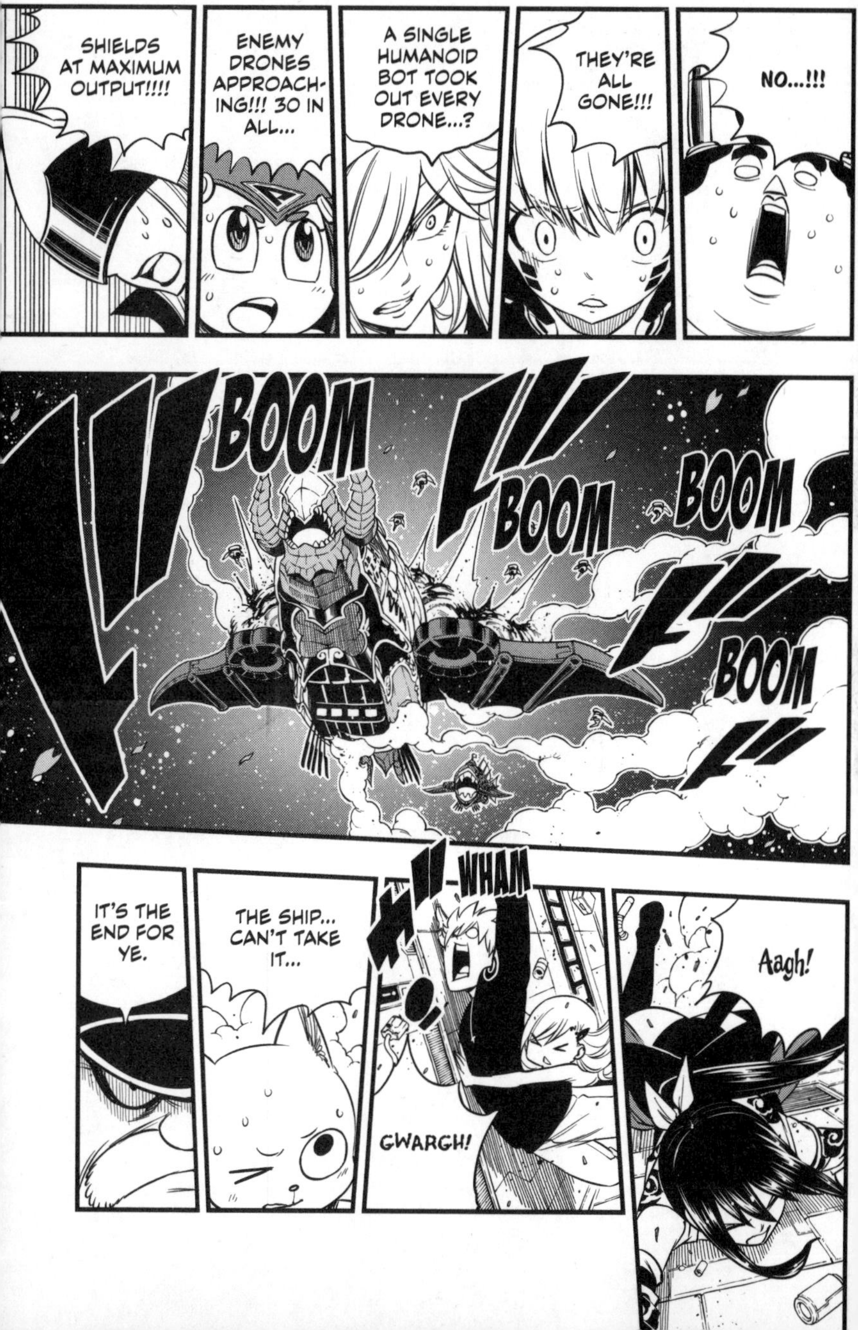
NO...!!!
THEY'RE ALL GONE!!!
A SINGLE HUMANOID BOT TOOK OUT EVERY DRONE...?
ENEMY DRONES APPROACHING!!! 30 IN ALL...
SHIELDS AT MAXIMUM OUTPUT!!!!
BOOM
BOOM
BOOM
BOOM
Aagh!
WHAM
GWARGH!
THE SHIP... CAN'T TAKE IT...
IT'S THE END FOR YE.

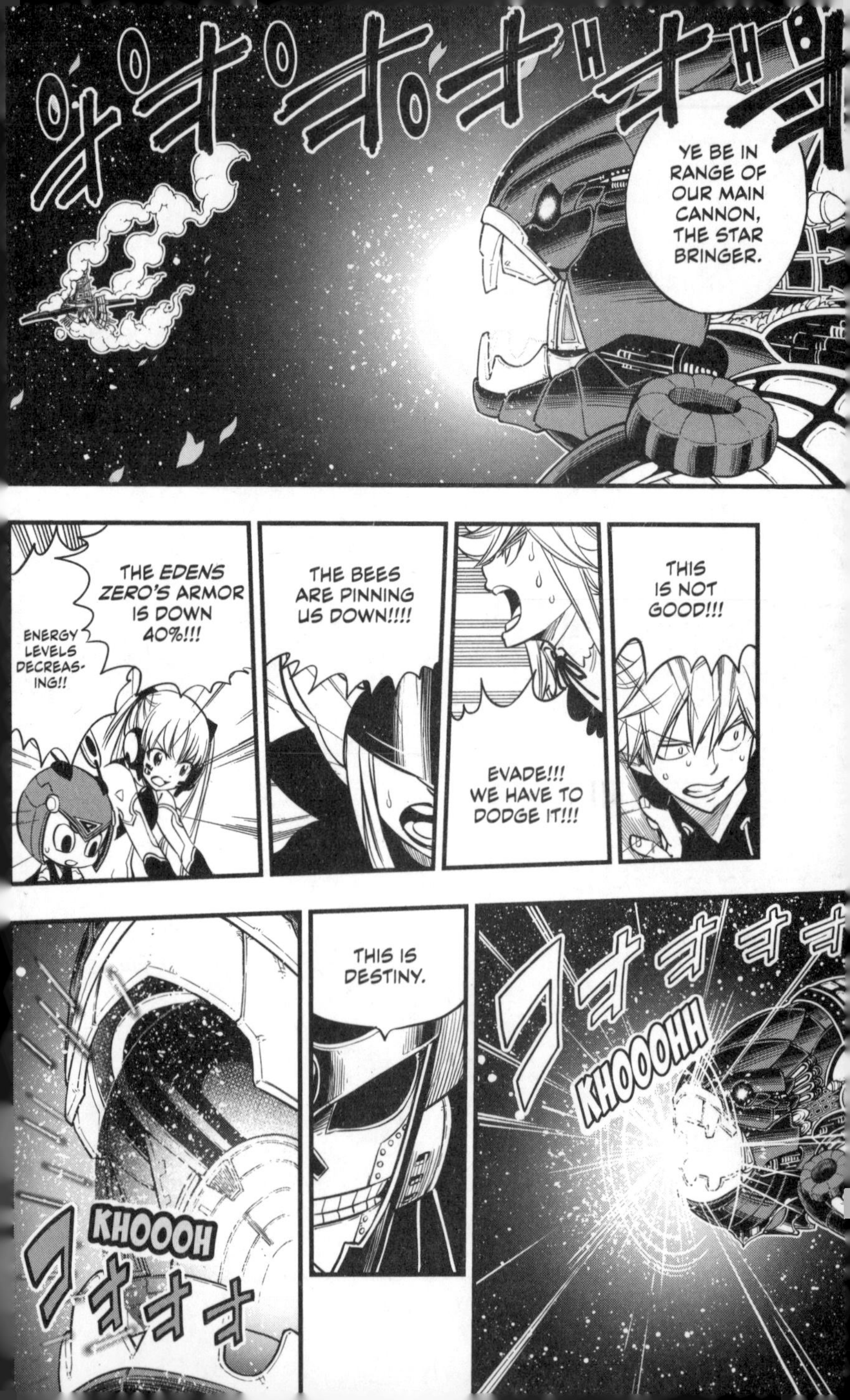
YE BE IN RANGE OF OUR MAIN CANNON, THE STAR BRINGER.
THIS IS NOT GOOD!!!
EVADE!!! WE HAVE TO DODGE IT!!!
THE BEES ARE PINNING US DOWN!!!!
THE EDENS ZERO'S ARMOR IS DOWN 40%!!!
ENERGY LEVELS DECREAS-ING!!
KHOOOHH
THIS IS DESTINY.
KHOOOH

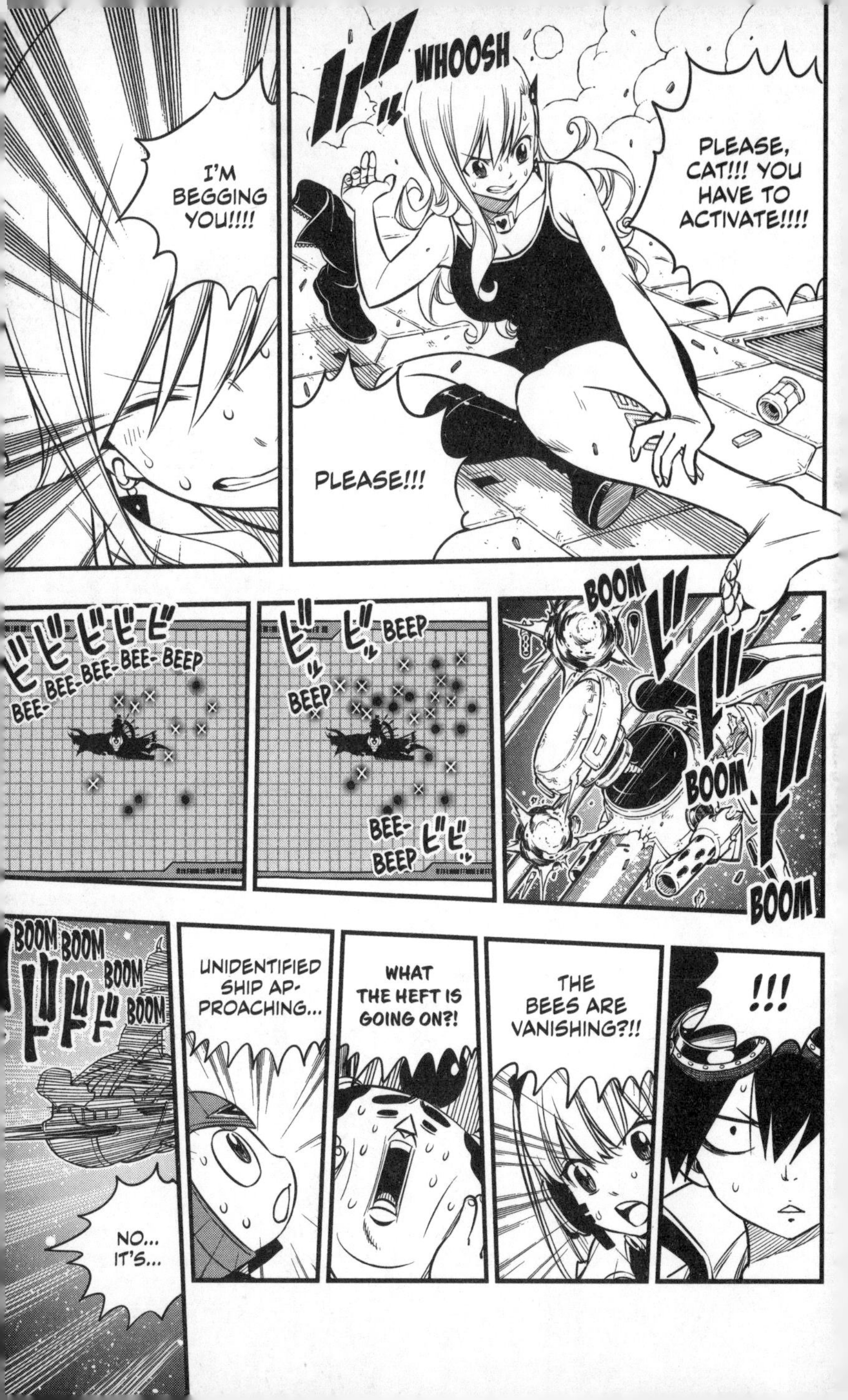
WHOOSH
PLEASE, CAT!!! YOU HAVE TO ACTIVATE!!!!
PLEASE!!!
I'M BEGGING YOU!!!!
BOOM
BOOM
BOOM
ビッ
BEEP
ビッ
BEEP
BEE-BEEP
ビビッ
ビビビビビ
BEE-BEE-BEE-BEE-BEEP
!!!
THE BEES ARE VANISHING?!!
WHAT THE HEFT IS GOING ON?!
UNIDENTIFIED SHIP AP-PROACHING...
BOOM BOOM BOOM BOOM
NO... IT'S...

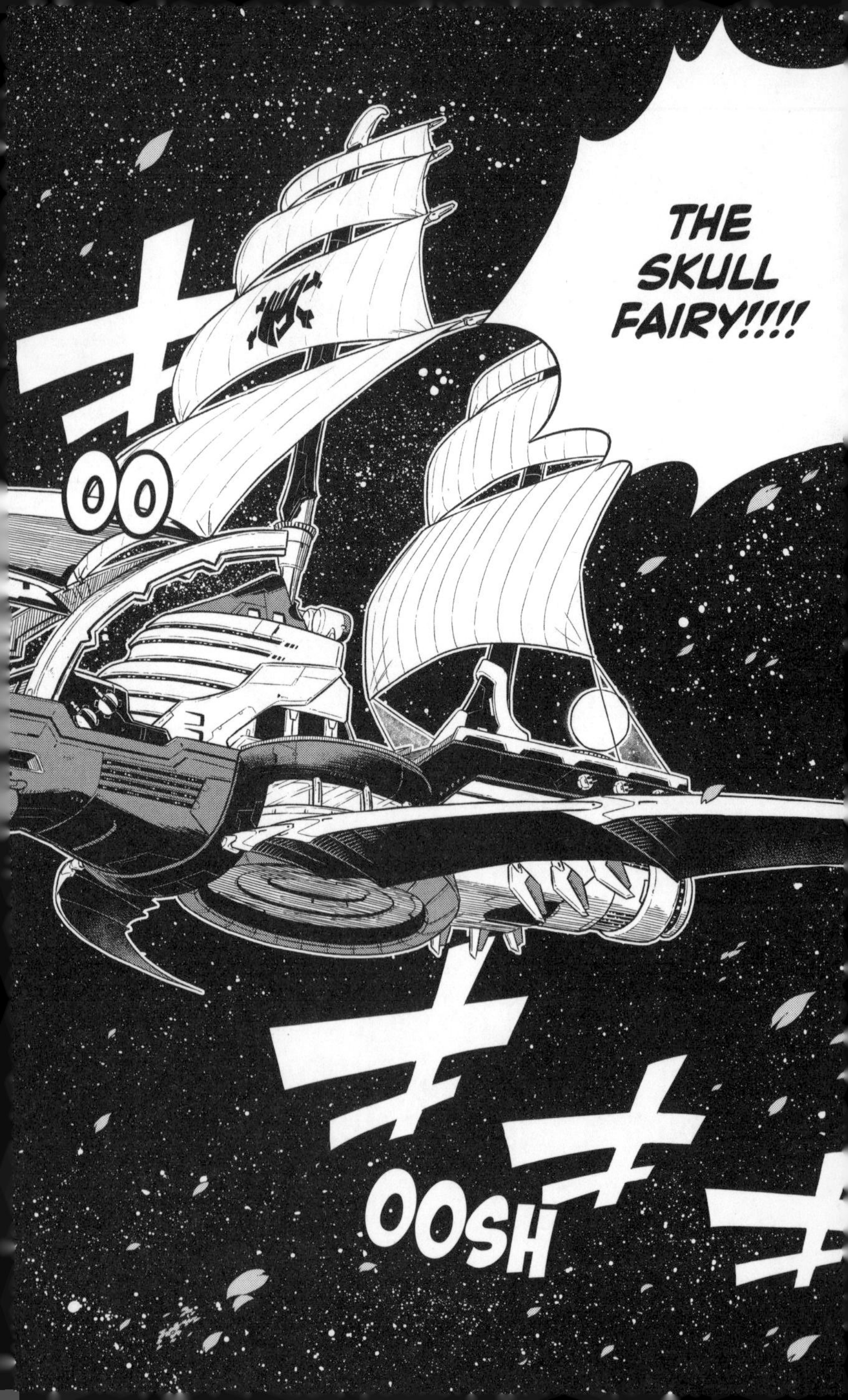
THE SKULL FAIRY!!!!
OOSH

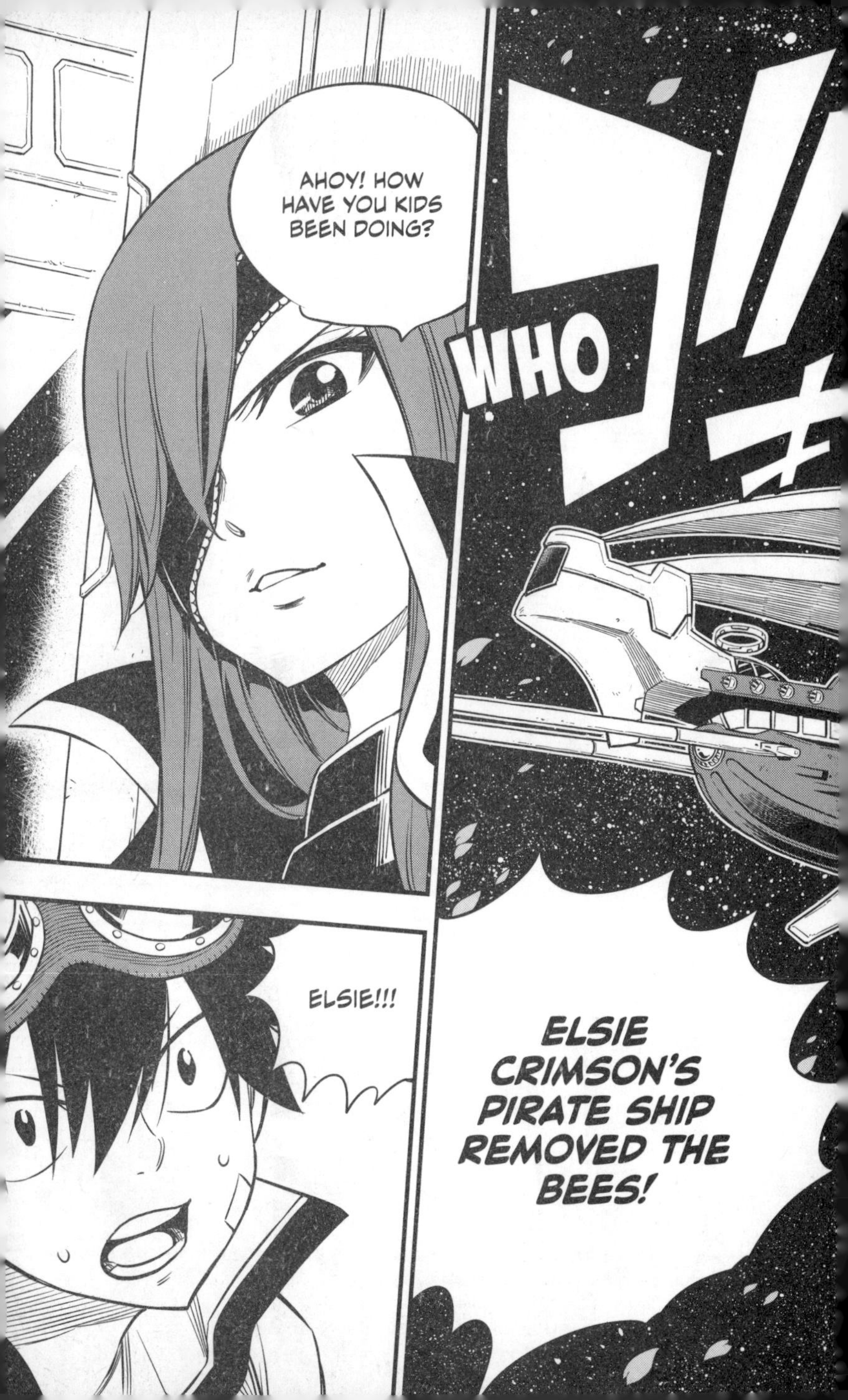
WHO
ELSIE CRIMSON'S PIRATE SHIP REMOVED THE BEES!
AHOY! HOW HAVE YOU KIDS BEEN DOING?
ELSIE!!!

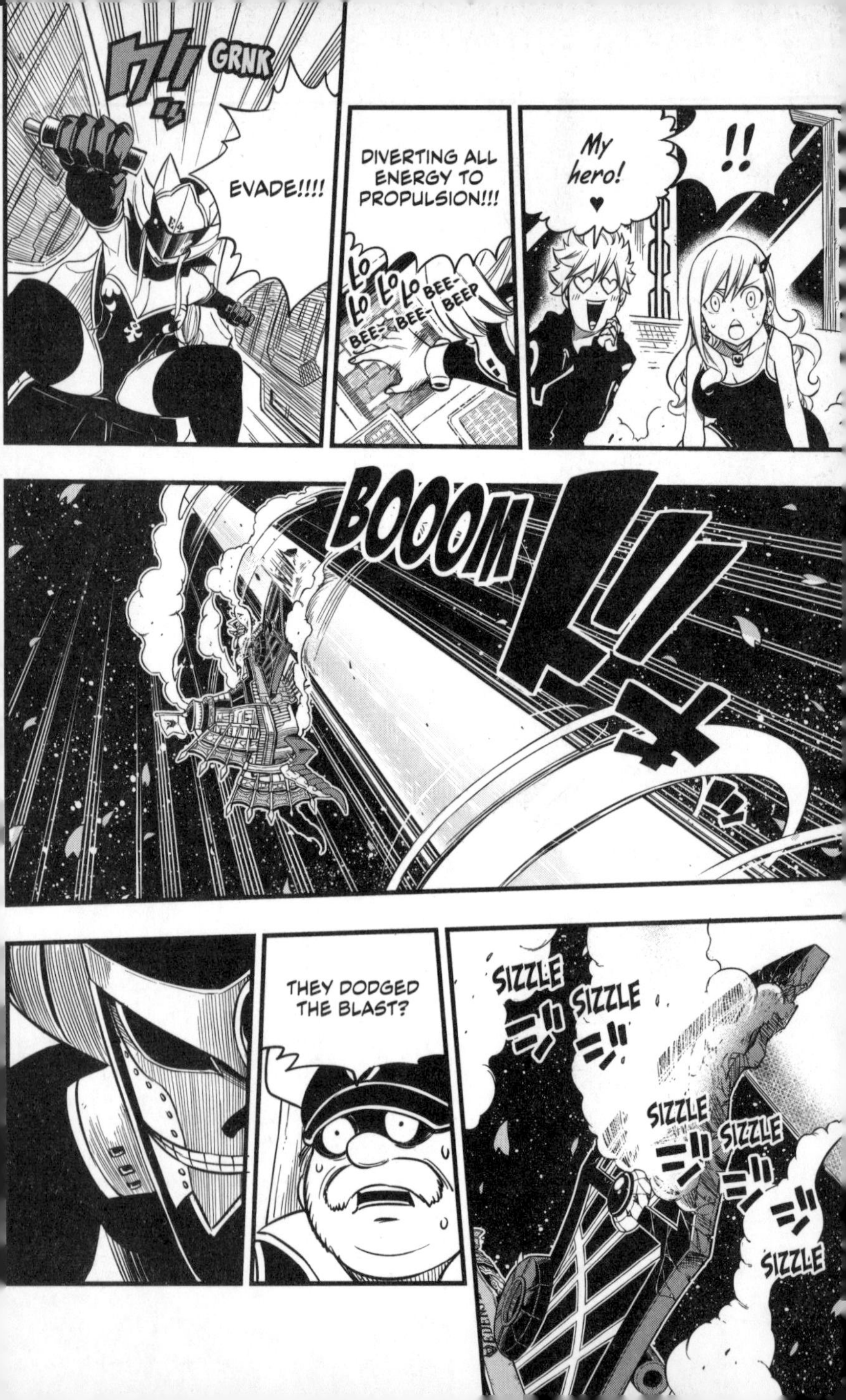
!!
My hero! ♥
DIVERTING ALL ENERGY TO PROPULSION!!!
BEE-BEEP
BEE-BEE-
GRNK
EVADE!!!!
BOOOM
SIZZLE
SIZZLE
SIZZLE
SIZZLE
SIZZLE
THEY DODGED THE BLAST?

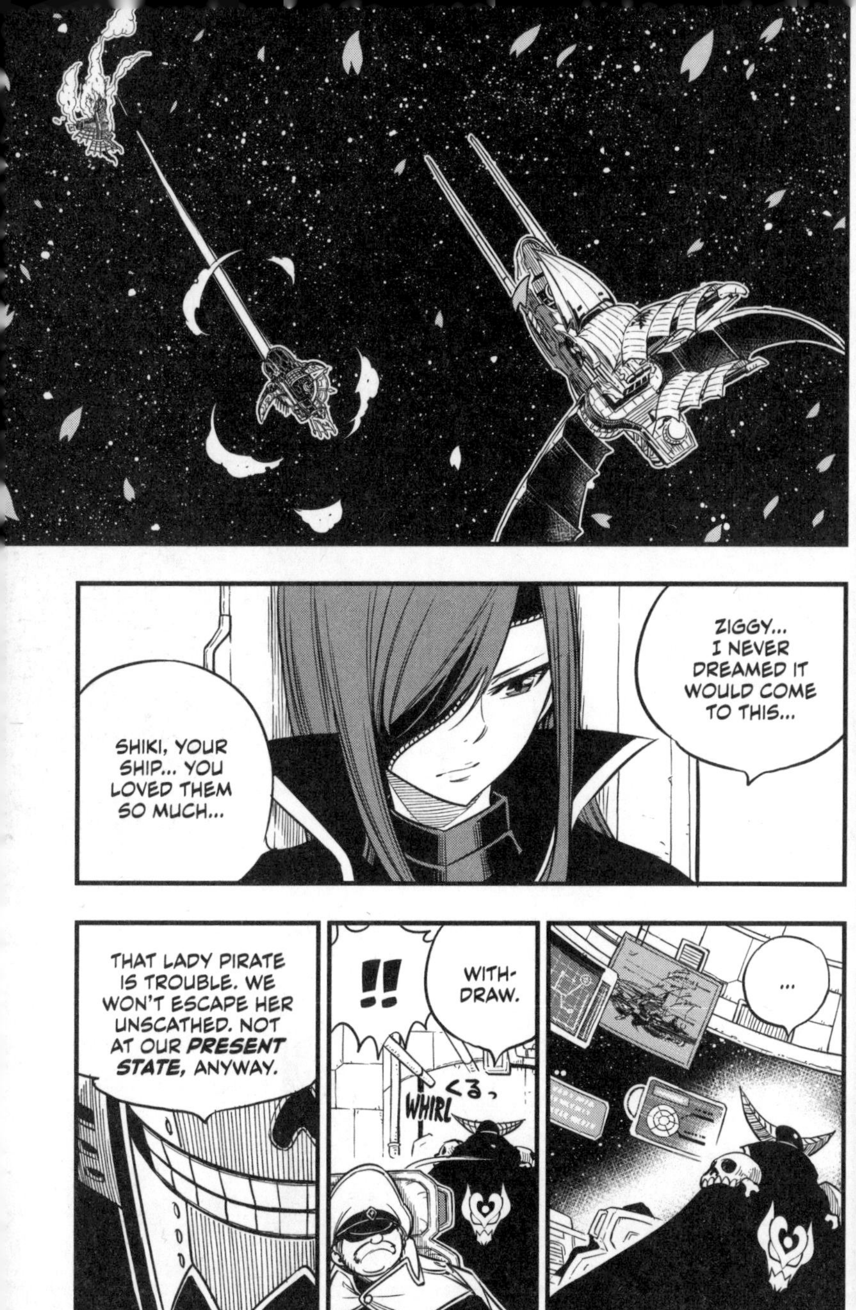
ZIGGY... I NEVER DREAMED IT WOULD COME TO THIS...
SHIKI, YOUR SHIP... YOU LOVED THEM SO MUCH...
...
WITH-DRAW.
!!
くるっ
WHIRL
THAT LADY PIRATE IS TROUBLE. WE WON'T ESCAPE HER UNSCATHED. NOT AT OUR ***PRESENT STATE,*** ANYWAY.

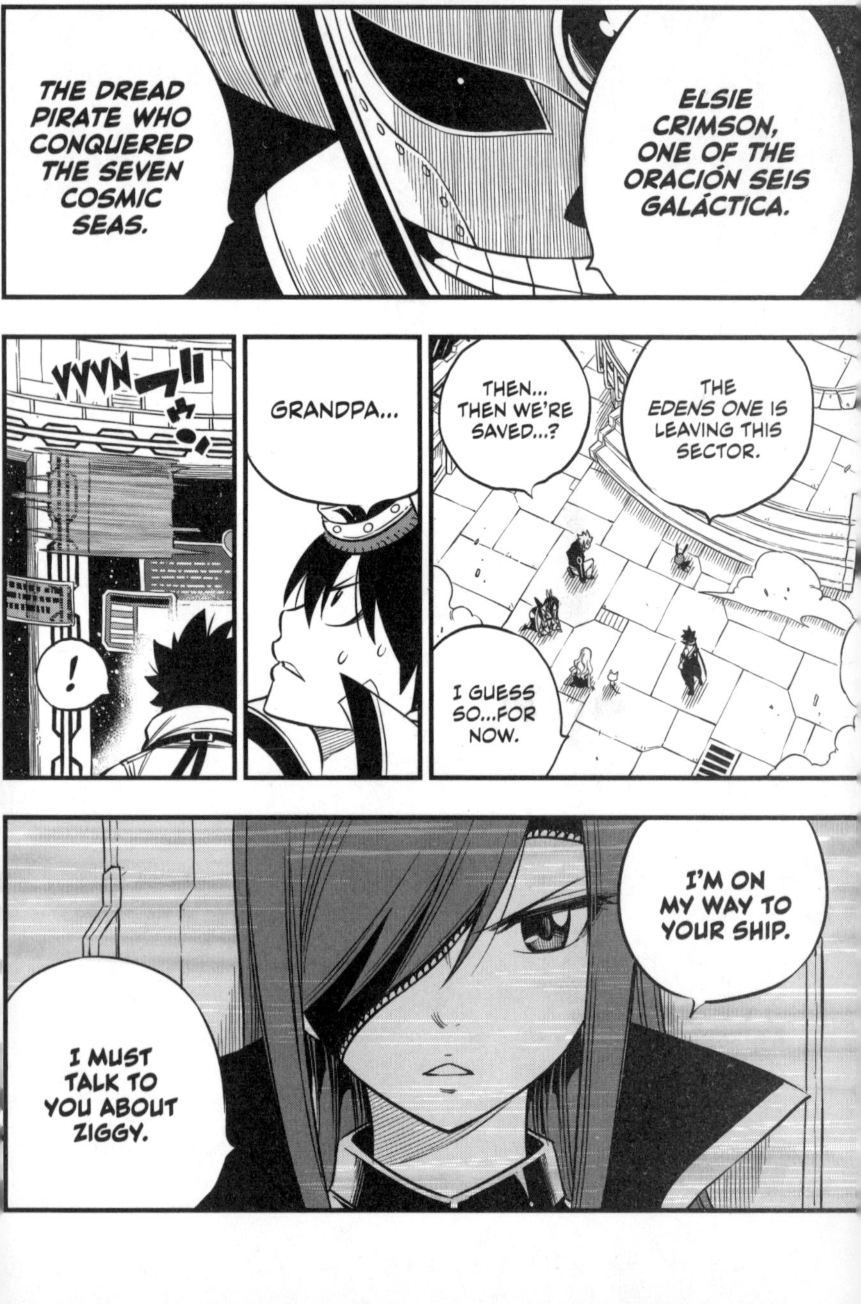
ELSIE CRIMSON, ONE OF THE ORACIÓN SEIS GALÁCTICA.
THE DREAD PIRATE WHO CONQUERED THE SEVEN COSMIC SEAS.
THE EDENS ONE IS LEAVING THIS SECTOR.
THEN... THEN WE'RE SAVED...?
I GUESS SO...FOR NOW.
GRANDPA...
VVVN
!
I'M ON MY WAY TO YOUR SHIP.
I MUST TALK TO YOU ABOUT ZIGGY.

CHAPTER 104: THE WOMAN THEY CALLED PIRATE

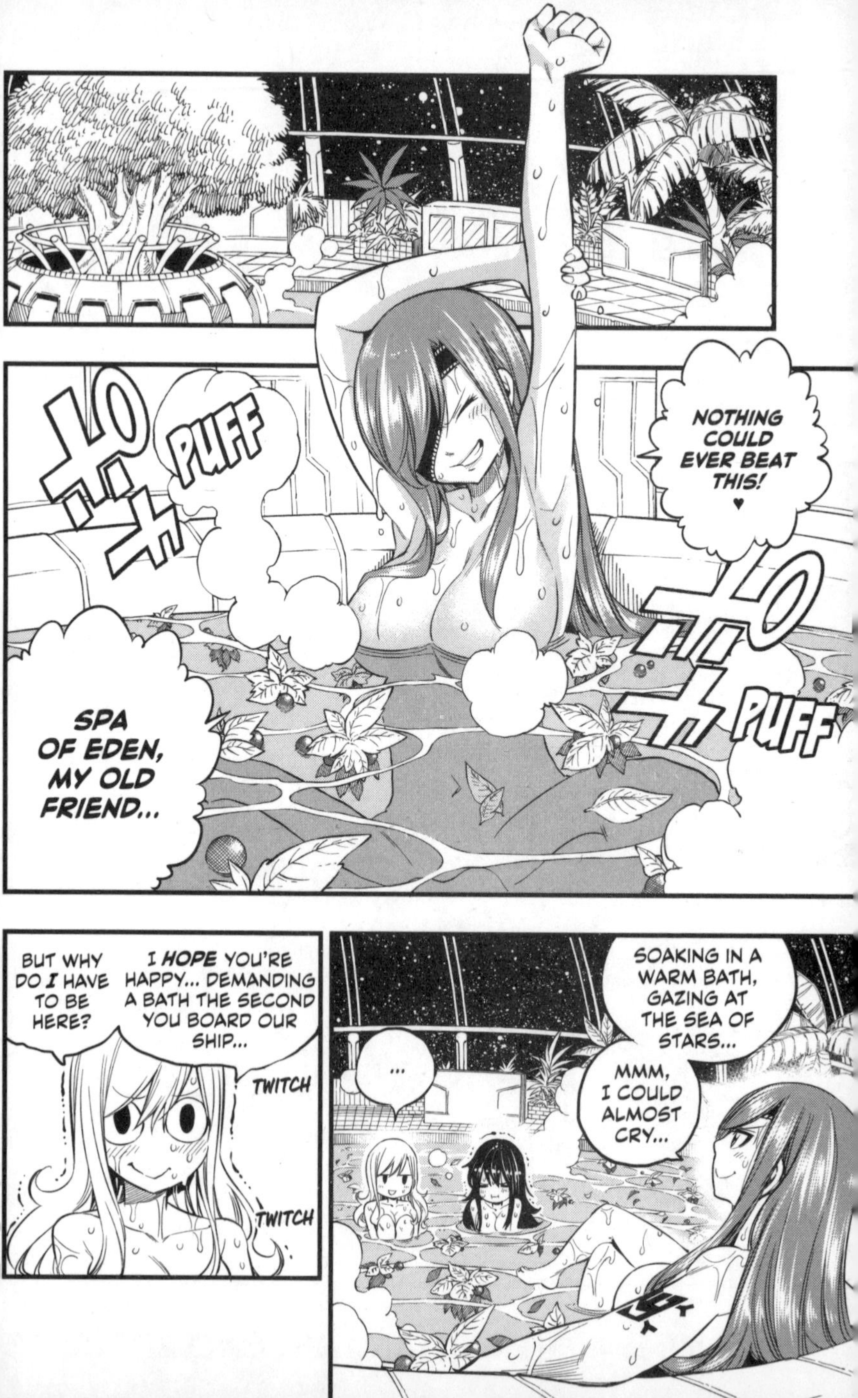
NOTHING COULD EVER BEAT THIS! ♥
PUFF
PUFF
SPA OF EDEN, MY OLD FRIEND...
SOAKING IN A WARM BATH, GAZING AT THE SEA OF STARS...
MMM, I COULD ALMOST CRY...
...
I HOPE YOU'RE HAPPY... DEMANDING A BATH THE SECOND YOU BOARD OUR SHIP...
BUT WHY DO I HAVE TO BE HERE?
TWITCH
TWITCH

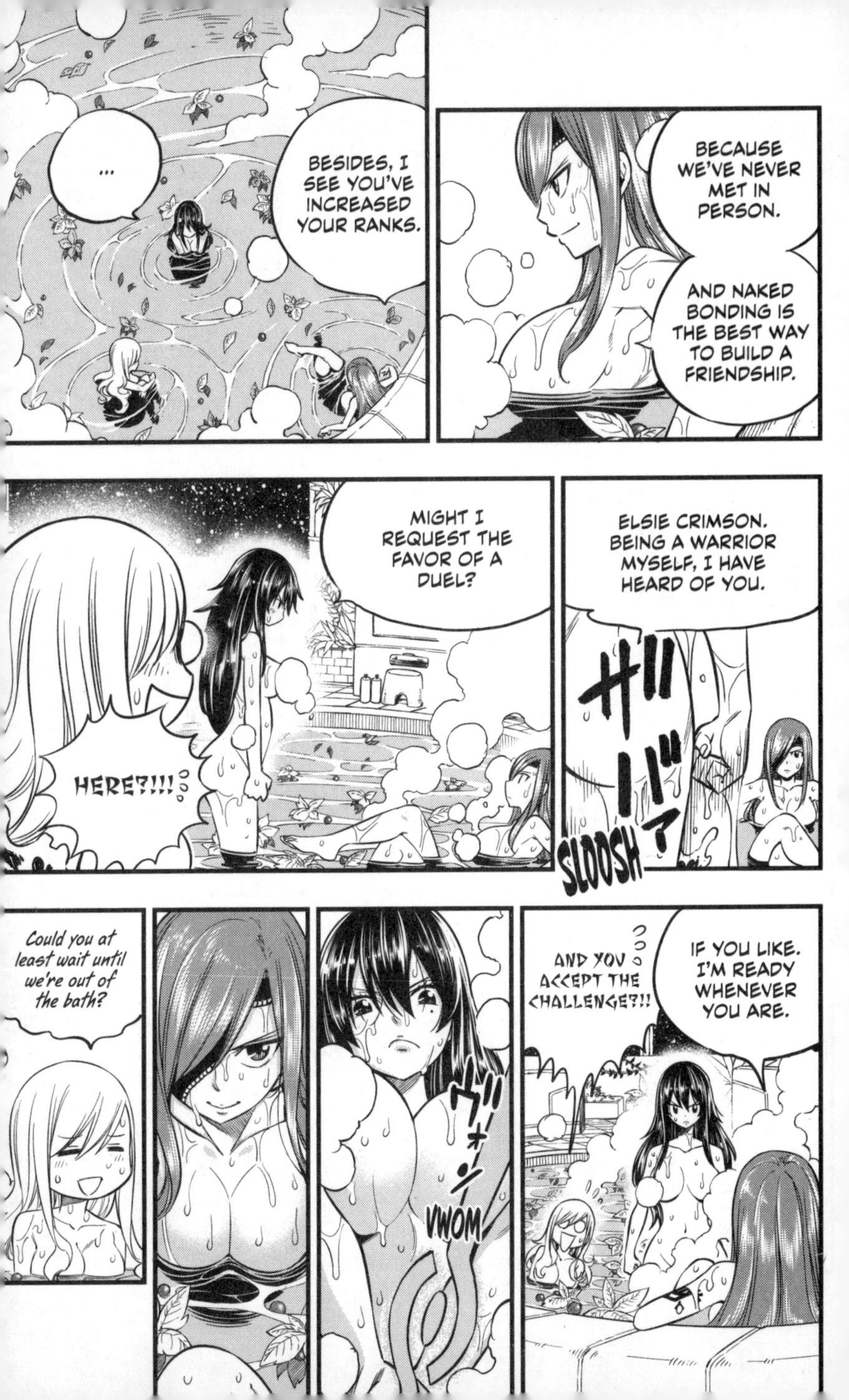
BECAUSE WE'VE NEVER MET IN PERSON.
AND NAKED BONDING IS THE BEST WAY TO BUILD A FRIENDSHIP.
BESIDES, I SEE YOU'VE INCREASED YOUR RANKS.
...
ELSIE CRIMSON. BEING A WARRIOR MYSELF, I HAVE HEARD OF YOU.
SLOOSH
MIGHT I REQUEST THE FAVOR OF A DUEL?
HERE?!!!
IF YOU LIKE. I'M READY WHENEVER YOU ARE.
AND YOU ACCEPT THE CHALLENGE?!!
VWOM
Could you at least wait until we're out of the bath?

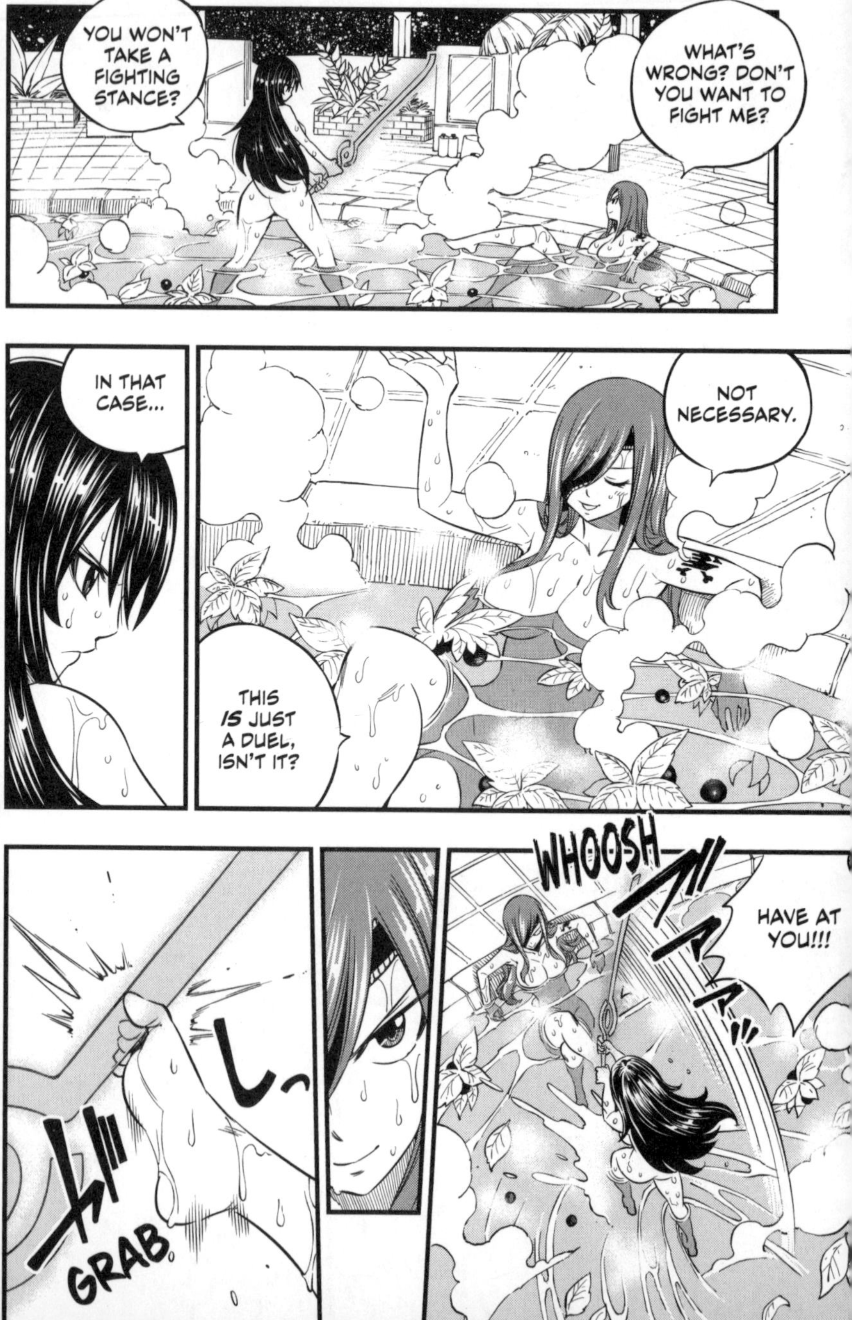
WHAT'S WRONG? DON'T YOU WANT TO FIGHT ME?
YOU WON'T TAKE A FIGHTING STANCE?
NOT NECESSARY.
THIS *IS* JUST A DUEL, ISN'T IT?
IN THAT CASE...
WHOOSH
HAVE AT YOU!!!
GRAB

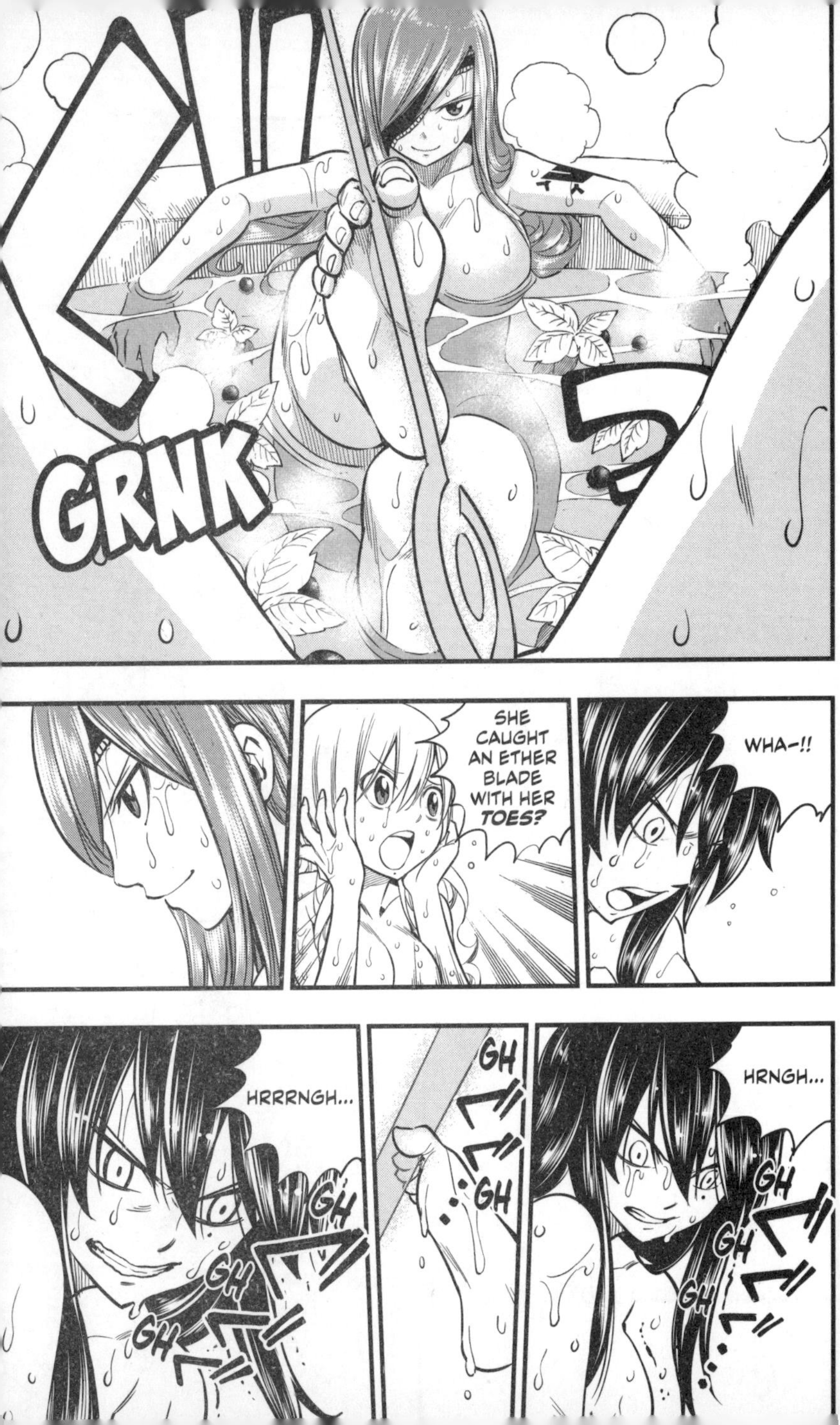
GRNK
WHA-!!
SHE CAUGHT AN ETHER BLADE WITH HER TOES?
HRNGH...
GH
GH
GH
GH
GH
HRRRNGH...
GH
GH
GH

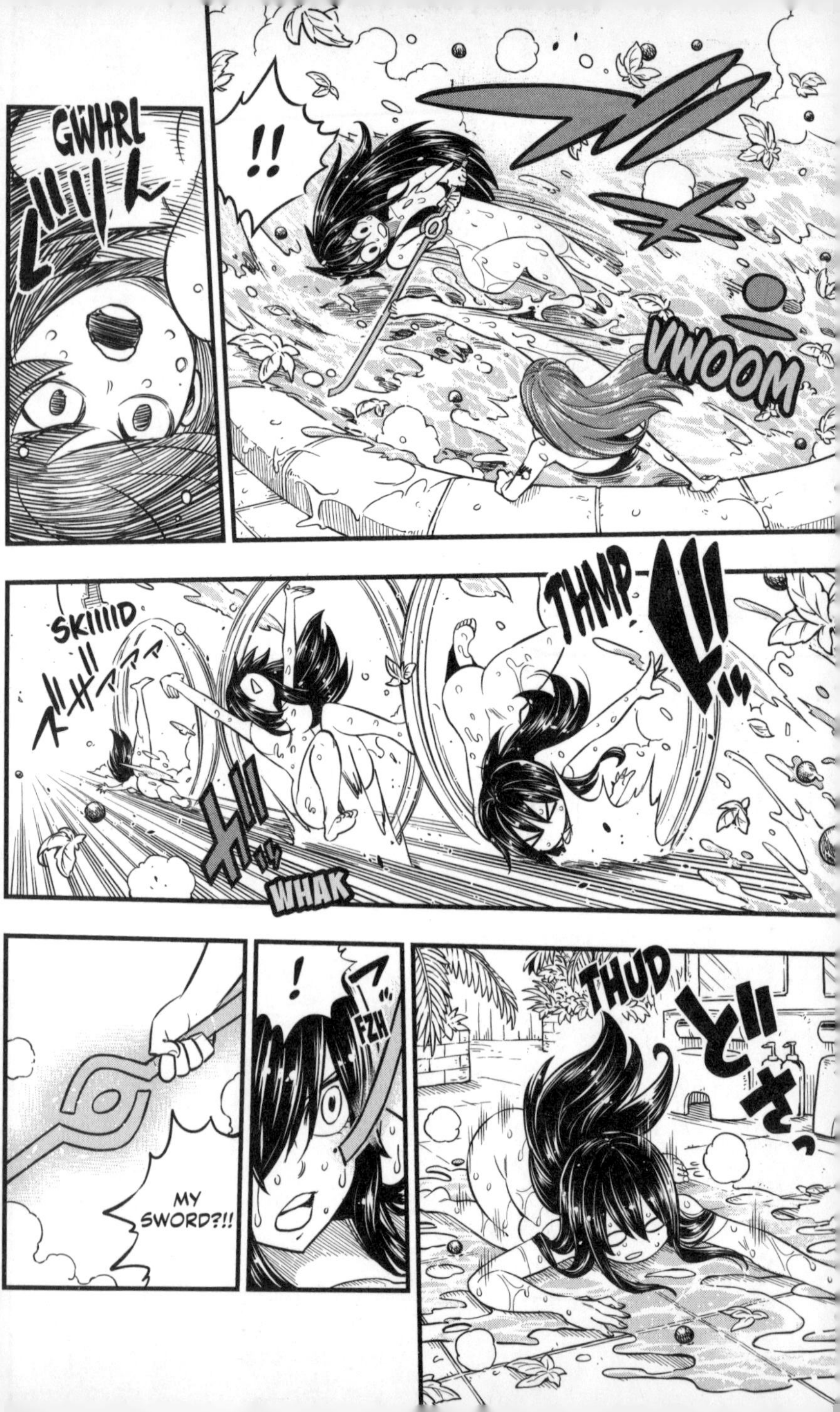
!!
VWOOM
GWHRL
THMP
ドッ
WHAK
SKIIIID
THUD
どさっ
!
FZH
MY SWORD?!!

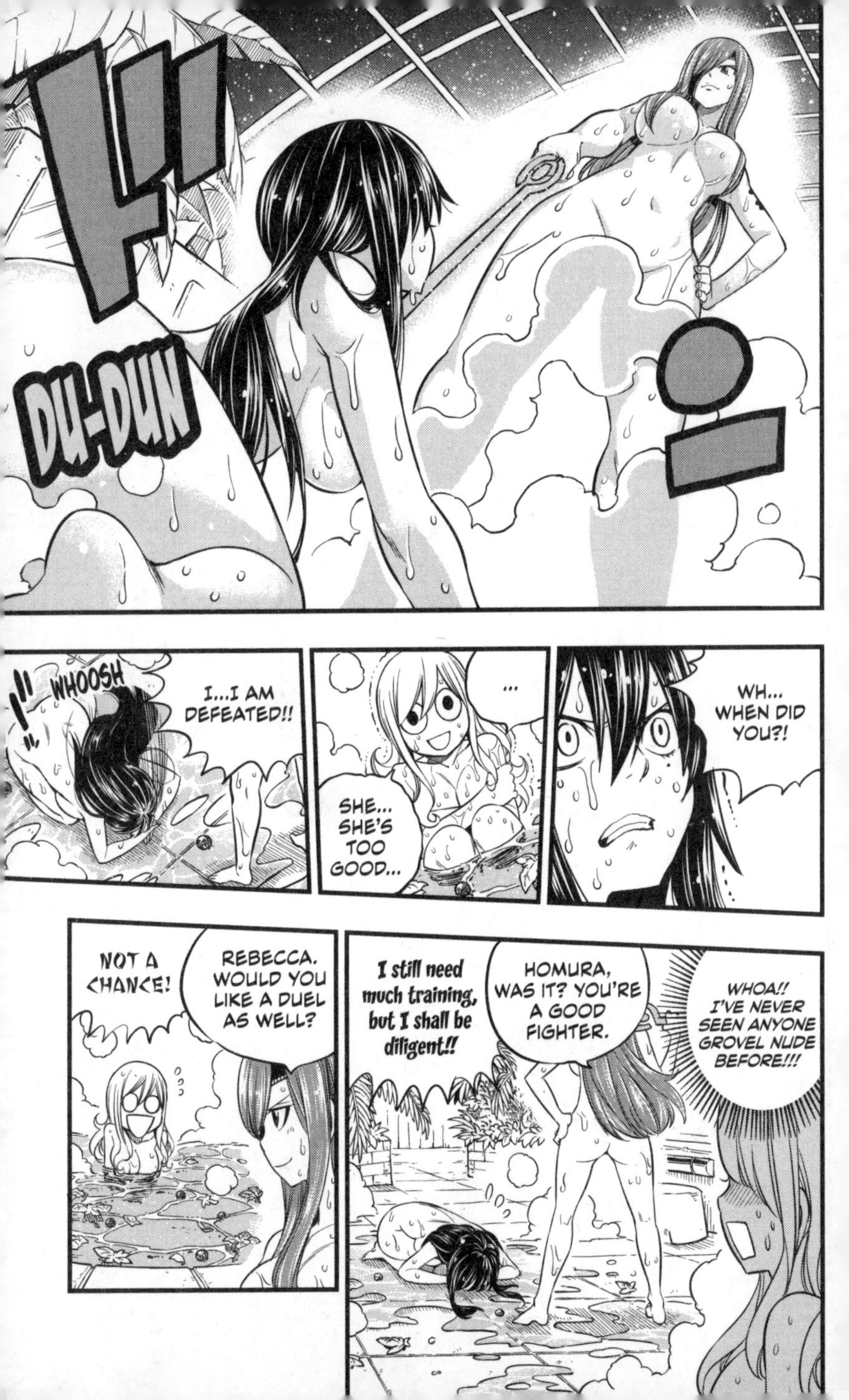
DU-DUN
WH... WHEN DID YOU?!
...
SHE... SHE'S TOO GOOD...
I...I AM DEFEATED!!
WHOOSH
WHOA!! I'VE NEVER SEEN ANYONE GROVEL NUDE BEFORE!!!
HOMURA, WAS IT? YOU'RE A GOOD FIGHTER.
I still need much training, but I shall be diligent!!
REBECCA. WOULD YOU LIKE A DUEL AS WELL?
NOT A CHANCE!

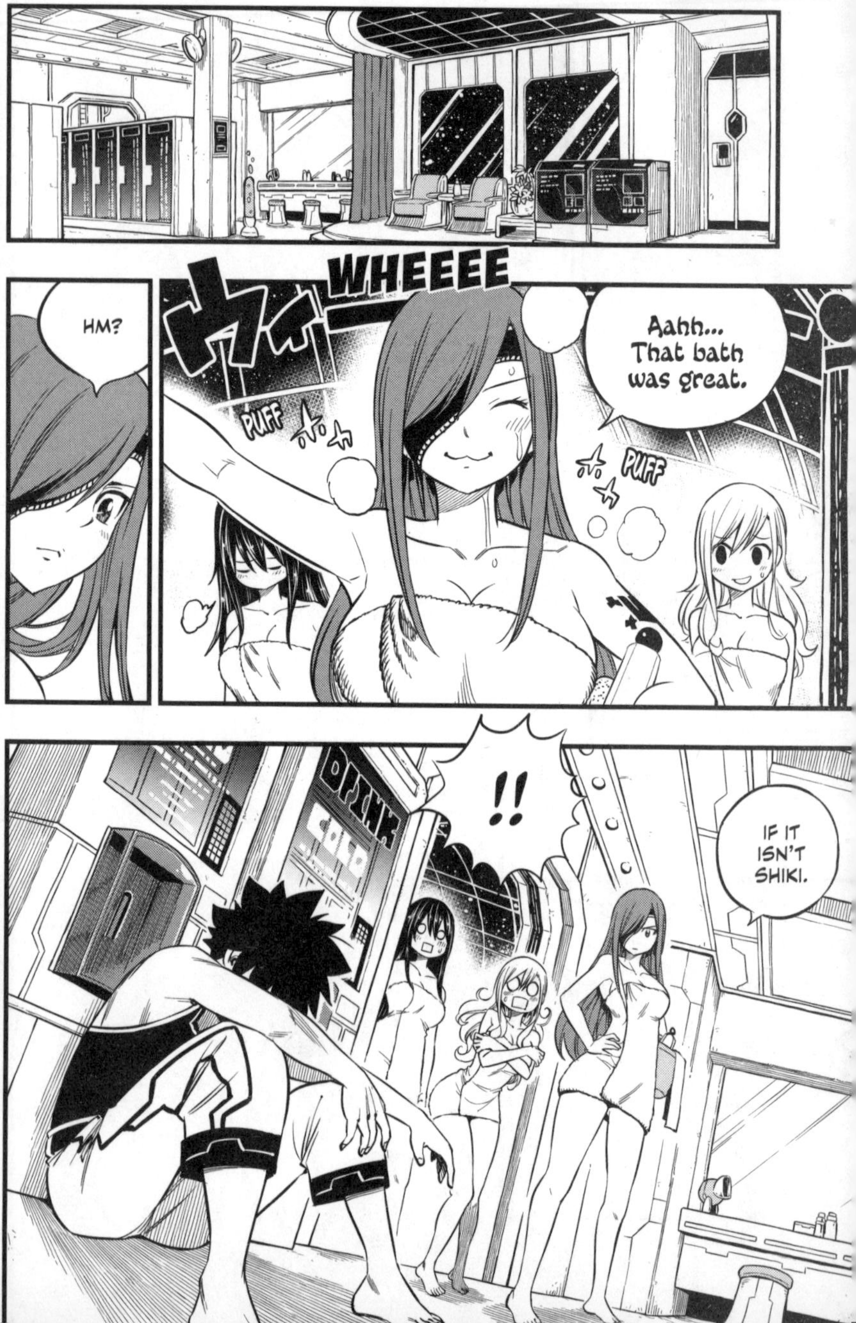
WHEEEE
Aahh... That bath was great.
PUFF
PUFF
HM?
!!
IF IT ISN'T SHIKI.

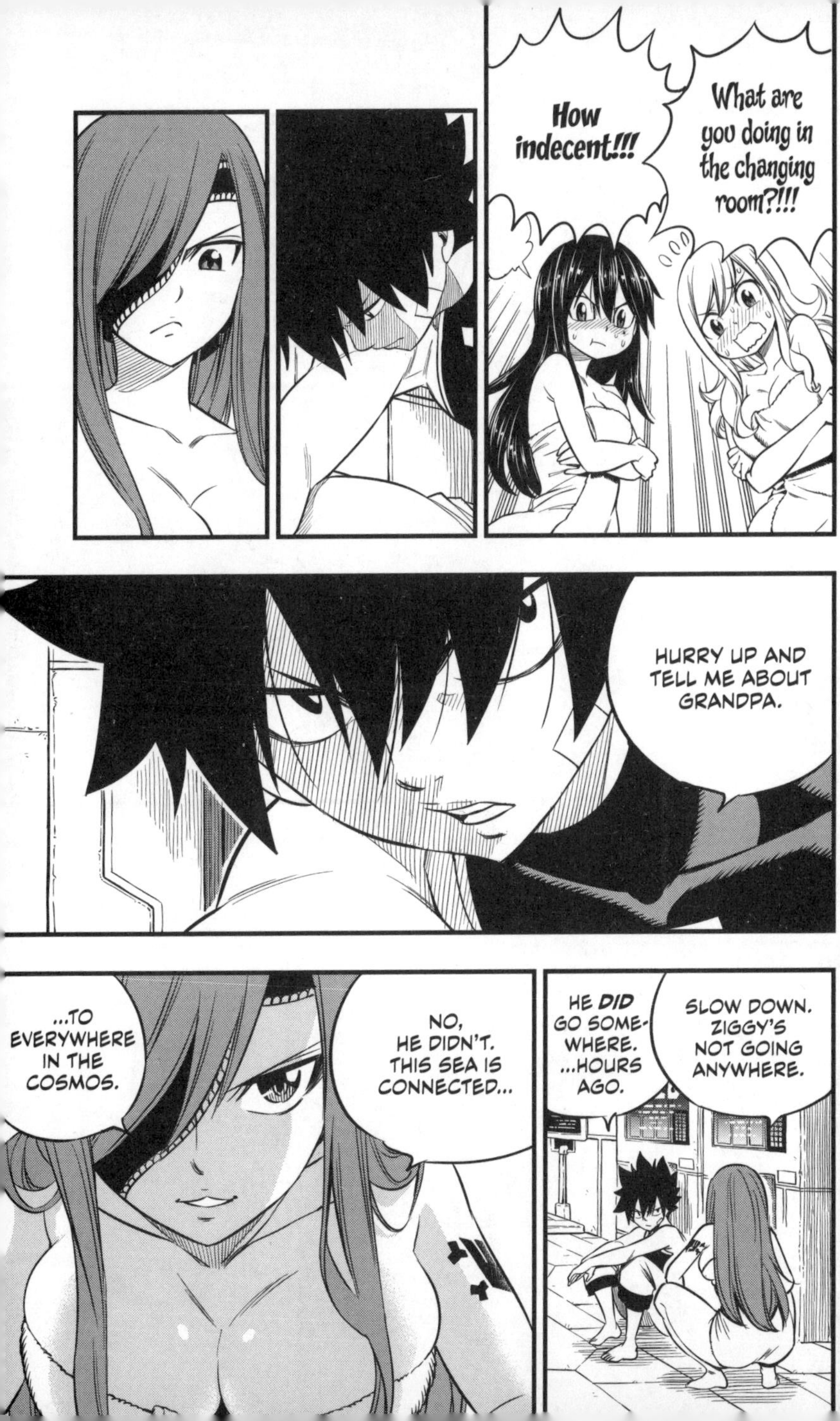
What are you doing in the changing room?!!!
How indecent!!!
HURRY UP AND TELL ME ABOUT GRANDPA.
SLOW DOWN. ZIGGY'S NOT GOING ANYWHERE.
HE DID GO SOMEWHERE. ...HOURS AGO.
NO, HE DIDN'T. THIS SEA IS CONNECTED...
...TO EVERYWHERE IN THE COSMOS.

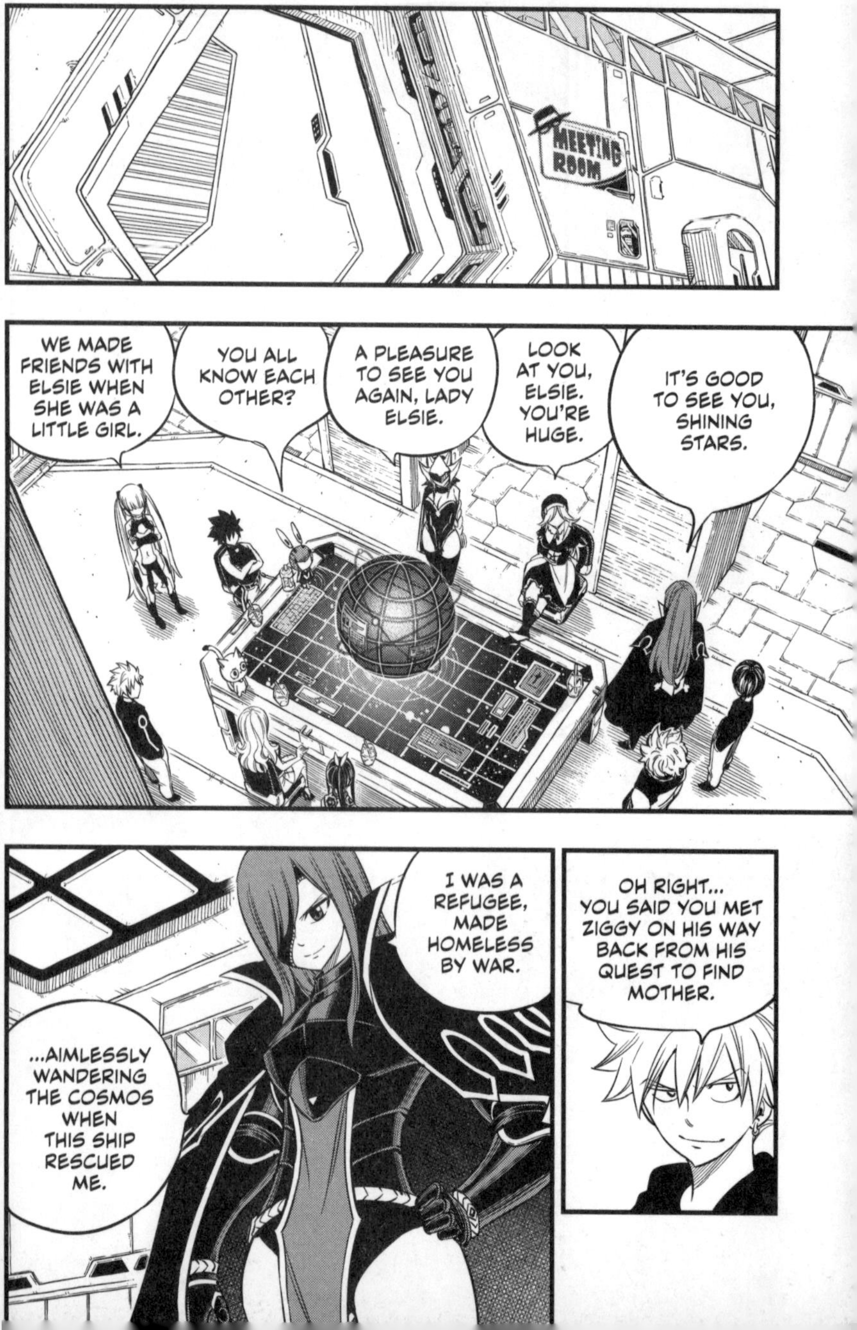
MEETING ROOM
IT'S GOOD TO SEE YOU, SHINING STARS.
LOOK AT YOU, ELSIE. YOU'RE HUGE.
A PLEASURE TO SEE YOU AGAIN, LADY ELSIE.
YOU ALL KNOW EACH OTHER?
WE MADE FRIENDS WITH ELSIE WHEN SHE WAS A LITTLE GIRL.
OH RIGHT... YOU SAID YOU MET ZIGGY ON HIS WAY BACK FROM HIS QUEST TO FIND MOTHER.
I WAS A REFUGEE, MADE HOMELESS BY WAR.
...AIMLESSLY WANDERING THE COSMOS WHEN THIS SHIP RESCUED ME.

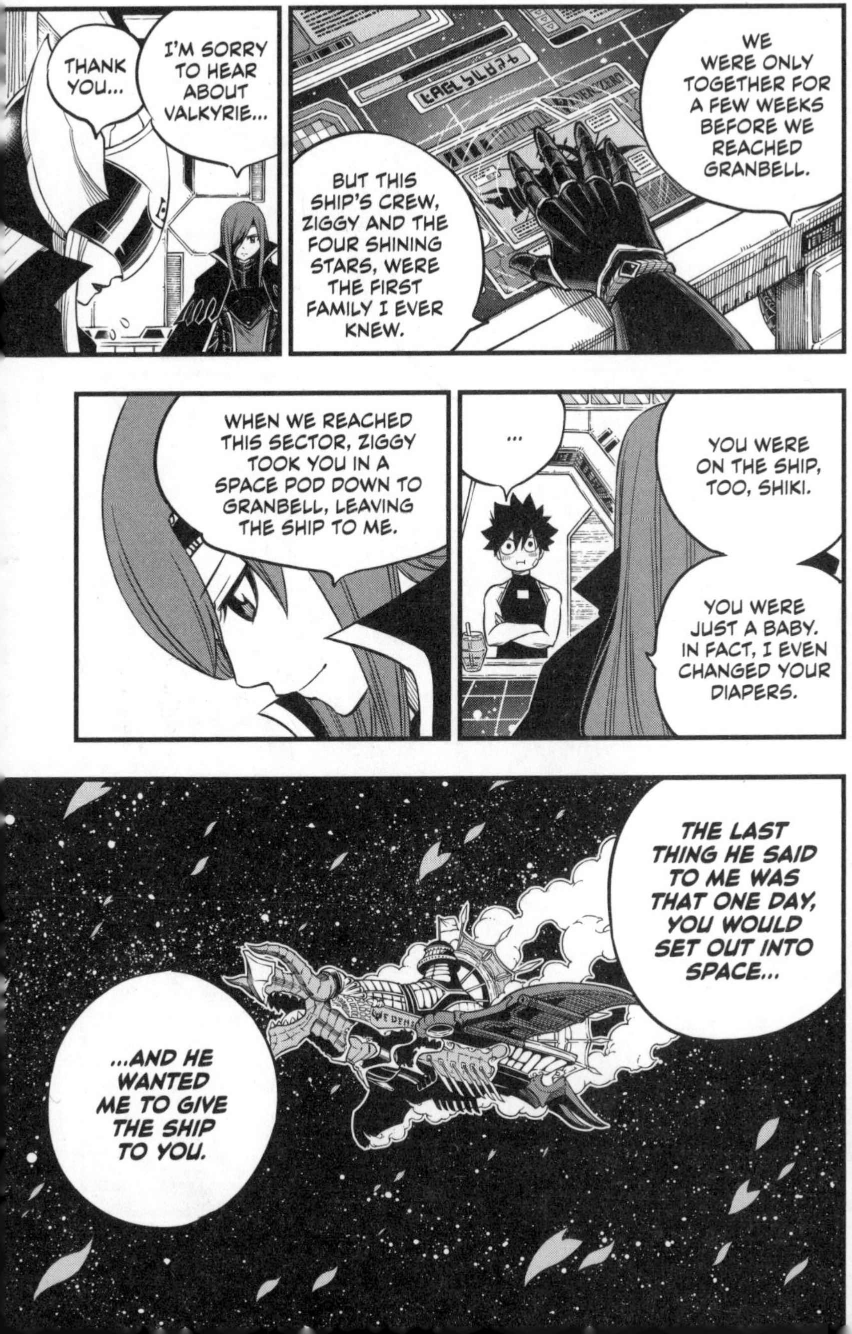
WE WERE ONLY TOGETHER FOR A FEW WEEKS BEFORE WE REACHED GRANBELL.
BUT THIS SHIP'S CREW, ZIGGY AND THE FOUR SHINING STARS, WERE THE FIRST FAMILY I EVER KNEW.
I'M SORRY TO HEAR ABOUT VALKYRIE...
THANK YOU...
YOU WERE ON THE SHIP, TOO, SHIKI.
...
YOU WERE JUST A BABY. IN FACT, I EVEN CHANGED YOUR DIAPERS.
WHEN WE REACHED THIS SECTOR, ZIGGY TOOK YOU IN A SPACE POD DOWN TO GRANBELL, LEAVING THE SHIP TO ME.
THE LAST THING HE SAID TO ME WAS THAT ONE DAY, YOU WOULD SET OUT INTO SPACE...
...AND HE WANTED ME TO GIVE THE SHIP TO YOU.

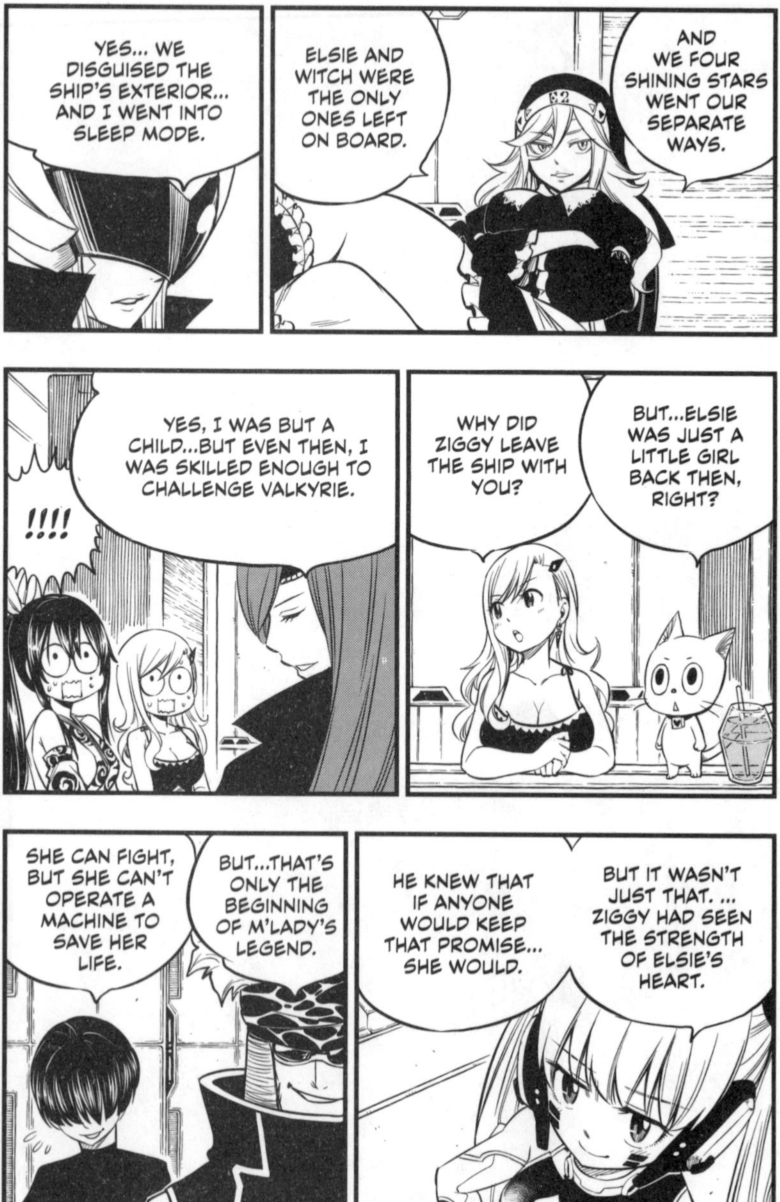
AND WE FOUR SHINING STARS WENT OUR SEPARATE WAYS.
ELSIE AND WITCH WERE THE ONLY ONES LEFT ON BOARD.
YES... WE DISGUISED THE SHIP'S EXTERIOR... AND I WENT INTO SLEEP MODE.
BUT...ELSIE WAS JUST A LITTLE GIRL BACK THEN, RIGHT?
WHY DID ZIGGY LEAVE THE SHIP WITH YOU?
YES, I WAS BUT A CHILD...BUT EVEN THEN, I WAS SKILLED ENOUGH TO CHALLENGE VALKYRIE.
!!!!
BUT IT WASN'T JUST THAT. ... ZIGGY HAD SEEN THE STRENGTH OF ELSIE'S HEART.
HE KNEW THAT IF ANYONE WOULD KEEP THAT PROMISE... SHE WOULD.
BUT...THAT'S ONLY THE BEGINNING OF M'LADY'S LEGEND.
SHE CAN FIGHT, BUT SHE CAN'T OPERATE A MACHINE TO SAVE HER LIFE.

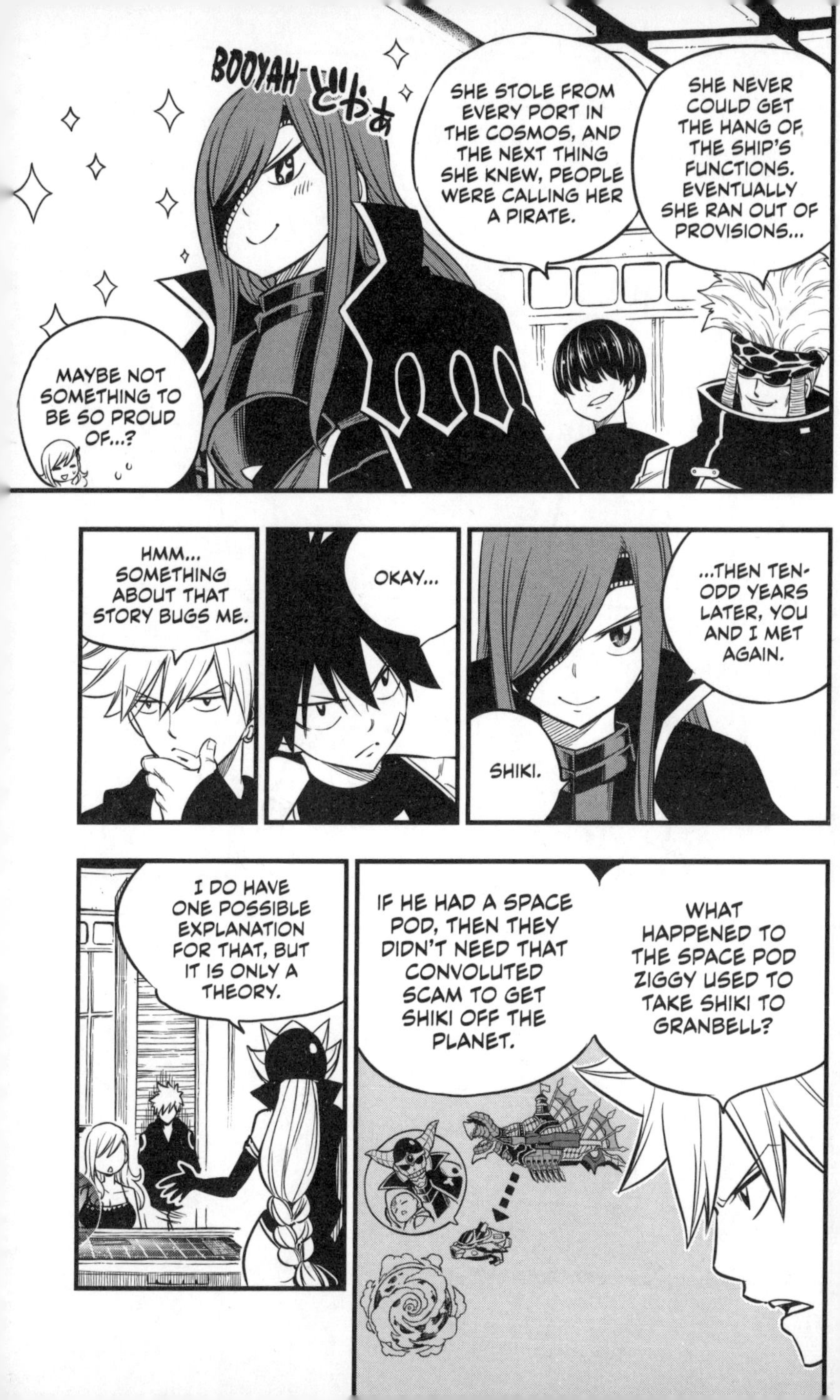
SHE NEVER COULD GET THE HANG OF THE SHIP'S FUNCTIONS. EVENTUALLY SHE RAN OUT OF PROVISIONS...
SHE STOLE FROM EVERY PORT IN THE COSMOS, AND THE NEXT THING SHE KNEW, PEOPLE WERE CALLING HER A PIRATE.
BOOYAH- どやぁ
MAYBE NOT SOMETHING TO BE SO PROUD OF...?
...THEN TEN-ODD YEARS LATER, YOU AND I MET AGAIN.
SHIKI.
OKAY...
HMM... SOMETHING ABOUT THAT STORY BUGS ME.
WHAT HAPPENED TO THE SPACE POD ZIGGY USED TO TAKE SHIKI TO GRANBELL?
IF HE HAD A SPACE POD, THEN THEY DIDN'T NEED THAT CONVOLUTED SCAM TO GET SHIKI OFF THE PLANET.
I DO HAVE ONE POSSIBLE EXPLANATION FOR THAT, BUT IT IS ONLY A THEORY.

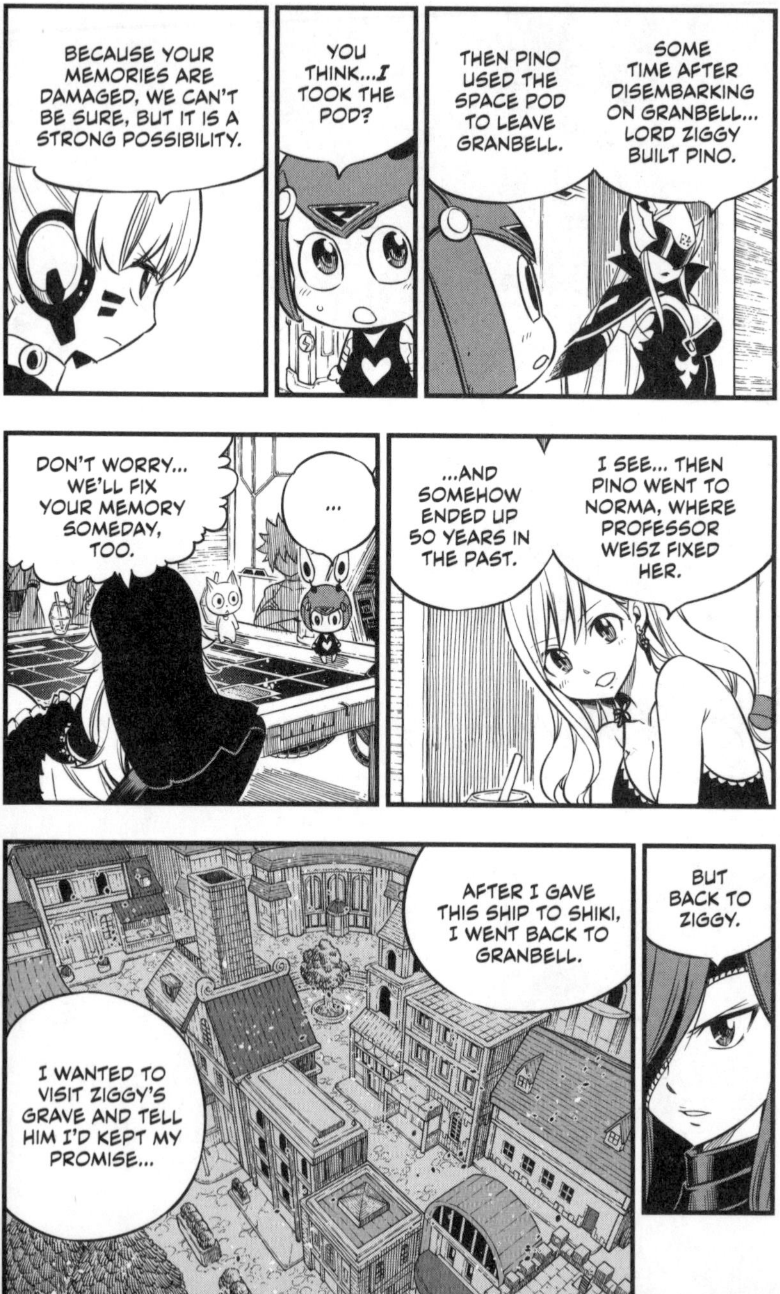
SOME TIME AFTER DISEMBARKING ON GRANBELL... LORD ZIGGY BUILT PINO.
THEN PINO USED THE SPACE POD TO LEAVE GRANBELL.
YOU THINK...I TOOK THE POD?
BECAUSE YOUR MEMORIES ARE DAMAGED, WE CAN'T BE SURE, BUT IT IS A STRONG POSSIBILITY.
I SEE... THEN PINO WENT TO NORMA, WHERE PROFESSOR WEISZ FIXED HER.
...AND SOMEHOW ENDED UP 50 YEARS IN THE PAST.
...
DON'T WORRY... WE'LL FIX YOUR MEMORY SOMEDAY, TOO.
BUT BACK TO ZIGGY.
AFTER I GAVE THIS SHIP TO SHIKI, I WENT BACK TO GRANBELL.
I WANTED TO VISIT ZIGGY'S GRAVE AND TELL HIM I'D KEPT MY PROMISE...

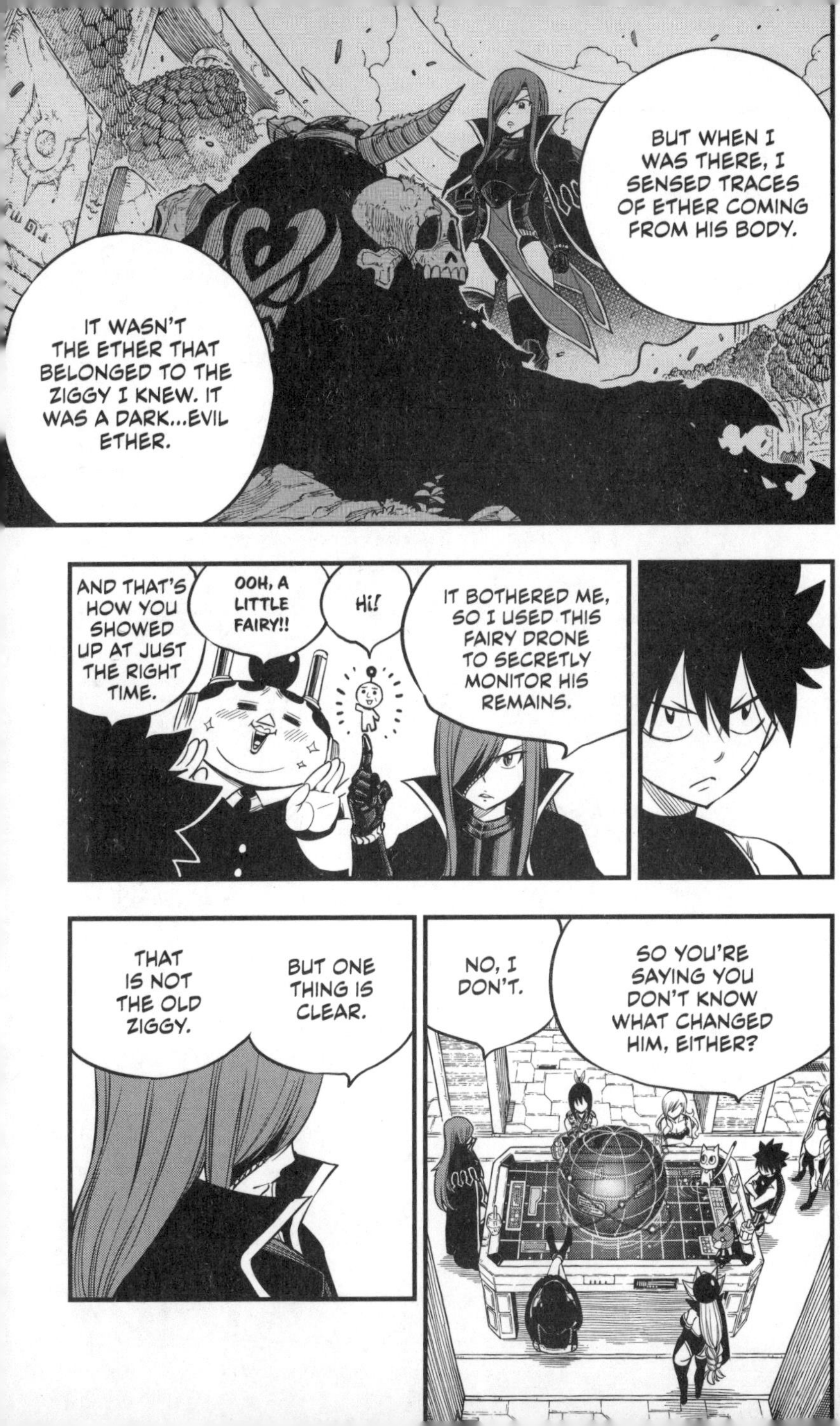
BUT WHEN I WAS THERE, I SENSED TRACES OF ETHER COMING FROM HIS BODY.
IT WASN'T THE ETHER THAT BELONGED TO THE ZIGGY I KNEW. IT WAS A DARK...EVIL ETHER.
IT BOTHERED ME, SO I USED THIS FAIRY DRONE TO SECRETLY MONITOR HIS REMAINS.
Hi!
OOH, A LITTLE FAIRY!!
AND THAT'S HOW YOU SHOWED UP AT JUST THE RIGHT TIME.
SO YOU'RE SAYING YOU DON'T KNOW WHAT CHANGED HIM, EITHER?
NO, I DON'T.
BUT ONE THING IS CLEAR.
THAT IS NOT THE OLD ZIGGY.

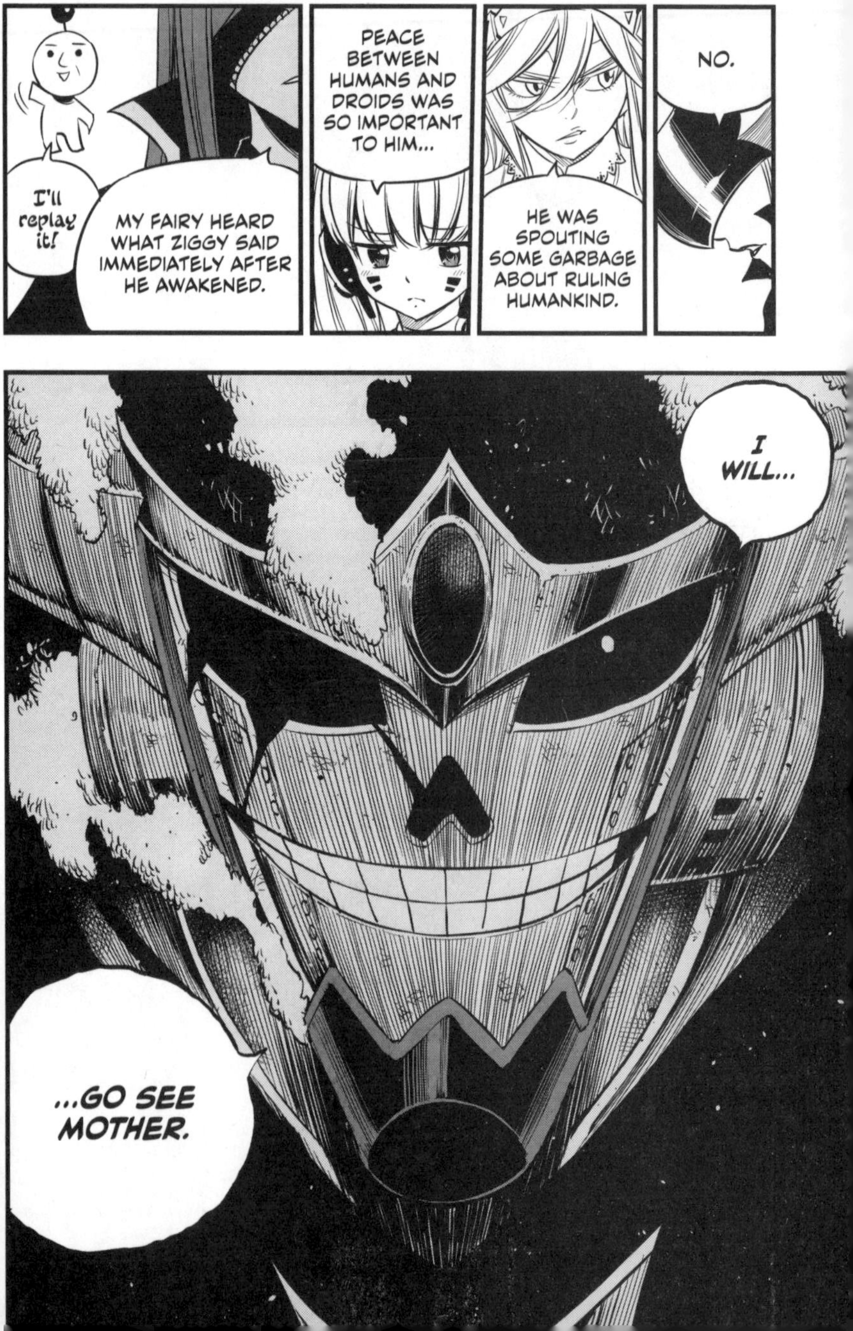
NO.
HE WAS SPOUTING SOME GARBAGE ABOUT RULING HUMANKIND.
PEACE BETWEEN HUMANS AND DROIDS WAS SO IMPORTANT TO HIM...
MY FAIRY HEARD WHAT ZIGGY SAID IMMEDIATELY AFTER HE AWAKENED.
I'll replay it!
I WILL...
...GO SEE MOTHER.

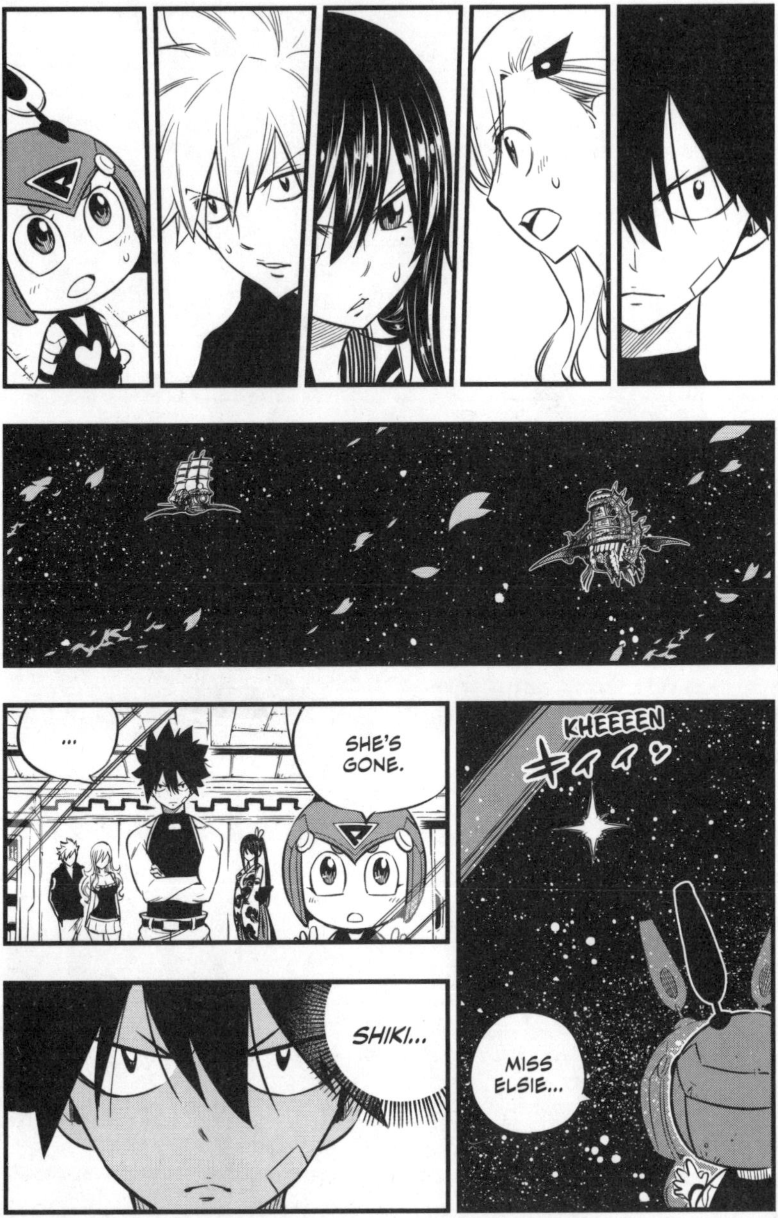
KHEEEEN
キィィ♡
MISS ELSIE...
SHE'S GONE.
...
SHIKI...

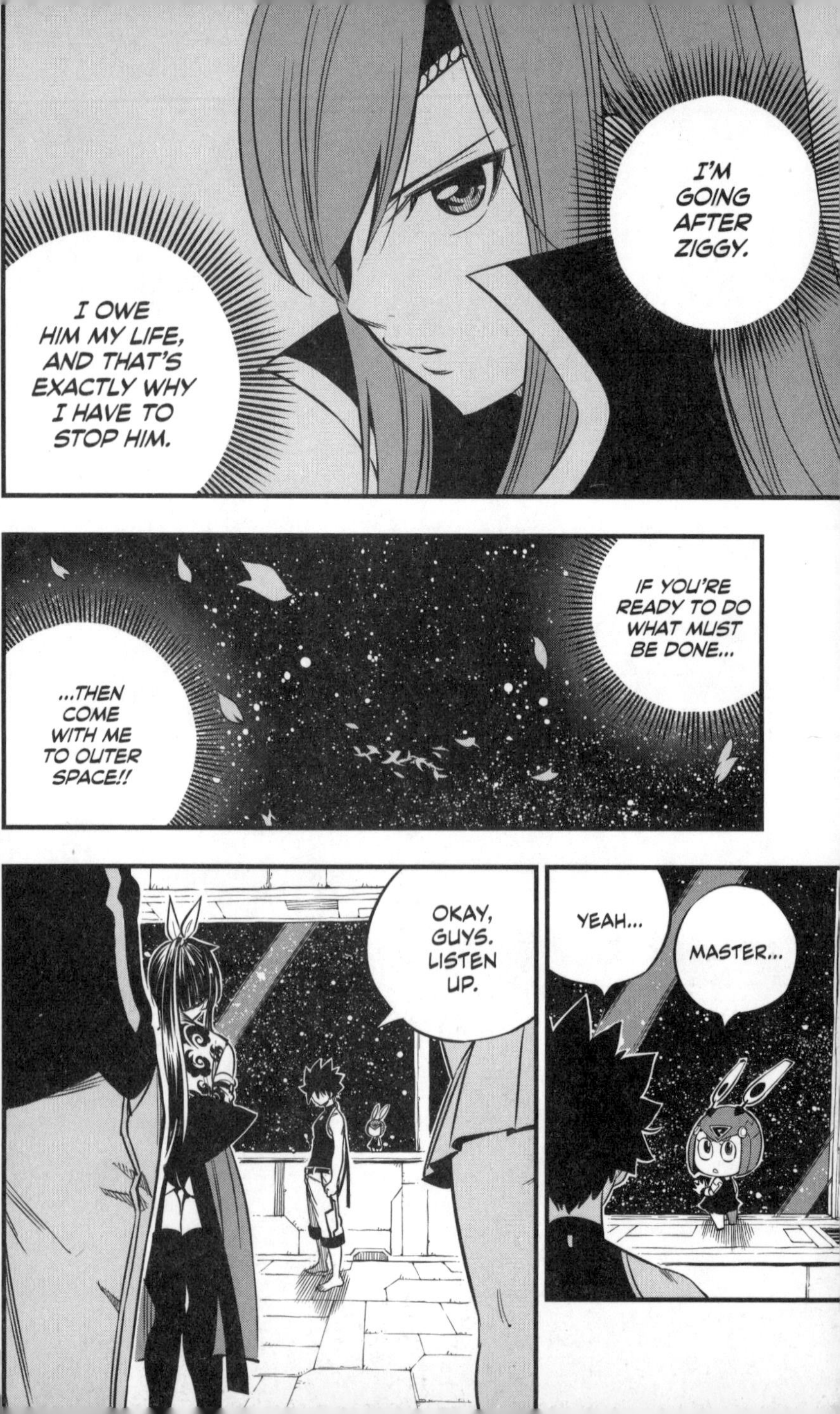
I'M GOING AFTER ZIGGY.
I OWE HIM MY LIFE, AND THAT'S EXACTLY WHY I HAVE TO STOP HIM.
IF YOU'RE READY TO DO WHAT MUST BE DONE...
...THEN COME WITH ME TO OUTER SPACE!!
MASTER...
YEAH...
OKAY, GUYS. LISTEN UP.

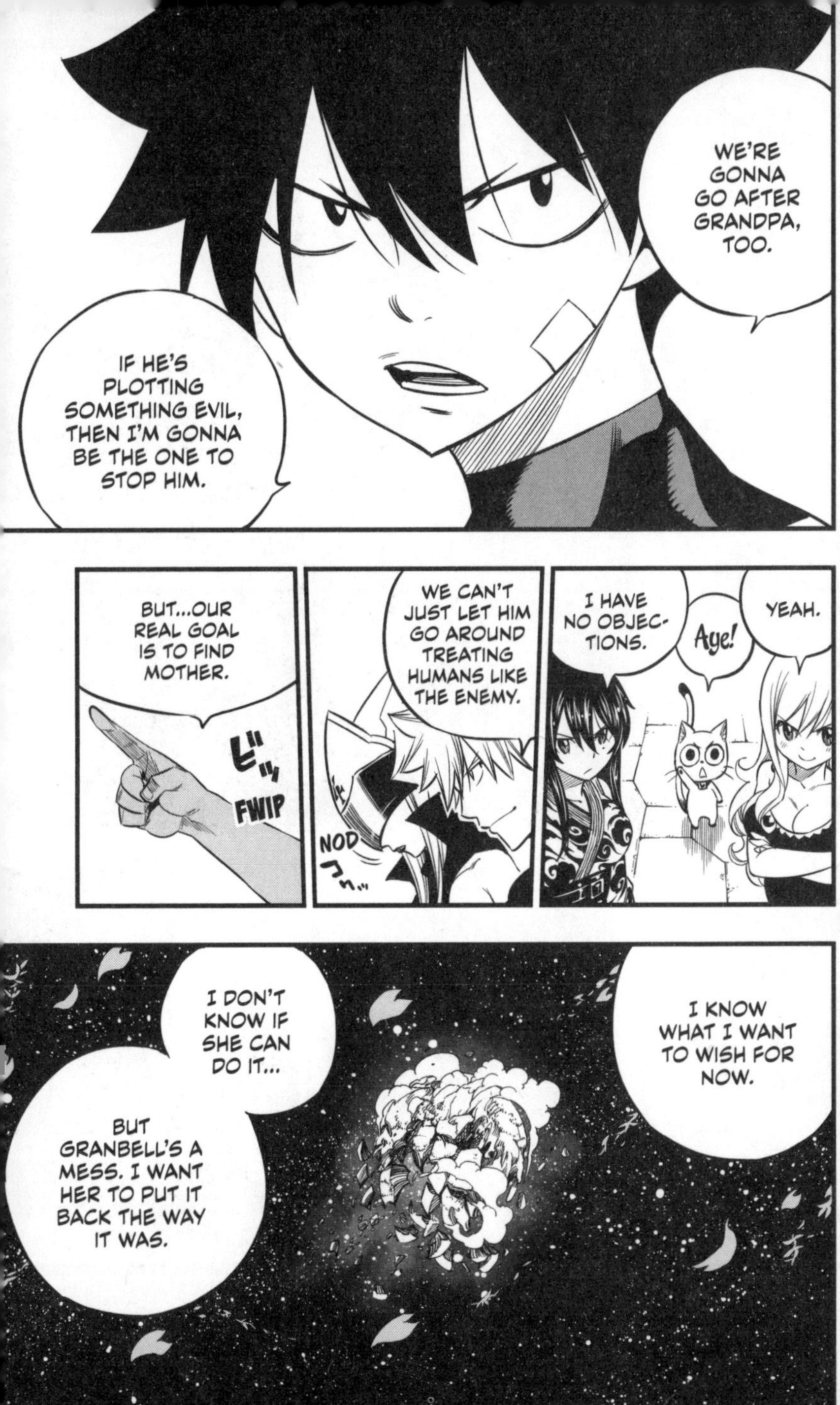
WE'RE GONNA GO AFTER GRANDPA, TOO.
IF HE'S PLOTTING SOMETHING EVIL, THEN I'M GONNA BE THE ONE TO STOP HIM.
YEAH.
Aye!
I HAVE NO OBJECTIONS.
WE CAN'T JUST LET HIM GO AROUND TREATING HUMANS LIKE THE ENEMY.
NOD
BUT...OUR REAL GOAL IS TO FIND MOTHER.
ビッ
FWIP
I KNOW WHAT I WANT TO WISH FOR NOW.
I DON'T KNOW IF SHE CAN DO IT...
BUT GRANBELL'S A MESS. I WANT HER TO PUT IT BACK THE WAY IT WAS.

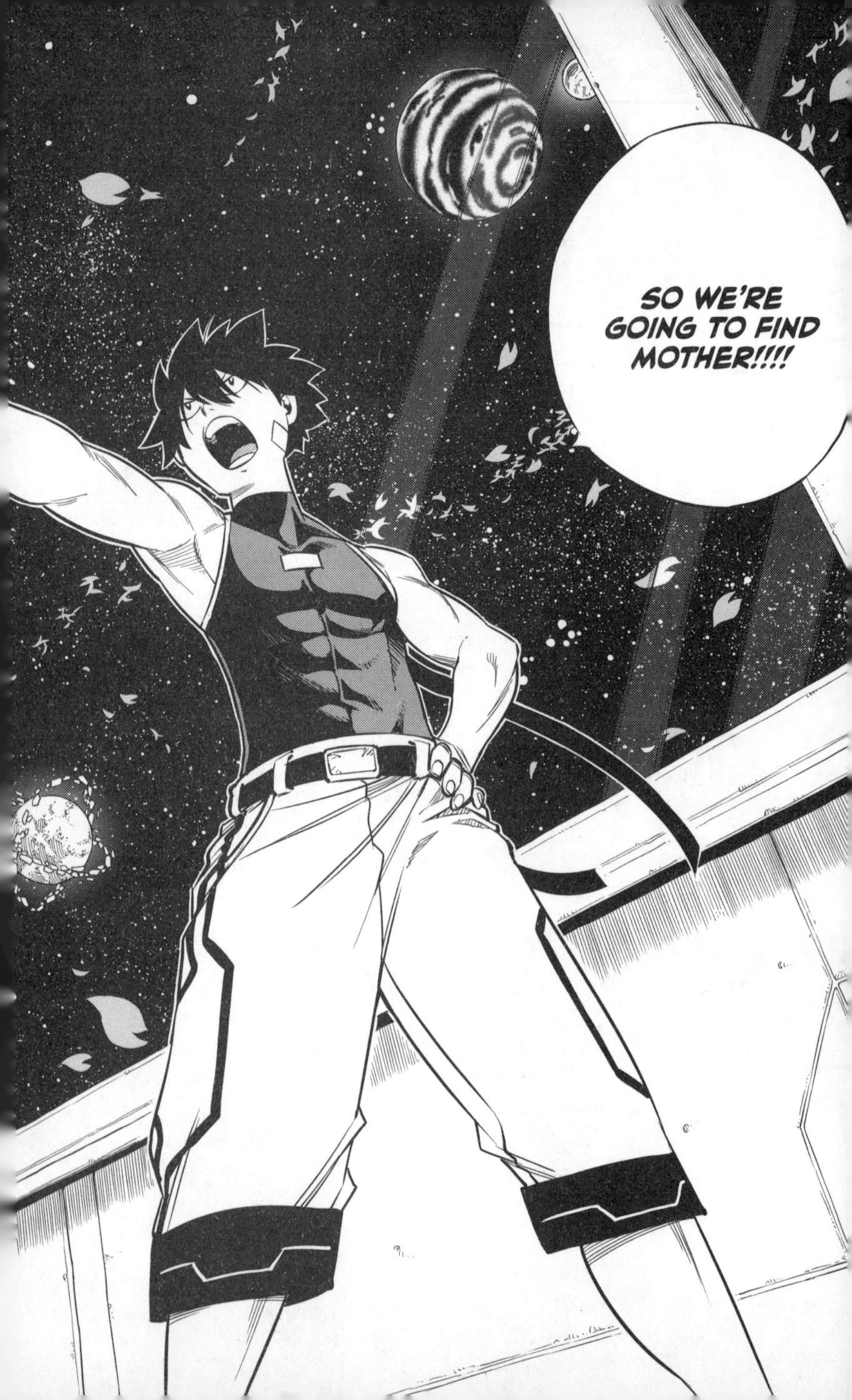
SO WE'RE GOING TO FIND MOTHER!!!!

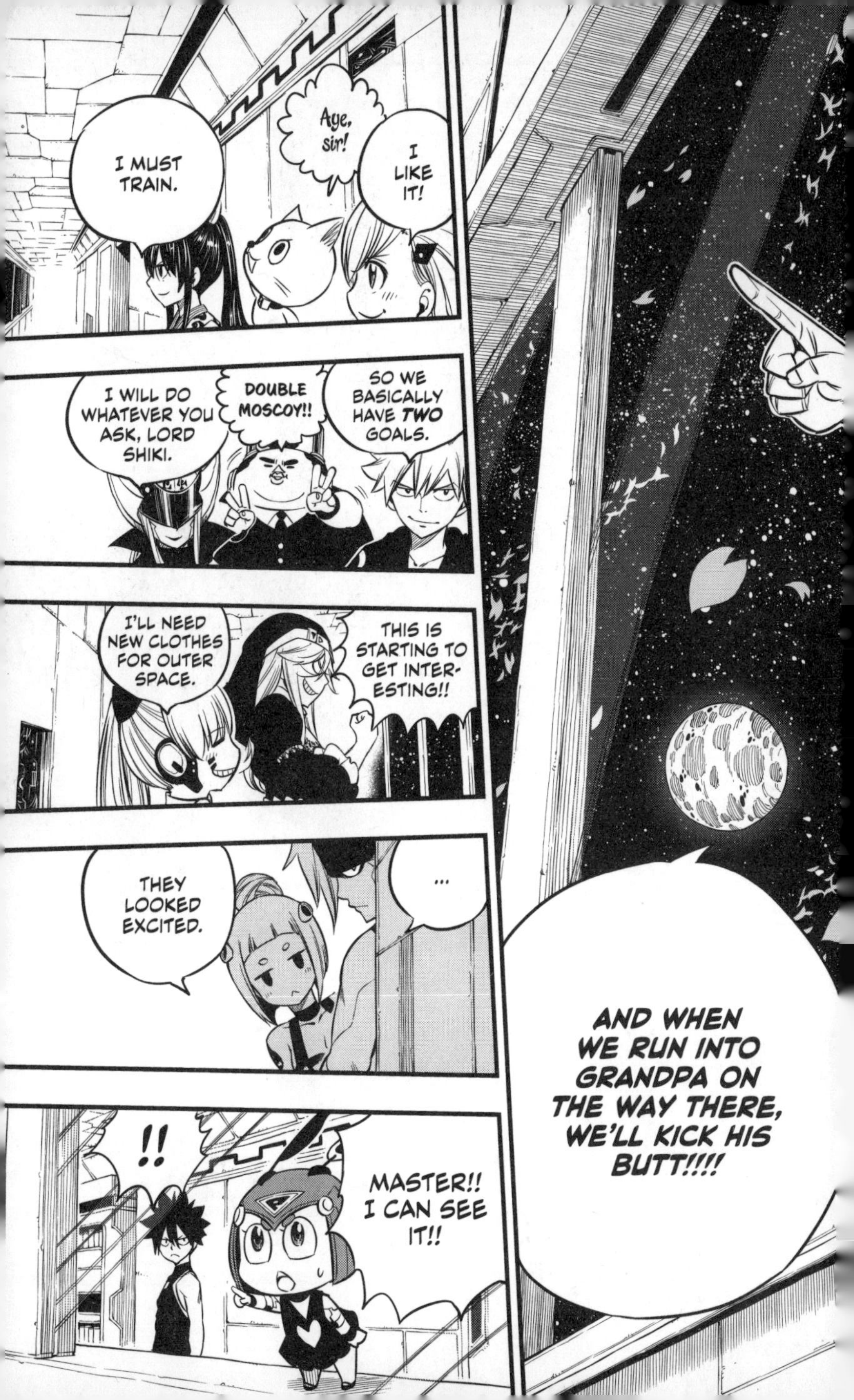
AND WHEN WE RUN INTO GRANDPA ON THE WAY THERE, WE'LL KICK HIS BUTT!!!!
I LIKE IT!
Aye, sir!
I MUST TRAIN.
SO WE BASICALLY HAVE TWO GOALS.
DOUBLE MOSCOY!!
I WILL DO WHATEVER YOU ASK, LORD SHIKI.
THIS IS STARTING TO GET INTER-ESTING!!
I'LL NEED NEW CLOTHES FOR OUTER SPACE.
...
THEY LOOKED EXCITED.
MASTER!! I CAN SEE IT!!
!!

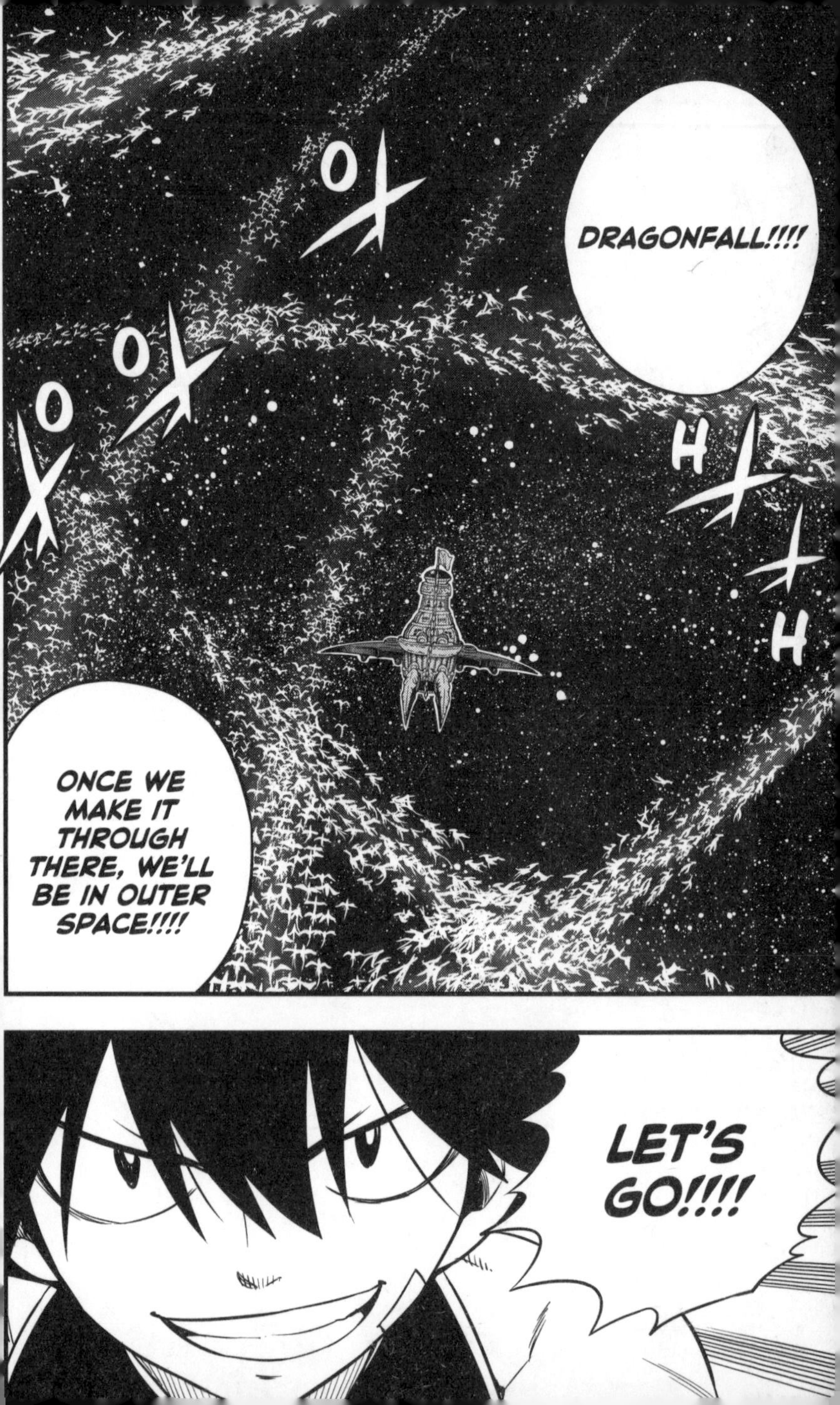
DRAGONFALL!!!!
ONCE WE MAKE IT THROUGH THERE, WE'LL BE IN OUTER SPACE!!!!
LET'S GO!!!!

AFTERWORD

First an anime, now a video game version of this series has been announced. I can't wait to play it. It's being made by Konami. I've actually worked with Konami for a while now—they made a game of my first series *Rave Master*, and my previous series *Fairy Tail*, and now they're working to produce a third game for one of my series. I'm honored to have been approached by a few game companies who wanted to make a game of *Edens Zero*. The other game companies' pitches were really great and appealing, but because of Konami's enthusiasm, and the sense of security that came from our history together, we decided to go forward with Konami's project. The main members of the development team include veterans who worked on the *Rave Master* game and young new recruits, so I'm extremely excited to see the finished product.

I can't tell you too much about what's going to be in the game yet, but it's going to be an action RPG, which is my favorite genre of video game. They especially put a lot of work into faithfully recreating the characters as 3D models, and I think the designs are exceptionally good.

Speaking of the designs, there are a lot of original costumes that I drew just for the game, and not only that, but there will be several costumes that appeared in the manga, costumes designed by Konami, and anyway, the abundance of costume variety is just one of the things I'm looking forward to.

Also, I personally am a huge fan of video games, so I made a lot of very gamer-geek type requests, and they're going to consider implementing whichever ones they can, which I really appreciate. They're working on a game that will be fun not just for *Edens Zero* fans, but for gamers, too, so I hope you look forward to hearing more about it and buying the game when it comes out.

Now, the series is finally entering a new arc. There will be a lot of new places and new characters to see, so I hope you look forward to that, too!

A Kodansha Comics Trade Paperback Original
EDENS ZERO 12 copyright © 2020 Hiro Mashima
English translation copyright © 2021 Hiro Mashima

Published in the United States by Kodansha Comics, an imprint of Kodansha USA Publishing, LLC, New York.

Publication rights for this English edition arranged through Kodansha Ltd., Tokyo.

First published in Japan in 2020 by Kodansha Ltd., Tokyo.

ISBN 978-1-64651-151-8

Original cover design by Narumi Miura (G x complex).

Printed in the United States of America.

www.kodansha.us

2nd Printing
Translation: Alethea Nibley & Athena Nibley
Lettering: AndWorld Design
Editing: David Yoo
Kodansha Comics edition cover design by Phil Balsman

Publisher: Kiichiro Sugawara

Director of publishing services: Ben Applegate
Associate director of operations: Stephen Pakula
Publishing services managing editors: Alanna Ruse, Madison Salters
Production managers: Emi Lotto, Angela Zurlo